# AGGREGATE MONEY DEMAND FUNCTIONS

## Empirical Applications in Cointegrated Systems

# AGGREGATE MONEY DEMAND FUNCTIONS

## Empirical Applications in Cointegrated Systems

**Dennis L. HOFFMAN**
*Arizona State University*
*Tempe, Arizona, USA*

**Robert H. RASCHE**
*Michigan State University*
*East Lansing, Michigan USA*

KLUWER ACADEMIC PUBLISHERS
Boston/London/Dordrecht

**Distributors for North America:**
Kluwer Academic Publishers
101 Philip Drive
Assinippi Park
Norwell, Massachusetts 02061 USA

**Distributors for all other countries:**
Kluwer Academic Publishers Group
Distribution Centre
Post Office Box 322
3300 AH Dordrecht, THE NETHERLANDS

---

**Library of Congress Cataloging-in-Publication Data**

Hoffman, Dennis L.
Aggregate money demand functions : empirical applications in cointegrated systems / Dennis L. Hoffman, Robert H. Rasche.
p. cm.
Includes bibliographical references and indexes.

ISBN-13: 978-94-010-7308-0 e-ISBN-13: 978-94-009-1814-6
DOI: 10.1007/978-94-009-1814-6

1. Demand for money--Econometric models. I. Rasche, Robert H. II. Title.
HG226.5.H62 1996
332.4'14--dc20 96-468
CIP

---



*Printed on acid-free paper.*

# Contents

# Preface

The econometric consequences of nonstationary data have wide ranging implications for empirical research in economics. Specifically, these issues have implications for the study of empirical relations such as a money demand function that links macroeconomic aggregates: real money balances, real income and a nominal interest rate. Traditional monetary theory predicts that these nonstationary series form a cointegrating relation and accordingly, that the dynamics of a vector process comprised of these variables generates distinct patterns. Recent econometric developments designed to cope with nonstationarities have changed the course of empirical research in the area, but many fundamental challenges, for example the issue of identification, remain.

This book represents the efforts undertaken by the authors in recent years in an effort to determine the consequences that nonstationarity has for the study of aggregate money demand relations. We have brought together an empirical methodology that we find useful in conducting empirical research. Some of the work was undertaken during the authors' sabbatical periods and we wish to acknowledge the generous support of Arizona State University and Michigan State University respectively. Professor Hoffman wishes to acknowledge the support of the Fulbright-Hays Foundation that supported sabbattical research in Europe and separate support of the Council of 100 Summer Research Program at Arizona State University.

During our work we have benefited from discussions with a number of individuals and we wish to thank Richard Anderson, Richard Baillie, Michael Bergman, John Carlson, William Crowder, Thomas Cooley, Neil Ericsson, Clive Granger, Dennis Jansen, Søren Johansen, Katarina Juselius, Robert King, Bent Nielsen, Kevin Reffet, Donald Schlagenhauf, John Taylor, Keshin Tswei, Jeffrey Wooldridge, Mark Watson, James Stock, Anders Warne, Mark Wohar, and Su Zhou.

Special thanks goes to Mr. Richard Laborin who supplied typographic assistance. The manuscript was prepared for LaTeXusing Scientific Word 2.01. We also wish to acknowledge the patience and support of our respective families during our work on this project.

DENNIS L. HOFFMAN
*Arizona State University*

ROBERT H. RASCHE
*Michigan State University*

# Chapter 1

# BACKGROUND

The object of this study is to utilize the tools of modern time series analysis to determine the role of an aggregate demand for real balances in the generation of macroeconomic time series. A significant distinguishing characteristic of this research is that we undertake the identification and estimation of this demand function in a multivariate framework, in contrast to most existing studies that concentrate on a single equation framework.

Chapter 2 provides a broad review of the existing empirical literature on the demand for real balances in the United States. The focus of this review is the specification and identification assumptions that characterize previous studies. Frequently these issues are not fully articulated. However, in many cases recognition of these assumptions is critical to an understanding of the specification failures that are so abundant in this literature.

Empirical research in macroeconomics has taken a number of forms in recent years. Despite the diversity in approach, the fundamental problem of identification remains a challenge that is central to all of this work. In particular, the literature on money demand provides an illustration of how identification is an essential ingredient in establishing the nature of a relation linking monetary aggregates, prices, a scale variable such as income and a measure of the opportunity cost of holding a portion of wealth as money balances. Traditionally, identification issues are addressed prior to the estimation of an aggregate money demand function, because knowledge of the structure that embodies the relation dictates the instruments used to estimate its parameters. Debates over the stability of relations estimated in this manner are essentially disputes over fundamental structure or ultimately questions of identification.

Recently empirical work has made the distinction between monetary relations that are presumed to prevail over the long run and relations that characterize the short run. This study builds on this distinction and is directed at an audience of readers interested in exploring the concept of a long-run empirical money demand relation. However, the technical discussion is applicable to other aggregate relations. Emphasis on the long run shifts concern away from the problem of instrument choice. Nevertheless, the quality of estimates and accuracy of statistical inference regarding parameters encountered in the "long-run" arena depends upon the proper consideration of nonstationarity that is characteristic of time series data on macroeconomic aggregates.

In Chapter 3 we examine how a long-run money demand function can be identified and estimated as a cointegrating relation from a vector process comprised of integrated variables that, at a minimum, includes real money balances, real income and a nominal interest rate. Several alternative estimation procedures are considered as are accompanying techniques designed to gauge the precision of each estimator.

The overall question of identification is hardly settled with the estimation of a long-run money demand relation. Indeed, a cointegrating relation that displays the characteristics of a long-run money demand function can serve as a fundamental "anchor" for a vector process and opens the door to the exploration of dynamic structure. This investigation can proceed in stages and can be tailored to suit the tastes of those willing to impose minimal structure, but enough to provide an interpretation of the long-run dynamics that prevail. Alternatively, the exercise can proceed until the entire structure of the system is established. In Chapter 3 we confine our discussion to a research methodology suited to those applications that do not undertake complete structural identification but choose to focus exclusively on the long-run characteristics of the system. In Chapter 4 we explore conditions that allow identification of the entire system structure, emphasizing the role played by knowledge of cointegration rank in achieving identification.

In one sense the analysis below reveals that empirical research remains constrained by the the fundamental prescriptions for structural identification set out in the work of the Cowles Commission. Indeed, the discussion of Chapter 4 reveals that though the form and source of restrictions required to identify structural innovations in contemporary models is quite different from the exclusion restrictions outlined in traditional textbook treatment of rank and order conditions, the number of identifying restrictions is precisely the same. Knowledge of cointegration rank facilitates the task by reducing the number of arbitrary restrictions required to accomplish structural identification, but outside information in the form of structural restrictions is still required.

The process of structural identification pursued throughout our analysis presumes that the link between fundamental innovations that govern dynamic behavior of the economy can be represented by invertible Wold representations. In Chapter 5 we provide an example of a prototype economic model designed to be representative of the type of aggregate structure that serves as the point of departure for numerous applications. The model is based upon a "textbook" aggregate structure and incorporates a rational expectation solution to obtain a relation linking permanent innovations that are real and nominal in origin to the long-run behavior of a vector time series processes that contain variables that appear in a money demand relation specified in the models.

The model in Chapter 5 and the methodology set out in Chapters 3 and 4 provide the foundation for the applications in Chapters 6 through 8. We begin in Chapter 6 by noting the importance of estimating the money demand relation as a long-run cointegrating relation. In this discussion, we compare our findings with those authors who have not found evidence of a stable cointegrating relation. Once the case for cointegration is established, we proceed to identify the fundamental innovations that underlie a simple vector process characterized by a long-run money demand function. Subsequently we discuss the dynamic characteristics of the data series that are constrained by the long-run demand function for real balances. Minimal models are investigated in this chapter. The emphasis here is on the importance of functional form in the analysis of cointegration and the robustness of the basic results to different frequency of data.

In Chapters 7 and 8 we extend the analysis to systems of larger dimension. We examine whether these broader systems include additional cointegrating relations in the form of either a Fisher relation that links nominal interest rates and inflation or a term structure relation that links nominal rates of differing maturities. The dynamics of the broader systems are shown to be consistent with the results obtained from the simple system investigated in Chapter 6. In addition the increased dimension of the systems permits identification of some of the transitory shocks that drive the behavior of the included time series.

Our discussion presumes that empirical time series models can adequately summarize the structure of the economy and can be used to represent the link between economic theory and empirical observation. In this setting the task of empirical research is to identify structure and to test hypotheses that can be examined in the context of a particular structure. In addition, we assume that sufficient constancy prevails to ensure that the exercise is meaningful. Constancy of long-run structure is testable as discussed in Chapter 3. We acknowledge that this view is not shared by all macroeconomists and in Chapter 4 we outline some of the challenges faced by structural VAR modelers at this time. Our goal is to determine how the identity of cointegrating relations that link macro aggregates facilitates understanding of dynamic structure. The centerpiece of our applications is the aggregate money demand function though the technical approach generalizes to other aggregate relations as illustrated in Chapters 7 and 8.

Though microfoundations portrayed in "dynamic general equilibrium literature" are not addressed explicitly in our discussion, we do not believe that the representation of an aggregate money demand relation, a Fisher relation that links expected inflation and nominal interest rates, or a relation linking interest rates across different maturities are at odds with the microfoundations literature. Indeed, Lucas (1988) acknowledges the important work of Meltzer (1963) on monetary aggregates by deriving the aggregate relation using a dynamic optimization problem cast in a representative agent setting. Once the relations that link aggregates are in place, we establish a road map to follow in determining whether a chosen identification scheme reveals useful insights about the innovations that govern a particular time series process. The methodology discussion in Chapters 3 and 4 reveals how knowledge of the number and form of these fundamental aggregate "anchors" can facilitate this process.

The technical discussion in Chapters 3 and 4 reflects material that has been developed by numerous authors and appears in published work or has been circulated in working papers. We have selected an outline for the technical discussion that brings together a set of important contributions in this area. We tackle the issues by considering the sequence of estimation, inference, and dynamic analysis in turn. The central theme of identification runs throughout. Due to space constraints we have not been able to include all of the work in the area and the discussion should not be considered as a "survey" of the literature. The discussion is "complete" only in the sense that it provides a unified approach to dealing with the econometric issues inherent in the consideration of nonstationary macroeconomic aggregates. We know of no other single resource that treats all of these issues comprehensively, with accompanying illustration.

# Chapter 2

# THE DEVELOPMENT AND FAILURES OF THE EMPIRICAL LITERATURE ON THE DEMAND FOR MONEY

It is quite likely that no subject has attracted more attention, consumed more pages in economic journals, nor resulted in more mining and remining of the same data sets as the search for a satisfactory empirical representation of the demand function for real balances. The high point in this effort was realized in the early 1970s when, in summarizing the literature to that date, Boorman (1976) could claim:

> "The first and most important result of this survey is that the evidence supporting the existence of a reasonably stable demand for money function would seem to be overwhelming. This is true both of long-term evidence covering the last seventy years or so and of the evidence from the postwar period until 1973. Second, and perhaps next in importance for the conduct of monetary policy, the vast majority of this same evidence supports the hypothesis that the nominal interest rate plays a significant role in the determination of the public's desired money balances has been fairly narrowly circumscribed, with the best possible results suggesting an elasticity of about - 0.2 for the short rate and approximately - 0.7 for the long rate." (p. 356)

From that point to the present, more and more studies have appeared which cast doubt on the optimism in the above quotation. After approximately twenty years of additional data accumulation Friedman and Kuttner (1992) summarize the evidence on the same question as:

> "...the evidence in favor of the kind of long-run stability of the money-income relationship that cointegration represents has become weaker over time, so much that any presumption in favor of such a relationship must reflect prior beliefs, rather than evidence contained in the data now available." (p. 490)

The question that we seek to address in this chapter is the cause of the dramatic decline in confidence about our understanding of the relationship among real balances, real income and nominal interest rates at the aggregate level. Much of the attention in the literature of the past twenty years is directed toward documenting the breakdown of some past empirical study and proposing a change in specification and or measurement to rehabilitate an estimated equation that failed with the availability of additional information. Little, if any, attention appears to have been given to the underlying causes of the continuing specification failures in this literature. Our approach is to reexamine some traditional specifications in light of recent insights into the problems of analyzing economic time series data and developments in applied econometrics that address the characteristics of these data.

In the first section, we reexamine some equilibrium studies that were published before 1970 in the attempt to determine if there were specification problems present in the data that were available at that time, but were overlooked by the authors and commentators, and which would suggest that the types of specification failures that are observed in later years were predictable. The particular studies that we examine are chosen because they are representative of broad classes of published studies, and because they are sufficiently well documented that we are quite confident that we are able to examine the original data. In the second section, we reexamine the partial adjustment model that became the standard framework for the analysis of the "short-run demand for money". We outline the justification for this specification and discuss the serious criticisms that this approach has generated. In the third section we review some of the diagnostic tools that have been applied to testing empirical money demand specifications for the U.S. We show that in some cases the approach to specification testing has tended to obfuscate predictable specification problems.

In the final section we reestimate some historical money demand specifications using the original data sets, but apply modern econometric techniques designed to address the specification problems in the original analyses.

## 2.1 Some Equilibrium Money Demand Studies

Attempts to construct empirical representations of aggregate money demand functions prior to the mid 1960s in large part concentrated on the estimation of a "long-run" specification. The important aspect of this specification is that it assumed that the data generating process traced out intersections of demand

and supply curves for real balances; namely that the observed quantity of real money balances corresponded to the quantity of real balances that are desired at the current values of the arguments of the demand function.[1] A confusing aspect of this literature is that the vast majority of the studies that adopted this specification assumption also chose data that were generated over a long period of time. Thus a common confusion in this literature is to interpret "long-run" as a reference to the time span of the data series rather than to the equilibrium assumption of the specification.

The two most famous studies in the class of models are those by Meltzer (1963) and Chow (1966). Both studies focus primarily on the role of wealth or permanent income as an argument of the equilibrium demand for real balances. Indeed, Meltzer's primary conclusion is that "the theory and empirical evidence support the view that the long-run demand function is consistent with the quantity theory of money and contains two principal arguments of almost equal explanatory power: interest rates and non-human wealth" (Meltzer (1963), p. 227). Chow concludes "Our own findings regarding the long-run demand function are, first, that permanent income is a better explanatory variable that both wealth and current income; second, that, while wealth is a slightly better variable than current income, the latter does contribute significantly to the explanation of money stock in addition to the effect of wealth ..." (Chow (1966), p. 127). For our purposes, the information that is of interest in these studies are the relations between money (defined as currency plus demand deposits), income (defined as net national product) and interest rates (defined as long-term bond rates).

The money income regressions reported by Meltzer and Chow are almost identical in construction. The major differences are that Chow uses a consumer price index to deflate nominal balances and net national product, while Meltzer uses a NNP deflator, and slightly different choices of sample periods: Chow starts with 1897 and excludes the war years 1917-19 and 1941-45, while Meltzer starts his sample in 1900 and includes all years.

We have obtained the data from the original sources listed in Chow (1966) and reproduced some of the regressions that he reports. Our estimates are given in Table 2.1. The first equation in Table 2.1 is a reestimation of equation 1.9 in Chow (1966), Table 1. Essentially we reproduce the original estimates exactly, which is quite remarkable given the well known difficulties in reproducing published econometric results (DeWald, Anderson and Thursby (1986)), and the changes in estimation technology that have occurred over the past twenty-five years. The second equation indicates that these results are invariant to the deflation of nominal balances and net national product. This can be anticipated, since the income elasticity in the nominal equation is very close to one, and not significantly different from one by the conventional "$t$"-ratio.

The third and fourth equations in this table indicate that the inclusion or exclusion of the two sets of war years does not affect the inference from the re-

[1] Early exceptions to this assumption are Bronfenbrenner and Mayer(1960) and Teigen(1964)

Table 2.1: Equilibrium Money Demand Functions for Real Balances

(Double Log Specification)

| Sample Period | Spec, | Const | Income | Interest Rate | $R^2$ | SSE | DW | $\rho$ |
|---|---|---|---|---|---|---|---|---|
| 1897-1958 (ex. 17-19,41-45) | Nom. | -.2386 (.1956) | .9890 (.0133) | -.5396 (.0647) | .993 | .0901 | .75 | - |
| 1897-1958 (ex. 17-19,41-45) | Real | -.2334 (.2148) | .9827 (.0225) | -.5427 (.0673) | .982 | .0902 | .74 | - |
| 1897-1958 | Nom. | -.1703 (.2027) | .9850 (.0139) | -.5676 (.0616) | .991 | .0964 | .66 | - |
| 1897-1958 | Real | -.1629 (.2252) | .9766 (.0237) | -.5733 (.0656) | .965 | .0965 | .65 | - |
| 1900-1958 | Real | .1236 (.2470) | .9463 (.0260) | -.6215 (.0665) | .979 | .0934 | .69 | - |
| 1900-1929 | Real | 1.0089 (.3205) | .7137 (.0689) | -.1432 (.1566) | .900 | .0673 | .80 | - |
| 1930-1958 | Real | .6002 (.4560) | .8722 (.0491) | -.5110 (.1076) | .958 | .0904 | .64 | - |
| Autoregressive Transformation (Maximum Likelihood) | | | | | | | | |
| 1900-1958 | Real | 3.4891 (.8526) | .4171 (.0897) | -.2803 (.1165) | .995 | .0565 | 1.65 | .992 (.017) |
| 1900-1929 | Real | 1.5044 .5208) | .5970 (.0861) | .0661 (.1807) | .936 | .0538 | 1.94 | .695 (.160) |
| 1930-1958 | Real | 2.9810 (1.1435) | .5334 (.1382) | -.3564 (.1584) | .980 | .0626 | 1.63 | .963 (.054) |
| First Difference Regressions | | | | | | | | |
| 1901-1958 | Real | .0241 .0074) | .2788 (.0912) | -.3330 (.1082) | .270 | .0526 | 1.65 | - |
| 1901-1929 | Real | .0233 (.0103) | .2113 (.1250) | -.2386 (.1812) | .127 | .0478 | 1.95 | - |
| 1931-1958 | Real | .0234 (.0120) | .3521 (.1458) | -.3395 (.1443) | .306 | .0575 | 1.62 | - |

gressions. From the perspective of the entire sample period it appears that the income elasticity of the demand for real balances is not significantly different from unity, so that these equations can be interpreted as velocity relationships. The estimated elasticity of velocity with respect to the long-term nominal interest rate appears to be on the order of .5 to .6. The final three equations in the table reestimate the real balance specification on the three sample periods reported in Meltzer (1963), Table 2 (his equation 8). The estimated coefficients are somewhat different from those reported by Meltzer, presumably because of the different deflator. However, the inference from these three regressions is the same as that from Meltzer's Table 2: judged by the conventional "$t$"-ratios the income elasticity is significantly less than one in the 1900-29 subsample, and on this basis, the interest elasticity is not significantly different from zero during this subsample.

The supplementary information included in Table 2.1 that is not available in the original sources is the information on the serial correlation of the residuals. In all of the regressions reported here, the Durbin-Watson statistics indicate strong positive serial correlation in the residuals. In all cases, the goodness-of-fit measures are extremely high. This combination of diagnostics is symptomatic of Granger and Newbold's (1974) caution about "spurious regression". "It would, for example, be easy to quote published equations for which the $R^2 = .997$ and the Durbin-Watson statistic ($d$) is .53. The most extreme example we have met is an equation for which $R^2 = .99$ and $d = .093$. However, we shall suggest that cases with much less extreme values may well be entirely spurious" (p. 111). The consequences of this "spurious regression" problem is that the estimates of the regression coefficients are inefficient and the conventional significance tests are invalid. The autocorrelation problem, even at the extreme case where the variables that enter the regression are nonstationary (have a unit root) does not mean that the standard ordinary least squares estimator is inconsistent–though substantial finite sample bias may remain. Under conditions of nonstationarity it has been shown (Stock (1987)) that this estimator is "superconsistent". The fundamental problem is determining the appropriate estimator of the standard errors of the OLS coefficients so that correct inference can be made.

The traditional way of dealing with severe autocorrelation in the estimated regression residuals is to estimate the equation subject to a first order autoregressive transformation, or simply to construct the regression in first differences. We have reestimated the real balance equation for a number of sample periods with a first order autoregressive specification of the disturbance term using a maximum likelihood estimator. The results are reported in the center portion of Table 2.1. The estimated autocorrelation parameter is not significantly less than one in two of the three samples reported there. The estimated real income elasticities are much smaller than the ordinary least squares estimates in the top part of the table, as are the absolute values of the interest rate elasticities. Once again, the estimated interest elasticity is not significantly different from zero in the 1900-29 sample period.

First differenced regressions are reported in the bottom portion of Table 2.1. Here the point estimates of the coefficients on the differences of real income and the differences of interest rates are much more stable across the various sample periods than is the case with either the ordinary least squares or the AR specifications. The absolute value of the estimated interest rate coefficients are comparable to those from the AR estimator, but the estimated real income coefficients are smaller than those in the other parts of the table. The estimates for the 1900-29 sample period suggest that during this period real balances are a random walk.

The variety of parameter estimates that are produced using traditional techniques to deal with the evident serial correlation in the regression residuals leaves considerable uncertainty as to both the stability of an equilibrium demand function for real balances and the magnitude of the parameters of such a specification. We return to the problem of testing of this specification in section 2.4 after discussing the partial adjustment model that eclipsed the equilibrium model in the mid 1960s.

## 2.2 Partial Adjustment Models

Chow (1966) introduced a "stock adjustment" model that became the basis for several decades of empirical research into a "short-run demand for money" function. His original formulation:

$$M_t - M_{t-1} = c(M_t^* - M_{t-1}) + d(A_t - A_{t-1}) \tag{2.1}$$

incorporated two elements in the adjustment of nominal money balances. The first element, $c(M_t^* - M_{t-1})$, is meant to reflect the adjustment of past nominal balance holdings to current desired money balances ($M_t^*$), the second element is meant to reflect the change in total assets ($A_t$) that accumulates as money holdings. Desired money balances were modeled by the same specifications used in previous "long-run" specifications. The second adjustment element was not pursued in subsequent empirical studies.

Such stock adjustment or "partial adjustment" specifications typically are motivated by cost minimizing behavior in the presence of quadratic costs of adjustment. An explicit derivation of a function such as (2.1) is found in Goldfeld and Sichel (1987), where agents are presumed to face a trade off between opportunity costs associated with holding money balances that differ from their desired holdings on the one hand, and explicit costs of moving from their previous cash position on the other hand.

Initially two variants of the "partial adjustment" model existed in the literature: an arithmetic adjustment process illustrated by (2.1) and a proportional adjustment process:

$$M_t/M_{t-1} = (M_t^*/M_{t-1})^c \tag{2.2}$$

that states that a certain percentage, rather than a certain fraction of the discrepancy between past money holdings and current desired holdings is adjusted in a particular time period. This latter formulation became the preferred specification since it is straightforward to transform it into the log-linear specification:

$$\ln M_t - \ln M_{t-1} = c(\ln M_t^* - \ln M_{t-1}) \tag{2.3}$$

This specification is convenient since generally it is accepted that the elasticity of desired money holdings with respect to an appropriate scale variable such as income or wealth is constant. In the framework of the proportional adjustment mechanism of (2.3), this constant elasticity hypothesis generates a simple linear (in the parameters) estimating equation.

Early specifications of partial adjustment models (Chow (1966); Modigiani, Rasche and Cooper (1970)) applied hypotheses such as (2.1) or (2.3) in which agents were assumed to adjust their nominal money holdings. This approach contrasts and conflicts with earlier specifications of equilibrium money demand models, and with the theories that justified these equilibrium models, where the theoretical and empirical emphasis is on agents' demand for real balances. In the early 1970s this contradiction was recognized and gave rise to two alternative "short-run money demand" specifications: a "real partial adjustment mechanism" and a "nominal partial adjustment mechanism" (Goldfeld (1973)).

Both of these specifications applied the same equilibrium hypothesis that agents had desired real balances, $m_t^* = \ln((M/P)_t^*)$, as suggested by the available theoretical models. The models differ with respect to how agents are presumed to behave when the real value of actual money holdings differs from equilibrium real balances. In the "real partial adjustment model" agents are presumed to adjust their real balances to eliminate a proportion of the discrepancy between their current desired real balances and their previous real balance holdings (valued at the previous price level):

$$\ln(M/P)_t - \ln(M/P)_{t-1} = c(m_t^* - \ln(M/P)_{t-1}) \tag{2.4}$$

The "nominal partial adjustment mechanism" presumes that agents adjust their nominal cash balances by some proportion of the difference between their previous nominal balances and the nominal value of their current equilibrium real balances (valued at the <u>current</u> price level):

$$\ln(M_t) - \ln M_{t-1} = c(m_t^* + \ln P_t - \ln M_{t-1}) \tag{2.5}$$

The difference between these two hypotheses can be seen clearly by subtracting the inflation rate (measured as the log difference in the price level) from both sides of equation (2.5) and rearranging terms to obtain:

$$\ln(M/P)_t - \ln(M/P)_{t-1} = c(m_t^* - \ln(M/P)_{t-1}) - (1-c)(\ln P_t - \ln P_{t-1}) \tag{2.6}$$

Thus the difference between the real partial adjustment specification and the nominal partial adjustment specification is solely the question of what constraint should be applied to the coefficient of the log change in the price level in the estimating equation: in the former case the coefficient on this variable is constrained to zero; in the latter case it is constrained to $-(1-c)$. Neither model allows the estimation of this coefficient as a free parameter.

Very little attention has been given in the literature to the implicit valuation assumptions that are applied in the two models. An alternative, and possibly more appropriate, valuation assumption in the real adjustment model is to assume that agents adjust a portion of the discrepancy between their current equilibrium real balances and the real value of their past nominal balances in terms of current prices. The specification of such a hypothesis is:

$$\ln(M/P)_t - \ln M_{t-1} + \ln P_t = c(m_t^* - \ln M_{t-1} + \ln P_t) \tag{2.7}$$

Some simple algebraic manipulation of (2.7) produces equation (2.6). Thus it appears appropriate to conclude that there is no fundamental difference in economic behavior presumed but the two specifications. Rather, the difference in the estimating equations arises from arbitrary (and typically unstated) assumptions about the price level that agents apply in converting nominal balances at different points in time into purchasing power equivalents. If nominal balances are converted to real values using consistent assumptions, then the two models are observationally equivalent.

A second identification problem that arises in the context of partial adjustment models is discussed by Goldfeld and Sichel (1987). They address the issue of whether the rate of inflation has a role in determining agents' equilibrium holdings of real balances independent of and in addition to any impact through the inflation premium built into nominal interest rates. They note that it is impossible discriminate between the two partial adjustment mechanisms (equation (2.4) and (2.7)) unless it is assumed that the inflation rate has no independent role in the determination of equilibrium real balances. Alternatively, without an assumption on the form of the adjustment model, it is impossible to test for an independent role of inflation in the equilibrium demand for real balances.

In the early applications of the partial adjustment models it was recognized that these models imposed very specific constraints on the dynamics (distributed lag responses) of real balances to the variables that were presumed to affect the equilibrium demand for real balances. A typical specification of the latter is:

$$m_t^* = a + b_1 \ln Q_t - b_2 \ln R_t \tag{2.8}$$

where $Q$ is a "scale variable" such as real income or real wealth and $R$ is a measure of nominal interest rates (or a vector of such rates). When this expression is substituted into (2.6) the resulting equation expressed in lag operator notation is:

$$[1-(1-c)L]\ln(M/P)_t = ca + cb_1 \ln Q_t - cb_2 \ln R_t + c[1-L]\ln P_t \tag{2.9}$$

Clearly the partial adjustment model imposes identical geometrically declining distributed lags on ln$Q$, ln$R$ and the inflation rate (for the nominal adjustment or respecified real adjustment mechanism) for $0 < c < 1$. The implicit steady state elasticities with respect to $Q$, and $R$ are $b_1$ and $b_2$ respectively. One implication of the specification that is apparent from (2.9) is that it is very difficult if not impossible to discriminate in the partial adjustment framework between a demand for real balances that depends on current income and one that depends on "permanent income" (Feige (1967); Modigliani, Rasche and Cooper (1970)). The traditional implementation of a time series measure of "permanent income" is a weighted moving average of current and past income, with geometrically declining weights (Friedman (1956), Chapter V). Since the time series of a weighted geometric moving average of income closely follows that of a weighted arithmetic average of the same income series, (2.9) can be interpreted as a traditional "permanent income" specification of the demand for real balances that allows for a distributed lag response to interest rates and the inflation rate.

Recognition of the near equivalence of the implicit distributed lag on real income in the partial adjustment model to the traditional measure of "permanent income" raises the question of whether estimates of equations such as (2.4) or (2.6) really reflect an adjustment mechanism. Inclusion of the lagged dependent variable in the estimating equation to generate the distributed lag on real income, imposes the same distributed lag on all other regressors. Thus studies that present "partial adjustment model" estimates do not provide a test of the short-run model against an equilibrium specification in which demand for real balances depends upon "permanent income" and contemporaneous interest rates. This point was made by Feige (1967) who also noted that a distributed lag on short-term interest rates could be interpreted as a measure of average expected future long-term interest rates.

There is a simple method of testing the partial adjustment model against the alternative "permanent income" equilibrium hypothesis that as far as we can determine does not appear in the literature. Augment the estimating equation (2.4) or (2.6) with an additional regressor: $\ln R_{t-1}$. If the estimated coefficient on $\ln R_t$ is $a_2$ and the estimated coefficient on $\ln R_{t-1}$ is $a_3$, then a test of the maintained partial adjustment model against the alternative equilibrium model is a test of the nonlinear restriction $a_3 = -a_2(1-c)$. If this restriction cannot be rejected, then the coefficients on all lagged values of the interest rate are not significantly different from zero. A similar nonlinear coefficient restriction can be applied to current and lagged inflation rates in the nominal adjustment specification. Feige (1967) constructed a regression similar to the experiment described here using annual data from 1915-63. His conclusion is that the data from this sample reject the partial adjustment hypothesis in favor of an equilibrium hypothesis where real balances depend on expected income measured as a geometrically weighted moving average of current and lagged real income and on contemporaneous short-term interest rates.

A experiment of the type suggested here appears in Goldfeld (1973), Table 6, Equation B, including one quarter lags on real income and interest rates in addition to the contemporaneous variables and the lagged dependent variable. The estimated coefficient on the lagged income term is not significantly different from zero in this regression, but the estimated coefficients on the lagged interest rate terms have the same sign as the estimated coefficients on the contemporaneous interest rate variables. The test proposed here is not constructed for the reported regression, but Goldfeld notes that "satisfactory estimation of [this] equation ... is impeded by pronounced multicollinearity" (p. 601). Hence it is not apparent from the available information that the "permanent income" equilibrium specification would be rejected in favor of the partial adjustment model for this data sample.

There are some results available that relax the assumption that of a common geometrically declining distributed lag pattern in the coefficients of all regressors in the estimating equation. Typically such studies do not estimate unrestricted distributed lag regressions, but impose some kind of smoothness restrictions on the lag patterns. Frequently this was implemented by forcing the coefficients of the distributed lags to lie on a low order polynomial using "Almon lag" estimates (Modigliani, Rasche and Cooper (1970); Goldfeld (1973)). Even with these restrictions, the estimated shapes of the interest rate lag patterns are quite different from those of real income, the estimated lengths of the interest rate lags are shorter than the real income lags, and the estimated mean response time of real balances to interest rate changes is smaller than the estimated mean response time to real income changes.

In some early implementations of the partial adjustment specification the evidence of a unitary long-run income elasticity (a long-run velocity - interest rate relationship) from several empirical studies of equilibrium models of the demand for real balances was incorporated into the adjustment specification. From (2.9) it can be seen that this restriction requires that the ratio $b_1/(1-c)$ be constrained to 1.0. This restriction is implemented easily in the estimating equation using the transformation:

$$\begin{aligned} \ln(M/P)_t &= ca - cb\ln R_t - (1-c)(\ln(M/P)_{t-1} - \ln Q_t) \\ &\quad +(1-c)(\ln P_t - \ln P_{t-1}), \end{aligned} \tag{2.10}$$

where the inflation rate term is included or excluded depending on whether the a nominal or real adjustment mechanism is hypothesized (Modigliani, Rasche and Cooper (1970)).

Since its earliest implementation, the partial adjustment specification has been extremely controversial. Laidler (1980,1982,1985) has been a persistent critic of these specifications. Laidler claims that there is a fallacy of composition in the aggregation of a hypothesis such as (2.4) or (2.5) from the level of an individual agent (his individual experiment) to the aggregate economy (his market experiment). Laidler argues that at the individual level the decision variable is the size of nominal balances and the price level is an exogenous variable. Therefore in terms of microeconomic behavior, adjustment of real balances to desired real balances must occur through changing the amount of nominal balances held in the individual portfolio. When the aggregate nominal money stock is set exogenously by the monetary authority, adjustment of aggregate real balances to the aggregate of individual equilibrium real balances must occur through adjustments in the price level, since under this monetary regime there is nothing that private agents can do to affect the aggregate nominal money stock. Laidler argues that under these circumstances equations such as (2.4) and (2.5) cannot represent an aggregate short-run demand for real balances, but rather reflect the adjustment process of the price level in the economy where a disequilibrium occurs between the real value of aggregate nominal balances and the aggregate of individual equilibrium real balances.

A monetary regime in which the nominal money stock is truly exogenous probably has never been observed. First, historically central banks have focused most frequently on controlling the behavior of interest rates, not monetary aggregates. Second, the monetary aggregates that are analyzed most frequently in money demand functions include among their components both inside and outside money, so that their behavior fundamentally is endogenous in the aggregate economy. Laidler also argues that endogeneity of the monetary aggregate does not validate partial adjustment specifications as aggregate short-run money demand functions. If the monetary aggregate is endogenous, then the observed combinations of aggregate real balances, aggregate real income and interest rates reflect movements of both aggregate supply and aggregate demand curves. Under these conditions it is necessary to specify the short-run money supply function, including the monetary rule implicit in the actions of the central bank, in order to identify the short-run demand for money. In the absence of adequate identifying restrictions, the dynamics estimated from specifications such as (2.4) and (2.5) are at best linear combinations of the supply and demand dynamics.

The second type of criticism leveled against partial adjustment models is that the estimated dynamics suggest speeds of adjustment that are implausibly slow. Goldfeld (1973), Table 16 reports quarterly adjustment parameter estimates ($c$) from a low of .06 to a high of .34 per quarter depending on which interest rate(s) are used in the real adjustment model. Judd and Scaddings (1982) report quarterly speeds of adjustment from a number of different published studies ranging from a low of .02 to a high of .27 per quarter.

Goodfriend (1985) developed an entirely different criticism of partial adjustment models. He argues that the observed adjustment relationship represented by the estimated coefficient of the lagged dependent variable may have nothing to do with deviations from equilibrium real balances at either the individual or aggregate economy levels, but may be an artifact of errors in the measurement of the arguments of the demand for real balances.

Goodfriend proposes an explanation of the typical partial adjustment model estimates in terms of an equilibrium model, measurement errors, and autocorrelated time series. He assumes that the true data generating process between observed aggregate real balances and the arguments of the aggregate demand function is:

$$\ln(M/P)_t = a + b_1 \ln Q_t^* - b_2 \ln R_t^* + e_t, \tag{2.11}$$

where $e_t$ is a white noise disturbance term. He further assumes that the true values of $\ln Q_t^*$ and $\ln R_t^*$ are not observed directly, but are measured by $\ln Q_t$ and $\ln R_t$ with serially correlated (AR(1)) measurement errors. The measurement errors are assumed to be uncorrelated, and uncorrelated with $e_t$. Under these assumptions he shows that a regression of real balances on $\ln Q_t$, $\ln R_t$ and the lagged real balances will produce a positive coefficient on the lagged dependent variable even though there is no partial adjustment in terms of the correctly measured variables (2.11). In addition the estimated coefficients on $\ln Q_t$ and $\ln R_t$ are biased towards zero relative to the true parameter values, $b_1$ and $b_2$. It can be shown that if the long-run variance of $\ln Q^*$ and $\ln R^*$ is held constant, the size of the estimated coefficient on lagged dependent variable increases as the autocorrelation coefficient on either $\ln Q^*$ or $\ln R^*$ increases. An increase in the autocorrelation of $\ln Q^*$ [$\ln R^*$], with a constant long-run variance and a constant autocorrelation of $\ln R^*$ [$\ln Q^*$] increases the bias of the estimated coefficient of the proxy variable $\ln Q$ [$\ln R$].

Goodfriend derives a particularly interesting result for the single regressor case ($b_2 = 0$), when the true regressor $\ln Q^*$ is nonstationary (the AR coefficient is 1.0 so $\ln Q^* \sim I(1)$). Since the measurement error in these models is assumed to be stationary, nonstationarity of $\ln Q^*$ implies nonstationarity of the observable variable $\ln Q$. Since $e_t$ is assumed stationary, nonstationarity of $\ln Q$ in (2.11) implies that real balances is also a nonstationary (integrated) time series. Thus the Goodfriend model with a unit root in $\ln Q^*$ is an example of the "spurious regression" problem discussed by Granger and Newbold (1974). Goodfriend shows (his equations (26) and (27)) that under these conditions estimating the model:

$$\ln(M/P)_t = h_0 + h_1 \ln Q_t + h_2 \ln(M/P)_{t-1} + \varepsilon_t \tag{2.12}$$

will produce an estimate for $h_2$ that is greater than zero and an estimate of $h_1$ that is biased towards zero from the true parameter value $b_1$ in (2.11). His most interesting result is that under these conditions $h_1/b_1 + h_2 = 1.0$, so that $b_1 = h_1/(1 - h_2)$. The implication of this result is that the inappropriate inclusion of a lagged dependent variable in regressions where the time series are nonstationary and measured with error will result in the false conclusion that there is a distributed lag relationship between the dependent and independent variables and will bias the estimated impact effect towards zero. However, it is only the timing of the effect of the independent variable that is subject to this bias. The estimated steady-state response to a change in $\ln Q^*$ in the misspecified regression is $h_1/(1-h_2)$, which is the true steady-state (instantaneous) response of $\ln(M/P)$ to $\ln Q^*$. Goodfriend's result for the single regressor model can be shown to generalize to two regressors when both regressors are nonstationary and at least one of them is subject to measurement error (see Appendix A).

## 2.3 Specification Testing - The U.S. Experience

Beginning in the early 1970s, partial adjustment models were commonly evaluated on the basis of a particular type of specification test. This technique is dynamic simulation analysis, applied either within sample or in true post-sample forecasting experiments. An early example of this approach to specification testing is given in Table 4 of Goldfeld (1973) where root-mean-squared errors are tabulated for four quarter ahead dynamic simulations for a number of nonoverlapping periods both within and post sample periods. In the early 1970s these forecasting experiments generally indicated very small bias and were judged to validate the partial adjustment model.

Beginning in the middle 1970s, post sample forecasts from partial adjustment models began to exhibit systematic bias. This was noted by Goldfeld (1976) who labelled the problem one of "missing money", since the dynamic forecasts typically overestimated the real balances that were actually observed. The pattern observed by Hein (1980) and reproduced in Table 2.2 is typical of many reported dynamic simulation experiments during this period. A second problem that was observed was parameter instability in recursive regressions as the estimation period was extended through the mid 1970s. The parameter instability typically took the form of increases in the estimated coefficient on the lagged dependent variable (decreases in the speed of adjustment) or increases in the estimated autoregressive coefficient of the disturbance specification as the sample period was extended. Examples of this type of parameter instability can be found in Hafer and Hein (1980), Tables 1 and 2. In particular note that these equations can be written in the form of a transfer function (Box and Jenkins (1976)) in which the autoregressive part of the data generating process for real balances is second order with coefficients $(1 - (s + z)L + szL^2)$ where $L$ is the usual lag operator. As the sample period is extended beyond 1974, the coefficients of this polynomial estimated by Hafer and Hein (1980) indicate either a unit root, or that the polynomial is not invertible.

The rationalizations proposed for these instabilities were of two types. One school of thought argued that the observations reflected substantive changes in economic behavior as a result of financial innovation (for examples see Garcia and Pak (1979) and Porter, Simpson and Mauskopf (1979)). A second group of critics argued that the instabilities reflected problems in the stock adjustment specification.

Financial innovations were alleged to create two types of problems for the hypothesis of a stable demand function for aggregate real balances. The first problem cited was a measurement problem. Increases in nominal interest rates associated with rising inflation in the 1970s generated profitable opportunities to create and market new financial instruments that were not restricted by the interest rate regulations that were imposed on bank deposits by the banking legislation adopted during the 1930s. NOW accounts, share drafts and bank repo arrangements are all examples of such instruments. Proponents of the financial innovation hypothesis noted that such assets were efficient substitutes for cash and checkable deposits, but were excluded from the contemporaneous definitions and official measures of "money". Even if there were no change in the demand for money at the individual or aggregate level, available measures of "money" understated the true size of assets that were demanded as "money". Hence, according to this view, there really was "missing money" from the official definitions.

In 1974 the Board of Governors of the Federal Reserve appointed a special advisory committee to study the existing measures of monetary aggregates and to make recommendations for improved measures. The report of the Advisory Committee on Monetary Statistics, Improving the Monetary Aggregates was published in June, 1976. In 1980 the Board of Governors of the Federal Reserve System began publishing revised official measures of the various monetary aggregates that in large part conformed to the recommendations of the advisory committee. These new official statistics either incorporated, or provided information that measured the impact of many of the newly created financial instruments (see Simpson (1980)). The new measures of money did not alleviate the parameter instability in the partial adjustment model specifications (see Hafer and Hein (1982), Table 1).

The second element of the financial innovation hypothesis was that portfolio behavior of agents really was changing during this period. Therefore, even if "money" was correctly measured, post-sample forecasts using parameters estimated from the 50s and 60s would still overestimate the correctly measured aggregate real balances. The foundation of this argument derives from Tobin's (1956) transactions theory of money demand that postulates both fixed and proportional transactions costs. The financial innovation hypothesis argued that the increases in interest rates in the 70s raised the opportunity costs of holding real balances to the extent that the savings in opportunity costs from permanently restructuring portfolios more than offset the fixed costs of making such fundamental changes in behavior. Changes in corporate compensating balance arrangements are cited as an example of such fundamental shifts in portfolio behavior.

The financial innovations hypothesis viewed the problems observed in partial adjustment models of aggregate money demand as a continuing process. This was supported by reference to dynamic simulation results such as those reported in Table 2.2 where the forecast errors become larger (in absolute value) as the forecasting horizon increases. The alternative view of the parameter instability observed in the 70s is that the observed specification problems are not consistent with an evolutionary process and that there is something fundamental wrong with the partial adjustment specification itself.

It is not widely understood that forecast errors such as those in Table 2.2 do not necessarily imply a continuing process of change, but are also consistent with a one-time permanent shock to the demand for real balances. Assume that for a sample period (ending at $T$) the relationship between $Y$ and $X$ is:

$$Y_t = a + bX_t + cY_{t-1} + e_t \tag{2.13}$$

Dynamic forecasts starting at period $T+1$ are constructed as:

Table 2.2: Real Adjustment Version(Log Level Equation)

| | | Coefficients (t-stats in parentheses) | | | | | diagnostics | | |
|---|---|---|---|---|---|---|---|---|---|
| Est. | Sample | Const | ln $y_t$ | ln(cpr)$_t$ | ln(Rtd)$_t$ | ln(mp)$_{t-1}$ | Durb-h | $\rho$ | SSE* |
| CORC | 55:2-62:4 | -0.644 | 0.140 | -0.017 | -0.034 | 0.698 | -.03 | .26 | .38 |
| | | (2.30) | (2.75) | (4.11) | (2.39) | (7.51) | | | |
| CORC | 55:2-63:4 | -0.838 | 0.169 | -0.018 | -0.038 | 0.710 | .03 | .33 | .38 |
| | | (3.13) | (3.39) | (4.07) | (2.61) | (7.64) | | | |
| CORC | 55:2-64:4 | -0.962 | 0.184 | -0.018 | -0.040 | 0.742 | .18 | .37 | .37 |
| | | (3.93) | (3.92) | (4.08) | (2.81) | (8.17) | | | |
| CORC | 55:2-65:4 | -0.954 | 0.186 | -0.019 | -0.041 | 0.716 | .37 | .30 | .38 |
| | | (4.37) | (4.28) | (4.29) | (3.08) | (8.25) | | | |
| CORC | 55:2-66:4 | -0.755 | 0.154 | -0.021 | -0.032 | 0.724 | .61 | .44 | .41 |
| | | (3.40) | (3.44) | (4.08) | (2.32) | (7.59) | | | |
| CORC | 55:2-67:4 | -0.842 | 0.170 | -0.021 | -0.037 | 0.708 | .57 | .41 | .40 |
| | | (4.43) | (4.34) | (4.48) | (2.95) | (8.07) | | | |
| CORC | 55:2-68:4 | -0.893 | 0.179 | -0.021 | -0.039 | 0.703 | .75 | .42 | .40 |
| | | (4.90) | (4.72) | (4.49) | (3.27) | (8.27) | | | |
| CORC | 55:2-69:4 | -0.905 | 0.181 | -0.023 | -0.040 | 0.698 | .81. | .42 | .39 |
| | | (5.04) | (4.88) | (5.09) | (3.36) | (8.53) | | | |
| CORC | 55:2-70:4 | -0.916 | 0.184 | -0.022 | -0.040 | 0.688 | .93 | .42 | .38 |
| | | (5.23) | (5.09) | (5.13) | (3.53) | (8.71) | | | |
| CORC | 55:2-71:4 | -.9016 | 0.179 | -0.017 | -0.040 | 0.661 | 1.38 | .43 | .41 |
| | | (4.89) | (4.84) | (4.22) | (3.38) | (8.12) | | | |
| CORC | 55:2-72:4 | -0.861 | 0.177 | -0.016 | -0.040 | 0.665 | 1.32 | .44 | .40 |
| | | (5.18) | (5.04) | (4.57) | (3.51) | (8.36) | | | |
| CORC | 55:2-73:4 | -.0867 | 0.180 | -0.016 | -0.040 | 0.649 | 1.46 | .44 | .40 |
| | | (5.24) | (5.16) | (4.70) | (3.57) | (8.28) | | | |
| CORC | 55:2-74:4 | -0.703 | 0.145 | -0.022 | -0.032 | 0.732 | 1.13 | .60 | .46 |
| | | (3.90) | (3.87) | (4.88) | (2.48) | (8.54) | | | |
| CORC | 55:2-75:4 | -0.716 | 0.155 | -0.014 | -0.048 | 0.678 | .31 | .87 | .51 |
| | | (3.69) | (4.30) | (3.01) | (2.70) | (7.76) | | | |
| CORC | 55:2-76:4 | -0.702 | 0.156 | -0.013 | -0.050 | 0.652 | -.28 | .91 | .50 |
| | | (3.52) | (4.45) | (2.95) | (2.74) | (7.70) | | | |
| CORC | 55:2-77:4 | -0.688 | 0.156 | -0.013 | -0.050 | 0.632 | -.39 | .93 | .50 |
| | | (3.41) | (4.50) | (2.88) | (2.72) | (7.51) | | | |
| HILU | 55:2-78:4 | -0.919 | 0.190 | -0.014 | -0.045 | 0.583 | -.39 | .98 | .51 |
| | | (2.43) | (3.47) | (3.15) | (2.33) | (6.78) | | | |

Note:The SSE's are $\times 10^{-3}$

$$Y^f_{T+1} = a + bX_{T+1} + cY_T \tag{2.14}$$

$$Y^f_{T+2} = a + bX_{T+2} + cY^f_{T+1} = a + bX_{T+2} + c[a + bX_{T+1} + cY_T]$$

$$= a(1+c) + bX_{T+2} + bcX_T + c^2Y_T \tag{2.15}$$

and in general:

$$Y^f_{T+i} = a\sum_{j=0}^{i-1} c^j + b\sum_{j=0}^{i-1} c^j X_{T+i-j} + c^j Y_T \tag{2.16}$$

As long as the structure of the relationship between $Y$ and $X$ remains unchanged, the actual post-sample generating process for $Y$ is given by:

$$Y_{T+i} = a\sum_{j=0}^{i-1} c^j + \sum_{j=0}^{i-1} c^j X_{T+i-j} + c^j Y_T + \sum_{j=0}^{i-1} c^j e_{T+i-j} \tag{2.17}$$

Therefore the dynamic simulation errors are:
$Y_{T+i} - Y^f_{T+i} = \sum_{j=0}^{i-1} c^j e_{T+i-j}$ and

$$E[Y_{T+i} - Y^f_{T+i}] = \sum_{j=0}^{i-1} c^j E[e_{T+i-j}] = 0 \tag{2.18}$$

Now assume there is a one-time permanent changes in the constant term of (2.13), and assume that this change is not known nor considered in constructing the post-sample dynamic simulations (see Hein (1980)). The actual data generating process after T is not (2.13) but rather:

$$Y_{T+i} = a^* + bX_{T+i} + cY_{T+i-1} + e_{T+i},\ i > 0 \tag{2.19}$$

for $a^*$ not equal to a. Then

$$Y_{T+i} = a^*\sum_{j=0}^{i-1} c^j + b\sum_{j=0}^{i-1} c^j X_{T+i-j} + c^j Y_T + \sum_{j=0}^{i-1} c^j e_{T+i-j} \tag{2.20}$$

Under these conditions, the dynamic simulation errors are:

$$Y_{T+i} - Y^f_{T+i} = (a^* - a)\sum_{j=0}^{i-1} c^j + \sum_{j=0}^{i-1} c^j e_{T+i-j} \tag{2.21}$$

Since $\sum_{j=0}^{i-1} c^j = (1 - c^j)/(1 - c)$, as the forecast horizon becomes longer, the dynamic simulation errors will fluctuate around $(a^* - a)/(1 - c)$ after the one-time change in the constant term. This is the general pattern of the dynamic forecast errors from the equations in Table 2.2.

Additional evidence that is consistent with the specification error explanation of the "missing money" phenomenon is found in Tables 5 and 6 of Hafer and Hein (1980). There authors estimated first differences of the standard partial adjustment models. Implicit in this transformation is the assumption that shocks to real balances are "permanent". Under this transformation, the estimated parameters of both the real and nominal adjustment equations remain stable as recursive regression samples are extended through the 60s and 70s, and there is no evidence of serial correlation in the residuals. Hafer and Hein (1980) include a lagged real balance term in their first difference specification. The interpretation of the coefficient on this lagged dependent variable is problematic, since the partial adjustment model specifies a relationship between the levels of actual real balances and the levels of the determinants of equilibrium real balances, but all information on relationships among levels of variables is lost in the differencing process.

Hafer and Hein (1982) provide additional support for their conclusion that the breakdown of the partial adjustment model in the mid 1970s is a result of a one-time permanent shock to the level of real balances through an analysis of covariance on a traditional log-linear specification of a real partial adjustment model that allows for changes in both the intercept and slopes of the regression model in the second quarter of 1974. They conclude that there is no evidence in favor of the hypothesis that the slopes of the regression change, but that there is a significant negative shift in the regression intercept at this time. They conclude

> "changes in money demand since II/1974 can be explained by changes in the exogenous variables without relying on tenuous assertions that the underlying economic relationships have degenerated. Although previous analyses have suggested that there has been a continuous, unexplained deterioration of the money demand function after 1973, our analysis suggests that marginal relationships have remained stable over the I/1960 - IV/1979 period, providing useful information in estimating the level of money demand" (Hafer and Hein (1982), p. 16).

This conclusion appears to have been premature. Their estimate of the real partial adjustment model over the sample period 60:1 - 73:4 is quite similar to previously published studies for this sample period, even though the data on nominal money balances used in this study are the new measures introduced by the Board of Governors in 1980. When the sample period is extended through 1979, allowing for a shift in the regression intercept in 74:2, the estimated coefficient on lagged real balances is approximately .92 that implies a speed of adjustment of only eight percent per quarter. This is extremely low, even when compared with the estimates from the data of the 50s and 60s. The estimated standard error on the coefficient of the lagged dependent variable is .057, suggesting that it may not be significantly less than unity and that the autoregressive part of the estimated process generating real balances may not be invertible. In light of the results from Goodfriend's measurement error model, the estimated steady-state parameters from the Hafer and Hein regression are particularly interesting. The point estimate of the equilibrium real income elasticity is .92 (that is probably not significantly less than unity, though there is insufficient information in the published results to confirm this conjecture) and the sum of the steady-state interest elasticities with respect to the commercial paper rate and the time deposit rate is .49. These estimates of the steady-state elasticities are much larger than any of the estimates derived from partial adjustment models estimated over pre 1974 sample periods, and are quite similar to elasticities estimated from equilibrium specifications on samples of annual data over half a century.

The final collapse of the partial adjustment specification occurred in the early 1980s. At this time there was a significant change in the time series behavior of M1 velocity (Haraf (1985)). During the 1950s - 1970s this time series appeared to behave like a random walk (I(1)) process with a positive drift (deterministic trend) of around three percent per year. It is this property of this velocity measure that is the basis for the Andersen-Jordan (1968) equation of the relationship between measures of monetary and fiscal policy variables and nominal economic activity. Sometime in the early 80s, most likely in late 1981, the deterministic trend changed, and since that time the deterministic trend has been zero or slightly negative. This change contrasts with the hypothesis of a change in the level of real balances for a given level of real income that is alleged to have occurred in the mid 70s.

After an analysis of partial adjustment models on a sample of U.S. data for the period 1974-83, Roley (1985) concluded:

> "Empirical results concerning the partial adjustment model also were rather pessimistic. In particular, it is not clear that the partial adjustment model – either in real or nominal terms – should be preferred over specifications simply accounting for serially correlated residuals. The robustness of the partial adjustment model – at least when estimated over the 1974-83 period – again may be questioned on the basis of estimation results obtained after differencing the specifications" (p. 635).

In a subsequent analysis Rasche (1987) found that a relationship between the first difference of real balances, a distributed lag on first differences of real income, and a distributed lag of first differences of interest rates could be found for samples that ended in the mid 70s. In addition, it was shown that the estimates of the parameters of this equation remained stable when the sample was extended through 1981. This is consistent with the results from the first differences of the lagged dependent variable specification used by Hafer and Hein (1980). However, it was also determined that for the parameter estimates to remain stable when the sample was extended to include 1982-5, it was necessary to allow for a shift in the intercept term (the deterministic drift) at the end of 1981.

In contrast to the geometric distributed lag restriction implied by the lagged dependent variable specification, Rasche (1987) utilized unrestricted finite distributed lags. He found that the restriction of unity on the sum of the coefficients in the real income changes in general could not be rejected, regardless of sample period or degree of time aggregation. This contrasts with the first difference specifications of Hafer and Hein (1980) with the lagged dependent variable, in which the implicit sum of the distributed lag coefficients on real income is generally in the range of .4 to .5. In Rasche's equations, the sum of the unrestricted estimated distributed lag coefficients on the interest rate is uniformly small, which is consistent with the results from the geometric lag results on first differenced variables.

## 2.4 Another Look at U.S. Money Demand

In light of the criticisms and shortcomings of the partial adjustment models discussed in the preceding section, a reexamination of some of the published estimates of these models is warranted. We consider both the sample of annual data that was used in Chow (1966) and the sample of pre-1973 quarterly data that was used in Goldfeld (1973).

Chow (1966) reported estimates of both an equilibrium (long-run) money demand specification (his Table 1) and a partial adjustment (short-run) money demand equation (his Table 2). In contrast to the reported equilibrium parameters in Table 1, the speeds of adjustment implicit in the partial adjustment models are extremely slow, ranging from .1 to .5 per annum. In a number of cases, the regressions reported in Table 2 differ only from the equilibrium equation reported in Table 1 by the addition of the lagged dependent variable. In these cases it is possible to compare the estimated steady-state coefficients under the two specifications. For the models that include only one scale variable (permanent income, wealth or current income) the steady-state coefficients obtained from the partial adjustment model are very similar to the coefficient estimates in the comparable equilibrium model. For the double log specifications, the implied steady-state income coefficient from the partial adjustment model is slightly larger than that of the equilibrium model and the absolute value of the implied steady-state interest coefficient from the partial adjustment model is slightly smaller than that of the equilibrium model. However, in these cases the results are generally consistent with the outcome predicted by the Goodfriend (1985) nonstationary errors-in-variables model for the partial adjustment regression. In those cases where more than one scale variable is included in the regressions, there does not appear to be any systematic relationship between the steady-state coefficient estimates from the two specifications.

Goldfeld (1973) does not report any regression results for an equilibrium specification on the sample of quarterly data. We have reconstructed these data from the sources reported in his Appendix, with the exception of the commercial bank time deposit rate that was generously supplied by Professor Goldfeld. Using these data, we have essentially reproduced the partial adjustment model

Table 2.3: Estimated Demand for Real Balances (M1): 1952:1-1972:4

| Const | ln(Q) | ln(RCP) | ln(RTD) | $\ln(M/P)_{t-1}$ | $\bar{R}^2$ | SSE | DW | $\rho$ |
|---|---|---|---|---|---|---|---|---|
| .4250 | .1921<br>(.0349)<br>{.6143} | -.0188<br>(.0032)<br>{-.0601} | -.0456<br>(.0110)<br>{-.1458} | 0.6873<br>(.0670) | .994 | .0044 | 1.77 | .43 |
| .3430 | .1788<br>(.0293)<br>{.6387} | -.0198<br>(.0025)<br>{-.0707} | -.0423<br>(.0089)<br>{-.1511} | .7201<br>(.0556) | .993 | .0049 | 1.13 | - |
| 1.7320 | .5483<br>(.0017) | -.0269<br>(.0042) | -.1519<br>(.0050) | – | .979 | .0085 | .70 | - |
| -.0936 | .0436<br>(.0071)<br>{1.406} | -.0178<br>(.0027)<br>{-.5742} | – | .9690<br>(.0203) | .991 | .0055 | 1.13 | - |
| 3.2578 | .2851<br>(.0273) | -.0397<br>(.0145) | – | – | .742 | .0296 | .07 | - |
| **Estimates with Real Output as Dependent Variable** | | | | | | | | |
| -2.8443 | -1.0000<br><br>{.5683} | .0534<br>(.0070)<br>{-.0303} | .2786<br>(.0061)<br>{-.1583} | 1.7594<br>(.0376)<br>{-1.0000} | .995 | .0152 | .73 | - |
| -4.1309 | -1.0000<br>·<br>{.4964} | .0267<br>(.2714)<br>{-.1347} | – | 2.0141<br>(.1928)<br>{-1.000} | .876 | .0787 | .20 | - |
| **Estimates with the Commercial Paper rate as Dependent Variable** | | | | | | | | |
| 17.145 | 7.865<br>(1.034)<br>{.6190} | -1.0000<br><br>{.0768} | -1.849<br>(.325)<br>{-.1455} | -12.707<br>(1.972)<br>{-1.000} | .808 | .184 | .58 | - |
| -1.0207 | 2.0665<br>(.2031)<br>{.9679} | -1.0000<br><br>{-.4683} | – | -2.1350<br>(.7796)<br>{-1.0000} | .912 | .125 | .34 | - |

for M1 reported in that study as indicated in the first equation of Table 2.3. The numbers in parentheses under the coefficient estimates are the conventional estimated standard errors, while the numbers in braces are the estimated steady-state coefficients. The second equation in that table shows that for this sample, the results are quite insensitive to the inclusion of an AR(1) disturbance structure. For all practical purposes, all that is accomplished by the addition of the autoregressive coefficient is to reduce the serial correlation in the estimated residuals and improve the efficiency of the coefficient estimates. In both cases the estimated speed of adjustment is moderately slow, on the order of thirty percent per quarter.

The steady-state estimates that are implied by the partial adjustment model in the first two equations of Table 2.3 are quite similar to the steady-state estimates that are obtained from an equilibrium specification, as indicated in the third equation in the table. This result is again consistent with Goodfriend's non-stationary errors-in-variables hypothesis. In all three cases the estimated equilibrium income elasticity is on the order of .6 and the sum of the estimated equilibrium interest elasticities is on the order of .2. These estimates are substantially smaller than the equilibrium elasticities reported by Chow and Meltzer for annual data.

The fourth and fifth equations reported in Table 2.3 indicate that the estimates from this quarterly sample are very sensitive to the exclusion of the time deposit interest rate. In those cases where the time deposit rate is included, the partial elasticity with respect to this rate is always much larger in absolute value than the partial elasticity with respect to the commercial paper rate. Without the time deposit rate and with no correction for autocorrelated residuals, the estimated coefficient on the lagged dependent variable is not significantly less than unity, which is consistent with the view that real balances are nonstationary. (The comparable result, with the autoregressive adjustment is reported in Goldfeld (1973), Table 16). When both the time deposit rate and the lagged dependent variable are excluded from the regression, the estimated income elasticity is less than .3 and the estimated coefficient on the commercial paper rate is barely significant measured against the conventional "$t$"-test.

If the variables involved in these regressions are really nonstationary, and if there exists a stationary linear combination of the variables, then a regression of levels upon levels of the variables is a consistent single equation estimator of the long-run relationship among the variables, though not an efficient estimator (Engle and Granger (1987); Stock (1987)). However, from this limited information perspective, there is no reason to prefer one normalization of the regression over any other normalization. In the classical regression model, with only two regressors, reversing the normalization of the regression is a traditional method of bounding the least squares bias generated by simultaneity or errors-in-variables. This technique has also been applied in the multivariable case generated by money demand specifications (e.g. Poole (1970), Goldfeld (1973)). Cooley and LeRoy (1981) have shown that in the multivariable regression, least squares coefficient bias is not bounded by this technique.

In the middle of Table 2.3, estimates of the equilibrium specification normalized for the log of real output are reported. In the bottom part of the table the same equations with a commercial paper rate normalization are reported. The renormalized coefficients are reported in braces under the standard errors of the estimated coefficients.

Normalization by real output has no effect on the inference about the steady-state relationship among these variables. Again the implicit steady-state real income elasticity is on the order of .5 - .6 and the sum of the steady-state interest elasticities is on the order of .2 to .3. Normalization on the log of the commercial paper rate produces dramatically different results depending on whether the time deposit rate is included or excluded from the specification. When the time deposit rate is included, the renormalized estimates are quite similar to those reported in the first two sections of the table. When the time deposit rate is excluded from the specification the implied real income elasticity

Table 2.4: Equilibrium Demand Functions for Real Balances (M1) 1900-1956: DOLS Estimates with Two Lags

| Const | ln(M/P)) | ln(Q) | ln(R) | $\overline{R}^2$ | SSE | DW |
|---|---|---|---|---|---|---|
| | | Real M1–Real Income | | | | |
| .4484 | -1.000 | .9337 | -.7556 | .993 | .0525 | 1.09 |
| | | (.022) | (.059) | | | |
| -.4285 | 1.0681 | -1.0000 | .7972 | .984 | .0694 | 1.19 |
| | (.0299) | | (.091) | | | |
| | {-1.0000} | {.9362} | {-.7464} | | | |
| .7585 | -1.2197 | 1.1202 | -1.0000 | .905 | .071 | .75 |
| | (.1233) | (.1409) | | | | |
| | {-1.0000} | {.9184} | {-.8199} | | | |
| | | Nominal M1–Nominal Income | | | | |
| .2720 | -1.0000 | .9676 | -.7269 | .996 | .0604 | .74 |
| | | (.0210) | (.0930) | | | |
| -.3374 | 1.0370 | -1.0000 | .7652 | .993 | .0749 | .93 |
| | (.0212) | | (.1011) | | | |
| | {-1.0000} | {.9643} | {-.7379} | | | |
| .5613 | -1.2841 | 1.2313 | -1.0000 | .881 | .0799 | .59 |
| | (.1540) | (.1651) | | | | |
| | {-1.0000} | {.9589} | {-.7788} | | | |

**Note:** Numbers in {} indicate renormalization.

is close to 1.0 and the implied commercial paper rate elasticity is about .5.

The interpretation of these estimates as coefficients of a steady-state demand equation for real balances when the time series are really nonstationary requires that the residuals of the estimated relationship be stationary. In a number of cases in Table 2.3, the low estimated Durbin-Watson statistics suggest that such stationary is problematic. The problem here is that the number of observations in the sample is so small, and the span of the data is so short that the available tests of stationarity or nonstationary are likely to have very low power against the respective alternative hypothesis.

We tried one other specification using the Goldfeld data set. In their study of short-run demand functions for broadly defined money in the U.K., Artis and Lewis (1976) argue that the implicit assumption in the standard partial adjustment model that interest rates are free to adjust to equilibrium rates in the short run is not appropriate. They argue that the operating procedures used by the Bank of England preclude short-term nominal rates from quickly adjusting to the market clearing rates, and therefore a more appropriate specification is to imbed the equilibrium demand for real balances in a partial interest rate adjustment model. The argument that they present for the Bank of England operating procedures are reasonable to apply to interest rate behavior under the various historical Federal Reserve operating procedures. The difference in the specification from the ones that have been discussed here is that the equation is estimated with an interest rate as the dependent variable and includes a lagged interest rate variable rather than the lagged real balance variable. When estimates of this specification were constructed from the Goldfeld data, the estimated speed of interest rate adjustment is still very slow (.2 per quarter) and the estimated coefficient on real balances is so small that the estimated long run income and interest elasticities of the demand for real balances are completely nonsensical.

In our final attempt at single equation estimation, we assumed that the data series in both samples are generated by a nonstationary process, and attempted to estimate a stationary relationship among the three variables using different normalizations for estimation. The estimates are obtained using Stock and Watson's (1993) dynamic ordinary least squares (DOLS) estimator that under restrictive assumption about the data generating process, produces an efficient estimate of a stationary linear combination of the variables, if such exists, and appropriate estimates of the standard errors of the nonstandard distribution of the estimated coefficients.

The results of applying the DOLS estimator (with two lags) to the Chow data sample are reported in Table 2.4. The relationship between the log of money, the log of income and the log of the long-term interest rate was estimated in both real and nominal specifications as in the original article, and with each of the three variables, in turn, chosen as the dependent variable in the estimating equation. The results in Table 2.4 can be summarized very briefly: they all uniformly support the conclusion that the long-run income elasticity is approximately 1.0 and the long-run interest elasticity is .7 - .8. Furthermore, while the estimated Durbin-Watson statistics suggest that there is still substantial serial correlation in the residuals of the DOLS estimates, there is nothing to suggest that these residuals are nonstationary. Thus this approach appears to reinforce the conclusions that were reached from the original Chow equilibrium specification.

The DOLS estimates from the Goldfeld sample do not produce any consistent results. When the time deposit rate in included in the regressions, the estimates of the equilibrium real income and interest elasticities are little changed from those reported in Table 2.5, regardless of the normalization imposed on the estimation. In two of the three normalizations the estimated Durbin-Watson statistics are sufficiently small that the stationarity of the residuals is suspect. When the time deposit rate is omitted from the regression, the results change dramatically across normalizations. In the real balance normalization the estimated coefficient on the log of the commercial paper rate is not significantly different from zero. In the real output and interest rate normalizations, the estimates of the real income elasticity are on the order of 1.0 and the estimates of the interest elasticity are on the order of .3 - .4. In these last two cases the results are in line with the conclusions from the Chow sample of annual data. However, in five of the six specifications estimated the estimated Durbin-Watson statistics are sufficiently low to cast doubt on whether the residuals of

Table 2.5: Estimated Demand for Real Balances (M1) 1952:1-1972:2 ; DOLS Estimates with Two Lags

| | | Real M1–Real Income | | | | | |
|---|---|---|---|---|---|---|---|
| Const | ln(M/P)) | ln(Q) | ln(RCP) | ln(RTD) | $\overline{R}^2$ | SSE | DW |
| 1.5490 | -1.0000 | .5809 | -.0424 | -.1536 | .98 | .0074 | 0.43 |
| | | (.01313) | (.0160) | (.0109) | | | |
| 2.4344 | -1.0000 | .4384 | -.1263 | | .76 | .0270 | 0.16 |
| | | (.1660) | (.0901) | | | | |
| -2.5135 | 1.6899 | -1.0000 | -.0806 | -.2586 | .99 | .0123 | 0.42 |
| | (.1222) | | (.0285) | (.0283) | | | |
| | {-1.0000} | {.5918} | {-.0476} | {-.1515} | | | |
| | 1.1593 | -1.0000 | -.3816 | | .94 | .0524 | 0.21 |
| | (.4420) | | (.0507) | | | | |
| | {-1.0000} | {.8626} | {-.3292} | | | | |
| 12.7529 | -10.6305 | 6.8659 | -1.0000 | -1.4426 | .91 | .1265 | 1.01 |
| | (3.1296) | (1.6393) | | (.5174) | | | |
| | (-1.0000} | {.6459} | {-.0940} | {-.1357} | | | |
| -2.0856 | -2.1892 | 2.3035 | -1.0000 | | .89 | .1434 | 0.59 |
| | (1.0045) | (.2469) | | | | | |
| | {-1.0000} | {1.5022} | {-.4568} | | | | |

**Note:** Numbers in {}indicate renormalization.

these regressions are truly stationary.

We conclude from these experiments on two historical data sets that the single equation approach to estimating demand functions for real balances from short samples of quarterly data probably has never been particularly informative for the United States. Even for sample periods for which it appeared that a satisfactory statistical relationship had been uncovered, it appears that the traditional interpretation of the results are questionable. Partial adjustment specifications cannot be identified relative to errors-in-variables specifications. This is particularly telling, since many published studies utilize a variety of alternative measures of the regressors on the grounds that none of them measure the true arguments of the demand for real balances. Attempts to estimate equilibrium specifications on the traditional samples of data produce results that are not very robust and whose interpretation as estimates of parameters of a demand for money function are questionable.

# Chapter 3

# IDENTIFICATION, ESTIMATION, AND INFERENCE IN COINTEGRATED SYSTEMS

Chapters 3 and 4 provide technical background for the empirical applications conducted in Chapters 6-8. In this Chapter we examine identification, estimation and testing hypotheses in models characterized by long-run relations that may prevail in nonstationary time series data. The discussion does not break new ground, but brings together important points that span in a wide range of literature. At the same time, there is no attempt to incorporate all contributions that have been made in this area. The discussion is "complete" only in the sense that it provides a unified approach to dealing with the econometric issues inherent in the consideration of nonstationary macroeconomic aggregates. We tackle issues in the sequence they are typically encountered in applied work. The discussion spans issues of structural identification, estimation and inference, and structural stability while implications for dynamic analysis are discussed in Chapter 4. The discussion is aimed at those readers wishing to acquaint themselves with an econometric approach for empirical analysis of models characterized by integrated and cointegrated variables. In later chapters the techniques are illustrated with applications that pertain to a long–run money demand relation, but the methodology may be applied in a number of areas. Chapter 3 begins by providing background on nonstationarity and the implications that unit roots have for estimation of a stable long-run money demand function. In section 3.2 procedures designed to detect unit roots are discussed. The discussion primarily focuses on the detection of unit roots in a multivariate setting.

Some of the most recent advances designed to handle general and broken deterministic trend specifications are documented. In section 3.3 we turn our attention to the topic of long-run parameter identification that results in partial identification of a structural VAR. A discussion of complete identification in the context of the structural VAR associated with the time series representation of variables that comprise a money demand model is reserved for Chapter 4. Examples from existing literature are used to illustrate the concepts. In section 3.4 several of the popular approaches to estimating the cointegration space are examined including a section on overidentifying restrictions and a discussion of statistical inference. In Section 3.5 approaches designed to test "long-run" parameter constancy are explored.

## 3.1 Nonstationary and the Estimation of Money Demand Models

Recent developments in time series econometrics have underscored the notion that empirical analysis of variables that are inherently nonstationary requires special consideration. Excellent technical discussion of these issues appears in a number of papers and textbooks.[1] Below we sketch an outline for understanding the role played by nonstationarity in estimating a "long–run" money demand function. Our goal is to provide the intuition behind some of the techniques that have been applied to deal with observed nonstationarities while interested readers are referred to original sources for more technical treatment.

Covariance stationary processes have finite mean with variance and covariance that are both finite and "time invariant". A vector $z_t$, consisting of $p$ stationary time series may be represented in a multivariate vector autoregressive process as

$$z_t = \mu + \sum_{j=1}^{q} \Pi_j z_{t-j} + \varepsilon_t, \tag{3.1}$$

where $\mu$ denotes a vector of constants, $\Pi_j$ matrices of autoregressive coefficients and $\varepsilon_t$ is a $p$-dimensional random vector of serially uncorrelated disturbance or error terms.

Define the lag polynomial

$$\Pi(L) = I - \sum_{j=1}^{q} \Pi_j L^j \tag{3.2}$$

and note that when the roots of the characteristic equation

$$|\Pi(\zeta)| = 0 \tag{3.3}$$

[1] Surveys by Stock(1994), on unit root analysis, and Watson(1994) on the topic of cointegration provide firm technical foundation, as well as an excellent list of references, for much of the literature that serves as a basis for the techniques discussed in Chapter 3. In addition, texts by Banerjee et. al.(1993), on cointegration and error correction issues, and Hamilton(1994), on a wide range of time series topics, provide excellent treatment of these topics.

are outside the unit circle, there exists a $p \times p$ lag polynomial matrix $C(L)$ such that $C(L)\Pi(L) = I_p$ and the vector process has moving average representation

$$z_t = \mu + \sum_{j=0}^{\infty} C_j \varepsilon_{t-j}. \tag{3.4}$$

When these conditions apply, each element of $z_t$ is stationary. (see Fuller (1976), Hamilton (1994), or Watson (1994) for formal treatment)

Most conventional approaches to estimation and inference in time series models are based on this fundamental concept of stationarity. In practice, time series variables are assumed to be stationary or are simply integrated (differenced) until they exhibit the characteristics of stationarity.

### 3.1.1 Nonstationary Univariate Processes

Consider a univariate autoregressive representation of the $i^{th}$ element of random vector $z_t$; $z_{ti}$,

$$\Pi_i(L) z_{ti} = \mu_i + \varepsilon_{ti} \tag{3.5}$$

The degree of integration maintained by $z_{ti}$ depends upon the degree of nonstationarity or number of unit roots that prevail in the univariate polynomial

$$\Pi_i(\zeta) = 0 \tag{3.6}$$

When "$d$" roots of (3.6) are equal to 1, the univariate process is integrated of order $d$; $z_{ti} \sim I(d)$.

In contrast to variables that are covariance stationary, the higher moments of integrated time series depend upon $t$. We confine our discussion to situations where $z_{ti} \sim I(1)$ so that the time series maintains a single "unit root".[2] Then by definition, $\Delta z_{ti}$ is stationary and maintains a Wold representation[3]

$$\Delta z_{ti} = C_i(L)(\mu_i + \varepsilon_{ti}) = \gamma_i + C_i(L)\varepsilon_{ti} \tag{3.7}$$

As illustrated by Beveridge and Nelson (1981), among others, we may decompose the lag polynomial $C_i(L)$ as;

$$C_i(L) = C_i(1) + (1 - L)C_i^*(L) \tag{3.8}$$

so the "levels" of $z_{ti}$ may be expressed as

$$z_{ti} = z_{0i} + C_i(1)\left(\mu_i t + \sum_{s=1}^{t} \varepsilon_{si}\right) + C_i^*(L)\varepsilon_{ti} \tag{3.9}$$

---

[2] Some applications have focused on models that exhibit higher orders of integration (see Johansen (1992a)) while others have examined "fractionally integrated" systems(see Hamilton (1994)).

[3] We assume that the accompanying Wold representation is "invertible." In Chapter 4 we discuss the implications for conducting dynamic analysis with structures that exhibit "nonfundamental"(non–invertible) moving average representations. This issue is discussed by Lippi and Reichlin (1993), among others.

Equation (3.9) reveals that unless $C_i(1) = 0$, $z_{ti}$ will contain a random walk component that imparts nonstationarity to $z_{ti}$. Clearly, any innovation in this random walk; $\sum_{s=1}^{t} \varepsilon_{si}$, will leave a lasting imprint on the value maintained by $z_{ti}$ at any point in the future. It is the permanent imprint left by the history of innovations that characterizes integrated time series.

### 3.1.2 Nonstationary Vector Processes

Vector processes consisting of $p$ distinct and potentially $I(1)$ variables have attracted considerable attention in the literature. To facilitate the discussion, allow $z_t$ to consist of $p$ potentially integrated variables and write (3.1) in its now familiar "error correction" form by simply subtracting $z_{t-1}$ from each side of the equality and combining terms to obtain.

$$\Delta z_t = \mu + \sum_{i=1}^{q-1} \Pi_i^* \Delta z_{t-i} - \Pi z_{t-1} + \varepsilon_t \tag{3.10}$$

where $\Pi_i^* = -\Pi_{i+1} - .... - \Pi_q$, $i = 1, 2, ..., q-1$ and $\Pi = I - \Pi_1 - \Pi_2 - .... - \Pi_q$, so that the total impact matrix of the autoregressive representation, $\Pi$, appears as a coefficient on $z_{t-1}$. .

Representation (3.10) provides a useful framework for classifying the order of integration maintained by the variables that comprise $z_t$. When the rank of $\Pi$ equals $p$, the root condition, equation (3.3), is satisfied and the system represents $p$ distinct stationary processes. Alternatively; when the rank of $\Pi$ equals 0, the system is comprised of $p$ separate $I(1)$ processes driven by $p$ independent sources of nonstationarity. This is the implicit assumption maintained in conventional multivariate time series analysis where nonstationarity is addressed by simply "integrating" or differencing the vector process until stationarity is obtained. When the rank of $\Pi$ equals $r$ with $0 < r < p$, the system exhibits cointegration and $\Pi$ may be written as the product of two $p \times r$ matrices; $\Pi = \alpha\beta'$ that each exhibit rank $r$.[4] In the vernacular of the literature on error correction and cointegration the matrix $\alpha$ spans the "error correction" space while $\beta$ represents the "cointegration space." In this case the $r$ long–run relations imply that the only $p - r = k$ independent random walk components can produce the nonstationary behavior exhibited by the $p$-dimensional system.

### 3.1.3 Nonstationarity and the Estimation of Money Demand

As discussed in Chapter 2 much of the empirical literature on money demand either ignores the possibility of nonstationarity among variables that comprise the money demand model or implicitly assumes the variables can be differenced to achieve stationarity. In the latter case it is assumed that no information is

[4]The implications of this condition are defined in the Granger Representation Theorem. See Johansen (1991).

lost when empirical analysis is devoted exclusively to the differenced structures. However, representation (3.10) clearly illustrates that this practice ignores the role of the long–run information that prevails in the system when cointegration is observed ($\rho(\Pi) = r$). Indeed some of the conflicting results described in Chapter 2 may result from estimating an inherently long–run relation using a short–run specification. In many circumstances, cointegration provides evidence of long-run equilibria that are consistent with theories of the behavior of macroeconomic aggregates and therefore is central to understanding of macroeconomic relations. In Chapter 4 we see that knowledge of cointegration rank can pave the wave to an understanding of the dynamic underpinnings of important macro aggregates.

Economic theory clearly predicts a link between real balances, real income and a measure of opportunity cost for maintaining cash balances. The origin of this aggregate relation lies in the work of Baumol (1952), Tobin (1956) and Friedman (1956) while Lucas (1988) demonstrates how micro foundation for the relationship may be established in a representative agent setting. Considerable evidence (i.e., Johansen and Juselius (1990), Hoffman and Rasche (1991), King, Plosser, Stock and Watson (1991)) suggests that a cointegrating or long-run relation does indeed prevail among the variables that comprise a money demand model. Hendry and Ericsson (1991) and Ericsson, Hendry, and Tran (1993) provide excellent discussions of how money demand can be modelled in an error correction framework analogous to equation(3.10).

Despite this theoretical foundation, the evidence in favor of a stable long–run money demand relationship is not completely one-sided. Stock and Watson (1993) find instabilities in recursive samples estimated through the late 1970s with U.S. data, Friedman and Kuttner (1992) suggest that evidence of a long-run relationship among variables that comprise the money demand model is very weak once the sample spans the "New Operating Procedures" period of 1979-1982.[5] Both of these papers base conclusions on a semi-log specification that is consistent with most theoretical representations of the paradigm. Hoffman, Rasche, and Tieslau (1995) examine post war evidence from the U.S. and four other industrialized countries. Without reduction in the long-run parameter space, (e.g. a unitary income elasticity) the case for stability is mixed.

Though cointegration is a statistical property, whether it prevails among the variables that comprise the textbook money demand relation is a question that has important implications for understanding the behavior of real balances, real income and nominal interest rates. Cointegration simply implies that there exists a linear combination of these three variables that is stationary or exhibits "mean reversion." In the absence of cointegration, the random errors from a standard textbook money demand equation (or any other linear combination of real balances, real income and nominal interest rates) are nonstationary or have infinite variance. This suggests that any paradigm linking these variables has no empirical content in time series data, evidence that would serve as a strong rejection of popular explanations used to predict the behavior of money, prices, real income and nominal interest rates described in the money demand

[5]In Chapter 6 we examine the Friedman and Kuttner findings in considerable detail.

literature.

Statistical evidence in support of a cointegrating relation validates this body of theoretical literature and paves the way for further investigation of the dynamics and forecasting properties of a system anchored by a long–run money demand relation. Absence of cointegration poses a serious challenge to this literature. The question is clearly relevant for an improved understanding of relations among macro aggregates and, given the weight of the theoretical literature, empiricists rejecting the notion may be compelled to provide explanations for the observed instabilities. Two obvious explanations come to mind. Either fundamental changes in institutional or agent behavior have induced instability or the statistical tests designed to detect cointegration have failed to deliver accurate inference. Considerable effort has been put forth in recent years to develop tests for cointegration that yield improved inference under general deterministic trend specifications that may characterize aggregate money demand relations.

## 3.2 Nonstationarity in the Money Demand Model: Is There Evidence of Integration or Cointegration?

Beginning with the contributions of Nelson and Plosser (1982) considerable effort has been directed toward establishing whether macroeconomic time series exhibit stochastic trends as in equation (3.9). In some cases (e.g. GDP) this exercise is a means to an end because evidence of mean or trend reversion has interesting economic implications. In other circumstances it may be prudent to establish degree of integration prior to choosing a strategy for estimation and inference. As the traditional literature on money demand estimation illustrates, ignoring integration and cointegration can lead to spurious regression and misleading inference.

While there is considerable agreement that degree of integration provides useful information, there is substantial controversy regarding whether a definitive answer to the question may be obtained. A host of questions arise. Can the presence or absence of unit roots be established in a univariate context? Should nonstationarity or stationarity serve as the null hypothesis? What role should deterministic trend play in specifications designed to determine whether stochastic trends prevail? Perhaps the best strategy is to compare results obtained from several of these approaches and examine whether the preponderance of evidence makes a convincing case for stationarity, nonstationarity, or cointegration. At the same time it may prove very difficult to prove definitively whether stochastic or broken deterministic trends provide the best explanation for the behavior of a given series.[6] In this light it may be prudent to examine

[6]Perhaps the best example of this difficulty is a series such as the inflation rate($\ln(p/p_{-1})$) where it is unclear whether the underlying process($\ln(p)$) is I(1) with breaks in trend that correspond with major oil shock episodes or actually an I(2) process. In the later case,

the behavior of a vector process with and without maintaining the assumption of stochastic trends.

### 3.2.1 Univariate Unit Root Tests

The development of tests for a unit root in a univariate time series process dates from Fuller (1976) and Dickey and Fuller (1979). The literature is certainly voluminous and excellent surveys appear in Stock (1994) and Hamilton (1994). In this section we consider only two of the numerous approaches described in these references.

The basic framework for testing the hypothesis of a unit root can be obtained from the univariate representation for the $i^{th}$ element of $z_t$; $z_{ti}$

$$\Delta z_{ti} = \mu_{0i} + \mu_{1i}t + \rho z_{t-1,i} + \sum_{j=1}^{q-1} \gamma_j \Delta z_{t-j,i} + \varepsilon_t \text{ for } t = 1, ..., T \tag{3.11}$$

so that the unit root hypothesis is $H_0 : \rho = 0$ while stationarity requires $\rho < 0$. Dickey and Fuller demonstrate that under $H_0$, the distribution of ordinary least squares estimates of $\rho$ is nonstandard. Statistical inference in this setting is typically based on conventional "$t$"-ratios designed to test $H_0 : \rho = 0$ or the "normalized bias" test statistic $T(\rho - 1)$. Critical values for these statistics are simulated to account for the nonstandard distributions maintained under the null of nonstationarity (see Fuller (1976) p. 371 and 373). Critical values differ depending upon sample size and assumptions made regarding $\mu_{0i}$ and $\mu_{1i}$.

Numerous attempts to improve inference in unit root tests have been undertaken. Phillips (1987) and Phillips and Perron (1988) offer some of the most noteworthy contributions designed to accommodate more general serial correlation assumptions regarding the errors in (3.11). Schwert (1987) provides critical values for a wide range of unit root tests based upon (3.11) under general assumptions about serial correlation (specifically moving averages) in the error process.

An alternative approach is undertaken by Kiatkowski, Phillips, Schmidt and Shin (1992) where nonstationarity in $z_{ti}$ is represented by

$$z_{ti} = \mu_{0i} + \mu_{1i}t + x_{ti} + \varepsilon_{ti} \tag{3.12}$$

$$x_{ti} = x_{t-1,i} + \mu_{ti}$$

where $\varepsilon_t$ is a stationary error term and $x_{ti}$ is a random walk process. Stationarity requires $\sigma_\mu^2 = 0$. KPSS form an LM statistic that is based upon the partial sum process

$$S_t = \sum_{i=1}^{t} \widehat{\varepsilon}_{ti} \tag{3.13}$$

---

inflation rates are I(1).

where $\widehat{\varepsilon}_t$ is estimated directly from equation(3.12) under the null of stationarity. The LM test suggested by KPSS is

$$LM = \sum_{t=1}^{T} \frac{S_t^2}{\widehat{\sigma}_{\varepsilon_i}^2} \tag{3.14}$$

where $\widehat{\sigma}_{\varepsilon_i}^2$ is the estimated variance of the errors in equation (3.12). The distribution of the test in equation (3.14) is calculated by KPSS under the null of stationarity. KPSS tests serve as a useful comparison to tests based on the Dickey-Fuller formulation since they take stationarity as the null hypothesis while the Dickey-Fuller tests maintain the null of nonstationarity. KPSS performed simulations designed to accommodate serial correlation in the errors of (3.12).

### 3.2.2 Multivariate Analysis

Univariate tests are sometimes used as a precursor to subsequent multivariate analysis. In these cases the tests are intended to establish order of integration so that multivariate analysis is directed at sets of variables that contain the same order of integration. However, univariate analysis in isolation, might yield misleading conclusions if interest lies in the elements of a vector process because it inherently focuses on an underspecified model. Complex serial correlation patterns encountered in univariate analysis may signal omitted variables that appear in a multivariate specification. Attempts to accommodate serial correlation in the univariate setting may serve as inefficient proxies for the multivariate representation.

There are a number of cointegration(multivariate unit root) tests as in the case of the univariate tests described in the preceding section. Excellent surveys appear in Hamilton (1994), and Watson (1994). Many of the first tests where based upon simple applications of univariate tests to the residuals of presumably cointegrating regressions.(see Engle and Granger (1987) or Engle and Yoo (1987)). More recently these approaches have received less attention, primarily because of the development of Johansen's (1988) likelihood procedure designed to test cointegration rank.

Johansen's (1988) reduced rank procedure is based upon the maximum likelihood principle. It is designed to accommodate multivariate representations and is one of the most widely used approaches for detecting the number of unit roots in random vectors comprised of stationary, integrated and/or cointegrated variables. To illustrate, write a multivariate representation for the $p$–dimensional random vector $z_t$ in its error correction representation as in equation (3.10) above

$$\Delta z_t = \mu + \sum_{i=1}^{q-1} \Pi_i^* \Delta z_{t-i} - \Pi z_{t-1} + \varepsilon_t \tag{3.15}$$

where $\Pi$ and $\Pi^*$ are defined above in (3.10). When cointegration rank is zero, the elements of $z_t$ are determined by $p$ distinct unit roots and when cointegration rank is $p$, the system embodies no unit roots. If cointegration rank of $r$ is detected, long–run behavior of the vector process is determined by $k = p - r$ distinct unit roots. When all elements of $z_t$ are nonstationary *a priori*, and cointegration rank $r$ is detected, there are $r$ distinct cointegration vectors. However, cointegration rank of $r$ may also simply imply that $r$ stationary and $p - r$ nonstationary variables comprise $z_t$. In this case the "cointegrating vectors" are each comprised of a single nonzero entry. We examine methods that will allow tests that discriminate between these two outcomes in section 3.4.

Knowledge of the rank of $\Pi$ in (3.10) can help reveal both integration and cointegration properties among the elements of $z_t$. Johansen (1988) suggests two statistics that may be used to test hypotheses regarding the rank of $\Pi$ in practical applications. First, extract the estimated eigenvalues of $\Pi$ using Johansen's reduced rank regression. Once estimated, the eigenvalues are ordered from largest to smallest. Then Johansen obtains, using the likelihood ratio principle, the "trace" statistic for testing the degree of cointegration rank $r$ vs. the alternative of rank greater than $r$ is given by ,

$$-2 \ln Q\{H_0(r)|H_0(p)\} = -T \sum_{i=r+1}^{p} \ln(1 - \lambda_i) \tag{3.16}$$

where $\lambda_1 \geq \lambda_2 \geq ... \geq \lambda_p$. The distribution of this "trace" statistic is nonstandard. Critical values have been calculated for models with simple linear deterministic trends and separately for no deterministic trends by simulation in Osterwald-Lenum (1992) and for general deterministic trend (including broken trends) specifications by Johansen and Nielsen (1993). An alternative statistic that examines only the significance of the marginal eigenvalue is the maximum eigenvalue test ($\lambda$-max test) obtained by evaluating increments to the trace statistic at successive choices for $r$. Johansen's test takes no cointegration as the null hypothesis. In this case the vector is completely comprised of integrated, but not cointegrated, variables. The test then reveals whether cointegration rank of $r$ is rejected in favor of $r + 1$, $r + 2$,..., up to $p$ cointegration vectors. In the last case no unit roots prevail in the $p$-dimensional system.

Haug (1994) examines the small sample performance of a number of competing tests for cointegration.[7] His experiments reveal that the Johanson test exhibits the fewest size distortions of any of the techniques he examines but all tests display low power against relevant alternatives. It is perhaps not surprising that the most general tests for cointegration exhibit low power because the problem of discerning unit and near unit root specifications is pervasive. However, Horvath and Watson (1993) and Pesaran and Shin (1994) have taken steps toward obtaining sharper inference.

Horvath and Watson offer a test of cointegration, based upon the Wald principle, under the maintained hypothesis that some of the cointegration vectors are known. This allows the test statistics to compare specifications void of cointegration with models characterized by particular cointegration vectors. In

[7] Haug examines both single equation and "systems based" tests.

a similar vein, Pesaran and Shin construct likelihood ratio tests of hypotheses that pin down portions of the cointegration space while the remainder is unconstrained. They also offer algorithms designed to estimate unconstrained portions of the cointegration space while maintaining restrictions about certain parameters of the space. Reduction in the parameter space obtained by incorporating restrictions that are consistent with both underlying theory and the observation sample should lead to sharper inference. These developments are especially useful in those cases where theory delivers clear predictions of the precise form of the cointegration vector.

### 3.2.3 Dealing with Linear, Quadratic or Broken Deterministic Trends

While the existence of stochastic trends in time series variables may be easily tested in the absence of deterministic trend, complex deterministic trend structures can obscure the picture. Johansen (1992d) presents an approach that is designed to accommodate general deterministic trend specifications. The technical framework for this analysis is Johansen's reduced rank regression model with a very general specification for deterministic trends. Johansen defines a $p$-dimensional vector error correction model that allows for quadratic deterministic trends in the DGP and linear trends in cointegrating vectors as

$$\Delta z_t = \sum_{i=1}^{q-1} \Pi_i^* \Delta z_{t-i} - \Pi z_{t-1} + \mu_0 + \mu_1 t + \varepsilon_t \tag{3.17}$$

As before, cointegration rank "$r$" implies $\Pi = \alpha\beta'$ with $\alpha$, and $\beta$, $p \times r$ matrices with $\Pi$ and $\Pi^*$ defined as in equation (3.10). In this case Johansen demonstrates that, $z_t$ has representation

$$z_t = z_0 + C(1) \sum_{i=1}^{t} \varepsilon_i + \frac{1}{2}\tau_2 t(t-1) + \tau_1 t + \tau_0 + Y_t - Y_0 \tag{3.18}$$

where from the Granger Representation Theorem,

$$\begin{aligned} C(1) &= \beta_\perp(\alpha'_\perp \Pi_1^*(1)\, \beta_\perp)^{-1}\alpha'_\perp, \\ \beta'_\perp \beta &= 0, \alpha'_\perp \alpha = 0, \\ \Pi_1^*(1) &= \Pi + I - \sum_{i=1}^{q-1} \Pi_i^* L^i, \tau_2 = C(1)\mu_1, \end{aligned}$$

and $Y_t$ is stationary with $\beta' z_0 = \beta' Y_0$. From Johansen (1992) coefficients $\mu_0$ and $\mu_1$ are defined as $(\alpha\beta_0 + \alpha_\perp\gamma_0)$ and $(\alpha\beta_1 + \alpha_\perp\gamma_1)$, respectively, where $\beta_0, \gamma_0, \beta_1$ and $\gamma_1$ are fixed constants. The values of $\tau_0$ and $\tau_1$ are $C^*(L)\varepsilon_t$ and $-C(1)\mu_0 - C^*(L)\mu_1$, respectively, where $C(L) = C(1) + C^*(L)$. Clearly $\tau_1$ depends upon the assumptions that prevail about $\beta_0$; $\gamma_0, \beta_1$ and $\gamma_1$.

Johansen separates the various trend specifications into five categories. $H_0(r)$ maintains the most general specification where $\beta_0, \gamma_0, \beta_1$ and $\gamma_1$ are all nonzero. In this case the cointegrating vector: $\beta$, removes stochastic and quadratic trend.

However, a linear trend of $\beta'\tau_1 t$ typically remains in $\beta' z_t$ since there is no reason for $\beta$ to be orthogonal to $C^*(L)$. In the case of $H_0^*(r)$, $\gamma_1 = 0$ and the DGP is inherently free of quadratic drift (since $C(1)\mu_1 = 0$), but both the data *and* the error correction term $\beta' z_t$ typically maintain deterministic drift since again $\beta'\tau_1 \neq 0$ unless $\beta' C^*(L) = 0$. For example, $H_0^*(r)$ could adequately depict $r$ trend stationary variables assembled in a $p$-dimensional vector along with $p - r$ variables that are nonstationary about linear trend. In this case no cointegration need prevail. Conventional strong form or "deterministic" cointegration is maintained by $H_1(r)$ where $\beta_1 = \gamma_1 = \mu_1 = 0$. Under $H_1(r)$, the cointegrating vector eliminates *both* stochastic and linear trends from the data as has been assumed by most cointegration applications. This occurs because $\mu_1 = 0$ so that $\tau_1$ is simply $C(1)\mu_0$ and then clearly $\beta'\tau_1 = 0$. When $\gamma_0 = 0$ as well, there is no deterministic drift in the data and a constant term is easily estimated and $E(\beta' z_t) = \beta_0$. This is described by Johansen as $H_1^*(r)$ and Johansen and Juselius (1990) provide an example. Under $H_2(r)$, *all* stationary components have mean zero.[8]

The order of cointegration for these alternative models is established from the standard trace and $\lambda$-max statistics. Critical values for $H_0(r)$ and $H_0^*(r)$ are given in Johansen (1991) and critical values for $H_1(r)$ and $H_1^*(r)$ are given in Osterwald-Lenum (1992) and Johansen and Nielsen (1993).

Johansen (1991) shows that likelihood ratio tests for reduction in the degree of trend may be formed from the eigenvalues obtained from his well known reduced rank regression procedure. Denote the $p$ eigenvalues obtained under the various hypotheses as $\lambda_{0,i}$, $\lambda_{0,i}^*$, $\lambda_{1,i}$, $\lambda_{1,i}^*$ and $\lambda_{2,i}$, $i = 1, ..., p$ respectively and order each set of eigenvalues from largest to smallest. Then, the test statistics for testing $H_j^*(r)$ in $H_j(r)$ are

$$-T \sum_{i=r+1}^{p} \ln\{(1 - \lambda_{ji}^*)/(1 - \lambda_{ji})\} \sim \chi^2_{(p-r)}$$

for $j = 0, 1, 2$ and similar statistics for testing $H_j(r)$ in $H_{j-1}^*(r)$ are

$$T \sum_{i=1}^{r} \ln\{(1 - \lambda_{j,i}^*)/(1 - \lambda_{j-1,i}^*)\} \sim \chi^2_{(r)}$$

for $j = 1, 2$.[9]

Considerable effort has been devoted to models characterized by breaks in deterministic trend.[10] When breaks occur, the data may exhibit characteristics of stochastic trend when, in fact, stationarity actually prevails. Quite naturally, tests designed to detect the number of independent unit roots that prevail among a vector process will display lower power against alternatives characterized by stationarity about broken linear trend. This problem is discussed at length by

---

[8]This case was observed by Crowder and Hoffman(1995)

[9]The software package EVIEWS allows tests for cointegration in the presence of any of the five deterministic trend specifications.

[10]See the *Journal of Business and Economic Statistics*, July 1992, Vol. 10, No. 3 for a representative sample of recent papers. In addition, Stock(1994) provides an excellent survey.

Perron (1989) in the context of univariate representations. He simulates critical values (comparable to the Dickey-Fuller values) that may be applied to the standard augmented Dickey-Fuller normalized bias and t-tests when the alternative is stationarity about a known broken trend. Perron's empirical results provide evidence that many U.S. time series may be stationary about a linear trend that exhibits distinct breaks at the Great Depression and the energy shocks of the mid 1970s.[11]

Campos, Ericsson, and Hendry (1993) examine the properties of simple Granger/Engle two-step and error correction tests for cointegration in the presence of structural breaks. Johansen and Nielsen (1993) examine the performance of the likelihood ratio (trace) test for cointegration rank in the presence of general trend specifications. The latter paper is accompanied by a simulation program (DISCO) that may be used to formulate critical values that correspond to particular linear or broken trend specifications.

## 3.3 Identification of Long-Run Parameters from Knowledge of Cointegration Rank

The issue of identification in cointegrated systems is multi-faceted. First, identification of parameters that comprise the cointegration and error correction spaces can be conducted in an exercise that depends exclusively on the long–run properties of the system. This leads naturally to the question of identifying permanent structural innovations that are responsible for the nonstationarity that characterizes a cointegrated system. But, as we illustrate below and again in Chapter 4, establishing the identity of permanent structural innovations also serves to partially identify the complete structure of an economic model. In this chapter we focus exclusively on identification issues that pertain to the long–run character of the system. A discussion of complete system identification issues is reserved for Chapter 4.

Consider a $p$–dimensional vector process for random vector; $z_t$, in the form used by Zellner and Palm (1974)

$$H(L)z_t = \mu + F(L)v_t \tag{3.19}$$

where $H(L) = \sum_{i=0}^{q} H_i L^j$ and $F(L) = \sum_{i=0}^{s} F_i L^i$ and the vector of structural errors, $v_t$, satisfies classical conditions.

To allow for unit roots in the vector process, we depart from Zellner and Palm's assumption that all roots of the determinantal polynomial of $H(L)$ lie outside the unit circle. Instead assume that the $p$-dimensional process exhibits cointegration rank $r$, suggesting $p - r$ distinct unit roots prevail in the system. Let the contemporaneous coefficient matrix for (3.19); $H(0)$, be nonsingular and

[11]Some of the recent literature attempts to discern stochastic trends in models characterized by deterministic breaks at unknown points in the sample (see the *JBES*, 1992 or Stock(1994)).

write the reduced form for the system in notation comparable to that employed by Johansen (1988, 1991):

$$z_t = \mu + \sum_{i=0}^{q} \Pi_i z_{t-i} + \varepsilon_t = \mu + \Pi(L) z_t + \varepsilon_t \tag{3.20}$$

with $\Pi_i = H(0)^{-1} H_i$, $\mu = H(0)^{-1}\mu$ and $\varepsilon_t = H(0)^{-1} F(L) v_t$ and $\Sigma_\varepsilon$ is the covariance matrix of reduced form errors. In standard applications, the reduced form errors are assumed to be free of persistence so we depart further from Zellner and Palm in assuming $F(L) = I$. The reduced form error correction representation of this process is the now familiar error correction form

$$\Delta z_t = \mu + \sum_{i=1}^{q-1} \Pi_i^* \Delta z_{t-i} - \Pi z_{t-1} + \varepsilon_t \tag{3.21}$$

where and $\Pi_i^*$ and $\Pi$ are defined above.[12]

VAR methodologies that have dominated the literature over the last decade have directed the focus away from establishing the identity of $H(0)$(using exclusion or otherwise "incredible" restrictions) to disclose the structure of (3.19)– choosing instead to focus on reduced form representations of vector processes. But, structural innovations analysis that typically accompany these exercises are identification exercises that require demanding sets of restrictions in their own right. Below we see that a distinct set of identification issues arise in cointegrated systems even if we concentrate exclusively on the long–run properties of the data and make no attempt to identify the complete contemporaneous structure of the model. That is, identification remains crucial to the analysis even if the focus of the investigation is exclusively equation (3.21).

### 3.3.1 Identification of Long–Run Equilibria

When reduced from errors are free from persistence and homoskedastic (e.g. $F(L) = I$), equation (3.21) is equivalent to the specification examined by Johansen (1988, 1991). Cointegration rank $r$ implies $\Pi = \alpha\beta'$ where $\alpha$ denotes a $p \times r$ matrix of error correction coefficients and $\beta$ a $p \times r$ matrix of cointegration vectors. Without further information about the cointegration space, the elements of $\alpha$ and $\beta$ are *not* identified from $\Pi$ because there is an infinite number of $r$-dimensional nonsingular basis transformation matrices; $R$, such that $\alpha^* = \alpha R^{-1}$ and $\beta^* = \beta R$ are also consistent with the long–run information embedded in $\Pi$. That is, $\Pi = \alpha\beta' = \alpha^*\beta^{*\prime}$.

Restrictions that limit the choice of feasible transformation matrices; $R$, may be used to identify $\alpha$ and $\beta$. Rank and order conditions for identification of $\beta$ can be established in a direct application of Fisher (1966) and Rothenberg (1971) and have been discussed in the context of cointegrated systems by Park (1990), Johansen (1992), Hoffman and Rasche (1991) (1993) and recently by Pesaran

[12]Note that equation (3.21) could easily be expressed in a form that includes $z_{t-q}$ instead of $z_{t-1}$. This seems to be the preferred choice of Johansen. The long-run information in $\Pi$ is not influenced by this reformulation.

and Shin (1994). These papers reveal that the identity of the cointegration and error correction spaces may be established with access to $r^2$ independent restrictions ($r$ $(r-1)$ after arbitrary normalization of each vector in either $\alpha$ or $\beta$). Johansen's original suggestion for identifying $\beta$ is to orthogonalize the cointegration space while readily acknowledging that any transformation of the space by conformable basis transformation matrix is also cointegrating. Pesaran and Shin (1994) offer a clear statement of general conditions under which identification is obtained and how "cross vector" and nonlinear restrictions can be used to accomplish the task.

When the cointegration space, $\beta$, is identified, the reduced form error correction coefficients, $\alpha$, are easily obtained. Similarly, knowledge of $\alpha$ could be used to obtain $\beta$. If economic theory delivers more information about the long-run relations than it does for the short-run relations, the preferred path to identification may be to first establish the identity of the $\beta$ space. The conditions for identifying the cointegration space using simple linear restrictions on each vector of the space can be derived using an approach that dates from the work of the Cowles Commission. Consider the identification of $\beta'$ on a row by row basis (cointegration vector by cointegration vector). The first row is denoted $\beta_1'$ and let *a priori* homogeneous linear restrictions that apply to $\beta_1'$ be represented by a $p \times m$ restriction matrix; $\phi$, so that $\beta_1'\phi = 0$ defines $m$ homogeneous linear restrictions. Clearly, $\beta_1'$ is identified only when the set of feasible transformation matrices, $R$, is sufficiently limited by $\phi$. Normalize by one element of $\beta_1$ so that the first row of $R$ is $R_1 = \{1, R_1^*\}$ and then $\beta_1'$ is identified if and only if $R_1^*$ $= 0$ for all *feasible* basis transformation matrices, $R$. But, transformations are admissible if and only if the restrictions embodied in $\phi$ are maintained by $R_1\beta_1'$. This requires $R_1\beta_1'\phi = 0$ so that the *feasible* transformation corresponds with the *a priori* restrictions implied by theory.

The applicable rank and order conditions are obtained by defining $\beta_{1r}'$ as the "last" $r-1$ rows of $\beta'$ (excluding $\beta_1'$). Then redefine the restriction condition;

$$0 = R_1\beta_1'\phi = [1, R_1^*]\begin{bmatrix} \beta_1'\phi \\ \beta_{1r}'\phi \end{bmatrix} = R_1^*\beta_{1r}'\phi,$$

since $\beta_1'\phi = 0$ by definition. A necessary and sufficient condition for $R_1^*\beta_{1r}'\phi = 0$ to imply $R_1^* = 0$ is that the rank of $\beta_{1r}'\phi = r-1$. Since the rank of $\beta_{1r}'\phi$ equals the rank of $\beta'\phi$, the necessary and sufficient condition for the identification of the first equation is that the rank of $\beta'\phi = r-1$. The corresponding order condition requires that the column dimension of $\phi$ must equal or exceed cointegration rank less one; $m \geq r-1$.

When the identification conditions for all vectors in $\beta$ are satisfied, the error correction space is identified since $\alpha = \Pi\beta(\beta'\beta)^{-1}$. Any additional restrictions imposed on $\alpha$ or $\beta$ are overidentifying. When the set of independent linear restrictions on $\beta$ is insufficient to identify $\beta$, available restrictions on $\alpha$ can help identify $\beta$. Since $\alpha^* = \alpha R^{-1}$, $\beta^* = R\beta$, $\Pi = \alpha\beta' = \alpha^*\beta^{*\prime}$; restrictions on the structure of the error correction space $\alpha$ (or $\alpha^*$) may provide information that restricts the choices for $R^{-1}$. These restrictions may limit $R$ choices and be useful in cases where $\beta$ is not identified. Let $m_1$ denote the number of independent $\beta$ restrictions while $m_2$ denotes the number of independent $\alpha$ restrictions pertinent to $\beta$ identification. When $\alpha$ restrictions exist, a generalized order condition $m_1 + m_2 \geq r - 1$ is applicable.[13]

When identification is obtained using this standard linear "vector-by-vector" approach, matrix normalizations can play a useful role in cointegration vector identification. When initial estimates of $\beta$ are arbitrarily matrix normalized by the inverse of an $r \times r$ nonsingular submatrix, exactly $r - 1$ "zeros" appear in each vector of the transformed cointegration space. Instead of an arbitrary normalization, the matrix normalization can be chosen to reflect corresponding "zero" restrictions that prevail among the long-run equilibria that constitute $\beta$. These restrictions are presumably drawn from economic theory. Matrix normalizations employed in this manner retain the property of cointegration and no constraints are imposed on $\beta$ by the normalizations. However, once an estimated space is normalized to produce "zeros" that are suggested by a theory of the long run, the only transformation that preserves these theoretically consistent "zeros" is of course the identity matrix and the cointegration space is clearly identified.[14] In sum, matrix normalizations are arbitrary, but used in conjunction with theories that predict restrictions on the long-run equilibrium relations, they provide a framework for $\beta$ space identification that sets the stage for subsequent statistical inference regarding overidentifying restrictions.[15]

Long–run parameter identification can establish an important bridge between economic theory and cointegration applications. Theory typically predicts more than simply cointegration rank but also a particular functional form for certain cointegration vectors. These typically take the form of exclusion, or unitary long–run elasticity restrictions. When theory is sufficiently rich, the cointegration space can be parameterized uniquely and long–run identification is achieved. Investigation can then proceed with a series of statistical tests that can validate or reject any overidentifying restrictions implied by the theory.

### 3.3.2 Examples of Long-Run Parameter Identification

A simple example illustrates the basic principles of long-run parameter identification. King, Plosser, Stock, and Watson (1991) specify a simple three variable log-linear model consisting of consumption; $c$, investment; $i$, and output; $y$ (lower case denotes natural logs). KPSW argue that the nonstationary behavior

[13] See Pesaran and Shin for a detailed discussion of nonlinear and "cross–vector" identification restrictions. The conditions for long–run parameter identification in Pesaran and Shin are perfectly comparable to those in our simple example after accounting for the $r$ (one in each vector)normalization restrictions.

[14] In the notation of Park (1990) and Pesaran and Shin (1994), $r$ total restrictions are required for each vector and matrix normalization delivers them since the normalizing elements along the diagonal are counted as well.

[15] It is easy to think of identification restrictions that are not easily expressed by simple matrix normalization. However, if each vector is identified by linear restrictions, a suitable matrix normalization may be applied to a linear transformation of the system to obtain identification of each distinct long-run relation.

of the three variables is ultimately determined by the accumulated innovations of a single technology shock. The effect of this single shock is transmitted throughout the system by means of two long-run equilibria that restrict output, consumption, and investment growth to coincide in the long run. This yields the stationary "great ratios" $C/Y$ and $I/Y$ (upper case denotes levels of actual series) depicted by KPSW. If the data are consistent with this model, tests for cointegration applied to this trivariate system will reveal a cointegration rank of 2 and the estimated cointegration space will contain cointegration vectors that correspond to $c_t - y_t$ and $i_t - y_t$. If we order the data as $z_t = (c_t, i_t, y_t)'$, the cointegration space predicted by KPSW is

$$\beta' = \begin{bmatrix} 1 & 0 & -1 \\ 0 & 1 & -1 \end{bmatrix}.$$

In this case $p = 3$ and $r = 2$ so that identification is obtained when one $(r-1 = 1)$ exclusion restriction appears in each vector of the cointegration space $\beta$. But, this is precisely the number of restrictions implied by the "great ratios" story. In sum, any estimated $2 \times 3$ cointegration space can be matrix normalized to obtain

$$\beta' = \begin{bmatrix} 1 & 0 & \beta_{13} \\ 0 & 1 & \beta_{23} \end{bmatrix}.$$

But in this particular application, the "zeros" obtained in this normalization are consistent with a particular economic interpretation of the long-run equilibria and no additional transformation matrix (other than the identity matrix) can preserve the restrictions implied in this scenario. The cointegration space is then identified by these restrictions while the proximity of estimated values of $\beta_{13}$ and $\beta_{23}$ to "one" can be examined as evidence to support or contradict the complete "great ratios" story.[16]

The KPSW example clearly reveals that an alternative parameterization of the long run relations, i.e.,

$$\beta_A = \begin{bmatrix} 1 & \beta_{12} & -\beta_{13} \\ 0 & 1 & -1 \end{bmatrix}$$

does not allow identification of the first equilibrium relation since it does not preclude a feasible transformation obtained by choosing a basis transformation matrix

$$R = \begin{bmatrix} 1 & \beta^* \\ 0 & 1 \end{bmatrix}$$

so that

$$\beta_A^* = \begin{bmatrix} 1 & \beta^* \\ 0 & 1 \end{bmatrix} \begin{bmatrix} 1 & \beta_{12} & -\beta_{13} \\ 0 & 1 & -1 \end{bmatrix}$$

[16] While the normalized cointegration space can provide evidence in support of a particular economic model, it may at the same time support alternative economic interpretations (see Bergman, Blakemore and Hoffman (1995)). In this case, the same matrix normalization is consistent with two distinct theories of the long run.

is also cointegrating. In this case, the underlying economic theory presumably does not provide enough information to allow us to distinguish $\beta_{12}$ and $\beta_{13}$ from $\beta_{12} + \beta^*$ and $\beta_{13} + \beta^*$.

If no additional information about the long–run is forthcoming, the $\beta$ space will in general remain underidentified. As discussed above, restrictions on the space of feasible error correction parameters can sometimes be used to obtain identification. Suppose, for illustration, we knew nothing about the first cointegration vector. However, we had access to information that the $(2, 1)$ element is zero as above *and,* that no adjustments occur in investment as a result of "disequilibria" in the second vector. In this case the matrix of error correction coefficients is restricted, vis.

$$\alpha = \begin{bmatrix} \alpha_{11} & \alpha_{12} \\ \alpha_{21} & 0 \\ \alpha_{31} & \alpha_{33} \end{bmatrix}.$$

This zero restriction is not preserved by the transformation $R^{-1}$ associated with $\beta_A^*$ unless $\beta^* = 0$ since

$$\alpha R^{-1} = \begin{bmatrix} \alpha_{11} & -\beta^*\alpha_{11} + \alpha_{12} \\ \alpha_{21} & -\beta^*\alpha_{21} \\ \alpha_{31} & -\beta^*\alpha_{31} + \alpha_{32} \end{bmatrix}.$$

But if $\beta^* = 0$, $\beta$ is identified–as is $\alpha$. While potentially useful, $\alpha$ restrictions such as this may not be as forthcoming from economic theory as are predictions of long–run equilibria simply because $\beta$ restrictions must prevail only in the long–run while $\alpha$ restrictions pin down contemporaneous responses of the system to short–run deviations of the long–run equilibria.

## 3.4 Identifying the Source of Nonstationarity

Considerable recent work has examined the permanent and transitory dichotomy that prevails in cointegrated systems. An excellent summary of these contributions is found in Watson (1994) and papers by Gonzalo and Granger (1991); King, Plosser, Stock and Watson (1991); and Warne (1993) provide examples. Our discussion primarily follows the framework set out in KPSW.

The permanent/transitory dichotomy arises since cointegration rank of $r$ in a $p$-dimensional vector process implies that there exists a representation of the system in which a reduced number, $p - r = k$, distinct stochastic trends explain the long-run behavior of all $p$ variables in the system. The quest for the identity of these separate sources of nonstationarity is an identification problem that can be divorced from the exercise discussed above. In this case interest lies exclusively with the fundamental structural innovations that govern the long–run properties of the system.

To illustrate, express the system in (3.21) in its Wold representation.[17]

[17] The moving average representation in (3.22) is not obtained from a simple inversion of its

$$\Delta z_t = C(L)(\mu + \varepsilon_t) = \gamma + C(L)\varepsilon_t \tag{3.22}$$

Obtain a multivariate Beveridge-Nelson decomposition from (3.22) by separating the matrix polynomial into components associated with long-run and short-run information to obtain $C(L) = C(1) + C^*(L)(1-L)$ where $C(1)$ is the sum of the moving average coefficients and $C_i^* = -\sum_{i=j+1}^{\infty} C_i \; i = 1, 2, ....$ The representation obtained by multiplying (3.22) by $(1-L)^{-1}$ (e.g. accumulating the differences) is then

$$z_t = z_0 + C(1)\left(\mu t + \sum_{s=1}^{t} \varepsilon_s\right) + C^*(L)\varepsilon_t \tag{3.23}$$

The total impact matrix $C(1)$ clearly transmits the random walk information (permanent components) to the system while the transitory components of the system are confined to $C^*(L)\varepsilon_t$.

The Granger Representation Theorem (GRT) provides perspective for the permanent/transitory decomposition of (3.23). Using the notation of Johansen's (1991) proof of the GRT,

$$C(1) = \beta_\perp(\alpha_\perp' \Pi_1^*(1)\beta_\perp)^{-1}\alpha_\perp'$$

where $\beta_\perp$and $\alpha_\perp$ are $p \times k$ orthogonal complements for $\beta$ and $\alpha$ where $k = p - r$, and

$$\beta_\perp'\beta = \alpha_\perp'\alpha = 0,$$

$$\Pi(L) = \Pi(1) + \Pi_1^*(L)(1-L),$$

$$\Pi_1^*(L) = \Pi + I - \sum_{i=1}^{q-1} \Pi_i^* L^i,$$

and $(\alpha_\perp' \Pi_1^*(1)\ \beta_\perp)$ is nonsingular.[18] When the $p-$dimensional system exhibits cointegration rank $r$, the rank of $C(1)$ is $k$ and the nonstationary behavior of the system is determined by $k$ independent random walk components.[19] In concert with conclusions drawn from the autoregressive representation, when $r = 0$ no cointegration prevails, and each of the $p$ variables are determined by a distinct stochastic trend. When $r = p$, $C(1)$ has rank zero and the original data are not influenced by stochastic trends(stationarity prevails).

The term $C(1)\sum_{s=1}^{t} \varepsilon_{t-s}$ in (3.23) contains the linear combination of accumulated innovations responsible for the nonstationary behavior of the system.

---

autoregressive counterpart (3.21) owing to the unit roots in the matrix polynomial $\Pi(L)$. For details on the prescise relatinship between $\Pi(L)$ and $C(L)$ see Johansen (1991) or Boswijk (1992) or comparable proofs of the Granger Representation Theorem.

[18]Note that $\Pi_1^*(1) = \Pi_1 + 2\Pi_2 + 3\Pi_3 + ... + q\Pi_q$.

[19]This argument is carefully articulated by Stock and Watson (1988) and illustrated in King, Plosser, Stock, and Watson (1991).

Again appealing to the Granger representation Theorem, Johansen (1993) designates $\alpha_\perp'\left(\mu t + \sum_{s=1}^{t} \varepsilon_s\right)$ as the common trends that correspond to the system. This is consistent with the concept of common trends that appears in the KPSW application. Accordingly, $\beta_\perp(\alpha_\perp'\Pi_1^*(1)\,\beta_\perp)^{-1}$ measures the factor loading that transmits the effects of innovations in these trends to the elements of $z_t$ in the long run. Knowledge of cointegration rank; $r$ establishes that both $C(1)$ and $\alpha_\perp$ are of rank $k$, but there are an infinite number of candidates for the orthogonal spaces $\alpha_\perp$ and $\beta_\perp$even when their orthogonal complements; $\alpha$ and $\beta$, are identified. For example, without *a priori* restrictions it will be impossible to distinguish $\alpha_\perp'$ from $\alpha_\perp^{*\prime}$obtained by multiplying the $\alpha_\perp$ space by a $k-$dimensional nonsingular basis transformation matrix $R$ where $\alpha_\perp^{*\prime} = R\alpha_\perp'$. Hence $\alpha_\perp^{*\prime}\sum_{s=1}^{t}(\mu t + \varepsilon_s)$ is an alternative representation of the common trends in the model that is equally consistent with the long-run information conveyed by the Wold representation since

$$\begin{aligned} C(1) &= \beta_\perp(\alpha_\perp'\Pi_1^*(1)\beta_\perp)^{-1}R^{-1}R\alpha_\perp' \\ &= \beta_\perp(\alpha_\perp^{*\prime}\Pi_1^*(1)\beta_\perp)^{-1}\alpha_\perp^{*\prime} \end{aligned}$$

and $\beta_\perp(\alpha_\perp^{*\prime}\Pi_1^*(1)\beta_\perp)^{-1}$ and is the factor loading that corresponds to this system.

Without *a priori* restrictions on the relationship between innovations in these trends and the long-run response of certain elements of $z_t$, there is no mechanism to identify distinct economic roles for the trends. When $\alpha_\perp$ and the factor loading matrix can be identified in $C(1)$, the "nature" of the innovations that constitute the common trends can be separated distinctly from the "effect" of innovations in the trends as conveyed by the factor loading matrix.

To simplify notation, let the orthogonal space, $\beta_\perp$, represent the entire factor loading, $\beta_\perp(\alpha_\perp\Pi_1^*(1)\,\beta_\perp)^{-1}$, so that the problem of identifying $\beta_\perp$ and $\alpha_\perp$ in the total impact matrix; $C(1) = \beta_\perp\alpha_\perp'$, is clearly analogous to identifying $\alpha$ and $\beta$ in $\Pi$ discussed in section 3.3.1. Using the arguments applied to $\alpha$ and $\beta$ above, one approach would be to rely on economic theory to provide $k(k-1)$ linear restrictions (after normalization) on either $\alpha_\perp$ or $\beta_\perp$ or some combination thereof. Zero restrictions on $\alpha_\perp$ would imply certain elements of $\varepsilon_t$ do not contribute to the linear combination of reduced form innovations that are accumulated to form the common trend just as "zeros" in specified long-run equilibria eliminate certain variables from the cointegration vector.[20] Alternatively, identification can be obtained by employing restrictions on $\beta_\perp$. These restrictions define how permanent innovations, of unknown origin *a priori*, impact upon the $z's$ in the "long run". This strategy is pursued when economic theory provides insight about the long-run *effects* of nebulous stochastic impulses, while it may

[20]Zero restrictions on the error correction space associated with weak exogeneity of a portion of $z_t$ with respect to the remaining elements of the vector generally result in imposing zero restrictions on the common trend space, $\alpha_\perp$. This is examined in Chapter 4 and illustrated by Crowder and Hoffman (1995).

be difficult to isolate the *origin* of specific impulses. Regardless of the focus, $\beta_{\perp}$or $\alpha_{\perp}$, $k(k-1)$ restrictions are required if identification is obtained in this fashion.

In one popular approach to identification of the permanent innovations KPSW employ innovation independence restrictions combined with a limited number of exclusion(expressed as long–run neutrality) restrictions. In this case identification restrictions are imposed on $\beta_{\perp}$ and $\alpha_{\perp}$ simultaneously to identify the origin and long–run effect of the permanent innovations. The origin of nebulous innovations is not assumed known nor are they restricted to stem from any particular set of reduced form errors *a priori* but, in the spirit of structural VAR identification, the permanent innovations are assumed to be statistically independent so that feasible choices for $\alpha_{\perp}$ must maintain a diagonal covariance matrix ; $\alpha'_{\perp}\Sigma_{\varepsilon}\alpha_{\perp}$. This covariance information provides $k(k-1)/2$ restrictions that may be used to identify $\beta_{\perp}$and $\alpha_{\perp}$. KPSW obtain the $k(k-1)/2$ neutrality restrictions by assuming that the permanent innovations influence the variables in the system in a particular recursive pattern (i.e., innovation one influences both real and nominal variables while innovation two has no impact on real variables in the long run).

The application by KPSW illustrates how the elements of $C(1)$ may be identified by combining covariance restrictions with a recursive response pattern for innovations in the common trend. Covariance restrictions require that the covariance matrix of the permanent innovations, $\alpha'_{\perp}\Sigma_{\varepsilon}\alpha_{\perp}$, is diagonal. This delivers $k(k-1)/2$ restrictions useful in identifying $\beta_{\perp}$and $\alpha_{\perp}$. Then select an initial candidate for $\beta_{\perp}$, e.g. $\beta^0_{\perp}$, which exhibits $k(k-1)/2$ restrictions. In the KPSW application, restrictions in $\beta^0_{\perp}$ are chosen so that innovations in the common trends, $\alpha'_{\perp}\varepsilon_t$, influence the variables in a recursive pattern. This pattern imposes $k(k-1)/2$ long–run neutrality restrictions on $\beta^0_{\perp}$ that must be maintained in any transformation that insures the innovations are orthogonal. In addition, $\beta^0_{\perp}$ must satisfy the orthogonality condition, $\beta'\beta^0_{\perp}=0$. Now, set

$$\beta^0_{\perp}\alpha^{0\prime}_{\perp}=C(1),$$

so an initial estimate of the common trend space is given by

$$\alpha^{0\prime}_{\perp}=(\beta^{0\prime}_{\perp}\beta^0_{\perp})^{-1}\beta^{0\prime}_{\perp}C(1)$$

and the covariance matrix of the permanent innovations is given by

$$\Sigma_v=(\beta^{0\prime}_{\perp}\beta^0_{\perp})^{-1}\beta^{0\prime}_{\perp}C(1)\Sigma_{\varepsilon}C(1)'\beta^0_{\perp}(\beta^{0\prime}_{\perp}\beta^0_{\perp})^{-1}.$$

The covariance condition requires that $\Sigma_v$ is diagonal, but of course there is no guarantee this condition is satisfied for an arbitrary initial factor loading $\beta^0_{\perp}$. To impose innovation independence, obtain the unique $k-$dimensional lower triangular Cholesky factor $\Sigma_v$ and following KPSW, designate it as $\pi$ so that $\Sigma_v=\pi\pi'$. The lower triangular nature of $\pi$ insures that any recursive structure embedded in $\beta^0_{\perp}$ will be preserved in $\beta_{\perp}=\beta^0_{\perp}\pi$ and the neutrality restrictions embodied by $\beta^0_{\perp}$ will remain in $\beta_{\perp}$. Now,

$$\pi^{-1}(\beta^{0\prime}_{\perp}\beta^0_{\perp})^{-1}\beta^{0\prime}_{\perp}=(\beta'_{\perp}\beta_{\perp})^{-1}\beta'_{\perp}$$

and the covariance matrix of the permanent structural innovations,

$$(\beta_\perp'\beta_\perp)^{-1}\beta_\perp' C(1)\Sigma_\varepsilon C(1)'\beta_\perp(\beta_\perp'\beta_\perp)^{-1}$$

is diagonal by construction so the common trend space $\alpha_\perp$ is identified as $\pi^{-1}\alpha_\perp^{0\prime}$ or equivalently

$$\alpha_\perp' = (\beta_\perp'\ \beta_\perp)^{-1}\beta_\perp' C(1).$$

### 3.4.1 Examples of Common Trend Identification

KPSW's (1991) six variable model provides an illustration of the restrictions used to identify $\beta_\perp$ and $\alpha_\perp$ using this covariance restriction/long–run neutrality approach. The vector $z_t$ in this example contains six elements ordered as $(y, c, i, m-p, R, \Delta p)'$ for log income, log consumption, log investment, log real money balances, nominal interest rates and inflation respectively. The specified cointegration space is

$$\beta' = \begin{bmatrix} -1 & 1 & 0 & 0 & -\phi_1 & \phi_1 \\ -1 & 0 & 1 & 0 & -\phi_2 & \phi_2 \\ -\beta_y & 0 & 0 & 1 & \beta_R & 0 \end{bmatrix}$$

where the zeros in columns 2-4 provide the $r(r-1) = 6$ exclusion restrictions that identify each cointegration vector in the model while the zero in column 6 is overidentifying as are the restrictions on $\phi_1$ and $\phi_2$ across columns 5 and 6. The initial orthogonal complement specified for $\beta$ is given by KPSW as

$$\beta_\perp^0 = \begin{bmatrix} 1 & 0^* & 0^* \\ 1 & 0 & \phi_1 \\ 1 & 0 & \phi_2 \\ \beta_y & -\beta_R & \beta_R \\ 0 & 1 & 1 \\ 0 & 1 & 0^* \end{bmatrix}$$

so that the first common trend is identified exclusively as the accumulation of technology or "balanced growth" innovations, the second trend is then comprised of innovations in inflation that are reflected in nominal variables in the long–run but not in real variables, and the third trend represents the accumulation of innovations closely aligned with the real interest rate trend. The estimated factor loading matrix is obtained by post multiplying $\beta_\perp^0$ by the lower triangular Cholesky factor of

$$(\beta_\perp^{0\prime}\beta_\perp^0)^{-1}\beta_\perp^{0\prime} C(1)\Sigma_\varepsilon C(1)'(\beta_\perp^{0\prime}\beta_\perp^0)^{-1}\beta_\perp^0.$$

The zero's marked with $*$ in KPSW's choice for $\beta_\perp^0$ are preserved by any such transformation and, combined with the innovation independence assumptions, serve to identify the structural innovations that underlie the model. Innovations in the inflation trend are precluded from having any long–run effect on output—regardless of the observed Cholesky factor, $\pi$—while the real rate trend innovations have no influence on either real output or inflation in the long run. Unlike the remaining zeros in $\beta_{\perp}^{0}$, the $k(k-1)/2 = 3$ identifying restrictions are not testable in this model. In general no zeros appear in $\alpha_{\perp}$ when this approach is employed so that each independent common trend is comprised of a linear combination that includes all reduced form errors. Clearly, this approach identifies common trends by first assuming their innovations are independent and then distinguishing their effect on variables in the system. The nature of accumulated innovations may be obtained by solving for $\alpha_{\perp}$ after $\beta_{\perp}$ is identified.

The advantage of the KPSW approach is that the innovation independence assumption is conducive to standard innovations analysis.(impulse response and variance decomposition) Moreover, the number of underlying permanent innovations is governed by the cointegration rank that prevails in the system and the analysis focuses exclusively on the long run so that no contemporaneous restrictions need to be specified.[21] However, it is predicated on the notion that the underlying "structural" innovations that ultimately determine system nonstationarity are in fact statistically independent. Specifications that are based on non-orthogonal innovations or on structures that may not be expressed in invertible Wold representations are not conducive to this approach. In Chapter 4 we explore the role of cointegration in identifying the complete "structural" VAR and tackle some of these exceptions. As we will see, the restrictions required to identify the separate components in $C(1)$ combined with restrictions that link structural innovations to transitory movements in the data will identify the complete structural VAR. Knowledge of cointegration rank and an identified cointegration space can facilitate this process.

## 3.5 Estimation and Inference Regarding Long-Run Parameters

Concern about the quality of estimates obtained in the presence of integrated variables dates back to Yule (1926). Granger and Newbold (1974) echoed this theme in cautioning against "spurious" regressions where conventional procedures for estimation and inference paint a misleading picture of the statistical strength of relations that prevail among nonstationary variables. Phillips (1986) derives the asymptotic distribution of simple least squares estimators, providing a framework for analyzing the nonstandard behavior documented in earlier work.[22]

Our discussion focuses on situations where integrated variables are cointegrated so that long-run relationships generally exist, but optimal approaches to estimation and inference should be able to distinguish spurious relations from

[21] Faust and Leeper(1994) caution against exclusive reliance on long–run restrictions to achieve identification. We discuss criticisms raised by Faust and Leeper and others in Chapter 4.

[22] A useful summary of the evolution of thought regarding OLS on integrated systems appears in Watson (1994) and Boswijk (1992).

cointegrating relations. Cointegrating relationships yield disturbance terms that are stationary while error terms associated with spurious regressions are nonstationary. In Engle and Granger's (1987) original paper the suggested "test" for cointegration is a two-step procedure where residuals from a least squares projection of one nonstationary variable on one (or more) nonstationary variables are examined for stationarity using a battery of unit root tests. This approach can be frustrating in practice since the inference obtained may depend upon the arbitrary choice of regressor and regressand in the first stage regressions.[23] The problem may actually stem from the poor performance of least squares in estimating the cointegration space. Stock (1987) demonstrates that OLS is "super" consistent, but at the same time, may be less than satisfying in applications due to appreciable bias in the asymptotic distribution that remains in reasonably large samples. Watson (1994) summarizes the problem by noting that in general the mean of the asymptotic distribution is not centered at zero. Hence, OLS estimates with finite samples encountered in practice can be of questionable quality and there remains considerable interest in the development of alternatives to simple OLS.

Though a considerable number of estimation approaches have been developed in the last several years it may be useful to consider alternatives based upon two distinct parameterizations of a cointegrated system. Below we separately consider estimation of the cointegration space using the "triangular" representation popularized by Phillips (1987,1991) and the reduced rank approach of Johansen (1988,1991).

### 3.5.1 Estimation Based on the Triangularization Principle

Once cointegration rank of $r$ is established in a $p$-dimensional vector, of nonstationary data, $z_t$, the system may be represented in triangular form by dichotomizing $z_t$ into $p-r$ and $r$ subvectors to obtain

$$\begin{aligned} y_t - \beta x_t &= \eta_{1,t} \\ \Delta x_t &= \eta_{2,t} \end{aligned} \tag{3.24}$$

with $\eta \sim N(0, \Sigma^\eta)$. The vector $x_t$ is weakly exogenous in this system when the system can be dichotomized so that the "off-block" diagonal elements of $\Sigma^\eta$, $\Sigma^\eta_{12}$, are zero.[24] In this case, Park and Phillips (1989), Stock and Watson (1993), Sims, Stock, and Watson (1990) among others demonstrate that standard estimates of $\beta$ from (3.24) are a mixture of normals and conventional procedures for statistical inference apply to tests of hypotheses regarding $\beta$. But there is little reason to believe that a particular vector process can be dichotomized so that $\Sigma^\eta_{12} = 0$ so in general, OLS estimates obtained from (3.24) follow a nonstandard distribution. In this case optimal inference requires that conventional test statistics be compared with critical values that may approximate those simulated by Dickey and Fuller.

---

[23]This is not apparent in the original Engle and Granger (1987) consumption and income illustration.

[24]See Chapter 4 for a discussion of weak exogeneity.

Phillips (1991) suggests that the MLE in this case is equivalent to OLS estimates of $\beta$ obtained form the transformed model

$$y_t = \beta x_t + D\Delta x_t + \eta_{1\cdot 2,t} \tag{3.25}$$

where $D = \Sigma_{12}^{\eta}\Sigma_{22}^{\eta}{}^{-1}$ and $\eta_{1\cdot 2,t} = \eta_{1t} - \Sigma_{12}^{\eta}\Sigma_{22}^{\eta}{}^{-1}\eta_{2t}$. Phillips and Loritan (1991) and Stock and Watson (1993) demonstrate that the same principle may be applied to accommodate more general error structures in (3.24) such as $\eta_t = \theta(L)\varepsilon_t$ where $\varepsilon_t$ is a vector of *iid* random impulses and $\theta(L)$ defines a distributed lag process. In this case (3.25) is augmented with a finite number of lags and leads in $\Delta x_t$.

Stock and Watson (1993) demonstrate that by augmenting the "levels" regression in (3.24) with a "two sided" polynomial $D(L)\Delta x_t$, potential correlation between $\eta_1$ and $\eta_2$ is accommodated and OLS estimation on the augmented levels regression provides the basis for estimation and inference that is asymptotically equivalent to MLE. In practice, alternative lag lengths in $D(L)$ may be examined, but nevertheless, significant residual serial correlation will typically remain. Stock and Watson suggest several approaches for dealing with persistence in the errors. For example, their suggested "Dynamic ordinary least squares" (DOLS) applies OLS to the augmented "levels" equation in (3.25) that includes both lead and lag differences. Stock and Watson (1993) then suggest a simple AR procedure to adjust the conventional error variance estimate; $\sum \widehat{\eta}_{1\cdot 2,t}^2/(T-K)$, for possible serial correlation in the underlying errors by weighting it by $(1-\sum \widehat{\rho}_i)^{-2}$ where $\widehat{\rho}_i$ are least squares estimates of autocorrelation coefficients obtained from a simple distributed lag model in $\widehat{\eta}_{1\cdot 2,t}$. Alternative "sum-of-covariances" estimators also exist.[25] A second approach; DGLS, applies generalized least squares (i.e. Cochrane-Orcutt) to the same equation so that the serial correlation issue is addressed at the same time that estimates of $\beta$ are obtained. [26]

While convenient, DOLS and DGLS may depend upon choices made for lag length of the two sided polynomial and the specific approach used to deal with serial correlation. In practice, DOLS and DGLS can differ substantially. Also, the arbitrary choice of $y$ and $x$ in (3.24) imposes a matrix normalization that arbitrarily reduces the parameter space prior to estimation. In finite samples, very different estimates of the cointegration space may be obtained by altering the composition of $x_t$ and $y_t$ among $z_t$—an unpleasant remnant reminiscent of the original Engle-Granger procedure. Implicit in the triangular representation is that the chosen dichotomy confines the cointegration to the first "$r$" equations and the $x_t$ in the last "$k$" equations do not "cointegrate". Arbitrary dichotomization of $z_t$ can violate this basic assumption.

[25] e.g. Newey and West (1987).

[26] Pesaran and Shin (1995) propose a single equation autoregressive approach that is based upon the conventional distributed lag specification. The primary difference between this estimator and those of Phillips is that the distributed lag specification presumes that some degree of exogeneity can be established in the system *a priori*.

### 3.5.2 Reduced Rank Estimation of the Cointegration Space

Johansen (1988, 1991) provides a likelihood based approach to estimation of the cointegration space as well as a unified framework for testing cointegration rank and estimating the error correction space, $\alpha$. The approach applies principle of reduced rank regression to the autoregressive representation of the cointegrated system.

The Johansen approach is easily illustrated in the context of a general autoregressive representation of the potentially nonstationary vector $z_t$,

$$z_t = \mu + \sum_{j=1}^{q} \Pi_j z_{t-j} + \varepsilon_t, \tag{3.26}$$

where $\varepsilon_t$ satisfies classical conditions and the model may be expressed in the now familiar error correction form.

$$\Delta z_t = \mu + \sum_{i=1}^{q-1} \Pi_i^* \Delta z_{t-i} - \Pi z_{t-1} + \varepsilon_t$$

where $\Pi_i^*$ and $\Pi$ are defined in (3.10).

With knowledge of cointegration rank $r$, $\Pi$ may be expressed as the product of $p \times r$ matrices $\alpha$ and $\beta$ such that $\Pi = \alpha\beta'$ so that $\beta$ defines the cointegration space. Johansen suggests that the space $\beta$ can be estimated by application of the reduced rank regression procedure described in Anderson (1984). In this case sample moment matrices are formed from residuals obtained by regressing $\Delta z_t$ and $z_{t-1}$ on a regressor space comprised of a constant and $\Delta z_{t-1} ... \Delta z_{t-q-1}$ and any I(0) "exogenous" variables. Denote these moment matrices as $S_{00}, S_{01}, S_{10}$, and $S_{11}$ then the eigenvalues of $\Pi$ are estimated by solving the eigenvalue problem

$$|\lambda S_{11} - S_{10} S_{00} S_{01}| = 0 \tag{3.27}$$

Estimates of the cointegration space, $\beta$, are provided by the eigenvectors associated with the $r$ largest eigenvalues obtained by solving (3.27). Johansen identifies the cointegration space using the $r(r-1)$ restrictions obtained from the statistical othogonalization of the space so as to satisfy

$$\beta' S_{11} \beta = I_r$$

but any matrix normalization of this estimated space is of course "cointegrating".

Johansen's estimates are likelihood based and statistical inference regarding the estimated parameters can be based upon the likelihood principle. Johansen (1991) and Johansen and Juselius (1992) illustrate how likelihood ratio tests can be applied to tests of particular linear hypotheses that pertain to each vector in the cointegration space; $H_0 : K'\beta = 0$. These tests are designed to be invariant to the choice of identifying restrictions.

In practice, as illustrated in chapters 6-8, economic theory maintains hypotheses associated with particular elements of an individual cointegration vector or involving parameters shared across vectors. In this case statistical inference does depend upon how the identity of the parameters is established. While identifying restrictions are not testable, it is possible to test overidentifying restrictions that prevail in a suitably identified cointegration space. Again, inference obtained in this manner is contingent upon the original identifying restrictions.

One approach to testing overidentifying restrictions is simply to apply the likelihood ratio principle where the unrestricted maximum is obtained directly from Johansen's reduced rank procedure and the restricted likelihood is obtained with the restrictions in place. Pesaran and Shin (1994) offer two separate numerical procedures that can each accomplish the task. The idea is to augment the likelihood function with the set of restrictions conveyed in a standard Lagrangian representation. Then one approach relies upon first derivatives of the function and applies "back–substitution" to deal with $\lambda$. An alternative, which exhibits superior convergence properties in Pesaran and Shin's experiments, is a modified Newton–Raphson applied to a Taylor's series approximation of the restricted likelihood. This approach utilizes both first and second derivatives.

An alternative approach to inference regarding the cointegration space is based upon the Wald principle. Represent the original Johansen estimates as $\beta$ and choose a matrix normalization $\beta_C = \beta(C'\beta)^{-1}$ where $C' = [I_r, 0]$ and the data are arranged so that the $r(r-1)$ "zeros" that appear in $\beta_C$ conform to restrictions that identify the cointegration space according to a particular economic theory.[27] Johansen (1992e) shows that $T(\beta_C - \beta_C)$ is asymptotically mixed Gaussian with mean zero and variance that may be estimated by

$$\Omega = (I - \widehat{\beta}_c C')\nu\nu'(I - C\widehat{\beta}_c') \otimes (\widehat{\beta}'C)^{-1}(D^{-1} - I)^{-1}(C'\widehat{\beta})$$

where $\nu$ is a matrix comprised of the eigenvectors associated with the $k$ smallest eigenvalues obtained in the solution of (3.27) and $D$ is a diagonal matrix of the $r$ largest eigenvalues. The Wald statistic appropriate for testing linear hypotheses of the form $K'vec(\beta_c) = 0$ is

$$T(K'vec(\widehat{\beta}_c - \beta_c)'(K'\Omega K)(K'vec(\widehat{\beta}_c - \beta_c)).$$

This statistic follows $\chi^2_{\dim K}$ distribution under the null hypothesis. The extension to nonlinear tests of hypotheses is straightforward. When the cointegration space is identified, general hypothesis tests (including tests regarding the values of coefficients in particular vectors or across two or more vectors) may be applied. Unlike tests that apply uniformly to each cointegration vector($H_0 : K'\beta = 0$), statistical inference obtained from these tests clearly depends on the chosen normalization (identification scheme).[28]

[27]This matrix normalization strategy is pursued by Ahn and Riensel (1990).

[28]Johansen recommends normalization invariance tests of the form $K'\beta = 0$. This test applies identical restrictions to each row of the cointegration space so that inference is invariant to the chosen normalization.

### 3.5.3 Comparing Estimation Strategies

While numerous alternative estimation strategies exist, the "triangular-based" approach and the "reduced rank" approaches provide two reasonable alternatives for applied research. DOLS and DGLS are computationally convenient and deliver estimates that are asymptotically equivalent to MLE. Of course the standard expressions used by ordinary software to calculate estimator variance do not account for persistence in errors that remains in DOLS. This persistence must be taken into consideration to ensure that standard tests of hypothesis are not misleading. The Johansen approach has optimal asymptotic properties and is quite convenient, but does require access to software that can solve standard eigenvalue problems.[29]

Evidence base upon small sample experiments is mixed. Gonzalo (1994) finds that the Johansen technique based upon the maximum likelihood principle out–performs several "single–equation" alternatives(DOLS or DGLS were not examined). Gonzalo attributes the performance to the fact that the MLE incorporates all prior knowledge about the existence of unit roots in the system, estimates are median unbiased, and symmetrically distributed. Stock and Watson's (1993) experiments stand in sharp contrast. They find that DOLS and DGLS perform well in most cases based upon MSE criterion. Moreover, they find that the Johansen estimates are subject to "large outliers" in many cases.

In practice, the advantage of "least squares" approaches is revealed in the Monte Carlo evidence provided in Stock and Watson (1993) who demonstrate that, in contrast to Johansen's approach, DOLS and DGLS perform well in simulation and yield stable results in recursive samples. However, the likelihood-based approach is highly sensitive to small changes in sample information. Phillips (1994) sheds light on the issue by examining the exact distribution maintained by the reduced–rank and triangular–based estimators in finite samples. Phillips demonstrates that the "reduced–rank" estimators exhibit "Cauchy–like" tails and no finite moments of integer order. In contrast, MLE's estimated from triangular representations maintain "matrix t-distribution tails with finite integer moments." Reliance on MSE criterion and recursive samples to assess small sample performance will clearly penalize estimators that produce outliers and thereby casts the reduced rank procedure in an unfavorable light. Applications that are guided by a distinct set of identifying restrictions may benefit from incorporating the identifying restrictions *ex ante*. However, the particular choice of normalization does influence the estimates and any subsequent rotation(matrix transformation) of the cointegration space will depend upon this choice of initial triangular representation.

In contrast, the reduced rank procedure yields normalizations that are unique because all normalization is applied to the estimated cointegration space *ex post*.

---

[29]RATS or GAUSS can easily do this. MICROFIT3 contains a menu driven approach that can be used to determine cointegration rank, estimate vectors and test simple hypotheses regarding the parameters of cointegration vectors. EVIEWS offers similar options in a "Windows" environment. RATS 4.2 offers numerous options in an extensive program, CATS, written by Hendrik Hansen and Katarina Juselius.

Moreover, though the risk of outliers may be greater, some steps can be taken to eliminate the number of observed outliers as in the applications discussed in chapters 6-8. Also, ongoing investigation of small sample properties reveals that many triangular based estimators exhibit some of the same "downward bias" tendencies of OLS in finite samples(see Crowder and Hoffman (1995)).

In addition, the relative performance of DOLS and Johansen's technique in a money demand study of five OECD countries is undertaken by Hoffman, Rasche, and Tieslau (1995). They find that unrestricted likelihood estimates do indeed display more volatility in recursive estimation than do DOLS counterparts. But the volatility in recursive estimation is reduced substantially once the parameter space is constrained by a unitary income elasticity. In fact, with this restriction in place, the Johansen estimates display considerable stability in recursive samples. This parameter reduction is consistent with many theories of money demand behavior and tests found it to be generally consistent with the data. The fact that reduction of parameter space can lead to improved small sample performance is certainly to be expected, but the dramatic reduction of outliers observed in some applications is no doubt attributable to the *ex post* normalization that is typically undertaken in concert with the Johansen technique.

This literature does not provide a clear direction for choosing estimators for applied work. The key to understanding the difference in performance between the reduced rank and triangular representation estimators lies with the issue of cointegration space identification. The triangular based estimator explicitly incorporates identifying restrictions *a priori* while identification of a cointegration space estimated by Johansen's technique is addressed *ex post*. Knowledge of the identifying restrictions clearly makes a difference. A simple way to see this is to note that $r^2$ fewer estimates are required to estimate the cointegration vectors using a triangular representation. Outliers occur in the reduced rank approach any time that the estimated space is normalized *ex post* by an $r \times r$ matrix that is "near singular." [30]

## 3.6 Testing Constancy of the Cointegration Space

In several recent studies the constancy of an estimated cointegration space of money demand variables has been questioned. (see Friedman and Kuttner (1992) or Stock and Watson (1993)) This is particularly relevant to the study of money demand because it is useful to know whether a stable relation linking real balances, real income, and interest rates is consistent with time series data. Moreover, the issue is important in the context of reduced rank regression techniques that have been shown to exhibit tendencies to produce large outliers. As

[30] The same problem might occur with triangular based estimates if one attempted to renormalize the estimated cointegration space after estimating the original vector with a particular normalization.

discussed in the previous section, Stock and Watson (1993) illustrate the potential severity of the problem in the context of money demand estimation while Hoffman, Rasche and Tielsau (1995) and Crowder and Hoffman (1995) demonstrate how reduction in the parameter space can reduce frequency of outliers.

### 3.6.1 Testing Constancy in Recursive Samples

Hansen and Johansen (1993) propose an approach applicable to testing long-run constancy in recursive samples. The basic idea expressed by HJ is to "fix" estimates of parameters associated with the short run dynamics ($\Pi_i^*$ in the error correction representation presented above) at values they obtain in the full sample. The cointegration and error correction spaces are then estimated at each recursive sub-sample using full sample estimates of coefficients associated with the short-run dynamics. The advantage of this approach is that variation in nuisance parameters associated with the short–run dynamics is not allowed to occur in the recursive estimation.

In the context of reduced rank regression, this is accomplished by regressing the differenced vector $\Delta z_t$ and the lag levels vector $z_{t-1}$ on $\Delta z_{t-1}$,..., $\Delta z_{t-q-1}$ including constant, seasonal dummies or any I(0) "exogenous" variables over the full sample—exactly as prescribed by Johansen (1988). Denote the full sample residuals formed from the "difference" and "levels" regression as $R_{0t}$ and $R_{1t}$ respectively and form moment matrices at each recursive sample using the segment of these residuals that corresponds to the recursive sample. The standard eigenvalue problem can be solved using

$$|\rho b' S_{11}(t) b - b' S_{10}(t) S_{00}(t) S_{01}(t) b| = 0 \tag{3.28}$$

where $S_{ij}(t)$ , $(i = 0,\, 1)$ denote sample moment matrices formed from $R_{0t}$ and $R_{1t}$, and $b$ is a known $p \times r$ cointegration space that defines the hypothesized constancy. Values obtained for the "$r$" largest eigenvalues obtained by solving (3.28) are compared with a like number of eigenvalues (denoted $\lambda_i$) obtained by solving the unconstrained version of (3.28). In recursive samples this produces a sequence of likelihood ratio statistics

$$-2\ln(Q(H_\beta|\widehat{\beta}(t)) = t\sum_{i=1}^{r}\ln\left\{\frac{1-\widehat{\rho}_i(t)}{1-\widehat{\lambda}_i(t)}\right\} \quad t = T_0, ..., T \tag{3.29}$$

that follows $\chi^2_{(p-r)r}$ under the null hypothesis of parameter constancy. In practice HJ suggest that "$b$" can be set at values obtained in full sample estimation or at hypothesized values that are perhaps suggested by economic theory and hence, suitable candidates for constancy analysis. The choice will depend upon whether one is interested in knowing whether values obtained in the full sample reflect recursive estimates or whether all subsamples are consistent with a particular set of long-run estimates. By pinning the short-run estimates at values obtained over the full sample, HJ's technique can be expected to deliver sharper inference regarding constancy. (see Hoffman, Rasche, and Tieslau (1995) or Hoffman and Tahiri (1994) for examples)

### 3.6.2 Do Breaks in Deterministic Trend Imply Corresponding Breaks in the Constant Term of the Cointegration Vector?

The presence of deterministic trends in cointegrated systems can pose problems in applied research. In section 3.2.3 we examined how correct inference is obtained in the presence of deterministic trends. The discussion in section 3.2.3 also revealed that the estimated cointegration space can contain deterministic trend components in some specifications. Specifically broken deterministic trends can have an effect on the stability of the constant term in the cointegrating regression across the sample.

Johansen's (1992) framework is conducive to the study of constant terms in cointegration vectors. Again, the reduced form VECM is

$$\Delta z_t = \mu + \sum_{i=1}^{q-1} \Pi_i^* \Delta z_{t-i} - \Pi z_{t-1} + \varepsilon_t \tag{3.30}$$

where $\Pi$ is defined as in (3.10). From the Granger Representation Theorem (see Engle and Granger (1987) or Johansen (1991)) $z_t$ has representation

$$z_t = z_0 + C(1) \sum_{S=1}^{t} \varepsilon_S + \tau_1 t + \tau_0 + Y_t - Y_0 \tag{3.31}$$

where $Y_t \sim I(0)$, $\beta' z_0 = \beta' Y_0$, and $C(1) = \beta_\perp (\alpha'_\perp \Pi_1^*(1)\, \beta_\perp)^{-1} \alpha'_\perp$ with $\alpha' \alpha_\perp = \beta'\, \beta_\perp = 0$ and $\Pi_1^*(1) = \Pi + I - \sum_{i=1}^{q-1} \Pi_i^*$.

The relation between the drift term in (3.10) and the constant term in the cointegration vector, $\beta_0 = \beta' \tau_0$ is obtained by substituting (3.10) in (3.31) and equating coefficients on the constant term to obtain

$$\beta_0 = \beta' \tau_0 = -(\alpha'\alpha)^{-1} \alpha' \left[ I - (I - \sum_{i=1}^{q-1} \Pi_i^*) C(1) \right] \mu \tag{3.32}$$

In some cases the value of the mean of the cointegration vector will be of interest. For example, one might wish to examine whether the parameters of cointegration vector (including the constant term) are constant through time. Equation (3.32) reveals that constancy of the mean of $\beta' z_t$ will depend on nearly all the parameters that comprise the autoregressive representation of the model. Specifically, suppose the time series process for $z_t$ exhibits a shift in deterministic drift. That is $\mu = \mu_0 + \mu_1 D_t$ where $D_t = 0$ for $t \leq T^*$ and $D_t = 1$ for $t > T^*$. It is clear that $\beta_0$ will be affected by this shift unless $\alpha' \mu_1 - \left( I - \sum_{i=1}^{q-1} \Pi_i^* \right) C(1) \mu_1 = 0$. Estimates of $\mu_1$ are easily obtained by augmenting (3.21) with $D_t$ and a test of the proposition can be undertaken conditional on values of $\alpha$, $\Pi^*$, and $C(1)$. Of course sharper inference can be obtained by also allowing for uncertainty embedded in estimates of these parameters.

## 3.7 Conclusion

This chapter provides a methodology for testing, identifying, estimating, conducting inference assessing stability and exploring the dynamics of the long-run characteristics of a system characterized by cointegration. Our focus is exclusively on the long–run character of the system while issues that arise in the complete structural analysis of the system are reserved for Chapter 4. The discussion reviews a large body of literature and is, as far as we know, the only outlet where all of these topics appear in one place. The discussion is not structured as a survey of the literature but is confined to a set of techniques that we have found useful in conducting empirical applications in cointegrated systems.

# Chapter 4

# A FRAMEWORK FOR STRUCTURAL AND DYNAMIC ANALYSIS IN COINTEGRATED SYSTEMS

In recent years considerable effort has been focused on the link between shocks that impact the macroeconomy through time and the importance of these shocks in understanding aggregate behavior. As a result empirical research has been directed at disclosing the identity of fundamental structures that adequately described the behavior of the macro economy. To that end. many empiricists embraced the VAR methodology popularized in the work of Sims (1980) and others. This approach assumes that the dynamic behavior of the economy is indeed determined by fundamental structural innovations. The identity of these innovations is ascertained by expressing a vector process in a Wold representation and conducting "structural innovations analysis." This consists of an examination of the response patterns of certain variables to innovations associated with the Wold structure. The relative importance of the innovations is ascertained by measuring the proportion of forecast error variance that is attributable to each structural innovation.

Innovations analysis as a vehicle for understanding structure is now an integral element in the tool kit of the applied macroeconomic analyst. Some of the appeal of the approach is the that it presumably avoids the demanding(in Sims' characterization "incredible") restrictions that are a prerequisite for identification of traditional "structural" econometric models(e.g.Cowles Commission vintage). However, identification in the context of a structural VAR requires restrictions that are demanding in their own right.

In Chapter 3 we saw the role played by identification in distinguishing the relative performance of estimators based upon Johansen's reduced rank method from those that impose the "identifying" triangular representation *a priori*. Identification restrictions are also required to obtain useful estimates of an $r$ dimensional cointegration space and, to isolate the source of nonstationarity in a common trends representation of a cointegrated system. In this chapter we examine how knowledge of cointegration rank can facilitate the task of identifying both the long-run and short–run structure of an economic model. The discussion underscores the notion that the identity of system structure is required before we can establish the nature of the shocks that determine aggregate fluctuations. We view the task of identification(and the role played by cointegration) in the context of "Cowles structures" as well as structural VAR's. Though knowledge of cointegration rank can be useful, we illustrate that identification remains a serious challenge for empirical work.

Our point of departure is a structural representation of a vector process $z_t$. In section 1 the identification problem is carefully posed in the context of a traditional multivariate autoregressive model. Section 2 examines the alternative approaches to identification of this system. Though the path taken to achieve identification varies considerably across applications and the identifying restrictions take on many different forms, the fundamental challenge, and ultimately the number of restrictions required to accomplish the task, is the same. We illustrate how complete(both long–run and short–run) structural innovation identification is obtained in the context of a cointegrated system using models of transitory shock identification provided by Englund, Verdin, and Warne (1991) as well as the Blanchard-Quah (1989) application where cointegration is not recognized explicitly. In section 3 we review techniques designed to measure the performance of various structural VAR models. This discussion also contains a summary of the criticisms that have been leveled at structural VAR methodology in recent years. Evidence of weak exogeneity can also assist in the identification of structural VAR models. In section 4 we examine how knowledge of weak exogeneity can help in identifying the nature of structural shocks in cointegrated systems; explore relevant transformations of cointegrated models designed to explicitly exhibit weak exogeneity; and note the inherent endogenous/exogenous dichotomy that prevails even in applications that ostensibly focus exclusively on reduced form analysis.

## 4.1 Identification

The concept of identification in contemporary economic analysis has its origins in the work of the Cowles Commission (see Koopmans (1950) and Koopmans and Hood (1953)). Many of these contributions are presented comprehensively in Fisher (1966) and Rothenberg (1971). The traditional identification problem is to solve for the complete economic structure–as represented by a system of "structural equations" from the reduced form representation of the system. Our Chapter 3 discussion reveals that knowledge of a set of "long–run" identifying restrictions can reveal the long-run equilibrium relations as well as the corresponding "error correction" coefficients that characterize the economic system. A separate set of partial identifying restrictions can reveal both the identity and effect of innovations in the common stochastic trends that are responsible for the nonstationary behavior of the variables in the system. As we have seen, empirical analysis of the long-run equilibria and common trends may be undertaken without restrictions sufficient to deliver complete system identification. We now consider what additional restrictions are required to identify the entire economic structure associated with the system.

The nature of the identification problem may be illustrated in the context of the structural autoregressive representation

$$H(0)z_t = u + \sum_{i=1}^{q} H_i z_{t-i} + v_t \tag{4.1}$$

where the structural errors are assumed free from persistence and $V\{v_t\} = \Sigma_v$ for t=1,2,...T.[1] We now wish to examine circumstances that may allow us to ascertain the identity of the contemporaneous coefficient matrix; $H(0)$.

The structural VECM obtained from (4.1) is

$$H(0)\Delta z_t = H(0)\mu + H(0)\sum_{i=1}^{q-1} \Pi_i^* \Delta z_{t-i} - H(0)\Pi z_{t-1} + v_t \tag{4.2}$$

with $\Pi_i^*$ and $\Pi$ defined as in equation 3.10.

The analysis of Chapter 3, section 3, reveals that knowledge of cointegration rank $r$ and conditions for identification of the long-run parameters $\beta$ enable us to identify the reduced form matrix of error correction coefficients, $\alpha$. Equation (4.2) reveals that knowledge of $H(0)$ will be required to identify the matrix of structural error correction parameters; $H(0)\alpha$.

The structural multivariate permanent/transitory decomposition model is similarly defined as

$$z_t = z_0 + C(1)H(0)^{-1}H(0)\left(\sum_{s=1}^{t} \varepsilon_s + \mu t\right) + C^*(L)H(0)^{-1}H(0)\varepsilon_t$$

$$\equiv z_0 + S(1)\left(\sum_{s=1}^{t} v_s + \mu t\right) + S^*(L)v_t \tag{4.3}$$

where the $S$ matrices denote $C(1)H(0)^{-1}$ and $C^*(L)H(0)^{-1}$ respectively so that the structure of the model is dichotomized into permanent and transitory components. Our discussion in Chapter 3 also reveals conditions that allow identification of the factor loading $\beta_\perp$ and the common trend coefficients $\alpha'_\perp$ from knowledge of $C(1)$. Below we demonstrate that conditions that allow identification of these components identify $k$ rows of $H(0)$ that correspond to the permanent components in the system. Complete structural identification

[1] This is more restrictive than in the general model where structural errors are represented by $F(L)v_t$. The restriction presumes that $q$ may be set at a level that purges persistence from $v_t$.

is obtained when sufficient restrictions are employed to identify the portions of $H(0)$ that correspond to *both* permanent and transitory components.

# 4.2 Identification in the Structural VECM

Identification is achieved when $H(0)$ may be obtained from a combination of *a priori* restrictions and the reduced form information. There are many different forms of *a priori* restrictions that can be used to accomplish this task. However, each path to identification is a quest for $H(0)$ and each approach has its origin in fundamental principles addressed in the work of the Cowles Commission. This point may be obscured in applications directed at disclosing the identity of structural innovations where restrictions are translated into constraints on impulse response patterns at short or long–run horizons. In this case, the form of information required to obtain identification differs but the overall identification challenge may be equally demanding.

The traditional approach to identification of $H(0)$ appeals to economic theory for precise contemporaneous relations among variables in an economic model. These relations imply restrictions on feasible choices for $H(0)$. In general $p^2$ unknown parameters appear in $H(0)$, and $p(p-1)$ remain even after normalization by a single variable in each equation, so considerable information must be forthcoming to allow identification of $H(0)$.

## 4.2.1 Structural Identification Using Contemporaneous Restrictions

A common strategy in VAR models is to adopt Fisher's suggestions for identification by means of restrictions on error covariance matrices. This approach is attributable to Wold (1960). For example, suppose that the errors associated with the structural model equation (4.1) are uncorrelated. This assumption places $p(p-1)/2$ restrictions on $\Sigma_\upsilon$. The relationship between the matrix of reduced form and structural error covariance matrices; $\Sigma_\varepsilon$ and $\Sigma_\upsilon$, is

$$H(0)\Sigma_\varepsilon H(0)' = \Sigma_\upsilon \tag{4.4}$$

Equation (4.4) reveals that feasible choices for $H(0)$ must maintain the restrictions embodied in $\Sigma_\upsilon$, thereby delivering $p(p-1)/2$ pieces of information useful for identification of $H(0)$. In many VAR applications the remaining $p(p-1)/2$ restrictions are obtained by imposing a recursive ordering on the variables in $z_t$, making $H(0)$ a triangular matrix. When combined with $p(p-1)/2$ covariance restrictions the recursive structure delivers the required $p(p-1)$ independent pieces of information and satisfies conditions for identification in a recursive system specified in Fisher (1966), Theorem 4.1.

It is also possible to identify $H(0)$ using the assumption that a "block recursive" structure might prevail among the variables that comprise $z_t$. In this case suppose $z_t$ can be separated into $r$ and $k = p - r$ dimensional vectors $y_t$ and $x_t$ respectively(expressed traditionally as endogenous and exogenous variables respectively) and write the system coefficient matrix as $H(0) = \begin{bmatrix} H_{yy} & H_{yx} \\ H_{xy} & H_{xx} \end{bmatrix}$ so that block recursivity implies $H_{xy} = 0$ and $Cov(v_y v_x') = 0$ for a total of $2kr$ restrictions. Then focus attention exclusively on the conditional model

$$H_{yy}\Delta y_t + H_{yx}\Delta x_t - H_{yz}\sum_{i=1}^{q-1}\Pi_i^*\Delta z_{t-i} - H_{yz}\Pi z_{t-1} = v_{yt} \tag{4.5}$$

and assume that $H_{xx}$ in the remaining equations

$$H_{xx}\Delta x_t - H_{xz}\sum_{i=1}^{q-1}\Pi_i^*\Delta z_{t-i} - H_{xz}\Pi z_{t-1} = v_{xt} \tag{4.6}$$

is identified by $k(k-1)$ restrictions obtained by assuming the $x_t$ represents $k$ distinct processes or that the $x$ forms a separate recursive system. In either case, $H_{xx}$ in (4.6) is identified. Identification of $H_{yy}$ and $H_{yx}$ in (4.5) can proceed in the manner prescribed by most "textbook" applications of rank and order exclusion restrictions. Absent any information regarding the form of the $r$-dimensional error covariance matrix $\Sigma_{vy}$, use the information conveyed by the reduced form associated with (4.5) where $x_t$ is treated as "predetermined". In this case conventional rank and order conditions apply to the $r$ equations in (4.5) so that $r-1$ restrictions must apply to each equation in the "$y$" subsystem or $r(r-1)$ independent restrictions will be required to identify $H_{yy}$ and $H_{yx}$. Available covariance restrictions can reduce the need to impose exclusion restrictions on $H_{yy}$ and $H_{yx}$ but a total of $r(r-1)$ restrictions are required nonetheless. When combined with the $k(k-1)$ restrictions required for identification of $H_{xx}$ and the $2kr$ restrictions delivered by the assumption of block recursivity we have $p^2 - p$ total restrictions and $H(0)$ is identified.

### 4.2.2 Structural Identification Using Long-Run and Short-Run Restrictions

Our discussion in Chapter 3 concentrated exclusively on conditions that allow us to establish the identity of long–run relations that prevail in autoregressive representations of a vector process as well as the source of nonstationarity that characterizes common trends representations of an economic system. The discussion explicitly avoids designating endogenous and exogenous variables in the system and does not determine the contemporaneous structure of the entire model as in traditional structural identification exercises. This partial identification strategy may be motivated by the observation that there is less controversy about the identity of the long–run structure of the economy or similarly that the restrictions that provide complete structural identification are simply too demanding.[2] Regardless, we now consider the conditions for complete structural identification and the role played by knowledge of cointegration rank.

[2] Faust and Leeper(1994) illustrate that exclusive focus on the long–run may also prove to be misleading and caution against identification strategies based exclusively on restrictions imposed at the infinite forecast horizon. We outline the Faust and Leeper criticism in more detail in section 4.3

Over the last decade the quest for identification in structural models has disdained the "incredible" contemporaneous restrictions suggested in the applications that evolved from the work of the Cowles Commission. VAR methodology shifted the emphasis from contemporaneous structure to structural innovations and, more recently, these structural innovations have been identified by restrictions on the long–run character of the model. Even if there remains no interest in the identity of $H(0)$ per se, all of these efforts may all be viewed as quests for the identity of $H(0)$ because complete structural identification requires just as much information as that required to identify $H(0)$. This is clear from either (4.1) or (4.3) since knowledge of $H(0)$ identifies both contemporaneous structure or structural innovations respectively.

In Chapter 3, we used an example from KPSW (1991) to illustrate how knowledge of cointegration rank summarizes available long–run information and assists in the identification of the structural VECM by identifying the first $k$ rows of $H(0)$. Warne (1993) provides an excellent summary of KPSW while adding a role for transitory information so that $H(0)$ can be completely identified. KPSW illustrate that models with $k$ common trends require $k(k-1)/2$ identifying restrictions that are requirements for all feasible factor loading matrices, $\beta_{\perp}^{0}$. The origin of the restrictions is economic theory that ties long–run movements in certain time series to particular structural innovations. Illustrations are discussed in section (4.2.3). With these restrictions in place KPSW employ the innovation independence assumptions to identify $\beta_{\perp}$ as the linear transformation of $\beta_{\perp}^{0}$ that preserves the original restrictions while insuring that the permanent structural innovations, $\alpha_t'\varepsilon_t$ are linearly independent. This approach identifies $\beta_{\perp}$ and $\alpha_{\perp}$ as well as $k$ rows of $H(0)$; $H_k(0)$,

$$v_t^p = H_k(0)\varepsilon_t = (\beta_{\perp}'\beta_{\perp})^{-1}\beta_{\perp}'C(1)\varepsilon_t \equiv \alpha_{\perp}'\varepsilon_t \tag{4.7}$$

The common trend identifying restrictions may be combined with assumptions about the nature of transitory innovations to allow complete structural VAR identification. The total number of combined "permanent and transitory" restrictions required for identification is exactly the same as those required by structural models discussed in the original Cowles Commission work. However, knowledge of cointegration rank does serve an important role in accomplishing the task because it distinguishes the long-run and short-run dichotomy that characterizes a vector process.

Warne (1993) illustrates how both long-run and short-run restrictions can be combined in an identification scheme that exploits knowledge of cointegration rank as well as covariance restrictions across all structural innovations in a VAR. The restrictions required by the Warne approach are sufficient to identify $H(0)$ in (4.1). Denote the $r$ rows of $H(0)$ that remain undefined, after the identification of $H_k(0)$ in equation(4.7), as $H_r(0)$ and note that the independence of permanent, $v_t^P$, and transitory, $v_t^T$, structural innovations requires

$$Cov(v_t^P, v_t^T) = \alpha_{\perp}'\Sigma_{\varepsilon}H_r(0)' = 0.$$

This limits the choice of $H_r(0)$ to candidates that satisfy this condition. Warne suggests that choices for $H_r(0)$ be of the form $\alpha^0\Sigma_{\varepsilon}^{-1}$ where $\alpha^0$ denotes any space spanned by the columns of $\alpha$ so that $\alpha'_{\perp}\alpha^0 = 0$. When $H_r(0)$ is of the form $\alpha^0\Sigma_\varepsilon^{-1}$, the covariance between permanent and transitory innovations is zero by construction. Independence among the "$r$" transitory innovations implies that

$$Cov(v_t^T) = \alpha^0\Sigma_\varepsilon^{-1}\alpha^{0\prime}$$

is diagonal. Both sets of independence assumptions are obtained by setting

$$H_r(0) = Q_r^{-1}(\alpha^0)'\Sigma_\varepsilon^{-1}$$

where $Q_r$ is the lower triangular Cholesky factor of $(\alpha^0)'\Sigma_\varepsilon^{-1}\alpha^0$. Then $H_r(0)$ is identified when a unique solution can be obtained for $\alpha^* = \alpha^0(Q'_r)^{-1}$. Paralleling the discussion of permanent shock identification, this requires $r(r-1)/2$ restrictions on $\alpha^0$ that are preserved in $\alpha^*$.

In practice, the process of identifying the $r$ rows of $H(0)$ associated with the transitory components is analogous to the approach to $H_k(0)$ identification employed by KPSW. First select a candidate for $\alpha^0$. Warne recommends an $r \times p$ selection matrix $U$, chosen so that $\alpha^0 = \alpha(U\alpha)^{-1}$ with $U\alpha$ nonsingular. In practice, $U$ can be chosen so that $\alpha^0$ is simply a matrix normalization of the error correction space $\alpha$. This choice places $r(r-1)$ "zeros" in $\alpha^0$ and $r(r-1)/2$ remain in $\alpha^* = \alpha^0(Q'_r)^{-1}$ since the Cholesky factor, $Q_r$, is lower triangular. The choice of $U$ dictates where these "zero first period" effects of transitory shocks on variables in the system will prevail. Hence, the representation of structural transitory innovations as

$$v_t^T = H_r(0)\varepsilon_t = Q_r^{-1}(\alpha^0)'\Sigma_\varepsilon^{-1}\varepsilon_t \equiv (\alpha^*)'\Sigma_\varepsilon^{-1}\varepsilon_t \tag{4.8}$$

satisfies both sets of independence conditions.

Specification of the permanent and transitory innovations as in (4.7) and (4.8) identifies $H(0)$ as

$$H(0) = \begin{bmatrix} H_k(0) \\ H_r(0) \end{bmatrix} = \begin{bmatrix} (\beta'_{\perp}\beta_{\perp})^{-1}\beta'_{\perp}C(1) \\ Q_r^{-1}(\alpha^0)'\Sigma_\varepsilon^{-1} \end{bmatrix} = \begin{bmatrix} \alpha'_{\perp} \\ (\alpha^*)'\Sigma_\varepsilon^{-1} \end{bmatrix} \tag{4.9}$$

and the structural innovations $v_t = H(0)\varepsilon_t$, are particular innovations that satisfy innovation independence assumptions as well as restrictions on $\beta_{\perp}$ and $\alpha^*$ that insure the representation of $H(0)$ in (4.9) is unique. In the context of equation (4.1) the particular form reflected in (4.9) may not convey intuitive contemporaneous relations among the elements of $z_t$ as is often the case when contemporaneous exclusion restrictions are used to identify $H(0)$. However, identification in this manner connotes its own structural pattern. Here, all structural innovations are mutually independent while the separate long-run and transitory innovations influence the elements of $z_t$ in a block recursive fashion. Hence, exclusion restrictions will typically appear in $r-1$ of the last $r$ columns of $H(0)^{-1}$ and in $k-1$ of the $k$ columns of $\beta^*_{\perp}$. From a purely technical perspective, the $k(k-1)/2 + r(r-1)/2$ "non covariance" restrictions used to identify $H(0)$ are arbitrary, and experiments with alternative identifying restrictions will be useful in building a convincing case for the robustness of a particular structural representation. Alternatives to this approach exist. If, the $k(k-1)/2$ or $r(r-1)/2$ restrictions are chosen differently in distinguishing among the permanent and transitory structural innovations, an alternative to lower Cholesky factorization may be required to insure the restrictions remain in the orthogonalized structural innovations.[3] Of course, non-orthogonal structural innovation identification schemes may be chosen, but these may not be conducive to meaningful innovations analysis. In these cases variance decompositions and impulse response patterns must be interpreted carefully.

The relationship between identification of the complete $p$—dimensional structural VAR and the identification conditions discussed above is now easily seen. In standard VAR models $p(p-1)/2$ restrictions are required in addition to the $p(p-1)/2$ innovation orthogonality constraints to obtain the identification suggested by a Wold "causal" chain. In the case of integrated VAR systems we can first employ the $p(p-1)/2$ innovation independence restrictions. Knowledge of cointegration rank $r$ implies that $r$ structural innovations leave no long-run imprint on the variables in the system. These $pr$ homogeneous restrictions deliver an additional $kr$ independent restrictions that may be applied toward the identification of $H(0)$.[4] With the addition of the $k(k-1)/2$ and $r(r-1)/2$ restrictions required to sort out among the sets of permanent and transitory innovations respectively, the $p(p-1)/2$ additional restrictions necessary to identify $H(0)$ (under the assumption of structural innovation independence) are obtained. Knowledge of cointegration rank then reduces the number of restrictions required to identify $H(0)$ by $kr$. An additional advantage of recognizing cointegration rank is that it can confirm hypotheses about the number of distinct permanent innovations—sometimes asserted in structural VAR applications.

### 4.2.3 An Example of Structural Identification in a Vector Error Correction Model

Englund, Vredin and Warne (1991) provide an example of transitory innovation identification. In practice these restrictions imply that some of the transitory innovations have no effect on certain variables in the first period. While long-run constraints used to identify permanent innovations often find considerable support in economic theory, the case for transitory innovations may not be so compelling. As we have seen, this is essentially the quest for the remaining $r$ rows of $H(0)$. EVW examine an open economy model comprised of domestic output; $y$, money; $m_t$, interest rates; $r_t$, prices; $p_t$, government purchases; $g_t$, and a measure of world output; $y_t$. Among these six variables they observe three cointegration vectors and three independent common trends that are identified as accumulated domestic and foreign real shocks and a separate nominal shock.

[3]Gali (1992) provides an example of this approach to identification of $H(0)$. In his Table 1, long-run restrictions R1-R3 identify $H_k(0)$ as defined here, and short-run restriction R4-R5 identify $H_r(0)$ as defined here.

[4]See Quah (1991) for a detailed technical discussion.

In the spirit of Blanchard and Quah, EVW ascribe the common trends to technology innovations that have "real" effects and a separate impulse responsible for long-run movement in the nominal variables. The three transitory innovations;

$$v_t^T = Q_r^{-1}(\alpha' U)^{-1}\alpha'\Sigma_\varepsilon^{-1}\varepsilon_t = (v_{tp}^T, v_{tdd}^T, v_{tfd}^T)$$

are designated as a separate domestic policy shock and foreign and domestic "demand" shocks. $U$ is chosen to select out the error correction terms that correspond to the price, government policy, and foreign output equations. Then $\alpha^0$ is simply a matrix normalization (on these three variables) of the error correction space. EVW "order" the transitory shocks so that the domestic demand shock has no contemporaneous effect on government policy and that neither the domestic demand shock nor the policy shock has a contemporaneous influence on foreign (world) output. This is achieved by first ordering the variables so that $g$ and $y_t^*$ are the last two elements of $z_t$. Then $U$ is defined to select rows 4-6 in $\alpha$, $\alpha^0$ exhibits $r(r-1)$ zeros obtained by matrix normalization, and $r(r-1)/2$ of these remain in $Q_r^{-1}\alpha^0$ since $Q_r$ is a lower triangular Cholesky factor. These restrictions convey the recursive pattern specified for the transitory innovations *a priori* and the transitory innovations are identified.

The EVW application illustrates that the choice of $U$ is directed by the *a priori* transitory shock specification. Typically transitory effects will be identified from the first period movement of a subset of variables. The selection of $U$ designates this set. Clearly this selection is technically restricted to choices of $U$ that yield a normalization, $\alpha' U$, which has rank $r$. This requirement rules out transitory specifications that define roles for variables that are weakly exogenous since the corresponding row of $\alpha$ will be zero. A reasonable approach might be to define $U$ so that it selects variables whose forecast error variance is left unexplained by permanent innovations in the short run. However, the case for a particular transitory specification will depend ultimately on whether the implied short-run structure is consistent with a convincing economic explanation. In contrast to the relatively small number of plausible long–run scenarios that are well founded in theory, considerable debate remains about the origin and effect of transitory impulses—posing a serious challenge to specification of the short run.

### 4.2.4 Structural VAR Identification in Models Not Characterized by Cointegration

Even when cointegration rank is zero, structural VAR analysis can proceed in a manner consistent with the discussion in the previous section. In this case a $p$-dimensional nonstationary vector process can be represented by $p$ independent permanent components. Identification in this setting remains the quest for $H(0)$ in establishing the structural total impact matrix $C(1)H(0)^{-1}$. However, $\beta = 0$ in this case so no information is forthcoming from the orthogonality condition $\beta_\perp' \beta = 0$. Absent this information, $p(p-1)/2$ restrictions on $C(1)H(0)^{-1}$ will be required to identify the model in addition to the $p(p-1)/2$ implied by the conventional innovation independence assumption. A typical approach in this context would be to write the $\beta_{\perp}^{0}$ as a lower triangular matrix (now $k = p$ so this can be done) so that permanent shocks influence all variables in a recursive manner.[5]

In the well known structural VAR application by Blanchard and Quah (1989) the focus is on real output; $y$, and the unemployment rate; $un_t$. In this bivariate system; $z_t' = (y, un_t)$, BQ specify a single source of long–run behavior and a transitory "demand" impulse so $k = 1 < p$ with no explicit discussion of cointegration. However, BQ explicitly model the unemployment rate as a trend stationary process.[6] Though BQ do not discuss cointegration, a cointegration vector is implicit in their formulation. This is given $\beta' = (0, 1)$ and $\beta_{\perp}$ is then identified as $\beta_{\perp}' = (1, 0)$. The BQ results can then be duplicated using the outline of section 3.3 of Chapter 3.

Blanchard (1989) examines a five dimensional VAR that is identified with $p(p-1)/2 = 10$ contemporaneous restrictions in addition to the assumption of structural innovation independence. Bergman, Blakemore, and Hoffman (1995) demonstrate that a five dimensional model—in the spirit of Blanchard (1989)—exhibits cointegration rank 3. This information provides $rk = 6$ identifying restrictions—enabling complete identification to be achieved with access to only 4 additional restrictions. In the applications conducted in Chapters 6-8 we exploit knowledge of cointegration rank in identifying structural innovations in several models characterized by money demand relations.

## 4.3 Assessing Structural VAR Specifications

We have seen that identification in structural VAR models requires considerable information in the form of identifying restrictions. While identifying restrictions are not testable, there are a number of mechanisms that may be used to assess any maintained specification. One standard criterion is of course predictive performance. Once the contemporaneous coefficient matrix; $H(0)$, is identified, conditional forecasts may be obtained. The accuracy of these forecasts may be compared with those forthcoming from either an unconstrained VAR representation or the corresponding VECM. Use of contemporaneous conditioning information can be expected to improve contemporaneous forecasts but of course requires more information than is typically available in the reduced form VAR.

The most common form of structural VAR assessment is conventional innovations analysis. In this case the pattern of impulse responses are examined along with variance decompositions to determine whether certain innovations

[5]This discussion presumes that structural VAR identification is obtained using long–run restrictions. It is easy to show that exclusive focus on the short run components of the system without exploiting cointegration rank restrictions requires $p(p-1)/2$ restrictions–collapsing to the conventional VAR identification methodology. Gali(1992) combined short and long–run restrictions in this fashion without explicitly recognizing cointegration rank.

[6]Trend stationarity rather than stationarity about a constant is discussed in the context of cointegration of Johansen (1991).

actually display a response pattern, or explain forecast error variance, in a manner that is consistent with economic theory. The difficulties often encountered in this task are well documented in the applied VAR literature.

When identification is obtained using long-run restrictions in the structural VAR, (in the KPSW/Warne approach) the validity of long-run restrictions can be assessed in many cases. Theory may predict that permanent innovations explain substantial portions of the variance in some of the variables at even medium term horizons while effects on "unrelated" variables should dissipate quickly. The pattern of response to alleged transitory shocks should be equally plausible. In practice an intuitively appealing scenario for the role of transitory shocks may be soundly rejected by data that deliver implausible impulse response patterns. Of course there are no strict guidelines for choosing exactly which forecast horizon should exhibit a particular imprint and the exercise often reduces to trying to fit a set of irregularly shapes pieces into a unified puzzle.

This process of assessing the significance of response patterns may be guided by statistical inference. Warne (1993) offers analytic formulae for calculating confidence intervals for impulse response functions and variance decompositions in structural VAR's identified using knowledge of cointegration rank. Runkle (1987) offers a simulation approach that has been applied by numerous authors including KPSW. Either of these approaches can be used to establish the precision of response patterns obtained in innovations analysis.

In addition to conventional innovations analysis, continued empirical investigation may explore other avenues. This begins with recalling that the permanent and transitory innovations are formed from linear combinations of reduced form residuals in the VAR, so their true nature or identity may be difficult to ascertain. However, some insight may be gained by accumulating the structural innovations with estimated drift to obtain a "picture" of each stochastic trend.[7] The proximity of these nebulous trends to observed variables, in or out of the original model, may shed light on the nature of the underlying sources of system nonstationarity. Similarly, visual analysis of the transitory components may help reveal the origin of transitory behavior. Historical decomposition may be used in conjunction with this type of visual analysis. "In sample" forecast error comparison can reveal how well individual structural innovations explain the forecast errors of particular variables or crucial business cycle turning points or episodes.

The structural VAR approach provides one important avenue for applied research in macroeconomics. When theoretically motivated cointegration vectors are consistent with cointegration rank that is observed in the system, the task of identification in the structural VAR is facilitated. Statistical evidence of cointegration rank will reject some models out of hand. But, building a case in favor of a particular structural VAR model may in general prove more difficult. Definitive support for precise parameterizations will typically require a number of restrictions that may be too stringent for economists who are unwilling

[7] KPSW adopt this strategy when plotting permanent components against "Solow residuals." See Bergman, Blakemore and Hoffman(1995) for another application.

to accept the "zero" order restrictions employed in conventional "structural" econometric models. Of course the strength of the case and the credibility of a chosen specification may well depend on whether the resulting innovations analyses (impulse response patterns and variance decompositions) make a compelling case. The argument may be bolstered by extracting the common trends and comparing them with observable proxies for variables they purportedly represent. The most challenging part of the exercise may be settling on a satisfying parameterization for transitory innovations—simply because there are so many plausible avenues for transitory innovations to influence a vector time series. Without a compelling argument well founded in economic analysis and/or solid support from the data, it will be impossible to build a convincing case in favor of a chosen specification.

### 4.3.1 Structural VAR Challenges

Structural VAR methodology has faced a number of challenges in recent years and no discussion of the approach would be complete without documenting some of the serious objections to the approach. Since the common trends model is simply a structural VAR model applied in a cointegrated setting, many of these criticisms apply to the framework outlined above. A basic criticism is that any identification assumption that is used to sort out the independent contribution of the "structural innovations" may be challenged. By their very nature, identifying assumptions are nontestable so modelers face the challenge of linking identifying assumptions to established theory *a priori*. When no firm link can be established, the best course of action may be to present results derived from the set of identification schemes that span relevant alternatives and determine whether a persistent pattern emerges from the sets of innovations analysis. However, the issue of identification is generally unavoidable and those in search of an approach that allows analysis without having to take a stand on the issue may wish to choose other pursuits. The discussion above reveals that knowledge of cointegration rank can reduce the number of arbitrary restrictions required to identify structural innovations but this reduction is achieved only when the researcher has access to knowledge of cointegration rank *and* an identified cointegration space.

Another, somewhat related, line of criticism is that the link between economic theory and structural VAR representations is not sufficiently strong. Certain models, for example some that fall under the label of the "general equilibrium" approach to macro modeling, predict links between underlying structural shocks and economic variables that are not adequately captured by standard Wold representations. Cooley and Dwyer (1995) illustrate that application of standard structural VAR methodology to certain systems can lead to very misleading conclusions about the relative importance of "demand" or transitory shocks and relate their concerns to the issue of "identification failure". Essentially, CD demonstrate the importance of identifying restrictions in reaching conclusions and chastise the SVAR literature for not basing the approach on sufficient theory.[8]

A similiar line of criticism stems from the challenge raised by Hansen and Sargent (1991) and later by Lippi and Reichlin (1993) is that certain plausible economic models are characterized by shocks that simply cannot be represented by Wold structures. Technically these "nonfundamental" shocks are associated with moving average representations that are not "invertible." HS and LR provide examples of how "nonfundamental" representations can arise. Perhaps most troubling from the perspective of applications in cointegrated systems is the Blanchard and Quah (1993) example of how common trends representations can clearly exhibit "nonfundamentalness" under certain conditions. The problem is indeed serious in the sense that application of the standard methodology can lead to misleading conclusions if it is applied to systems inherently characterized by nonfundamental structures. Or equivalently, the severity of the problem can be expressed in the inability of the standard technology to adequately account for structural innovations that are inherently nonfundamental. As more refinement takes place in the development of models characterized by a well defined bridge between structural innovations and macro aggregates, the importance of the "nonfundamental challenge" can be better understood. At this point empiricists can only take solace in the notion that invertible Wold representations can indeed be used to describe a wide range of agent behavior and that nearly all of the established empirical literature is based upon the existence of "fundamental innovations."

Faust and Leeper (1994) take a very different approach in their criticism of structural VAR's that rely on long–run restrictions to achieve identification. The basic idea is that there is insufficient information in the finite samples econometricians have at their disposal to effectively discriminate among long–run representations that link theoretical innovations and data. That is, FL suggest that identification requires more than simply restrictions about the long–run and identification is actually obtained only when theory dictates finite horizon response patterns for the effects of "structural" innovations. Though FL acknowledge that the criticisms that they level to not render the long–run approach a completely ineffective avenue for identification, they clearly illustrate that long–run restrictions in isolation may not be the innocuous route many have characterized them to be in recent applications. FL provide yet one more way of illustrating the challenge that identification poses for structural modelers.

Applications by Bergman et. al. (1995) and Crowder el. al. (1995) illustrate that a complete interpretation of the permanent structural innovations requires more than simply imposing neutrality restrictions at the infinite forecast horizon. Imprints left at short and intermediate horizons will also be useful in establishing the identity of the innovation. Illustrations in Chapters 6-8 also provide examples.

Our discussion of structural VAR methodology illustrates that the route to quality empirical applications requires that the modeler successfully navigate a

[8]This criticism applied to the SVAR literature in general and is not directly exclusively on applications in cointegrated systems.

series of obstacles or hurdles. Hypotheses regarding the role of certain structural innovations can be rejected once cointegration rank is established, once the cointegration space is estimated, or even after innovation analysis has been conducted. But the challenges raised above often run a bit deeper, questioning whether it makes sense to even participate in this type of contest because winning is meaningless or perhaps even misleading. Empirical modelers will need to address this line of criticism to make a truly convincing case for the value of structural innovations analysis. To that end, theory that underlies the empirical models must be continually refined and we need to seek out testable hypotheses that can bolster the empirical case. Below we examine the role that observed "weak exogeneity" can play in this process.

## 4.4 Weak Exogeneity in Cointegrated Structural VAR Models

The property of cointegration among the variables in a nonstationary vector process was originally discussed (see Engle and Granger (1987)) in the context of a VAR model where the tradition is to designate *no* variables a "exogenous" *a priori*. In contrast, empirical research based on traditional "structural" macroeconomic models often makes an endogeneity/exogeneity distinction. In a discussion of structural VAR analysis it is useful to explore how "weak exogeneity" may be used to build a case or to reject certain structural VAR parameterizations.

Engle et. al. (1983) characterize situations where "weak exogeneity" prevails in a VAR system and Johansen (1992) discusses implications for cointegrated systems. If we dichotomize the $p$-dimensional process $z_t$ into vectors $y_t$ and $x_t$ of dimension $p_y$ and $p_x$ respectively, $x_t$ is weakly exogenous if narrowing the investigation to the $p_y$-dimensional partial system in the $y$'s yields all available information regarding the parameters of interest. In this case conditioning on the $x_t$ values does not result in the loss of information pertinent to efficient maximum likelihood estimation of relevant parameters–typically $\alpha$ and $\beta$.

Johansen (1992e) outlines this argument and specifies the conditions necessary for weak exogeneity. Without loss of generality, arbitrarily decompose the VECM $z_t$ represented in (4.1) into the conditional model for $y_t$ given $x_t$

$$\begin{aligned}\Delta y_t &= \omega\Delta x_t + (\alpha_y - \omega\alpha_x)\beta' z_{t-1} + \\ &\quad \sum_{i=1}^{q-1}(\Pi^*_{yi} - \omega\Pi^*_{xi})\Delta z_{t-i} + \mu_y - \omega\mu_x + \varepsilon_{yt} - \omega\varepsilon_{xt}\end{aligned} \tag{4.10}$$

and the marginal model of $x_t$

$$\Delta x_t = \alpha_x\beta' z_{t-1} + \sum_{i=1}^{q-1}\Pi^*_{xi}\Delta z_{t-i} + \mu_x + \varepsilon_{xt} \tag{4.11}$$

where $\omega = \Omega_{yx}\Omega_{xx}^{-1}$, and $\Omega_{ii}$, $i = x, y$, denotes appropriate submatrices formed from the system covariance matrix of system errors $\Omega$, and subscripts "$x$" and "$y$" denote portions corresponding portions of the parameter spaces respectively.

Our primary interest is with the cointegration vector $\beta$ and the error correction coefficients $\alpha_y$ and $\alpha_x$. In general, efficient estimation/inference on these parameters requires treatment of both the conditional and marginal model since parameters of interest are found in both (4.10) and (4.11). However, when $\alpha_x = 0$, estimation/inference on $\alpha_y$ and $\beta$ can be obtained directly from the conditional model. In this case $x$ is "weakly exogenous". The test for weak exogeneity is easily obtained from estimates of the full system VECM. A likelihood ratio test can be formed by estimating the system with and without imposing $\alpha_x = 0$. Alternatively, a Wald type test based on $H_0 : \alpha_x = 0$, can be constructed directly from the unrestricted VECM estimates of $\alpha_x$ in the full system.

Several authors have illustrated that weak exogeneity allows us to deliver efficient parameter estimates from exclusive focus on a partial system. Johansen (1992e) demonstrates that full MLE properties of estimators—including accurate inference can be obtained and Ericsson and Irons (1994) have assembled an entire volume of papers on the issue of exogeneity with considerable emphasis on its role in cointegrated systems.

### 4.4.1 Weak Exogeneity and Structural VAR Dynamics

In a $p$–dimensional VECM, knowledge that certain elements of the matrix $\alpha$ are "zero" can be revealing. As we will see, this information can help isolate the nature or source of nonstationarity in a cointegrated system. Also, the restrictions implied by weak exogeneity can facilitate the task of identifying the link between permanent and transitory innovations by pointing direction for the identifying restrictions discussed above.

First note that if $\alpha = \begin{bmatrix} \alpha_y \\ 0 \end{bmatrix}$ defines the matrix of error correction parameters under the assumption of weak exogeneity, the orthogonal complement matrix $\alpha_\perp$ may be expressed as $\alpha_\perp = \begin{bmatrix} 0 \\ \alpha_{\perp x} \end{bmatrix}$ where the subscripts "$y$" and "$x$" correspond to $r$ and $k$ rows of the $p \times r$ matrix $\alpha$ and the $p \times k$ matrix $\alpha_\perp$ respectively. Recall that from (4.7) the structural innovations associated with permanent components are given by

$$v_t^P = (\beta_\perp' \beta_\perp)^{-1} \beta_\perp' C(1) \varepsilon_t \equiv \alpha_\perp' \varepsilon_t$$

since $C(1) = \beta_\perp \alpha_\perp'$ so that $\beta_\perp = \beta_\perp^0 \pi$ clearly transmits innovations in the common trends $\alpha_\perp' \varepsilon_t$ to the variables in the model. In general $\alpha_\perp'$ contains no "zeros" so that $v_t^P$ is influenced by each element of the vector of reduced form innovations $\varepsilon_t$. However, when weak exogeneity prevails $\alpha_\perp' = \begin{bmatrix} 0 & \alpha_{\perp x}' \end{bmatrix}$, and the permanent innovations are comprised exclusively of reduced form shocks that emanate from the marginal model in $\Delta x_t$; the "weakly exogenous" variables. In this case, the reduced form errors in the first $p_y$ equations of the system do not play a role in the accumulated stochastic trend responsible for system nonstationarity. Hence, the ultimate source or nature of these nonstationarity inducing shocks emanates from the marginal model in $x_t$.

From the earlier discussion in section 4.2, $r(r-1)/2$ identifying restrictions are required to identify the transitory shocks using the Warne (1993) decomposition. In practice, transitory innovations are identified by distinguishing variables that respond immediately to shocks in purported transitory components from other variables that exhibit response only after several periods. These restrictions are conveyed in the specification of Warne's "$U$" in (4.8). Since it must be chosen so that $r(r-1)/2$ elements in $\alpha(U\alpha)^{-1}(Q_r')^{-1}$ are zero, *a priori* knowledge of zeros in $\alpha$ can expedite the task. Specifically, the rank of the $U\alpha$ must be $r$ so that if "$U$" defines a selection matrix, the existence of weak exogeneity will restrict choices of $U$ to only those submatrices of rank $r$ so this would preclude the transitory innovations from having an immediate impact on the $k$ "weakly exogenous" variables in the system. The initial effect of transitory innovations is then confined to the $r$ "endogenous" (not weakly exogenous) variables, $y_t$, and the task of separately identifying the transitory innovations can focus on these $r$ variables.

The role of weak exogeneity in structural VAR identification is not limited to sorting out the nature of permanent and transitory shocks. Knowledge of weak exogeneity can also help in disentangling the effects of permanent innovations. If a particular shock is comprised exclusively of innovations from $x$, one might expect that an innovation associated with one of the elements of $x$ is neutral in the long–run with respect to another element of $x$ since each of the $k$ elements of $x$ could be determined in the long run by an independent source of nonstationarity. For example, suppose that $x$ contains distinct nominal and real elements and shocks that are exclusively nominal in origin leave no permanent imprint on "real variables". As discussed in section 3.3, identification of the permanent components is obtained when available restrictions sufficiently reduce the choice of feasible orthogonal complements to the cointegration space $\beta$. If a particular shock is comprised exclusively of innovations from the marginal system, it may suggest zeros in $\beta_\perp$ that produce no long–run influence of permanent shocks on particular elements of $z_t$. In this light, weak exogeneity can help identify dynamics of the system as well as the nature of nonstationarity when the number of cointegrating vectors matches $p_y$ because in this case, the number of common trends is simply $p_x$.

### 4.4.2 Relevant Transformations of Cointegrated Systems

Many structural VAR applications proceed without explicit weak exogeneity assumptions. These include applications that explicitly incorporate knowledge of cointegration rank and those that do not. (see Blanchard and Quah (1989)). Indeed, the traditional advantage of VAR analysis is that it can be undertaken without taking a position on exogeneity. However, the concept is implicitly embedded in these applications. To illustrate, first note that any VECM can be transformed to a system that exhibits weak exogeneity by weighting the VECM by a nonsingular matrix

$$W = \begin{bmatrix} I_r & 0 \\ & \alpha'_\perp \end{bmatrix}.$$

This transformation leaves $r$ of the original $p$ variables unaltered. The remaining variables in the transformed system; $\alpha'_\perp z_t$, are weakly exogenous by construction. When the system is characterized by $p_y$ and $p_x$ endogenous and exogenous variables *a priori*, this transformation can be chosen so that it simply "orders" the data so that endogenous variables appear first. In practice, analysis of $\alpha_\perp$ may reveal interesting linear combinations of the x's as candidates for the weakly exogenous linear combinations of variables.

The common trends representation for this transformed system is simply

$$\begin{aligned} \begin{bmatrix} y_t \\ \alpha'_\perp z_t \end{bmatrix} &= \begin{bmatrix} I_r & 0 \\ & \alpha'_\perp \end{bmatrix} C(1) \sum_{s=1}^{t} \begin{bmatrix} \varepsilon_{sy} \\ \alpha'_\perp \varepsilon_{sz} \end{bmatrix} \\ &+ C^*(L) \begin{bmatrix} \varepsilon_{ty} \\ \alpha'_\perp \varepsilon_{tz} \end{bmatrix} \end{aligned} \tag{4.12}$$

where $y_t$ denotes the subset of $z_t$ that remains intact after transformation. Write the right-hand side coefficient matrix in (4.12) as

$$\begin{bmatrix} \beta_{\perp,r} \\ \alpha'_\perp \beta_\perp \end{bmatrix} \alpha'_\perp$$

where $\beta_{\perp,r}$ denotes the first $r$ rows of $\beta_\perp$. The factor loading matrix in this system may be normalized to obtain,

$$\beta^*_\perp = \begin{bmatrix} \beta_{\perp,r}(\alpha'_\perp \beta_\perp)^{-1} \\ I \end{bmatrix}$$

with corresponding representation of the $p - r$ common trends as;

$$\tau^* = (\alpha'_\perp \beta_\perp) \alpha'_\perp \varepsilon_t$$

This expression facilitates interpretation of the system. Innovations in each of the $k$ common trends; $\tau^*$ ultimately result in proportional responses in each of the $k$ weakly exogenous variables, $\alpha'_\perp z_t$. Moreover, normalization of the factor loading implies that considerable long–run neutrality prevails in the system so that each of the weakly exogenous variables is explained entirely by a single innovation in the long–run. One might expect that the early response of the $x's$ should be pronounced and considerable portions of their forecast error variance should be explained by shocks in permanent components, while the specification also allows a long-run response of the $y's$ to innovations in $\tau^*$ as measured by $\beta_{\perp,r}(\alpha'_\perp \beta_\perp)^{-1}$.

We have now seen that the nature of permanent components can always be traced to the errors in the equations that correspond to the "weakly exogenous" portion of the system; $\alpha'_\perp z_t$. Gonzalo and Granger (1991) denote; $x_t = \alpha'_\perp z_t$, as the common factor of the system. The common trend $\tau^*$ above is the random walk component of this common factor. However, there is typically no statistical basis for choosing a unique orthogonal complement $\alpha_\perp$ so that $x_t$ has a relevant economic interpretation. Economic theory can serve as a guide for choosing particular orthogonal complements and testing whether zero restrictions apply.

To illustrate, order the data so that the first $r$ elements of the vector; $z_t$, contain the alleged endogenous variables while the remaining $p-r$ variables, or linear combinations thereof, are plausibly exogenous. The VECM formed from this ordering yields estimates of the error correction terms $\alpha$. Now following Johansen (1991) form the orthogonal complement space of $\alpha$ by defining

$$b = \begin{bmatrix} I_r \\ 0 \end{bmatrix} \text{ and, } b_\perp = \begin{bmatrix} 0 \\ I_k \end{bmatrix}$$

Then

$$\widehat{\alpha}_\perp = b_\perp - b(\widehat{\alpha}'b)^{-1}\widehat{\alpha}'b_\perp.$$

While any choice of matrix $b$ that is of rank $r$ will yield an estimate of $\alpha_\perp$, this particular choice is conducive to testing whether the weakly exogenous variables; $x_t = \alpha'_\perp z_t$, are formed exclusively from the alleged exogenous set of variables. Inference on $\widehat{\alpha}_\perp$ is obtained directly from the distributional properties of $\widehat{\alpha}$. From Johansen (1993)

$$T^{1/2}(\widehat{\alpha} - \alpha) \longrightarrow N_{p\times r}\{0, \Sigma_{\widehat{\alpha}}\}$$

where $\Sigma_{\widehat{\alpha}}$ can be estimated by $\Sigma_\varepsilon \otimes (\widehat{\beta}' S_{kk} \widehat{\beta})^{-1}$.

The orthogonal complement formed in this manner contains a matrix normalization that defines a distinct role for each of the variables in the system and their accompanying reduced form innovations. Inference on the remaining elements of $\alpha_\perp$ can help define the role played by the remaining variables in $\alpha_\perp$ and hence their ultimate contribution to the common trends. When the system contains exactly $k = p - r$ exogenous variables *a priori*, the test of the $(p-r)r$ weak exogeneity restrictions; $\alpha_x = 0$, discussed in the previous section should deliver the same inference as the test of the $r(p-r)$ restrictions, $\alpha_{\perp y} = 0$ that leave no role for the endogenous variable innovations in the construction of the common trends. Hence, $\alpha_\perp$ normalizations may provide little additional information in situations where strict weak exogeneity applies *a priori*. However, focus on $\alpha_\perp$ can still be informative in establishing the nature of nonstationary impulses in models not characterized by weak exogeneity *a priori*.

If certain zero restrictions in $\alpha_\perp$ do apply, the corresponding factor loading; $\beta^*_\perp$ will contain overidentifying restrictions as revealed above. Recall that $k(k-1)/2$ of these restrictions are required to identify the permanent innovations. The validity of the remaining restrictions can be subjected to tests that can reveal whether the interpretation implied by the transformation has empirical content. When weak exogeneity applies *a priori*, $W$ is block diagonal when the weakly exogenous variables are placed after the remaining variables.

### 4.4.3 Weak Exogeneity and Conventional Structural VAR Applications

The discussion in the previous section demonstrates that there is an element of weak exogeneity in all common trends applications even if we are unwilling to make the exogeneity distinction among the elements of $z_t$ *a priori*. In this case, it is the source of nonstationarity or "common trends" themselves that are ultimately "weakly exogenous". These may be characterized as nebulous unobservables such as the pace of technology advances that ultimately determines real variables in the system, or an intangible nominal impulse that has its origin in product and/or labor market power or in "shocks" displayed by monetary aggregates.

The notion is illustrated by transforming (augmenting) the entire system by a $p + (k) \times p$ matrix;

$$W = \begin{bmatrix} I_p \\ \alpha'_\perp \end{bmatrix}$$

to obtain the $p+p-r$ dimension augmented error correction system where the common factors, $x_t \equiv \alpha'_\perp z_t$ are weakly exogenous by construction.

The common trends representation of this system is simply

$$\begin{bmatrix} z_t \\ x_t \end{bmatrix} = \begin{bmatrix} \beta_\perp(\alpha'_\perp\beta_\perp)^{-1} \\ I \end{bmatrix} (\alpha'_\perp\beta_\perp)\alpha'_\perp \left(\mu t + \sum_{S=1}^{t} \varepsilon_t\right) + C^*(L) \begin{bmatrix} \varepsilon_{tz} \\ \alpha'_\perp \varepsilon_{tz} \end{bmatrix}$$

so that the $r + k = p$ cointegrating relations formed by $\begin{bmatrix} \beta' & 0 \\ \alpha'_\perp & -I \end{bmatrix}$ eliminate the stochastic trends from the augmented system.

In this light, the original $p$-dimensional random vector remains entirely "endogenous" as in the VAR tradition. However, this represents a $p$-dimensional partial model conditioned on $p - r$ additional variables; $x_t = \alpha'_\perp z_t$ that are weakly exogenous by construction. The elements of $x_t$ may be conceptual proxies for inherently unobserved counterparts (a real/technological trend or a nominal trend) that would clearly be augmented to $z_t$ *a priori* to form a weakly exogenous system if the data were available *a priori*. The final $p - r$ "cointegrating" vectors in this system merely define $\alpha'_\perp z_t$ as the common factors of the system with $\alpha'_\perp \varepsilon_{tz}$serving as the $k$-dimension random walk component.

In the context of system transformations, the structural VAR of (4.1) can be interpreted as a transformation of a conventional (reduced form) VAR model. When $H(0)$ is identified as in (4.9) the "structure" is simply a transformed VECM with errors that are orthogonal by construction. Moreover, the structural error correction space of this particular transformed system is

$$H(0)\alpha = \begin{bmatrix} 0 \\ \alpha^{*\prime}\Sigma_\varepsilon^{-1}\alpha \end{bmatrix}$$

so that $k$ elements of the transformed system are weakly exogenous by construction.

## 4.5 Summary

The fundamental problem of identification continues to pose challenges for applied research. We have demonstrated how knowledge of cointegration rank can help researchers meet this challenge. Essentially this knowledge reduces the number of arbitrary restrictions required to identify fundamental innovations that underlie a time series structure. At the same time, this knowledge does not solve the identification problem. Considerable work in linking economic theory to empirical structures remains.

# Chapter 5

# A PROTOTYPE ECONOMIC MODEL CHARACTERIZED BY COINTEGRATION

In the previous two chapters, we discussed the econometric problems in drawing inferences from vector error correction models. The conclusion of that discussion is that the estimated parameters of the VECM, and in particular the estimated cointegrating vectors, cannot be given a unique interpretation absent an identified economic structure. In subsequent chapters, we present estimates of vector error correction models that we allege provide information about certain aspects of the aggregate economic structure of the economy, in particular about the character of the equilibrium aggregate demand for real balances. The purpose of this chapter is to discuss a rational expectations aggregate economic model that is characterized by both permanent (nonstationary) and transitory (stationary) shocks, derive the reduced form error correction representation of that model, show that the model is characterized by cointegration, and show that the estimated cointegrating vectors provide information on some of the equilibrium parameters of the economic model. In addition we derive moving average (Wold) representation of the model and interpret common trends representations of such structures.

The starting point for our analysis is a model developed by Bean (1983) and elaborated by Bradley and Jansen (1989) and Jansen and Kim (1993). The supply side of that model, in the most general form presented by Jansen and Kim consists of the following equations:

$$y_t = (1-a)l_t + u_{1t} \qquad (0 < a < 1) \qquad u_{1t} = \tau_1 + u_{1t-1} + \varepsilon_{1t} \tag{5.1}$$

$$w_t - p_t - b = al_t + u_{1t} \tag{5.2}$$

$$w_t - p_t = c + dl_t^s - e[r_t - p_{t+1/t} + p_t] + f[m_t - p_t] \qquad (d, e, f > 0) \tag{5.3}$$

$$w_t^* = p_t + \phi_1 + \phi_2 u_{1t} + \phi_3[r_t - p_{t+1/t} + p_t] + \phi_4[m_t - p_t] \tag{5.4}$$

$$\begin{aligned} \phi_1 &= (ac + bd)/(a + d), \\ \phi_2 &= d/(a + d); \\ \phi_3 &= ae/(a + d); \\ \phi_4 &= af/(a + d) \end{aligned}$$

$$w_t = w_{t/t-1}^* + \theta[p_t - p_{t/t-1}] \tag{5.5}$$

The notation $t/t-1$ represents a conditional expectation for period $t$ based on all information available in $t-1$. Equation (5.1) is a standard aggregate production function relating the log of real output ($y$) to the log of employment ($l$) and a permanent shock with drift $\tau_1$. Jansen and Kim (1993) specify the permanent shock here, but without the deterministic trend. Equation (5.2) is the marginal productivity condition equating the log of the real wage rate $[w_t - p_t]$ to a linear function of the log of employment. Equation (5.3) is the labor supply function, which is a generalization of a standard log-linear labor supply function with the additional arguments of the current period real balances $[m_t - p_t]$ and the current period real interest rate $[r_t - p_{t+1/t} + p_t]$.[1] Equation (5.4) defines the market clearing nominal wage rate and is constructed by equating $l_t^s$ in equation (5.3) with $l_t$ in equation (5.2) and solving equations (5.1) - (5.3)) for real output, employment, and the real wage rate. Equation (5.5) defines the actual real wage rate equal to the expectation of the period $t$ market clearing real wage based on information available during $t-1$ and an indexing of this contracted nominal wage rate to the actual rate of inflation during period $t$. Note that $p_t$ is the log of the price level, not the inflation rate. In the absence of indexing ($\theta = 0$) the nominal wage is predetermined for period $t$ by the information available in $t-1$.

For our prototype analysis, the role of the real interest rate and real money stock terms in the labor supply function are unimportant. Therefore we use a simpler structure with $e = f = 0$ and correspondingly $\phi_3 = \phi_4 = 0$.

The aggregate supply curve for this model is constructed by taking conditional expectations of equation (5.4), using the resulting expression for $w_{t/t-1}$ in equation (5.5) and then solving this equation plus equations (5.1) and (5.2)

[1]Note that the labor supply equation is a deterministic function. For reasons that will appear below, a stochastic term in this equation would never affect the behavior of the variables in the model.

for $y$ and $l$.[2] This supply curve is:

$$y_t = \beta(b - \phi_1) + (1+\beta)u_{1t} - \beta\phi_2 u_{1t/t-1} + \beta(1-\theta)[p_t - p_{t/t-1}] \qquad (5.6)$$

where $\beta = (1-a)/a$. This equation is quite standard in the macroeconomics rational expectations literature (perhaps with the exception of the indexing function).

We make substantive modifications on the demand side of the Jansen and Kim (1993) model. They specify both the IS curve and the demand for real balances as subject to permanent [$I(1)$] shocks. In our analysis, we specify shocks to the demand for real balances to be stationary:

$$mr_t = y_t - \alpha_2 r_t + \varepsilon_{3t} \qquad (5.7)$$

where $mr_t$ is the log of real balances. For simplicity we assume that the income elasticity of the demand for real balances is unity (a velocity specification). This restriction has no substantive effect on our conclusions.

We specify the IS curve as:

$$y_t = z_t - \alpha_1[r_t - p_{t+1/t} + p_t] \qquad (5.8)$$

where $z_t$ is a measure of the log of autonomous expenditures. We treat autonomous expenditures as an unobservable variable and assume that the ratio of autonomous expenditures to real output is an AR(1) process:

$$y(t) - z(t) = u_{3t} \qquad (5.9)$$

where $u_{3t} = \omega u_{3t-1} + \varepsilon_{4t}$ and $\varepsilon_{4t}$ is stationary.[3] Equation (5.9) can be thought of as a fiscal policy rule that says the share of government purchases in total output is an AR(1) process. We do not restrict $\omega$ to be $< 1$, thus allowing for either a stationary ( $\omega < 1$) or nonstationary ( $\omega = 1$) real rate of interest.

The final element needed to complete the model is a specification of the data generating process for nominal balances. The existing literature (Bean (1983), Bradley and Jansen (1989) and Jansen and Kim (1993)) assumes that nominal balances are generated by a deterministic rule or a stationary process. We complete the model (equations (5.7 through 5.9)) with an identity and a no feedback nonstationary stochastic process for nominal money growth:

$$mr_t \equiv u_{2t} - [p_t - p_{t-1}] + mr_{t-1} \qquad (5.10)$$

$$u_{2t} = \tau_2 + u_{2t-1} + \varepsilon_{2t} \qquad (5.11)$$

[2] Any stochastic form in the labor supply curve [equation (5.3)] would appear in equation (5.4) along with the productivity shock, $u_{1t}$. As long as the conditional expectation is of such a shock is zero, it would not affect the supply curve (5.6).

[3] The question of how to measure autonomous expenditure generated a heated debate in the 1960s (Friedman and Meiselman (1963, 1965), Ando and Modigliani (1965), Deprano and Mayer (1965) and Hester (1964). Subsequently the issue was handled by specifying large and detailed econometric models. Since such models have gone out of fashion the measurement problem appears to be largely ignored.

In these two equations, $u_{2t}$ is the growth rate of nominal money balances. Real balances are defined as nominal money growth less the inflation rate plus lagged real balances. $\Delta m_t = u_{2t}$, so $\Delta^2 m_t = \Delta u_{2t} = \tau_2 + \varepsilon_{2t}$. Hence this specification implies an I(2) process for the log of the nominal money stock.

This type of monetary policy rule is a restricted version of the rule proposed by Meltzer (1987). Meltzer proposes that nominal monetary base growth ($\Delta \ln B_t$) be adjusted up or down around a trend ($\tau_2$) as a lagged moving average of velocity growth decreases or increases. We translate this deterministic rule in terms of the money stock to allow for fluctuations in the base multiplier that cannot be perfectly offset by the monetary authorities. For simplicity of presentation we assume a lagged one period moving average in velocity growth:

$$(1-L)\ln M_t = \tau_2 - [(1-L)y_{t-1} + (1-L)p_{t-1} - (1-L)\ln M_{t-1}] + \varepsilon_{2t} \quad (5.12)$$

This policy rule can be generalized to allow differential feedback from observed real output growth and inflation:

$$\begin{aligned}(1-L)\ln M_t &= \tau_2 - \lambda_1(1-L)y_{t-1} - \\ &\quad \lambda_2(1-L)p_{t-1} + (1-L)\ln M_{t-1} + \varepsilon_{2t} \end{aligned} \quad (5.13)$$

or

$$(1-L)^2 \ln M_t = \tau_2 - \lambda_1(1-L)y_{t-1} - \lambda_2(1-L)p_{t-1} + \varepsilon_{2t} \quad (5.14)$$

Under the restrictions $\lambda_1 = \lambda_2 = 0$ (no feedback) this rule is the one employed here.[4] If the assumption that $\lambda_1 = 0$ were relaxed, and $(1-L)y_t$ is a stationary process with trend, then $\ln M_t$ remains an $I(2)$ process with trend. In contrast, if $\lambda_2 \neq 0$ so feedback from the inflation rate to adjust the rate of base growth is permitted, then it is possible to observe $\ln M_t$ as an $I(2)$ process with trend and $y_t$ and $P_t$ both as $I(1)$ processes with trend.

The model as specified has five equations in five endogenous variables: $y_t$, $r_t$, $z_t$, $mr_t$, and $(p_t - p_{t-1})$. Since $(p_t - p_{t/t-1})$ can be rewritten as $(p_t - p_{t-1}) - (p_{t/t-1} - p_{t-1})$, the model contains the expected rate of inflation for both t+1 and t based on information available at $t$ and $t-1$ respectively. The model is driven by two permanent shocks, $u_{1t}$ a productivity shock and $u_{2t}$, a money growth shock and by a transitory money demand shock $\varepsilon_{3t}$, and a fiscal shock that may be either stationary or nonstationary and is determined by $\varepsilon_{4t}$.

## 5.1 Solution of the Rational Expectations Model

Define $\rho_t = p_t - p_{t-1}$ as the actual inflation rate. Then from equation (5.10) we have:

[4] McCallum (1988) proposes a varient of Meltzer's policy rule which adds an adjustment of base growth to deviations of real output from a linear trend. Under this specification $\ln M_t$ would not exhibit the I(2) characteristic of the policy rule used here.

$$\rho_t = u_{2t} - (mr_t - mr_{t-1}) \tag{5.15}$$

and therefore the expected rates of inflation are defined as:

$$\rho_{t/t-1} = u_{2t/t-1} - (mr_{t/t-1} - mr_{t-1}) \tag{5.16}$$

$$\begin{aligned}
\rho_{t+1/t} &= u_{2t+1/t} - (mr_{t+1/t} - mr_t) \\
&= \tau_2 + u_{2t} - (mr_{t+1/t} - mr_t) \\
&= \tau_2 + (\tau_2 + u_{2t-1} + \varepsilon_{2t}) - (mr_{t+1/t} - mr_t) \\
&= 2\tau_2 + u_{2t-1} + \varepsilon_{2t} - (mr_{t+1/t} - mr_t)
\end{aligned} \tag{5.17}$$

Unexpected inflation at time $t$ is:

$$\rho_t - \rho_{t/t-1} = \rho_t - u_{2t/t-1} + (mr_{t/t-1} - mr_{t-1}) \tag{5.18}$$

With these definitions, the model can be written in matrix form as:

$$\begin{bmatrix} 1.0 & 0 & 0 & -\beta(1-\theta) \\ 0 & \alpha_1 & -\alpha_1 & 0 \\ -1.0 & \alpha_2 & 1.0 & 0 \\ 0 & 0 & 1.0 & 1.0 \end{bmatrix} \begin{bmatrix} y_t \\ r_t \\ mr_t \\ \rho_t \end{bmatrix}$$

$$= \begin{bmatrix} \Lambda_1 \\ -\omega u_{3t-1} - \varepsilon_{4t} + \alpha_1 u_{2t+1/t} - \alpha_1 mr_{t+1/t} \\ \varepsilon_{3t} \\ u_{2t} + mr_{t-1} \end{bmatrix}$$

where

$$\begin{aligned}
\Lambda_1 &= \beta(b - \phi_1) + (1+\beta)u_{1t} - \beta\phi_2 u_{1t/t-1} \\
&\quad -\beta(1-\theta)u_{2t/t-1} + \beta(1-\theta)(mr_{t/t-1} - mr_{t-1}).
\end{aligned}$$

The determinant of the coefficient matrix on the left hand side of this equation is

$$\alpha_1[1 + \alpha_2 + \beta(1-\theta)]$$

that is greater than zero for all values of the model parameters. The adjoint of the left hand side matrix is:

$$\begin{bmatrix} \alpha_1(1+\alpha_2) & \alpha_2\beta(1-\theta) & -\alpha_1\beta(1-\theta) & \alpha_1(1+\alpha_2)\beta(1-\theta) \\ \alpha_1 & 1+\beta(1-\theta) & \alpha_1 & \alpha_1\beta(1-\theta) \\ \alpha_1 & -\alpha_2 & \alpha_1 & \alpha_1\beta(1-\theta) \\ -\alpha_1 & \alpha_2 & -\alpha_1 & \alpha_1(1+\alpha_2) \end{bmatrix}$$

Therefore the reduced form equation for $mr_t$ is:

$$\begin{aligned}
&[\alpha_1 + \alpha_1\alpha_2 + \alpha_1\beta(1-\theta)]mr_t \\
= \; &\alpha_1\Lambda_1 + \alpha_2\omega u_{3t-1} + \alpha_2\varepsilon_{4t} \\
&-\alpha_1\alpha_2 u_{2t+1/t} + \alpha_1\alpha_2 mr_{t+1/t} + \alpha_1\varepsilon_{3t} \\
&+\alpha_1\beta(1-\theta)u_{2t} + \alpha_1\beta(1-\theta)mr_{t-1}
\end{aligned} \tag{5.19}$$

or

$$\begin{aligned}
& -\alpha_1\alpha_2 mr_{t+1/t} - \alpha_1\beta(1-\theta)mr_{t/t-1} + \alpha_1[1+\alpha_2+\beta(1-\theta)]mr_t \\
= \; & \alpha_1\beta(b-\phi_1) + \alpha_1(1+\beta)u_{1t} - \alpha_1\beta\phi_2 u_{1t/t-1} - \alpha_1\beta(1-\theta)u_{2t/t-1} \\
& +\alpha_2\omega u_{3t-1} + \alpha_2\varepsilon_{4t} - \alpha_1\alpha_2 u_{2t+1/t} + \alpha_1\varepsilon_{3t} + \alpha_1\beta(1-\theta)u_{2t} \qquad (5.20)
\end{aligned}$$

Note that $u_{1t} = \tau_1 + u_{1t-1} + \varepsilon_{1t}$ and $u_{2t} = \tau_2 + u_{2t-1} + \varepsilon_{2t}$ so we can substitute $u_{1t/t-1} = \tau_1 + u_{1t-1}$and $u_{2t+1/t} = \tau_2 + u_{2t} = 2\tau_2 + u_{2t-1} + \varepsilon_{2t}$ and obtain:

$$\begin{aligned}
& -\alpha_1\alpha_2 mr_{t+1/t} - \alpha_1\beta(1-\theta)mr_{t/t-1} + \alpha_1[1+\alpha_2+\beta(1-\theta)]mr_t \\
= \; & \alpha_1\beta(b-\phi_1) + \alpha_1(1+\beta)(\tau_1 + u_{1t-1} + \varepsilon_{1t}) - \alpha_1\beta\phi_2(\tau_1 + u_{1t-1}) \\
& -\alpha_1\beta(1-\theta)(\tau_2 + u_{2t-1}) + \alpha_2\omega u_{3t-1} + \alpha_2\varepsilon_{4t} + \alpha_1\varepsilon_{3t} \\
& -\alpha_1\alpha_2(2\tau_2 + u_{2t-1} + \varepsilon_{2t}) + \alpha_1\beta(1-\theta)(\tau_2 + u_{2t-1} + \varepsilon_{2t}) \qquad (5.21)
\end{aligned}$$

We postulate a solution for $mr_t$ of the form:

$$\begin{aligned}
mr_t \; = \; & \Pi_0 + \Pi_1 u_{1t-1} + \Pi_2 u_{2t-1} \\
& +\Pi_3\omega u_{3t-1} + \Pi_4\varepsilon_{1t} + \Pi_5\varepsilon_{2t} + \\
& \Pi_6\varepsilon_{3t} + \Pi_7\varepsilon_{4t} \qquad (5.22)
\end{aligned}$$

Then

$$mr_{t/t-1} = \Pi_0 + \Pi_1 u_{1t-1} + \Pi_2 u_{2t-1} + \Pi_3\omega u_{3t-1} \qquad (5.23)$$

$$\begin{aligned}
mr_{t+1} \; = \; & \Pi_0 + \Pi_1 u_{1t} + \Pi_2 u_{2t} + \Pi_3\omega u_{3t} + \Pi_4\varepsilon_{1t+1} \\
& +\Pi_5\varepsilon_{2t+1} + \Pi_6\varepsilon_{3t+1} + \Pi_7\varepsilon_{4t+1} \qquad (5.24)
\end{aligned}$$

and

$$\begin{aligned}
mr_{t+1/t} \; = \; & \Pi_0 + \Pi_1 u_{1t} + \Pi_2 u_{2t} + \Pi_3\omega u_{3t} \\
= \; & (\Pi_0 + \Pi_1\tau_1 + \Pi_2\tau_2) + \Pi_1 u_{1t-1} \\
& +\Pi_2 u_{2t-1} + \Pi_3\omega^2 u_{3t-1} \\
& +\Pi_1\varepsilon_{1t} + \Pi_2\varepsilon_{2t} + \Pi_3\omega\varepsilon_{4t} \qquad (5.25)
\end{aligned}$$

Substituting for $mr_{t+1/t}$ and $mr_{t/t-1}$ in equation (5.21) gives:

$$\begin{aligned}
& -\alpha_1\alpha_2(\Pi_0 + \Pi_1\tau_1 + \Pi_2\tau_2) - \alpha_1\alpha_2\Pi_1 u_{1t-1} \\
& -\alpha_1\alpha_2\Pi_2 u_{2t-1} - \alpha_1\alpha_2\Pi_3\omega^2 u_{3t-1} \\
& -\alpha_1\alpha_2\Pi_1\varepsilon_{1t} - \alpha_1\alpha_2\Pi_2\varepsilon_{2t} - \alpha_1\alpha_2\Pi_3\omega\varepsilon_{4t} \\
& -\alpha_1\beta(1-\theta)\Pi_0 - \alpha_1\beta(1-\theta)\Pi_1 u_{1t-1} - \alpha_1\beta(1-\theta)\Pi_2 u_{2t-1} \\
& -\alpha_1\beta(1-\theta)\Pi_3\omega u_{3t-1} \\
& +\alpha_1[1+\alpha_2+\beta(1-\theta)]\Pi_0 + \alpha_1[1+\alpha_2+\beta(1-\theta)]\Pi_1 u_{1t-1} \\
& +\alpha_1[1+\alpha_2+\beta(1-\theta)]\Pi_2 u_{2t-1} + \alpha_1[1+\alpha_2+\beta(1-\theta)]\Pi_3\omega u_{3t-1} \\
& +\alpha_1[1+\alpha_2+\beta(1-\theta)]\Pi_4\varepsilon_{1t} + \alpha_1[1+\alpha_2+\beta(1-\theta)]\Pi_5\varepsilon_{2t} \\
& +\alpha_1[1+\alpha_2+\beta(1-\theta)]\Pi_6\varepsilon_{3t} + \alpha_1[1+\alpha_2+\beta(1-\theta)]\Pi_7\varepsilon_{4t} \\
= \; & [\alpha_1\beta(b-\phi_1) + \alpha_1[1+\beta(1-\phi)\tau_1] - 2\alpha_1\alpha_2\tau_2] \\
& +\alpha_1(1+\beta)\varepsilon_{1t} + [\alpha_1(1+\beta) - \alpha_1\beta\phi_2]u_{1t-1} \\
& -[\alpha_1\beta(1-\theta) + \alpha_1\alpha_2 - \alpha_1\beta(1-\theta)]u_{2t-1} + \alpha_2\omega u_{3t-1} \\
& +\alpha_1\varepsilon_{3t} + \alpha_2\varepsilon_{4t} + [\alpha_1\beta(1-\theta) - \alpha_1\alpha_2]\varepsilon_{2t} \qquad (5.26)
\end{aligned}$$

The undetermined coefficients solutions from this equation are:

$\Pi_1 = 1 + \beta(1-\phi_2) > 0$
$\Pi_2 = -\alpha_2 < 0$
$\omega\Pi_3 = (\alpha_2/\alpha_1)\omega/[1+\alpha_2(1-\omega)] \geq 0$
$\Pi_4 = [1+\beta+\alpha_2\{1+\beta(1-\phi_2)\}]/[1+\alpha_2+\beta(1-\theta)] > 0$
$\Pi_5 = [\beta(1-\theta) - \alpha_2(1+\alpha_2)]/[1+\alpha_2+\beta(1-\theta)]$
$\Pi_6 = 1/[1+\alpha_2+\beta(1-\theta)] > 0$
$\Pi_7 = \alpha_2[1+\alpha_2\omega/\{1+\alpha_2(1-\omega)\}]/\alpha_1[1+\alpha_2+\beta(1-\theta)] > 0$

## 5.2 The Vector Error Correction Representation

The construction of a VECM for the observable variables $y_t, r_t, mr_t$ and $\rho_t$ is facilitated by considering $u_{1t}, u_{2t}$ as latent variables, and defining a third variable,

$$\begin{aligned}
u_{4t} \equiv \; & \beta(b-\phi_1) - \beta\phi_2\tau_1 + \beta(1-\theta)\varepsilon_{2t} + (1+\beta)u_{1t} - \beta\phi_2 u_{1t-1} \\
& -\beta(1-\theta)\Pi_4\varepsilon_{1t} - \beta(1-\theta)\Pi_5\varepsilon_{2t} - \beta(1-\theta)\Pi_6\varepsilon_{3t} - \beta(1-\theta)\Pi_7\varepsilon_{4t}.
\end{aligned}$$

These three variables are exogenous with respect to the observable variables, so we can construct a marginal submodel in $u_{1t}, u_{2t}$ and $u_{4t}$ as:

$$\begin{bmatrix} 1.0 & 0 & 0 \\ 0 & 1.0 & 0 \\ -(1+\beta) & 0 & 1.0 \end{bmatrix} \begin{bmatrix} u_{1t} \\ u_{2t} \\ u_{4t} \end{bmatrix} = \begin{bmatrix} 1.0 & 0 & 0 \\ 0 & 1.0 & 0 \\ -\beta\phi_2 & 0 & 0 \end{bmatrix} \begin{bmatrix} u_{1t-1} \\ u_{2t-1} \\ u_{4t-1} \end{bmatrix}$$

$$+ \begin{bmatrix} 1.0 & 0 \\ 0 & 1.0 \\ -\beta\phi_2 & 0 \end{bmatrix} \begin{bmatrix} \tau_1 \\ \tau_2 \end{bmatrix} + \begin{bmatrix} \varepsilon_{1t} \\ \varepsilon_{2t} \\ -\beta(1-\theta)\Lambda_2 \end{bmatrix} + \begin{bmatrix} 0 \\ 0 \\ \beta(b-\phi_1) \end{bmatrix} \tag{5.27}$$

where $\Lambda_2 = \Pi_4\varepsilon_{1t} + (\Pi_5 - 1)\varepsilon_{2t} + \Pi_6\varepsilon_{3t} + \Pi_7\varepsilon_{4t}$. This model can be written in error correction form as:

$$\begin{bmatrix} 1.0 & 0 & 0 \\ 0 & 1.0 & 0 \\ -(1+\beta) & 0 & 1.0 \end{bmatrix} \begin{bmatrix} \Delta u_{1t} \\ \Delta u_{2t} \\ \Delta u_{4t} \end{bmatrix} = \begin{bmatrix} 0 & 0 & 0 \\ 0 & 0 & 0 \\ 1+\beta(1-\phi_2) & 0 & -1 \end{bmatrix} \begin{bmatrix} u_{1t-1} \\ u_{2t-1} \\ u_{4t-1} \end{bmatrix}$$

$$+ \begin{bmatrix} 1.0 & 0 \\ 0 & 1.0 \\ -\beta\phi_2 & 0 \end{bmatrix} \begin{bmatrix} \tau_1 \\ \tau_2 \end{bmatrix} + \begin{bmatrix} 0 \\ 0 \\ \beta(b-\phi_1) \end{bmatrix} + \begin{bmatrix} \varepsilon_{1t} \\ \varepsilon_{2t} \\ -\beta(1-\theta)\Lambda_2 \end{bmatrix} \tag{5.28}$$

so there is a single cointegrating vector spanning the space of $(u_{1t}, u_{2t}, u_{4t})$. The moving average (Wold) representation of the marginal submodel can be constructed directly by writing the model in lag operator notation:

$$\begin{bmatrix} (1-L) & 0 & 0 \\ 0 & (1-L) & 0 \\ -(1+\beta)+\beta\phi_2 L & 0 & 1 \end{bmatrix} \begin{bmatrix} u_{1t} \\ u_{2t} \\ u_{4t} \end{bmatrix} = \begin{bmatrix} 1.0 & 0 \\ 0 & 1.0 \\ -\beta\phi_2 & 0 \end{bmatrix} \begin{bmatrix} \tau_1 \\ \tau_2 \end{bmatrix}$$

$$+ \begin{bmatrix} 0 \\ 0 \\ \beta(b-\phi_1) \end{bmatrix} + \begin{bmatrix} \varepsilon_{1t} \\ \varepsilon_{2t} \\ -\beta(1-\theta)\Lambda_2 \end{bmatrix} \tag{5.29}$$

The determinant of the above polynomial matrix is $(1-L)^2$ and the adjoint matrix is:

$$(1-L) \begin{bmatrix} 1.0 & 0 & 0 \\ 0 & 1 & 0 \\ 1+\beta(1-\phi_2 L) & 0 & (1-L) \end{bmatrix}$$

So after canceling the common unit root factors the moving average representation of the marginal submodel is:

$$\begin{bmatrix} \Delta u_{1t} \\ \Delta u_{2t} \\ \Delta u_{4t} \end{bmatrix} = \begin{bmatrix} \tau_1 \\ \tau_2 \\ [1+\beta(1-\phi_2)]\tau_1 \end{bmatrix} +$$

$$\begin{bmatrix} \varepsilon_{1t} \\ \varepsilon_{2t} \\ [1+\beta(1-\phi_2 L)]\varepsilon_{1t} - \beta(1-\theta)(1-L)\Lambda_2 \end{bmatrix} \tag{5.30}$$

This representation will be useful in constructing the VECM and moving average representations of the conditional submodel in the four observable variables.

The conditional submodel in terms of the variables $y_t, r_t, mr_t$ and $\rho_t$ can be constructed from equations (5.7) - (5.9) and two identities: $y_t \equiv u_{4t}$ and (5.10). In matrix notation:

$$\begin{bmatrix} 1.0 & 0 & 0 & 0 \\ 0 & \alpha_1 & -\alpha_1 & -\alpha_1 \\ -1.0 & \alpha_2 & 1.0 & 0 \\ 0 & 0 & 1.0 & 1.0 \end{bmatrix} \begin{bmatrix} y_t \\ r_t \\ mr_t \\ \rho_t \end{bmatrix} = \begin{bmatrix} 0 & 0 & 0 & 0 \\ 0 & 0 & -\alpha_1 & 0 \\ 0 & 0 & 0 & 0 \\ 0 & 0 & 1.0 & 0 \end{bmatrix} \begin{bmatrix} y_{t-1} \\ r_{t-1} \\ mr_{t-1} \\ \rho_{t-1} \end{bmatrix}$$

$$+ \begin{bmatrix} 0 & 0 & 1 \\ 0 & 0 & 0 \\ 0 & 0 & 0 \\ 0 & 1 & 0 \end{bmatrix} \begin{bmatrix} u_{1t} \\ u_{2t} \\ u_{4t} \end{bmatrix} + \begin{bmatrix} 0 & 0 & 0 \\ -\alpha_1\Pi_1 & -\alpha_1\Pi_2 & 0 \\ 0 & 0 & 0 \\ 0 & 0 & 0 \end{bmatrix} \begin{bmatrix} \Delta u_{1t} \\ \Delta u_{2t} \\ \Delta u_{4t} \end{bmatrix}$$

$$+ \begin{bmatrix} 0 \\ \alpha_1\tau_2 \\ 0 \\ 0 \end{bmatrix} + \begin{bmatrix} 0 & 0 & 0 & 0 \\ \alpha_1\Pi_4 & \alpha_1\Pi_5 & \alpha_1\Pi_6 & \xi \\ 0 & 0 & 1.0 & 0 \\ 0 & 0 & 0 & 0 \end{bmatrix} \begin{bmatrix} \varepsilon_{1t} \\ \varepsilon_{2t} \\ \varepsilon_{3t} \\ \varepsilon_{4t} \end{bmatrix} \tag{5.31}$$

where $\xi = \alpha_1\Pi_7 - (1-\omega L)^{-1} - \alpha_1\Pi_3\omega[1-(1-\omega)L(1-\omega L)^{-1}]$. This can be written as a structural VECM form by adding and subtracting lags of the vector $(y_t, r_t, mr_t, \rho_t)'$:

$$\begin{bmatrix} 1.0 & 0 & 0 & 0 \\ 0 & \alpha_1 & -\alpha_1 & -\alpha_1 \\ -1.0 & \alpha_2 & 1.0 & 0 \\ 0 & 0 & 1.0 & 1.0 \end{bmatrix} \begin{bmatrix} \Delta y_t \\ \Delta r_t \\ \Delta mr_t \\ \Delta \rho_t \end{bmatrix}$$

$$= \begin{bmatrix} 0 & 0 & 0 & 0.0 \\ 0 & -\alpha_1 & 0 & \alpha_1 \\ 1.0 & -\alpha_2 & -1.0 & 0 \\ 0 & 0 & 1.0 & 0 \end{bmatrix} \begin{bmatrix} \Delta y_{t-1} \\ \Delta r_{t-1} \\ \Delta mr_{t-1} \\ \Delta \rho_{t-1} \end{bmatrix} +$$

$$\begin{bmatrix} 0 & 0 & 0 & 0 \\ 0 & -\alpha_1 & 0 & \alpha_1 \\ 1.0 & -\alpha_2 & -1.0 & 0 \\ 0 & 0 & 0 & 0 \end{bmatrix} \begin{bmatrix} y_{t-2} \\ r_{t-2} \\ mr_{t-2} \\ \rho_{t-2} \end{bmatrix} +$$

$$\begin{bmatrix} 0 & 0 & 1.0 \\ -\alpha_1\Pi_1 & -\alpha_1\Pi_2 & 0 \\ 0 & 0 & 0 \\ 0 & 1.0 & 0 \end{bmatrix} \begin{bmatrix} \Delta u_{1t} \\ \Delta u_{2t} \\ \Delta u_{4t} \end{bmatrix} +$$

$$\begin{bmatrix} 0 \\ \alpha_1\tau_2 \\ 0 \\ 0 \end{bmatrix} + \begin{bmatrix} 0 & 0 & 0 & 0 \\ \alpha_1\Pi_4 & \alpha_1\Pi_5 & \alpha_1\Pi_6 & \xi \\ 0 & 0 & 1.0 & 0 \\ 0 & 0 & 0 & 0 \end{bmatrix} \begin{bmatrix} \varepsilon_{1t} \\ \varepsilon_{2t} \\ \varepsilon_{3t} \\ \varepsilon_{4t} \end{bmatrix} \quad (5.32)$$

The reduced form VECM in $(y_t, r_t, mr_t, \rho_t)'$ is constructed by multiplying the structural VECM in these variables by the inverse of the coefficient matrix on the left hand side of that system:

$$\begin{bmatrix} \Delta y_t \\ \Delta r_t \\ \Delta mr_t \\ \Delta \rho_t \end{bmatrix} = \begin{bmatrix} 0 & 0 & 0 & 0 \\ 0 & -1.0 & 1.0 & 1.0 \\ 1.0 & 0 & -(1+\alpha_2) & -\alpha_2 \\ -1.0 & 0 & 2+\alpha_2 & \alpha_2 \end{bmatrix} \begin{bmatrix} \Delta y_{t-1} \\ \Delta r_{t-1} \\ \Delta mr_{t-1} \\ \Delta \rho_{t-1} \end{bmatrix}$$

$$+ \begin{bmatrix} 0 & 0 \\ -1.0 & 0 \\ \alpha_2 & 1.0 \\ -\alpha_2 & -1.0 \end{bmatrix} \begin{bmatrix} 0 & 1 & 0 & -1 \\ 1 & -\alpha_2 & -1 & 0 \end{bmatrix} \begin{bmatrix} y_{t-2} \\ r_{t-2} \\ mr_{t-2} \\ \rho_{t-2} \end{bmatrix} + \begin{bmatrix} 0 \\ \tau_2 \\ -\alpha_2\tau_2 \\ \alpha_2\tau_2 \end{bmatrix}$$

$$+ \begin{bmatrix} 0 & 0 & 1.0 \\ -\Pi_1 & (1-\Pi_2) & 0 \\ \alpha_2\Pi_1 & \alpha_2\Pi_2 - \alpha_2 & 1.0 \\ -\alpha_2\Pi_1 & -\alpha_2\Pi_2 + (1-\alpha_2) & -1.0 \end{bmatrix} \begin{bmatrix} \Delta u_{1t} \\ \Delta u_{2t} \\ \Delta u_{4t} \end{bmatrix}$$

$$+ \begin{bmatrix} 0 & 0 & 0 & 0 \\ \Pi_4 & \Pi_5 & \Pi_6 & \xi/\alpha_1 \\ -\alpha_2\Pi_4 & -\alpha_2\Pi_5 & -\alpha_2\Pi_6 + 1 & -\alpha_2\xi/\alpha_1 \\ \alpha_2\Pi_4 & \alpha_2\Pi_5 & \alpha_2\Pi_6 - 1 & \alpha_2\xi/\alpha_1 \end{bmatrix} \begin{bmatrix} \varepsilon_{1t} \\ \varepsilon_{2t} \\ \varepsilon_{3t} \\ \varepsilon_{4t} \end{bmatrix} \quad (5.33)$$

From the marginal submodel (5.30) the vector $(\Delta u_{1t}, \Delta u_{2t}, \Delta u_{4t})'$ depends only on the vector $(\varepsilon_{1t}, \varepsilon_{2t}, \varepsilon_{3t}, \varepsilon_{4t})'$, its first difference and the vector $(\tau_1, \tau_2)'$. Therefore, as long as $\omega < 1$ so that the real interest rate is stationary, there are two cointegrating vectors spanning the space of $(y_t, r_t, mr_t, \rho_t)'$.

It is clear from the reduced form VECM representation (5.33) that $y_t$ is exogenous. With perfect indexing ($\theta = 1$) real output is an ARIMA (0,1,0) process in the single shock $\varepsilon_{1t}$. With less than perfect indexing ($0 \leq \theta < 1$) there are transitory effects of all the other shocks ($\varepsilon_{2t}, \varepsilon_{3t}$,and $\varepsilon_{4t}$) on real output. The size of the initial response of real output relative to the long-run (permanent) response to an $\varepsilon_{1t}$ shock depends on the degree of indexing. The greater the degree of indexing ($\theta$) the larger the impact effect; when $(1-\theta) = \phi_2$ the impact and long-run effects of an $\varepsilon_1$ shock are equal.

Note that in (5.33) the rows of the error correction matrix corresponding to $mr_t$ and $\rho_t$ are of opposite sign and equal in absolute value. Thus the sum of these variables is weakly exogenous. This follows from (5.10) since the sum of the growth of real balances and the inflation rate is the growth rate of nominal balances plus the growth of lagged real balances.

Three rows of the "error correction" matrix are unequal to zero. In the common terminology of vector error correction models the elements of these rows would be interpreted as speeds of adjustment of the respective variables to the disequilibrium in real balances and real interest rates. Such an interpretation is not appropriate for this model. The structure of the model by construction has no partial adjustment mechanisms. Expectations are formed rationally with full information of the policy rule, and there is no asymetry in the information sets available to the monetary authorities and private agents. The only parameters in this matrix are those of the equilibrium demand for real balances. The "error correction" mechanism here is analogous to that in the rational expectations model of the term structure (Campbell and Shiller (1987)).

Finally, in (5.33) the matrix of cointegrating vectors has rank = 2. There are three linear restrictions among the elements of the first cointegrating vector and two linear restrictions among the elements of the second cointegrating vector. These restrictions satisfy the rank and order conditions for identification of the long-run economic relations from the VECM.

In the original model, the *ex ante* real interest rate is specified as a stationary variable for $\omega < 1$ (equations (5.8)-(5.9)). In the VECM we observe *contemporaneous values* of the nominal interest rate and the *actual rate of inflation.* This respecification produces a new cointegrating vector

$$-\alpha_1[r_t - \rho_t] = -\alpha_1[r_t - \rho_{t+1/t} + (\rho_{t+1/t} - \rho_t)] = u_{3t} - \alpha_1(\rho_{t+1/t} - \rho_t) \quad (5.34)$$

Given the mean of the *ex ante* real interest rate $\mu_3 = Eu_{3t}$, there is a larger constant term in the stationary relationship between $r_t$ and $\rho_t$. The difference in these constants is equal to the deterministic trend in expected inflation. The constant term in the VECM contains components generated by the trends in the nonstationary processes and the means of the cointegrating vectors (Yoshida and Rasche (1990)).

Write (5.33) as:

$$\Delta z_t = \Gamma_1 \Delta z_{t-1} - \alpha\beta' z_{t-2} + \mu + Q(L)\varepsilon_t \quad (5.35)$$

where $z_t' = (y_t, r_t, mr_t, \rho_t)'$ and

$$\mu = \begin{bmatrix} \Pi_1\tau_1 \\ -\Pi_1\tau_1 - (\Pi_2 - 1)\tau_2 + \tau_2 \\ \alpha_2[\Pi_1\tau_1 + (\Pi_2 - 1)\tau_2] + [\Pi_1\tau_1 - \alpha_2\tau_2] \\ -\alpha_2[\Pi_1\tau_1 + (\Pi_2 - 1)\tau_2] - [\Pi_1\tau_1 - \alpha_2\tau_2] + \tau_2 \end{bmatrix}$$

The deterministic trends of the nonstationary processes are:

$$\mu_0 = \begin{bmatrix} \Pi_1\tau_1 \\ \tau_2 \\ \Pi_1\tau_1 - \alpha_2\tau_2 \\ \tau_2 \end{bmatrix}$$

and the decomposition of the constant term in the VECM is:

$$\mu = (I - \Gamma_1)\mu_0 + \alpha\beta_0' \tag{5.36}$$

where $\beta_0'$ is the vector of means of the cointegrating vectors.[5] From the values of $\mu$ and $\mu_0$ above and using $\Gamma_1$ from (5.33) $\alpha\beta_0'$ can be computed as:

$$\alpha\beta_0' = \mu + (\Gamma_1 - I)\mu_0 = \begin{bmatrix} 0 \\ \tau_2 \\ -\alpha_2\tau_2 \\ \alpha_2\tau_2 \end{bmatrix} = \begin{bmatrix} 0 & 0 \\ 1 & 0 \\ -\alpha_2 & 1 \\ \alpha_2 & -1 \end{bmatrix} \begin{bmatrix} \tau_2 \\ 0 \end{bmatrix} \tag{5.37}$$

### 5.2.1 Vector Error Correction Models and the "Lucas Critique"

Lucas (1976) criticizes the prevailing use of econometric models for policy evaluation on the grounds that the existing models are "reduced forms" that embed in their estimated parameters the structure of the policy rules in force during the estimation sample period. He argues that simulation of such models under alternative specifications of policy rules produces inappropriate inferences, since it does not allow for the differences in model parameters that would be observed in a sample of data drawn from the economy operating under the alternative policy regime. The "Lucas Critique" is widely cited in macroeconometric studies, but equally widely ignored or dismissed as a minor consideration in the analysis.

The VECMs derived above (both the "structural" VECM (5.32) and the reduced form VECM (5.33)) are "reduced forms" in the sense of Lucas, since they are derived under the assumption of rational expectations, and the expectations variables have been eliminated from the model specifications. Therefore the Lucas critique is relevant for these models, and is an important consideration in both estimation and analysis of these structures.

A simple example illustrates this point. Consider two different policy regimes, both of which are nofeedback monetary growth rules such as (5.11). The only difference in the two policy regimes is the deterministic trend in the money growth rate, $\tau_2$. Assume that in regime 1 this drift is positive, while in regime 2 it is zero. From equation (5.36) and (5.32) it can be seen that this change in policy regime affects the constant term in the VECM through two different mechanisms. First, with $\tau_2 = 0$, the deterministic trends in inflation, nominal rates and real balances all change; the trends in nominal interest rates and inflation are reduced to zero and the trend in real balances is increased. The changes in these trends are not independent, since the slope coefficients in the demand functions for real balances and the IS curve are assumed invariant to the changes in policy regime. Thus the cointegrating vectors in the model are maintained. Therefore the change in the trends of inflation and nominal rates must be equal and the change in the trend of real balances must equal $-\alpha_2$ times the change in the nominal money growth trend.

[5] See Yoshida and Rasche (1990) or Johansen (1991), equation 4.9.

Second, the policy regime change affects the constant term in the *ex post* real rate cointegrating vector in this model. A reduction in the deterministic trend in money growth unambiguously decreases the constant term in this cointegrating vector.

In the empirical work reported in subsequent chapters we observe that both these effects within the samples we analyze.

## 5.3 Moving Average (Wold) Representation

One way to construct the Wold representation of the variables $y_t, r_t, mr_t$ and $\rho_t$ is to write the structural error correction model (5.32) in lag operator notation as:

$$\begin{bmatrix} (1-L) & 0 & 0 & 0 \\ 0 & \alpha_1\kappa & -\alpha_1(1-L) & -\alpha_1\kappa \\ -\kappa & \alpha_2\kappa & \kappa & 0 \\ 0 & 0 & (1-L)^2 & (1-L) \end{bmatrix} \begin{bmatrix} y_t \\ r_t \\ mr_t \\ \rho_t \end{bmatrix} = \begin{bmatrix} 0 \\ \alpha_1\tau_2 \\ 0 \\ 0 \end{bmatrix}$$
$$+ \begin{bmatrix} 0 & 0 & 1.0 \\ -\alpha_1\Pi_1 & -\alpha_1\Pi_2 & 0 \\ 0 & 0 & 0 \\ 0 & 1.0 & 0 \end{bmatrix} \begin{bmatrix} \Delta u_{1t} \\ \Delta u_{2t} \\ \Delta u_{4t} \end{bmatrix}$$
$$+ \begin{bmatrix} 0 & 0 & 0 & 0 \\ \alpha_1\Pi_4 & \alpha_1\Pi_5 & \alpha_1\Pi_6 & \xi \\ 0 & 0 & 1.0 & 0 \\ 0 & 0 & 0 & 0 \end{bmatrix} \begin{bmatrix} \varepsilon_{1t} \\ \varepsilon_{2t} \\ \varepsilon_{3t} \\ \varepsilon_{4t} \end{bmatrix} \tag{5.38}$$

where $\kappa = (1-L) + (1-L)L + L^2 = 1.0$. The determinant of the polynomial matrix on the left hand side of (5.38) is $\alpha_1[1-L]^2$ and the adjoint matrix is $(1-L)A^*(L)$ where $A^*(L)$ is:

$$\begin{bmatrix} \alpha_1 & 0 & 0 & 0 \\ 0 & (1-L) & 0 & \alpha_1 \\ \alpha_1 & -\alpha_2(1-L) & \alpha_1(1-L) & -\alpha_1\alpha_2(1-L) \\ -\alpha_1(1-L) & \alpha_2(1-L)^2 & -\alpha_1(1-L)^2 & \alpha_1[1+\alpha_2(1-L)] \end{bmatrix}.$$

Multiply (5.38) by $\alpha_1^{-1}A^*(L)$ to get the MA (Wold) representation as:

$$\begin{bmatrix} \Delta y_t \\ \Delta r_t \\ \Delta mr_t \\ \Delta \rho_t \end{bmatrix} = [\Lambda_3] \begin{bmatrix} \Delta u_{1t} \\ \Delta u_{2t} \\ \Delta u_{4t} \end{bmatrix} + [\Lambda_4]\,(1-L) \begin{bmatrix} \varepsilon_{1t} \\ \varepsilon_{2t} \\ \varepsilon_{3t} \\ \varepsilon_{4t} \end{bmatrix} \tag{5.39}$$

where

$$\Lambda_3 = \begin{bmatrix} 0 & 0 & 1.0 \\ -\Pi_1(1-L) & -\Pi_2(1-L)+1 & 0 \\ \alpha_2\Pi_1(1-L) & \alpha_2\Pi_2(1-L)-\alpha_2 & 1.0 \\ -\alpha_2\Pi_1(1-L)^2 & 1+\alpha_2[1-L][1-\Pi_2(1-L)] & -(1-L) \end{bmatrix}$$

and

$$\Lambda_4 = \begin{bmatrix} 0 & 0 & 0 & 0 \\ \Pi_4 & \Pi_5 & \Pi_6 & (\xi/\alpha_1) \\ -\alpha_2\Pi_4 & -\alpha_2\Pi_5 & \Lambda_5 & -\alpha_2(\xi/\alpha_1) \\ \alpha_2\Pi_4(1-L) & \alpha_2\Pi_5(1-L) & -\Lambda_5(1-L) & \alpha_2(\xi/\alpha_1)(1-L) \end{bmatrix}$$

where

$$\Lambda_5 = (1 - L - \alpha_2\Pi_6)$$

Substitute for $(\Delta u_{1t}, \Delta u_{2t}, \Delta u_{4t})'$ from (5.30):

$$\begin{bmatrix} \Delta y_t \\ \Delta r_t \\ \Delta mr_t \\ \Delta\rho_t \end{bmatrix} =$$

$$\begin{bmatrix} \Pi_1 & 0 \\ -\Pi_1(1-L) & 1-\Pi_2[1-L] \\ \Pi_1 + \alpha_2\Pi_1[1-L] & -\alpha_2(1-\Pi_2[1-L]) \\ -\Pi_1(1-L)[1+\alpha_2(1-L)] & 1+\alpha_2[1-(1-\Pi_2)(1-L)][1-L] \end{bmatrix} \begin{bmatrix} \tau_1 \\ \tau_2 \end{bmatrix} +$$

$$\begin{bmatrix} 1+\beta(1-\phi_2 L) - \beta(1-\theta)\Pi_4(1-L) \\ -\Pi_1(1-L) + \Pi_4(1-L) \\ \alpha_2(\Pi_1 - \Pi_4)(1-L) + 1 + \beta(1-\phi_2 L) - \beta(1-\theta)(1-L)\Pi_4 \\ -(1-L)^2(\alpha_2\Pi_1 + \frac{(1+\beta[1-\phi_2 L])}{(1-L)} - \beta(1-\theta)\Pi_4 - \alpha_2\Pi_4/(1-L)) \end{bmatrix} \varepsilon_{1t} +$$

$$\begin{bmatrix} \beta(1-\theta)(1-\Pi_5)(1-L) \\ 1-\Pi_2(1-L) + \Pi_5(1-L) \\ -\alpha_2 - \alpha_2(\Pi_5 - \Pi_2)(1-L) - \beta(1-\theta)(1-L)(\Pi_5 - 1) \\ 1 + (1-L)^2(\alpha_2\frac{(1-\Pi_2(1-L))}{(1-L)} + \beta(1-\theta)(\Pi_5 - 1) + \alpha_2\Pi_5) \end{bmatrix} \varepsilon_{2t} +$$

$$\begin{bmatrix} -\beta(1-\theta)\Pi_6(1-L) \\ \Pi_6(1-L) \\ -\beta(1-\theta)(1-L)\Pi_6 - \alpha_2\Pi_6(1-L) + (1-L)^2 \\ \beta(1-\theta)(1-L)^2\Pi_6 - (1-L-\alpha_2\Pi_6)(1-L) \end{bmatrix} \varepsilon_{3t} +$$

$$\begin{bmatrix} -\beta(1-\theta)\Pi_7(1-L) \\ (\xi/\alpha_1)(1-L) \\ -\beta(1-\theta)(1-L)\Pi_7 - (\alpha_2\xi/\alpha_1)(1-L) \\ \beta(1-\theta)(1-L)^2\Pi_7 + (\alpha_2\xi/\alpha_1)(1-L)^2 \end{bmatrix} \varepsilon_{4t} \qquad (5.40)$$

that is the MA (Wold) representation of the vector $(\Delta y_t, \Delta r_t, \Delta mr_t, \Delta\rho_t)'$.

From (5.41) the deterministic trends of the nonstationary processes can be determined by setting $L$=1 in the coefficient matrix on $(\tau_1, \tau_2)$ as:

$$\begin{bmatrix} 1+\beta(1-\phi_2) & 0 \\ 0 & 1 \\ 1-\beta(1-\phi_2) & -\alpha_2 \\ 0 & 1 \end{bmatrix} \begin{bmatrix} \tau_1 \\ \tau_2 \end{bmatrix} = \mu_0. \qquad (5.41)$$

The long run (permanent) effects of the shocks can be determined by setting $L$=1 in the coefficient matrices of the $\varepsilon_{it}$ in (5.40) as:

$$S(1)\begin{bmatrix}\varepsilon_{1t}\\ \varepsilon_{2t}\\ \varepsilon_{3t}\\ \varepsilon_{4t}\end{bmatrix} = \begin{bmatrix}1+\beta(1-\phi_2) & 0 & 0 & 0\\ 0 & 1 & 0 & 0\\ 1+\beta(1-\phi_2) & -\alpha_2 & 0 & 0\\ 0 & 1 & 0 & 0\end{bmatrix}\begin{bmatrix}\varepsilon_{1t}\\ \varepsilon_{2t}\\ \varepsilon_{3t}\\ \varepsilon_{4t}\end{bmatrix}$$

so the MA representation is consistent with the original economic structure that $\varepsilon_{3t}$ and $\varepsilon_{4t}$ are transitory shocks and only $\varepsilon_{1t}$ and $\varepsilon_{2t}$ have permanent effects. The accumulation of $\varepsilon_{1t}$, adjusted for the drift $\tau_1$, is the "real common trend" and the accumulation of $\varepsilon_{2t}$, adjusted for the drift $\tau_2$ is the "nominal common trend."

## 5.4 Impulse Response Functions

The coefficient vectors on the $\varepsilon_{it}$ in equation (5.40) represent the impulse response functions (dynamic multipliers) of the various variables with respect to the permanent and transitory shocks. The impulse response functions for $\Delta y_t$ depend on the degree of indexing of the nominal wage rate. If indexing is complete, then real output is insulated from permanent money growth shocks and from transitory shocks to real interest rates and the demand for real balances. Under these conditions, the response of the growth of real output to productivity shocks ($\varepsilon_{1t}$) is a first order moving average process. The impact response $(1+\beta)$ is partially offset after one period $(-\beta\phi_2)$ at which time the permanent response is established at $1+\beta[1-\phi_2]$.

In an economy with less than complete indexing there is an additional transitory component in the response function of $\Delta y_t$ that reflects the sources of inflation expectations error. This transitory component is a weighted sum of the four shocks to the economy:

$$\beta(1-\theta)(1-L)[\Pi_4, (\Pi_5-1), \Pi_6, \Pi_7][\varepsilon_{1t}, \varepsilon_{2t}, \varepsilon_{3t}, \varepsilon_{4t}]'.$$

Since

$$\begin{aligned}\Pi_5 - 1 &= \beta(1-\theta) - \alpha_2(1+\alpha_2)][1+\alpha_2+\beta(1-\theta)]^{-1} - 1\\ &= [\beta(1-\theta) - \alpha_2(1+\alpha_2) - \beta(1-\theta) - (1+\alpha_2)][1+\alpha_2+\beta(1-\theta)]^{-1}\\ &= -[1+\alpha_2]^2/[1+\alpha_2+\beta(1-\theta)] < 0\end{aligned}$$

and $\Pi_4 > 0$, $\Pi_6 > 0$, and $\Pi_7 > 0$. Note that

$$(\Pi_5 - 1) = -(1+\alpha_2)^2\,\Pi_6 < 0.$$

The impact effect of this transitory component on $\Delta y$ is positive for $\varepsilon_{1t}, \varepsilon_{3t}$ and $\varepsilon_{4t}$ shocks and negative for $\varepsilon_{2t}$ shocks. The only impact of this transitory component is contemporaneous to the shocks; it is completely reversed in the succeeding period.

The impulse response functions for the growth of real balances indicate permanent responses to both $\varepsilon_{1t}$ and $\varepsilon_{2t}$ shocks that impact with a one period lag and transitory responses that are fully offset after one period to all four shocks. This pattern is that assumed by the postulated solution of the rational expectations model in equation (5.22) for $mr_t$.

The impulse responses for $\Delta\rho_t$ are determined by the postulated solution for $mr_t$ and the identity $\Delta mr_t - \Delta mr_{t-1} + \Delta\rho_t = \tau_2 + \varepsilon_{2t}$. Consequently the transitory response of $\Delta\rho_t$ to each of the four shocks is a second order moving average process that dies out completely after two periods and the permanent response of the change in the inflation rate to $\varepsilon_{1t}$ is $-\Pi_1$, and to $\varepsilon_{2t}$ is 1.0.

Finally, the impulse response functions for $\Delta r_t$ satisfy the demand for money function restriction: $-\alpha_2\Delta r_t = \Delta mr_t - \Delta y_t - \Delta\varepsilon_{3t}$. This result that identifies the $\varepsilon_{3t}$ shock with the impulse response function of the cointegrating vector $mr_t - y_t + \alpha_2 r_t$ is specific to this model, and not a general characteristic of models that possess stationary money demand disturbances. The unique association of $\varepsilon_{3t}$ with the impulse response function of $mr_t - y_t + \alpha_2 r_t$ results from the absence of any dynamics in the money demand function (5.7). A more general specification that relaxed the assumption that the short-run and equilibrium aggregate demands for real balances are identical would generate a different MA representation for all four variables and typically would produce an impulse response function for the money demand cointegrating vector that is a function of all the shocks to the model.

## 5.5 Reduced Model VECM

Consider the equations represented by the 2nd and 4th rows of equation (5.31). Multiply the fourth row of (5.31) by $\alpha_1$ and add the resulting equation to the second row of (5.31). The resulting equation is:

$$\begin{aligned} \alpha_1 r_t &= \alpha_1 u_{2t} - \alpha_1\Pi_1\Delta u_{1t} - \alpha_1\Pi_2\Delta u_{2t} + \alpha_1\tau_2 \\ &\quad + \alpha_1\Pi_4\varepsilon_{1t} + \alpha_1\Pi_5\varepsilon_{2t} + \alpha_1\Pi_6\varepsilon_{3t} + \xi\varepsilon_{4t} \end{aligned}$$

This equation plus the first and third rows of (5.31) give a three equation conditional submodel in $y_t, r_t$ and $mr_t$:

$$\begin{bmatrix} 1.0 & 0 & 0 \\ 0 & \alpha_1 & 0 \\ -1.0 & \alpha_2 & 1.0 \end{bmatrix} \begin{bmatrix} y_t \\ r_t \\ mr_t \end{bmatrix} = \begin{bmatrix} 0 & 0 & 1 \\ 0 & \alpha_1 & 0 \\ 0 & 0 & 0 \end{bmatrix} \begin{bmatrix} u_{1t} \\ u_{2t} \\ u_{4t} \end{bmatrix}$$

$$+ \begin{bmatrix} 0 & 0 & 0 \\ -\alpha_1\Pi_1 & -\alpha_1\Pi_2 & 0 \\ 0 & 0 & 0 \end{bmatrix} \begin{bmatrix} \Delta u_{1t} \\ \Delta u_{2t} \\ \Delta u_{4t} \end{bmatrix} + \begin{bmatrix} 0 \\ \alpha_1\tau_2 \\ 0 \end{bmatrix}$$

$$+\begin{bmatrix} 0 & 0 & 0 & 0 \\ \alpha_1\Pi_4 & \alpha_1\Pi_5 & \alpha_1\Pi_6 & \xi \\ 0 & 0 & 1.0 & 0 \end{bmatrix}\begin{bmatrix} \varepsilon_{1t} \\ \varepsilon_{2t} \\ \varepsilon_{3t} \\ \varepsilon_{4t} \end{bmatrix} \tag{5.42}$$

This can be written as a structural VECM by differencing the first and second equations and adding lags of the variables in the third equation (recognizing $u_{4t-1} = y_{t-1}$)

$$\begin{bmatrix} 1.0 & 0 & 0 \\ 0 & \alpha_1 & 0 \\ -1.0 & \alpha_2 & 1.0 \end{bmatrix}\begin{bmatrix} \Delta y_t \\ \Delta r_t \\ \Delta mr_t \end{bmatrix} = \begin{bmatrix} 0 & 0 & 0 \\ 0 & 0 & 0 \\ 1.0 & -\alpha_2 & -1.0 \end{bmatrix}\begin{bmatrix} y_{t-1} \\ r_{t-1} \\ mr_{t-1} \end{bmatrix}$$

$$+\begin{bmatrix} 0 & 0 & 1.0 \\ -\alpha_1\Pi_1(1-L) & \alpha_1 - \alpha_1\Pi_2(1-L) & 0 \\ 0 & 0 & 0 \end{bmatrix}\begin{bmatrix} \Delta u_{1t} \\ \Delta u_{2t} \\ \Delta u_{4t} \end{bmatrix}$$

$$+(1-L)\begin{bmatrix} 0 & 0 & 0 & 0 \\ \alpha_1\Pi_4 & \alpha_1\Pi_5 & \alpha_1\Pi_6 & \xi \\ 0 & 0 & 1.0 & 0 \end{bmatrix}\begin{bmatrix} \varepsilon_{1t} \\ \varepsilon_{2t} \\ \varepsilon_{3t} \\ \varepsilon_{4t} \end{bmatrix} \tag{5.43}$$

The inverse of the left hand side matrix is:

$$\alpha_1^{-1}\begin{bmatrix} \alpha_1 & 0 & 0 \\ 0 & 1.0 & 0 \\ \alpha_1 & -\alpha_2 & \alpha_1 \end{bmatrix}$$

So the reduced form VECM is:

$$\begin{bmatrix} \Delta y_t \\ \Delta r_t \\ \Delta mr_t \end{bmatrix} = \begin{bmatrix} 0 \\ 0 \\ 1 \end{bmatrix}[1.0 - \alpha_2 - 1.0]\begin{bmatrix} y_{t-1} \\ r_{t-1} \\ mr_{t-1} \end{bmatrix} +$$

$$\begin{bmatrix} 0 & 0 & 1 \\ -\Pi_1(1-L) & 1-\Pi_2(1-L) & 0 \\ \alpha_2\Pi_1(1-L) & -\alpha_2[1-\Pi_2(1-L)] & 1 \end{bmatrix}\begin{bmatrix} \Delta u_{1t} \\ \Delta u_{2t} \\ \Delta u_{4t} \end{bmatrix} +$$

$$\frac{(1-L)}{\alpha_1}\begin{bmatrix} 0 & 0 & 0 & 0 \\ \alpha_1\Pi_4 & \alpha_1\Pi_5 & \alpha_1\Pi_6 & \xi \\ -\alpha_2\alpha_1\Pi_4 & -\alpha_2\alpha_1\Pi_5 & \Lambda_7 & -\alpha_2\xi \end{bmatrix}\begin{bmatrix} \varepsilon_{1t} \\ \varepsilon_{2t} \\ \varepsilon_{3t} \\ \varepsilon_{4t} \end{bmatrix} \tag{5.44}$$

where $\Lambda_7 = -\alpha_2\alpha_1\Pi_6 + \alpha_1$

### 5.5.1 Moving Average (Wold) Representation of the Reduced Model

Write the structural error correction model (5.43) in lag operator notation:

$$\begin{bmatrix} 1-L & 0 & 0 \\ 0 & \alpha_1(1-L) & 0 \\ -(1-L)-L & \alpha_2(1-L)+\alpha_2 L & (1-L)+L \end{bmatrix} \begin{bmatrix} y_t \\ r_t \\ mr_t \end{bmatrix} =$$

$$\begin{bmatrix} 0 & 0 & 1.0 \\ -\alpha_1\Pi_1(1-L) & \alpha_1[1-\Pi_2(1-L)] & 0 \\ 0 & 0 & 0 \end{bmatrix} \begin{bmatrix} \Delta u_{1t} \\ \Delta u_{2t} \\ \Delta u_{4t} \end{bmatrix} +$$

$$(1-L)\begin{bmatrix} 0 & 0 & 0 & 0 \\ \alpha_1\Pi_4 & \alpha_1\Pi_5 & \alpha_1\Pi_6 & \xi \\ 0 & 0 & 1.0 & 0 \end{bmatrix} \begin{bmatrix} \varepsilon_{1t} \\ \varepsilon_{2t} \\ \varepsilon_{3t} \\ \varepsilon_{4t} \end{bmatrix} \tag{5.45}$$

The determinant of the polynomial matrix on the left hand side of (5.45) is $\alpha_1(1-L)^2$ and the adjoint matrix is:

$$(1-L)\begin{bmatrix} \alpha_1 & 0 & 0 \\ 0 & 1.0 & 0 \\ \alpha_1 & -\alpha_2 & \alpha_1(1-L) \end{bmatrix} = (1-L)A^* \tag{5.46}$$

Multiply (5.45) by $\alpha_1^{-1}A^*$ to get the MA(Wold) representation as:

$$\begin{bmatrix} \Delta y_t \\ \Delta r_t \\ \Delta mr_t \end{bmatrix} = \begin{bmatrix} 0 & 0 & 1.0 \\ -\Pi_1(1-L) & 1-\Pi_2(1-L) & 0 \\ \alpha_2\Pi_1(1-L) & -\alpha_2[1-\Pi_2(1-L)] & 1.0 \end{bmatrix} \begin{bmatrix} \Delta u_{1t} \\ \Delta u_{2t} \\ \Delta u_{4t} \end{bmatrix}$$

$$+(1-L)\begin{bmatrix} 0 & 0 & 0 & 0 \\ \Pi_4 & \Pi_5 & \Pi_6 & \alpha_1^{-1}\xi \\ -\alpha_2\Pi_4 & -\alpha_2\Pi_5 & -\alpha_2\Pi_6+(1-L) & -\alpha_2\alpha_1^{-1}\xi \end{bmatrix} \begin{bmatrix} \varepsilon_{1t} \\ \varepsilon_{2t} \\ \varepsilon_{3t} \\ \varepsilon_{4t} \end{bmatrix} \tag{5.47}$$

that are exactly the first three rows of (5.39). Substitute for $(\Delta u_{1t}, \Delta u_{2t}, \Delta u_{4t})'$ from (5.30):

$$\begin{bmatrix} \Delta y_t \\ \Delta r_t \\ \Delta mr_t \end{bmatrix} = \begin{bmatrix} \Pi_1 & 0 \\ 0 & 1 \\ \Pi_1 & -\alpha_2 \end{bmatrix} \begin{bmatrix} \tau_1 \\ \tau_2 \end{bmatrix}$$

$$
+\begin{bmatrix} 1+\beta(1-\phi_2 L)-\beta(1-\theta)(1-L)\Pi_4 \\ -(\Pi_1-\Pi_4)(1-L) \\ \alpha_2(\Pi_1-\Pi_4)(1-L)+1+\beta(1-\phi_2 L)-\beta(1-\theta)(1-L)\Pi_4 \end{bmatrix}\varepsilon_{1t}
$$
$$
+\begin{bmatrix} -\beta(1-\theta)(1-L)(\Pi_5-1) \\ 1+(\Pi_5-\Pi_2)(1-L) \\ -\alpha_2-\alpha_2(\Pi_5-\Pi_2)(1-L)-\beta(1-\theta)(1-L)(\Pi_5-1) \end{bmatrix}\varepsilon_{2t}
$$
$$
+\begin{bmatrix} -\beta(1-\theta)(1-L)\Pi_6 \\ \Pi_6(1-L) \\ -\beta(1-\theta)(1-L)\Pi_6-\alpha_2\Pi_6(1-L)+(1-L)^2 \end{bmatrix}\varepsilon_{3t}
$$
$$
+\begin{bmatrix} -\beta(1-\theta)(1-L)\Pi_7 \\ \alpha_1^{-1}\xi(1-L) \\ -\beta(1-\theta)(1-L)\Pi_7-\alpha_2\alpha_1^{-1}\xi(1-L) \end{bmatrix}\varepsilon_{4t}. \qquad (5.48)
$$

The long-run (permanent) effects of the shocks can be determined by setting $L$=1 in the coefficient matrices of $\varepsilon_{it}$ in (5.48) as:

$$
S(1)=\begin{bmatrix} \varepsilon_{1t} \\ \varepsilon_{2t} \\ \varepsilon_{3t} \\ \varepsilon_{4t} \end{bmatrix}=\begin{bmatrix} 1+\beta(1-\phi_2) & 0 & 0 & 0 \\ 0 & 1.0 & 0 & 0 \\ 1+\beta(1-\phi_2) & -\alpha_2 & 0 & 0 \end{bmatrix}\begin{bmatrix} \varepsilon_{1t} \\ \varepsilon_{2t} \\ \varepsilon_{3t} \\ \varepsilon_{4t} \end{bmatrix} \qquad (5.49)
$$

Note that the equations in (5.48) are exactly the same as the first three equations in (5.40), even though the reduced form VECM for the three variable model (5.44) is considerably simpler (in particular it is lower order) than the reduced form VECM for the four variable model (5.33).

A comparison of equations (5.48) and (5.45) suggests several hypotheses that can be tested in terms of VECMs of different dimensions. If the dimension of the VECM is increased and the number of cointegrating vectors increase accordingly (so that the number of permanent shocks remains unchanged), then the impulse responses of the variables included in all the VECMs with respect to correctly identified permanent shocks should remain unchanged as the size of the VECM increases. Second, in a VECM with only one transitory shock, the impulse responses of the variables to this transitory shock are linear combinations of all the transitory shocks that impact upon the economy. As the dimension of the VECM is increased, it may be possible to separate out the impulse responses to particular transitory shocks if adequate identifying information for the dynamics of the economy is available (see Chapter 4).

# Chapter 6

# ANALYSIS OF THREE VARIABLE VECM MODELS INCLUDING DEMAND FUNCTIONS FOR REAL BALANCES

The review of the existing literature on empirical money demand functions presented in Chapter 2 suggests that very little confidence is derived from existing single equation estimates, either with respect to the existence of a stable aggregate demand function for real balances, or with respect to the magnitude of the parameter values of such a function, should it exist. In Chapters 3 and 4 newly developed techniques for multiequation analysis are discussed. The purpose of this and subsequent chapters is to apply these techniques to investigations into the existence of long-run aggregate demand functions for real balances. The analyses involve testing for cointegrating vectors among macroeconomic data series and identification of a long-run demand function for real balances among those cointegrating vectors. The identified long-run money demand functions are examined for stability across various sample periods, particularly the periods of "missing money" and those of velocity trend shifts. The robustness of the long-run money demand function is examined with respect to the dimension of the multivariate process and the number of cointegrating vectors. Finally, various techniques of identifying permanent and transitory "economic shocks" are applied to the vector error correction (VECM) models containing the money demand equation, and the resulting dynamic patterns are analyzed.

The minimum practical VECM model for the investigation of long-run money demand functions requires three variables: real balances, real income, and a nominal interest rate variable. In principle a two variable model involving only velocity and a nominal interest rate could be estimated. However, such a model not only constrains the equilibrium income elasticity of the demand for real balances to unity, but also imposes severe restrictions on the adjustment dynamics to real income and real balance changes. Since various theories of the demand for money provide little insight into the dynamics of adjustment, and since the dynamics of a VECM structure represent reduced form responses, we regard the *a priori* restriction of the dynamic structure unwarranted. Hence we start our analyses with three equation structures.

The existence of a cointegrating vector among real M1, real income and a nominal interest rate in the U.S. is the subject of some controversy. Hoffman and Rasche (1991) found such a relationship in monthly data spanning 1953-88. Hafer and Jansen (1991) found such a relationship for M1 in postwar U.S. quarterly data, but concluded that the evidence is very weak when the sample is extended to include the interwar years. Friedman and Kuttner (1992) address several issues including the question of stationary long-run relationships for several monetary and credit aggregates. They conclude that such relationships are sample specific and in particular that they "disintegrate when the sample extends into the 1980s" (p.490 ).

## 6.1 The Friedman–Kuttner Challenge

The purpose of this section is to show that the conclusions of Friedman and Kuttner are specific to their choice of functional form and testing strategy. In particular, they limit their analysis to specifications that are semi-logarithmic. This specification imposes higher long-run interest elasticities at higher interest rates. The imposition of a particular functional form can have a critical impact on conclusions about the stability of results across sample periods, since in the 1980s average short-term nominal interest rates were higher than in previous decades and for some of these years the rates were well outside of the range of previous observation.

### 6.1.1 Empirical Analysis

Our cointegration tests in this section are based on data that span 60:2 - 90:4 using series supplied by Friedman and Kuttner. The technical framework for the analysis is Johansen's reduced rank regression model with a very general specification for deterministic trends.

Our consideration of M1 begins with the notion that M1 velocity is nonstationary. This is clearly demonstrated by Friedman and Kuttner (among others) and apparently is a noncontroversial result. What remains is whether there exists a stationary long-run relationship between M1-income velocity and a measure of nominal interest rates. Friedman and Kuttner use a semi-log money demand specification to illustrate that once the experience of the 1980s is added to their sample, no evidence of stationarity in such a relationship prevails.

Granger (1992) argues that it is important to explore nonlinearities in the testing for cointegrating relationships. We reexamine Friedman and Kuttner's results with this notion in mind, particularly since the literature on money demand functions treats both semi-log and double log specifications. Our primary interest remains with the unitary income elasticity specification following the suggestion of Lucas (1988) and Poole (1988).

We examine two alternative M1-money demand specifications that may be compared with the Friedman and Kuttner semi-log model; the log-log (the natural log of M1 velocity and the natural log of the commercial paper rate) and following Granger (1992) the log-inverse specification (the natural log of velocity and the inverse of the commercial paper rate). A lag length of 4 in the VECM models ($k$=5 in Johansen's notation) is maintained throughout the analysis to facilitate comparison with the results of Friedman and Kuttner. The unitary income elasticity restriction can be imposed in two ways. First we focus on the specification of a bivariate system, M1 velocity and the commercial paper rate, so the unitary income elasticity is imposed prior to estimation of the VECM and the adjustment dynamics are restricted. We then examine a trivariate system of real M1 balances, real income and the commercial paper rate. The unitary income elasticity is then imposed after the VECM is estimated, but prior to the calculation of the Johansen test statistics (for details see Johansen and Juselius (1990)). The validity of the income elasticity restriction may be tested in the trivariate system.

Trace and maximum eigenvalue tests for cointegration in the unrestricted trivariate M1 model reveal no strong evidence of cointegration over the 60:2-90:4 period regardless of trend specification or functional form of the interest rate. This is consistent with the results reported by Friedman and Kuttner in their Table 10. However, there is also no evidence against the unitary income elasticity hypothesis (tests yield $\chi^2_{(1)}$ statistics of 3.19, 1.47 and .19 for the three alternative interest rate specifications). Cointegration tests obtained with the unitary income elasticity in place appear in Table 6.1. There is substantial evidence of a single cointegrating vector in the 60:2-90:4 sample period regardless of the *ex ante*(bivariate model) or *ex post* (trivariate model) imposition of the income elasticity restriction in the log-log and log-inverse interest rate specifications. Interestingly, there is some evidence of cointegration even in the semi-log model when the income elasticity is imposed *ex post.*

Tables 6.1 and 6.1 reveal the robustness of this finding and stability of the estimated interest rate effect "$\gamma$" over the alternative samples examined by Friedman and Kuttner. Substantial evidence of cointegration prevails regardless of sample or interest rate specification. Moreover, the estimated interest rate effects are virtually unaffected by excluding substantial portions of the sample, though the precision of the estimates is reduced in the shorter samples. Estimated standard errors for the coefficients reveal that they are statistically significant even in most of the shortest samples.[1] The $\gamma$ estimates and the es-

[1]Standard error estimates are obtained using a Wald test from variance estimates taken from Corollary 4, p. 398 of Johansen (1991). Precision estimates are virtually identical to

Table 6.1: M1-Money Demand Models: Estimates Across Alternative Samples(60:2-90:4), Bivariate Model

| | | Real M1–Real Income | | | |
|---|---|---|---|---|---|
| Specification | Sample | Trace Test | $\lambda - \max test$ | $\widehat{\gamma}$ | SE($\widehat{\gamma}$) |
| r | 60:2-90:4 | 15.49 | 12.74 | -.095 | .020 |
| r | 60:2-90:4 | 28.28* | 26.03* | -.118 | .017 |
| log(r) | 60:2-90:4 | 20:13* | 17.29* | -.600 | .079 |
| log(r) | 60:2-90:4 | 25.49* | 22.92* | -.684 | .084 |
| log(r) | 60:2-79:3 | 22.90* | 22.30* | -.553 | .071 |
| log(r) | 70:3-90:4 | 19.59* | 14.68* | -.531 | .134 |
| $r^{-1}$ | 60:2-90:4 | 19.92* | 17.02* | 3.328 | .407 |
| $r^{-1}$ | 60:2-90:4 | 19.07* | 16.40* | 3.500 | .484 |
| $r^{-1}$ | 60:2-79:3 | 20.22* | 19.83* | 2.709 | .346 |
| $r^{-1}$ | 70:3-90:4 | 24.84* | 19.94* | 4.244 | .899 |

Note * indicates significant rejection of the null of no cointegration at the 5% level.

Table 6.2: M1-Money Demand Models: Estimates Across Alternative Samples(60:2-90:4), Trivariate Model

| | | Real M1–Real Income | | | |
|---|---|---|---|---|---|
| Specification | Sample | Trace Test | $\lambda - \max test$ | $\widehat{\gamma}$ | SE($\widehat{\gamma}$) |
| r | 60:2-90:4 | 16.71* | 13.39 | -.128 | .028 |
| r | 60:2-90:4 | 19.89* | 17.81* | -.128 | .020 |
| r | 60:2-79:3 | 27.52* | 22.02* | -.126 | .016 |
| r | 70:3-90:4 | 13.20 | 8.92 | -.193 | .199 |
| log(r) | 60:2-90:4 | 20.85* | 16.06* | -.741 | .095 |
| log(r) | 60:2-90:4 | 18.39* | 15.56* | -.738 | .094 |
| log(r) | 60:2-79:3 | 26.12* | 20.90* | -.623 | .077 |
| log(r) | 70:3-90:4 | 17.07* | 11.54 | -.870 | .305 |
| $r^{-1}$ | 60:2-90:4 | 20.24* | 14.33* | 3.809 | .478 |
| $r^{-1}$ | 60:2-90:4 | 15.71* | 12.33 | 3.718 | .519 |
| $r^{-1}$ | 60:2-79:3 | 22.36* | 18.48* | 2.878 | .380 |
| $r^{-1}$ | 70:3-90:4 | 22.47* | 16.72* | 5.173 | 1.070 |

Note * indicates significant rejection of the null of no cointegration at the 5% level.

timator precision compare favorably with those obtained using Stock and Watson's DOLS approach and an autoregressive spectral procedure for estimating the standard errors (see Hoffman, Rasche and Tieslau (1995), and Stock and Watson (1993)).

There are two critical steps in this analysis. First, we note that cointegration tests that fail to impose unitary income elasticity may have low power. With this restriction (that is not rejected by the data) in place, there is considerable evidence against the null of no cointegration, regardless of sample size.[2] Second, we note that the absence of cointegration in a semi-log specification is not sufficient to rule out cointegration between the log of velocity and interest rates. The data generating process (DGP) does not unequivocally support a long-run relationship between velocity and interest rates when the interest elasticity is larger the higher the interest rate. It does support a long-run relationship with a constant interest elasticity, or an interest elasticity that is larger the lower the interest rate (the log-inverse model).

### 6.1.2 Functional Form: Why Does it Matter?

The question that is provoked by the evidence discussed above is why are the Friedman and Kuttner conclusions so specific to the semi-log functional form? Our view is that Friedman and Kuttner's result reflects the inadequacy of the semi-log functional form in the face of the high nominal interest rates of the early 1980s. The maximum value of the commercial paper rate prior to 79:4 was 11.53 percent (74:3). In 81:3 this rate achieved a post 79:3 maximum of 16.21 percent.

We reexamined the full sample (60:2 - 90:4) for each functional form excluding 79:4 - 82:2 the period of the "New Operating Procedures" (the "Early Volcker Years"). These results are included in Tables 6.1 and 6.2. The conclusions for the double log and inverse rate functional forms are unaffected by the exclusion of these observations. The Friedman and Kuttner conclusions for the semi-log functional form are not robust, and are completely reversed when the early 1980s are excluded from the sample. Without these observations, there is strong evidence for one cointegrating vector between the log of M1 velocity and the level of the commercial paper rate, from both the trace and maximum eigenvalue tests. The effect of the early 1980s observations can be seen clearly in Figure 6.1 where the deviations of actual M1 velocity from the cointegrating vector implied by the bivariate specifications in Table 6.1 are plotted.[3] The ab-

those obtained from likelihood ratio tests suggested by Johansen and Juselius (1990).

[2]Analysis of the estimated "log-log" and "log-inverse" velocity "equilibria" using standard univariate unit root tests yields the same statistical inference delivered by Johansen's multivariate test. Augmented Dickey-Fuller tests for a unit root, $\tau_\mu$, are -3.59 and -4.20 respectively for the log-log and log-inverse models estimated over the full sample for the bivariate model. Corresponding normalized bias test statistics (using autoregressive weights suggested by Phillips) are -41.69 and -55.78, respectively, while the respective first order autocorrelation coefficients are .833 and .805. Univariate tests on subsamples also point to rejections of the null of nonstationarity at conventional significance levels.

[3]These deviations are $\ln GNP_t - \ln M1_t + \gamma R_t - \alpha$ where $R$ represents the commercial

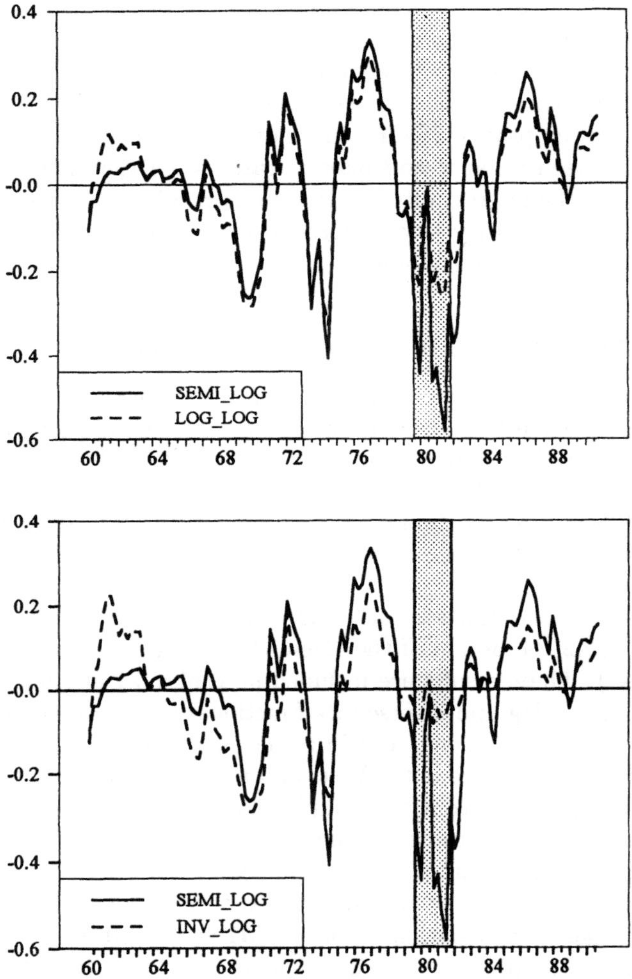


Figure 6.1: Velocity Deviations from Semi-Log and Log-Log Equilibria(top panel) and Velocity Deviations from Semi-Log and Log-Inv. Equilibria(bottom panel): Estimation Sample 60:2-90:4

solute deviations from the semi-log specification are extremely large during this period, based on the full sample estimates that reject cointegration. The absolute deviations from the double log specification are large, but no larger than those observed during 3-4 other periods within the sample. Absolute deviations from the inverse rate specification are relatively small during this period.[4]

The same deviations, based on the parameter estimates excluding the 79:4 - 82:2 observations, are plotted in Figure 6.2. The deviations from double log and inverse rate functional forms are not substantially changed by the sample truncation, neither during the shortened sample, nor during the omitted quarters.[5] The deviations from the semi-log functional form change dramatically. By excluding the 79:4 - 82:2 period, the maximum absolute deviation for this specification (during 81) increases by a factor of 1/3 (from approximately -0.6 to approximately -0.8). At 16.21 percent, the equilibrium interest elasticity of velocity implied by the semi-log functional form computed from estimates excluding 79:4 - 82:2 is 1.92. This compares with the constant elasticity of .68 from the double log functional form and .22 from the inverse rate functional form.

An alternative approach to evaluate the appropriateness of the functional forms for high interest rate regimes is shown in Figure 6.3. There the deviations from equilibrium velocity (again based on estimates excluding 79:4-82:2) are plotted for 78-85 with an estimated 95 percent confidence interval. The confidence interval is constructed from an estimated long-run variance from a fifth order autoregression of the deviations of velocity from the estimated equilibrium velocity of each functional form, excluding the 79:4 - 82:2 observations.[6] The only functional form for which the estimated deviations approach or fall outside of the confidence bounds in the 79-82 period is the semi-log form chosen by Friedman and Kuttner.

---

paper rate, its log, or its inverse for the semi-log, log and inverse specifications respectively. $\gamma$ is from Table 6.1. $\alpha$ is the mean of the sample deviations.

[4]In 1974, when the commercial paper rate peaked at 11.53 percent, the same characteristics are observed in the deviations from equilibrium velocity of the three functional forms, though not as extreme as in 80-81.

[5]These deviations are $\ln GNP_t - \ln M1_t + \gamma R_t - \alpha$ where $R$ represents the commercial paper rate, its log, or its inverse for the semi-log, log and inverse specifications respectively. $\gamma$ is from Table 6.1. $\alpha$ is the mean of the sample deviations.

[6]We used a fifth order autoregressive spectral estimator of the error variance in forming the confidence intervals. This technique is designed to accomodate persistence in the data generating process and is suggested by Stock and Watson (1993) for obtaining accurate inferences in circumstances when errors are stationary, but highly persistent. We accounted for the degrees of freedom lost in estimating the cointegration vector in constructing our estimate of the error variance. Specifically, the variance estimate is simply the variance of the residuals obtained by regressing the cointegration "equilibrium" on a constant and five lagged "equilibria" weighted by the reciprocal of $(1 - \Sigma\beta_i)^2$ where $\beta_i$ are the autoregressive coefficient estimates in the auxiliary regression.

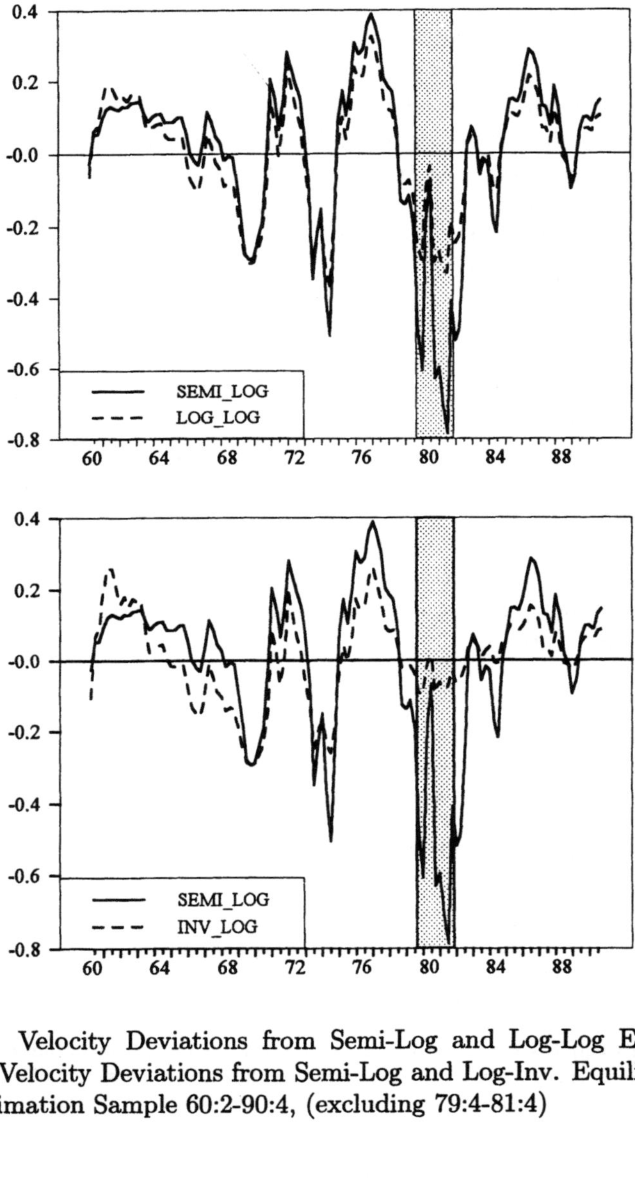


Figure 6.2: Velocity Deviations from Semi-Log and Log-Log Equilibria(top panel) and Velocity Deviations from Semi-Log and Log-Inv. Equilibria(bottom panel): Estimation Sample 60:2-90:4, (excluding 79:4-81:4)

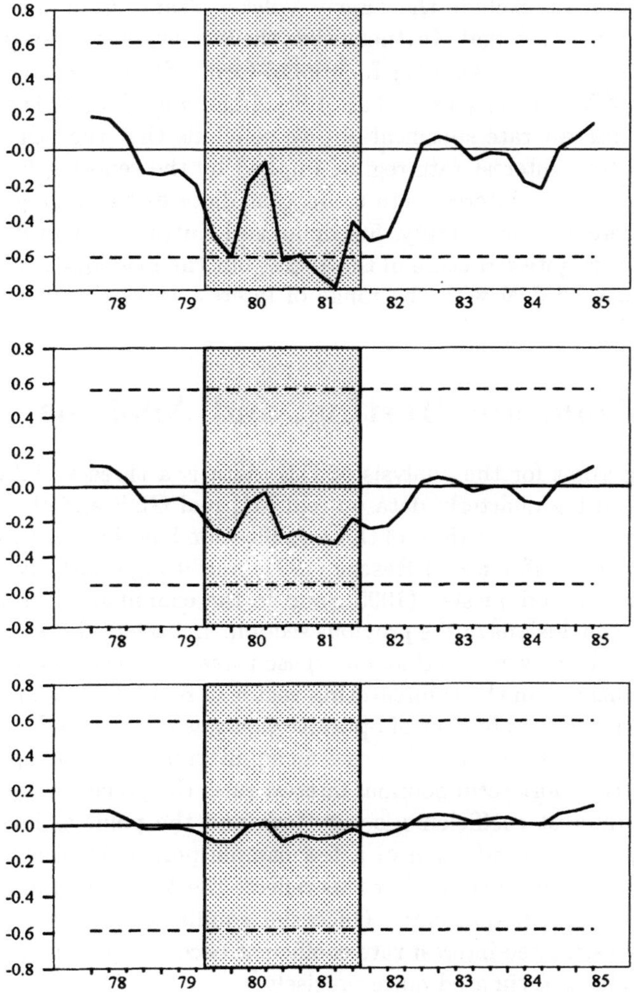


Figure 6.3: Velocity Equilibria 1978-1985: for the Semi-Log(top), Log-Log(middle) and Log-Inverse(bottom) Specification: Estimation Sample 60:2-90:4, (excluding 79:4-81:4).
Note: The figures include 95% confidence intervals for each of the equilibrium representations

### 6.1.3 Conclusion

Friedman and Kuttner (1992) find no statistical basis for a long-run relation between M1-velocity and the commercial paper rate in a semi-log model that employs data throughout the last three decades. Using log-log and log-inverse models of the long-run relationship between M1-velocity and interest rates, we find evidence that consistently supports the existence of such a long-run relationship. When we exclude the "Early Volcker Years" from the three decade sample that Friedman and Kuttner used, there is evidence of significant cointegration even with the semi-log functional form. Since the only difference in our analysis of M1-velocity from that of Friedman and Kuttner is the functional form of the interest rate specification, we conclude that the large elasticity of velocity in a high interest rate regime implied by the semi-log functional form does not capture the interest rate trend that dictates the aggregate of agent's long-run preferences for liquidity. Friedman and Kuttner's result does not reflect a change in aggregate structure in the 1980s, but the inadequacy of the semi-log functional form to deal with the range of interest rates that were observed in the early 1980s.

## 6.2 Estimation, Testing, and Analysis

Our starting point for the analysis of U.S. data is a three variable double log specification, using quarterly data on real M1, real GDP and the Treasury bill rate. The long-run implications of this specification have been investigated using monthly data in Hoffman and Rasche (1991) and using quarterly GNP data in Hoffman, Rasche and Tieslau (1995), and in the examination of the Friedman and Kuttner conclusions in the previous section. In each of those studies a single cointegrating vector was found among these three variables, and the hypothesis that the coefficients in the cointegrating vector of real balances and real income are equal in absolute value but of opposite sign was not rejected. In the absence of this linear restriction, which imposes an equilibrium relationship between M1-velocity and the short-term nominal interest rate, the precision of the estimated income and interest coefficients is very low, and the point estimates can vary considerably with the addition of a few sample points (Hoffman, Rasche and Tieslau (1995)). We conclude that this reflects the presence of multicollinearity in the data at low frequencies. Once the equilibrium velocity restriction is imposed, the estimated interest rate coefficient becomes quite stable in recursive regressions, and is estimated quite precisely.[7]

### 6.2.1 Estimation of Cointegrating Relationships

The only difference in the equilibrium estimates that are presented here from those in our previous work is that we have replaced the real GNP measure with

[7]It is important to note that the linear restriction is imposed only on the equilibrium relationship between velocity and interest rates. The dynamic specification of the VECM allows different responses to each of the three variables in each of the three equations.

GDP, and updated for the rebasing of the U.S. National Income and Product Accounts to 1987.[8] Since we have consistently failed to reject the equilibrium velocity restriction in previous analyses, we have imposed this restriction in all of the results discussed here. This analysis extends our previous work by examining the dynamics of the adjustment to the equilibrium that are implicit in the estimated VECM. The basic results are given in Table 6.3.

This table contains the results of recursive estimation of the double log VECM at interval of four quarters from 72:4 through 91:4. The lag length in the regressions is four quarters (three lagged differences). The initial sample period is the same (though with the current data revisions) as was used by Goldfeld (1973). The Johansen trace and maximum eigenvalue tests for cointegration applied to the sample strongly reject the hypothesis of no cointegration (trace =29.04; maximum eigenvalue = 19.5 with one percent critical values of 20.04 and 18.63 respectively).[9] This is noteworthy, since the span of the data is only 17 years at this point (66 quarterly observations). At this sample size, with quarterly macroeconomic data, the available studies on the power of unit root and cointegration tests suggest that the power to discriminate nonstationary time series from near nonstationary time series is quite low. The estimated long-run interest elasticity is .4054 from this specification. The estimated standard error of this elasticity from a Wald test of the hypothesis that the interest elasticity is zero is .0337. It is important to remember that this is an asymptotic test, and the computed value can have substantial bias as a measure of the standard error with such a small sample size. The interest elasticity is considerably larger than the estimated interest elasticities from the single equation partial adjustment models that are discussed in Chapter 2.

The important question is what happens as the sample period is extended through the 1970s, since it is during this period that the single equation "short-run money demand" specifications fail completely. As the sample period is lengthened, the trace and maximum eigenvalue tests provide consistent support for the hypothesis of a single cointegrating vector among the three variables. Extension of the sample period through the 70s does have some effect on the equilibrium interest elasticity estimate. As five additional years are added to the data set, the estimated equilibrium interest elasticity increases to .592, but then remains quite stable around .57 - .60 as the sample is extended through the 1980s. Thus, as far as the estimated equilibrium relationship is concerned, the period of the "missing money" has no effect on the stability of the VECM. After 1988, the estimated interest elasticity drifts steadily upward. For every sample

[8] While GDP is the concept that is featured in current press releases and discussions of macroeconomic performance in the U.S., the real GNP measure continues to be published for the new deflator base. Any differences between the equilibrium estimates reported here and those reported in our earlier research are more likely due to the rebasing of the implicit deflator than to the switch from the GNP to the GDP concept.

[9] The critical values are taken from Osterwald-Lenum (1992), using the values that are appropriate for a regression model that allows for deterministic trends, when the DGP includes deterministic trends. Johansen and Juselius (1992) utilize these same critical values for a VECM which includes a dummy variable, as is the case with the estimates considered here that incorporate data after 81:4.

Table 6.3: Estimates of Error Correction Parameters for Models that Contain, ln(M/P), ln(Y/P) and ln(Rtb): Recursive Samples Beginning 56:2

| End of Sample | Trace Tests r=0 | r≤0 | $\beta_c$ | | | $\beta_0$ | $\alpha_c$ | | | I-$\beta$'$\alpha$ |
|---|---|---|---|---|---|---|---|---|---|---|
| 72:4 | 29.1 | 9.5 | 1.0 | -1.0 | .405 | .89 | .034 | .062 | .504 | .82 |
| | | | | | (.034) | | (.017) | (.023) | (.386) | |
| 73:4 | 25.3 | 6.5 | 1.0 | -1.0 | .462 | .82 | .020 | .055 | .558 | .78 |
| | | | | | (.047) | | (.012) | (.017) | (.280) | |
| 74:4 | 21.9 | 2.4 | 1.0 | -1.0 | .525 | .73 | .013 | .046 | .495 | .77 |
| | | | | | (.058) | | (.009) | (.013) | (.205) | |
| 75:4 | 21.3 | .06 | 1.0 | -1.0 | .523 | .74 | .013 | .052 | .542 | .76 |
| | | | | | (.047) | | (.009) | (.012) | (.224) | |
| 76:4 | 20.6 | .41 | 1.0 | -1.0 | .544 | .72 | .011 | .046 | .445 | .79 |
| | | | | | (.052) | | (.008) | (.011) | (.177) | |
| 77:4 | 18.5 | .36 | 1.0 | -1.0 | .592 | .65 | .009 | .035 | .346 | .82 |
| | | | | | (.068) | | (.007) | (.009) | (.137) | |
| 78:4 | 22.0 | .69 | 1.0 | -1.0 | .584 | .67 | .003 | .037 | .346 | .83 |
| | | | | | (.058) | | (.006) | (.009) | (.134) | |
| 79:4 | 22.9 | .39 | 1.0 | -1.0 | .587 | .65 | .010 | .037 | .345 | .82 |
| | | | | | (.052) | | (.006) | (.009) | (.133) | |
| 80:4 | 23.4 | .95 | 1.0 | -1.0 | .578 | .66 | .015 | .040 | .398 | .80 |
| | | | | | (.048) | | (.007) | (.009) | (.142) | |
| 81:4 | 25.6 | 1.34 | 1.0 | -1.0 | .574 | .66 | .015 | .040 | .377 | .81 |
| | | | | | (.045) | | (.007) | (.009) | (.137) | |
| 82:4 | 29.1 | 2.0 | 1.0 | -1.0 | .593 | .62 | .011 | .042 | .349 | .82 |
| | | | | | (.05) | | (.007) | (.009) | (.13) | |
| 83:4 | 31.9 | 2.1 | 1.0 | -1.0 | .598 | .61 | .010 | .042 | .362 | .82 |
| | | | | | (.044) | | (.007) | (.008) | (.124) | |
| 84:4 | 31.4 | 1.3 | 1.0 | -1.0 | .587 | .64 | .011 | .041 | .384 | .80 |
| | | | | | (.040) | | (.007) | (.008) | (.122) | |
| 85:4 | 32.7 | 2.7 | 1.0 | -1.0 | .597 | .62 | .010 | .040 | .373 | .81 |
| | | | | | (.042) | | (.007) | (.008) | (.117) | |
| 86:4 | 29.0 | 3.2 | 1.0 | -1.0 | .594 | .63 | .012 | .037 | .0351 | .82 |
| | | | | | (.045) | | (.007) | (.009) | (.117) | |
| 87:4 | 26.2 | 2.7 | 1.0 | -1.0 | .606 | .62 | .008 | .034 | .317 | .83 |
| | | | | | (.052) | | (.007) | (.008) | (.110) | |
| 88:4 | 26.7 | 2.7 | 1.0 | -1.0 | .614 | .61 | .007 | .033 | .316 | .83 |
| | | | | | (.053) | | (.007) | (.008) | (.105) | |
| 89:4 | 26.7 | 2.2 | 1.0 | -1.0 | .624 | .59 | .006 | .032 | .301 | .84 |
| | | | | | (.053) | | (.007) | (.007) | (.100) | |
| 90:4 | 24.8 | 2.5 | 1.0 | -1.0 | .655 | .55 | .004 | .028 | .268 | .85 |
| | | | | | (.065) | | (.006) | (.007) | (.091) | |
| 91:4 | 21.5 | 3.5 | 1.0 | -1.0 | .692 | .49 | .005 | .022 | .200 | .88 |
| | | | | | (.090) | | (.005) | (.006) | (.079) | |

Table 6.4: Estimates of Error Correction Parameters, ln(M/P), ln(Y/P), lnRtb, Weak Exogeneity Restrictions on Real Balances (Recursive Estimation with Samples that begin in 1956:2)

| End of Sample | Trace Tests r=0 | r≤0 | | $\beta_c$ | | $\beta_0$ | | $\alpha_c$ | | I-$\beta$'$\alpha$ |
|---|---|---|---|---|---|---|---|---|---|---|
| 75:4 | 19.1 | .01 | 1.0 | -1.0 | .522 | .74 | 0.0 | .047 | .591 | .74 |
| | | | | | (.050) | | | (.016) | (.151) | |
| 80:4 | 18.9 | .69 | 1.0 | -1.0 | .566 | .68 | 0.0 | .035 | .403 | .81 |
| | | | | | (.052) | | | (.013) | (.106) | |
| 85:4 | 28.5 | .69 | 1.0 | -1.0 | .615 | .58 | 0.0 | .037 | .352 | .82 |
| | | | | | (.049) | | | (.012) | (.072) | |
| 91:4 | 18.0 | 0.9 | 1.0 | -1.0 | .733 | .42 | 0.0 | .019 | .179 | .89 |
| | | | | | (.05) | | | (.008) | (.05) | |

period there is strong evidence of a single cointegrating vector. The estimated values of the constant term in the cointegrating vector ($\beta_0$) are also included in Table 6.3. For the samples ending in 77-88 the estimated constant is quite stable in the range of .61 - .65. In the longest sample periods the estimated value becomes smaller as the sample is extended. There is no evidence of any major shift in this parameter at the beginning of the 1980s.

The values of the three "error correction coefficients" are also included in Table 6.3. These estimated coefficients are always positive, and the largest value is always that from the interest rate equation. The estimated error correction coefficient from the real balance equation is always the smallest of the three. The general conclusion that emerges from these estimates is that only real balances can be assumed "weakly exogenous". In particular, weak exogeneity of the nominal interest rate is strongly rejected, in spite of the attention of the Fed to setting short-run nominal interest rate targets during most of the sample period. Weak exogeneity of real balances is rejected in only three recursive estimations (72:4, 80:4 and 81:4) at conventional levels of significance. The estimated variance is constructed from the likelihood ratio test of Johansen ((1991), Theorem 3.2) that in this model is asymptotically distributed as $\chi^2_{(1)}$.

The tabulations in Table 6.4 show the estimated equilibrium parameters for selected years under the restriction that real balances are weakly exogenous. A comparison of these estimates with the corresponding values when the $\alpha_c$ vector is not restricted shows that the remaining parameter estimates are not affected in any economically or statistically significant way by the imposition of the weak exogeneity restriction (including those for the sample period ending in 80:4).

Frequently, the estimated coefficients of the error correction matrix ($\alpha_c$) are discussed as measures of "speeds of adjustment" towards the equilibrium relationship(s) determined by the cointegrating vector(s). Our view is that this interpretation is misleading. Consider the VECM structure discussed at length in Chapter 3:

$$\Delta z_t = \mu + \sum_{i=1}^{q-1} \Pi_i^* \Delta z_{t-i} - \alpha\beta' z_{t-1} + \varepsilon_t \tag{6.1}$$

Premultiply (6.1) by $\beta'$:

$$\beta' z_t - \beta' z_{t-1} = \beta'\mu + \sum_{i=1}^{q-1} \beta'\Pi_i^* \Delta z_{t-i} - \beta'\alpha\beta z_{t-1} + \beta'\varepsilon_t \tag{6.2}$$

and collect all the terms in $\beta' z_t$ on the left hand side:

$$[I - (I - \beta'\alpha)L]\beta' z_t = \beta'\mu + \sum_{i=1}^{q-1} \beta'\Pi_i^* \Delta z_{t-i} + \beta'\varepsilon_t \tag{6.3}$$

This reveals that $\beta' z_t$ is a first order vector autoregressive process with a moving average component determined by the stationary $\varepsilon_t$ processes, since $\Delta z_t$ has a Wold representation in terms of the $\varepsilon_t$ (see Chapter 3). Invertibility and the speed of adjustment of $\beta' z_t$ is determined by the eigenvalues of the matrix $(I - \beta'\alpha)$ (Hamilton (1994), pp. 11-16). In the model estimated here, $(I - \beta'\alpha)$ is a scalar, so the speed of adjustment is determined by the size of $(I - \beta'\alpha)$, which must be less than one in absolute value. This measure of the speed of adjustment is estimated at .80 - .85 for all but the longest sample period.

### 6.2.2 Estimates with a Dummy Variable for the Period After the "New Operating Procedures"

In much of our previous work (Hoffman and Rasche (1991)) we have included a dummy variable, D82, which is zero through the end of 1981 an is one thereafter. It is shown in Yoshida and Rasche (1990) that the inclusion of such a dummy variable in a VECM specification can represent changes in the intercepts (constants) of the cointegrating vectors, changes in the deterministic trends in the nonstationary portion of the data generating process, or a combination of the two. In our previous analysis of U.S. data we have not found any significant change in the intercept of the single cointegrating vector, and have concluded that the significant estimated coefficients on this dummy variable are attributable to shifts in the deterministic trends in the data generating process.

The existence of a single cointegrating vector for M1 velocity and short-term interest rates with no change in the slope coefficient or intercept during the sample period implies that there is only one (common) trend between M1 velocity and the short-term rate of interest. This implies that the observed deterministic trend in velocity is proportional to the short-term nominal interest rate during the sample period (Engle and Yoo (1987)). Therefore, a "shift in the drift" in velocity is the mirror image of a "shift in the drift" in nominal interest rates.

One hypothesis about the "shift in the drift" of M1 velocity, apparently initially advanced by Milton Friedman, is that the change in velocity behavior in the 1980s is a result of a break in inflation expectations. This hypothesis, among others, is investigated indirectly in Rasche (1987) using single equation techniques. Little support for that hypothesis was found. In the absence of direct effects of expected inflation in single equation estimates of the demand for real balances, there is no intuitive explanation of how a break in such expectations generates a "shift in the drift" of velocity.

The realization that any velocity shift is just the image of a shift in the deterministic trend of nominal interest rates provides the missing intuition for the expected inflation hypothesis. If the post-Accord period through the end of the 1970s is characterized by a steady upward drift in inflation expectations, then it is reasonable to conjecture that this drift is reflected in nominal interest rates.[10] If inflation expectations stabilized in the 1981-2 recession and subsequently remained constant, then a reasonable conjecture is that there is no drift in nominal interest rates during the 1980s.

One source of evidence consistent with the hypothesis of a break in the drift of inflation expectations around the end of 1981 is the Livingston survey data on inflation expectations. The survey dates from the late 1940s. The data on one year ahead inflation expectations show a general upward trend through 1980 and then a sharp downward break. Since 1982 the series has fluctuated without trend.[11]

If published inflation forecasts are taken as representative of inflation expectations there is a second source of evidence in support of a break in the drift of inflation expectations around the 1981-2 period. The annual CEA forecasts of the GNP deflator, as tabulated in McNees (1988), trend steadily upward from the first available observation in 1962 through 1981. then the forecast rates drop precipitously in 1981-2 and stabilize in the 3-4 percent range through the 1987. The forecasts for 1988 through 1991 in the respective Annual Reports of the Council of Economic Advisers are 3.9, 3,7 , 4.2 and 4.3 percent respectively. Belongia (1988) analyzes GNP deflator forecasts for the 1976-87 period from five sources: the CEA, the CBO, the ASA/NBER panel and from two major economic consulting firms. He finds that the forecasts of the latter four sources closely parallel those of the CEA. Thus the historical *ex ante* inflation forecasts are consistent with the hypothesis that inflation expectations stabilized in the early 1980s and have not drifted since.

This interpretation suggests that there are "Lucas effects" associated with the implementation of a credible disinflationary monetary policy. Under this hypothesis, when agents come to believe that the monetary policy regime has switched from one that permits accelerating inflation to one of stable or decelerating inflation, then the monetary authorities should expect that there will be a change in the average growth rate of the velocity of narrowly defined monetary aggregates. It this average growth rate declines, then it will not be necessary

[10]There are three cases consistent with this conjecture: a) expected inflation is stationary around a trend, so real rates are I(1); b) expected inflation is I(1) with drift and real rates are I(1); or c) expected inflation is I(1) and real rates are stationary. These alternatives are not identified in analyses that determine a single cointegrating vector between velocity and nominal interest rates. For tests of these computing hypotheses see Chapter 7.

[11]It would be interesting to know if these inflation expectations are an I(0) or an I(1) series. With only about 30 nonoverlapping observations it is unlikely that any test of the unit root hypothesis would provide a reliable discrimination between the two alternatives.

to slow the growth of the monetary aggregates as much as appears from an examination of the historical data generated by the accelerating inflation policy regime in order to accomplish the objective of a constant or declining rate of inflation. For example, using the data from the 60s and 70s it was generally believed that to stabilize the inflation rate in the U.S. at four percent per year, the Fed would have to achieve a long-run growth rate of M1 of the order of three percent per year to allow for the historical drift of M1 velocity of around three percent. If agents come to believe that inflation has stabilized, and this in turn eliminates the drift of M1 velocity by eliminating the drift in nominal interest rates, then a long-run growth objective of M1 of six percent per year will accomplish the objective of stable inflation at four percent per year.

Recursive regressions for samples ending in the fourth quarter of each year, 1982-91 with the dummy variable are given in at the top of Table 6.5. The inclusion of the dummy variable does not affect the inference that there is a single cointegrating vector among the three variables. In contrast to the estimates in Table 6.3, there is no drift in the estimated interest elasticity; it remains very stable at .58 as the sample period is extended through 91:4.

The estimated intercept of the cointegrating vector is the first value tabulated under $\beta_0$ in Table 6.5. The second value is the estimated shift in the intercept in the period subsequent to 81:4. With the exception of the sample period ending in 82:4, where the shift in the intercept is estimated on the basis of only four observations, the estimated shift is small in absolute value and fluctuates around zero. The estimated speed of adjustment parameter remains in the .80-.85 range, consistent with the values reported in Table 6.3 for the sample periods ending in the 1970s. The error correction model for sample periods ending in 82:4 - 91:4 was reestimated with the shift in the mean of the cointegrating vector restricted to zero. Results are tabulated at the bottom of Table 6.5. In all cases the likelihood ratio test comparing the restricted and unrestricted estimations fails to reject the restriction. None of the point estimates of $\alpha_c$ or $\beta_c$ are changed by the imposition of the restriction.

In this expanded VECM, weak exogeneity of real balances is rejected in the sample periods that end in the early 1980s. However, when the model is reestimated (Table 6.6) for selected sample periods subject to the restriction that real balances are weakly exogenous, the remaining parameter estimates are essentially unchanged from the values obtained without the $\alpha_c$ restriction. This is true of the sample period ending in 85:4 where the likelihood ratio test suggests a strong rejection of the restriction.

Our conclusion from the results reported in Table 6.5 is that all the characteristics of the cointegrating vector among real M1, real GDP, and the Treasury bill rate in the U.S., including the adjustment process of deviations from that cointegrating vector are extremely stable once the VECM specification allows for a shift in the drift of the nonstationary processes associated with the different inflation regime of the 80s compared to the inflation regime of the previous 25 years.

It should be noted that the weak exogeneity restrictions in Table 6.6 are not consistent with the weak exogeneity predicted for such a VECM by the ratio-

Table 6.5: Estimates of Error Correction Parameters, ln(M/P), ln(Y/P), lnRtb with D82 (Recursive Estimation with Samples that begin in 1956:2),

| End of Sample | Trace Tests r=0 | $r \leq 0$ | | $\beta_c$ | | $\beta_0$ | | $\alpha_c$ | | I-$\beta$'$\alpha$ |
|---|---|---|---|---|---|---|---|---|---|---|
| 82:4 | 26.4 | 1.2 | 1.0 | -1.0 | .575 | .66 | .015 | .041 | .367 | .81 |
| | | | | | (.04) | -.20 | (.007) | (.009) | (.137) | |
| 83:4 | 27.2 | 1.3 | 1.0 | -1.0 | .575 | .66 | .016 | .041 | .372 | .81 |
| | | | | | (.05) | -.09 | (.007) | (.009) | (.135) | |
| 84:4 | 27.8 | 1.3 | 1.0 | -1.0 | .577 | .66 | .017 | .040 | .362 | .81 |
| | | | | | (.044) | -.02 | (.007) | (.009) | (.132) | |
| 85:4 | 27.6 | 1.3 | 1.0 | -1.0 | .580 | .65 | .018 | .039 | .347 | .82 |
| | | | | | (.045) | -.02 | (.007) | (.009) | (.124) | |
| 86:4 | 25.0 | 1.3 | 1.0 | -1.0 | .586 | .64 | .020 | .034 | .306 | .83 |
| | | | | | (.050) | -.00 | (.007) | (.009) | (.126) | |
| 87:4 | 22.0 | 1.4 | 1.0 | -1.0 | .585 | .64 | .015 | .034 | .283 | .85 |
| | | | | | (.055) | .07 | (.007) | (.008) | (.123) | |
| 88:4 | 23.6 | 1.2 | 1.0 | -1.0 | .579 | .65 | .011 | .034 | .330 | .83 |
| | | | | | (.053) | .06 | (.007) | (.008) | (.117) | |
| 89:4 | 25.2 | 1.3 | 1.0 | -1.0 | .580 | .65 | .008 | .034 | .335 | .83 |
| | | | | | (.053) | .07 | (.007) | (.008) | (113) | |
| 90:4 | 23.2 | 1.4 | 1.0 | -1.0 | .577 | .66 | .007 | .032 | .337 | .83 |
| | | | | | (.056) | .08 | (.007) | (.008) | (.111) | |
| 91:4 | 19.5 | 1.4 | 1.0 | -1.0 | .580 | .65 | .009 | .027 | .281 | .86 |
| | | | | | (.066) | .10 | (.006) | (.007) | (.104) | |

($\beta_0$ Shift)

| End of Sample | Trace Tests r=0 | $r \leq 0$ | | $\beta_c$ | | $\beta_0$ | | $\alpha_c$ | | I-$\beta$'$\alpha$ |
|---|---|---|---|---|---|---|---|---|---|---|
| 82:4 | 26.2 | 1.2 | 1.0 | -1.0 | .576 | .65 | .015 | .041 | ..367 | .81 |
| | | | | | (.04) | .00 | (.007) | (.008) | (.128) | |
| 83:4 | 27.2 | 1.2 | 1.0 | -1.0 | .575 | .65 | .016 | .041 | .372 | .81 |
| | | | | | (.044) | .00 | (.007) | (.008) | (.124) | |
| 84:4 | 27.8 | 1.3 | 1.0 | -1.0 | .577 | .66 | .017 | .040 | .362 | .81 |
| | | | | | (.044) | .00 | (.007) | (.008) | (.120) | |
| 85:4 | 27.6 | 1.3 | 1.0 | -1.0 | .580 | .65 | .018 | .039 | .347 | .82 |
| | | | | | (.045) | .00 | (.006) | (.008) | (.118) | |
| 86:4 | 25.0 | 1.3 | 1.0 | -1.0 | .586 | .64 | .020 | .034 | .306 | .83 |
| | | | | | (.050) | .00 | (.006) | (.008) | (.114) | |
| 87:4 | 21.9 | 1.4 | 1.0 | -1.0 | .586 | .66 | .015 | .034 | .283 | .85 |
| | | | | | (.055) | .00 | (.007) | (.008) | (.110) | |
| 88:4 | 23.5 | 1.2 | 1.0 | -1.0 | .579 | .67 | .011 | .034 | .329 | .83 |
| | | | | | (.053) | .00 | (.007) | (.008) | (.112) | |
| 89:4 | 25.1 | 1.3 | 1.0 | -1.0 | .580 | .67 | .008 | .034 | .334 | .83 |
| | | | | | (.053) | .00 | (.007) | (.007) | (.107) | |
| 90:4 | 23.1 | 1.3 | 1.0 | -1.0 | .578 | .68 | .007 | .032 | .337 | .83 |
| | | | | | (.056) | .00 | (.007) | (.007) | (.105) | |
| 91:4 | 19.2 | 1.4 | 1.0 | -1.0 | .581 | .68 | .009 | .027 | .280 | .86 |
| | | | | | (.066) | .00 | (.006) | (.007) | (.098) | |

Table 6.6: Estimates of Error Correction Parameters, ln(M/P), ln(Y/P), ln(Rtb) with D82 and Indicated Restrictions on the Constant Term and Error Correction Parameter in the Real Balances Equation(Recursive Estimation with Samples that Begin in 1956:2)

| End of Sample | Trace Tests r=0 | $r\leq0$ | $\beta_c$ | | | $\beta_0$ | | $\alpha_c$ | | L.R.T. $H_0$ : $(\alpha_1 = 0)$ |
|---|---|---|---|---|---|---|---|---|---|---|
| 82:4 | 21.0 | 0.9 | 1.0 | -1.0 | .564 | .66 | .00 | .036 | .375 | 4.91 |
| | | | | | (.048) | .00 | | (.008) | (.131) | |
| 83:4 | 21.4 | 0.9 | 1.0 | -1.0 | .562 | .67 | .00 | .036 | .375 | 5.38 |
| | | | | | (.05) | .00 | | (.008) | (.128) | |
| 84:4 | 21.2 | 1.0 | 1.0 | -1.0 | .565 | .67 | .00 | .037 | .368 | 5.69 |
| | | | | | (.047) | .00 | | (.008) | (.123) | |
| 85:4 | 20.9 | 1.1 | 1.0 | -1.0 | .569 | .66 | .00 | .036 | .355 | 6.50 |
| | | | | | (.049) | .00 | | (.008) | (.121) | |
| 86:4 | 16.7 | 1.2 | 1.0 | -1.0 | .577 | .65 | .00 | .032 | .325 | 8.15 |
| | | | | | (.06) | .00 | | (.008) | (.117) | |
| 87:4 | 17.6 | 1.4 | 1.0 | -1.0 | .583 | .66 | .00 | .032 | .285 | 4.28 |
| | | | | | (.006) | .00 | | (.008) | (.113) | |
| 88:4 | 21.1 | 1.2 | 1.0 | -1.0 | .580 | .67 | .00 | .033 | .331 | 2.40 |
| | | | | | (.057) | .00 | | (.008) | (.110) | |
| 89:4 | 23.6 | 1.3 | 1.0 | -1.0 | .582 | .67 | .00 | .033 | .335 | 1.44 |
| | | | | | (.055) | .00 | | (.007) | (.106) | |
| 90:4 | 21.9 | 1.3 | 1.0 | -1.0 | .58 | .67 | .00 | .031 | .337 | 1.10 |
| | | | | | (.058) | .00 | | (.007) | (.105) | |
| 91:4 | 17.4 | 1.4 | 1.0 | -1.0 | .585 | .67 | .00 | .026 | .280 | 1.82 |
| | | | | | (.071) | .00 | | (.007) | (.098) | |

nal expectations model in Chapter 5 (equation 5.45). In addition to rational expectations and flexible prices, that model assumed natural output to be independent of the expected rate of inflation (equation 5.6) and monetary policy to be determined by an exogenous money growth rule (equation 5.11). Changes in these assumptions will alter the model predictions about weak exogeneity. Thus the estimates in Table 6.6 can be interpreted as a rejection of the joint hypothesis of exogenous natural output and no feedback money growth rule.

### 6.2.3 Semi–Log Functional Forms

It is constructive to undertake a careful analysis of a semi–log functional form for the demand for real balances a) because this functional form is more easily incorporated into the VECMs of higher dimension, b) because of the sensitivity of the Friedman-Kuttner conclusions to the choice of functional form and c) because of the widespread use of this functional form in theoretical analyses.

The basic results from recursive estimations are tabulated in Table 6.7. At first glance the estimates of the Johansen test statistics for the shortest sample periods suggest two cointegrating vectors between velocity and the Treasury bill rate. This implies that both variables are stationary, contrary to established univariate evidence on these time series. In other respects the results for the shorter samples are also peculiar. The estimated $\alpha_c$ values suggest that nominal interest rates are weakly exogenous (in contradiction to the inference that there

Table 6.7: Estimates of Error Correction Parameters, ln(M/P), ln(Y/P), Rtb (Recursive estimation with samples that begin in 1956:2-Excluding 79:4-81:4)

| End of Sample | Trace Tests r=0 | r≤0 | | $\beta_c$ | | $\beta_0$ | | $\alpha_c$ | | I-$\beta'\alpha$ |
|---|---|---|---|---|---|---|---|---|---|---|
| 72:4 | 30.3 | 11.1 | 1.0 | -1.0 | .095 | 1.1 | .048 | .048 | -.0001 | 1.0 |
| | | | | | (.008) | | (.018) | (.027) | (1.0) | |
| 73:4 | 29.0 | 10.6 | 1.0 | -1.0 | .107 | 1.0 | .037 | .056 | .847 | .92 |
| | | | | | (.010) | | (.016) | (.026) | (1.15) | |
| 74:4 | 25.9 | 5.1 | 1.0 | -1.0 | .124 | .92 | .029 | .050 | 1.01 | .90 |
| | | | | | (.011) | | (0.11) | (.015) | (.810) | |
| 75:4 | 21.5 | .13 | 1.0 | -1.0 | .129 | .90 | .025 | .055 | 1.18 | .88 |
| | | | | | (.011) | | (.009) | (.013) | (.785) | |
| 76:4 | 19.6 | .28 | 1.0 | -1.0 | .136 | .88 | .020 | .047 | .872 | .91 |
| | | | | | (.013) | | (.008) | (.012) | (.680) | |
| 77:4 | 17.4 | .05 | 1.0 | -1.0 | .149 | .83 | .015 | .033 | .800 | .90 |
| | | | | | (.018) | | (.006) | (.009) | (.515) | |
| 78:4 | 21.6 | .29 | 1.0 | -1.0 | .144 | .84 | .016 | .036 | .886 | .89 |
| | | | | | (.014) | | (.006) | (.009) | (.506) | |
| 79:3 | 21.2 | .59 | 1.0 | -1.0 | .137 | .86 | .016 | .037 | .864 | .90 |
| | | | | | (.013) | | (.006) | (.009) | (.532) | |
| 82:4 | 23.1 | 1.1 | 1.0 | -1.0 | .129 | .88 | .005 | .028 | .798 | .92 |
| | | | | | (.015) | | (.005) | (.006) | (.430) | |
| 83:4 | 25.7 | 1.3 | 1.0 | -1.0 | .130 | .87 | .004 | .028 | .838 | .92 |
| | | | | | (.015) | | (.004) | (.006) | (.412) | |
| 84:4 | 25.6 | 1.3 | 1.0 | -1.0 | .126 | .90 | .004 | .026 | 1.01 | .90 |
| | | | | | (.014) | | (.004) | (.006) | (.414) | |
| 85:4 | 26.6 | 2.4 | 1.0 | -1.0 | .131 | .87 | .003 | .024 | 1.02 | .89 |
| | | | | | (.016) | | (.004) | (.006) | (.391) | |
| 86:4 | 20.1 | 3.1 | 1.0 | -1.0 | .127 | .89 | .006 | .026 | .856 | .91 |
| | | | | | (.018) | | (.005) | (.007) | (.408) | |
| 87:4 | 16.6 | 2.7 | 1.0 | -1.0 | .138 | .86 | .001 | .016 | .716 | .92 |
| | | | | | (.027) | | (.004) | (.005) | (.343) | |
| 88:4 | 16.9 | 2.3 | 1.0 | -1.0 | .137 | .86 | .001 | .016 | .763 | .91 |
| | | | | | (.025) | | (.004) | (.005) | (.338) | |
| 89:4 | 17.3 | 2.1 | 1.0 | -1.0 | .139 | .86 | .001 | .016 | .766 | .91 |
| | | | | | (.023) | | (.004) | (.005) | (.333) | |
| 90:4 | 15.8 | 1.8 | 1.0 | -1.0 | .154 | .78 | .001 | .013 | .645 | .91 |
| | | | | | (.032) | | (.003) | (.004) | (.278) | |
| 91:4 | 14.4 | 3.1 | 1.0 | -1.0 | .175 | .67 | .001 | .009 | .458 | .93 |
| | | | | | (.053) | | (.003) | (.003) | (.218) | |

are two cointegrating vectors) and that real balances are not weakly exogenous, in contradiction to the results with the log linear specification. Finally, for the very shortest sample $I - \beta'\alpha$ is estimated at 1.0 that implies that adjustment does not occur to the specified cointegrating vector. Our interpretation of these results is that they are attributable to inadequate sample size.

This conclusion is supported by the behavior of the estimated results as the sample size is increased. Once the sample is extended beyond the end of 1974, the Johansen test statistics consistently support the hypothesis of one cointegrating vector, the value of the estimated interest rate semielasticity becomes quite stable in the range of .13-.14, and the estimated constant of the cointegrating vector becomes stable at approximately .85. $I - \beta'\alpha$ is estimated at approximately .90, implying a somewhat slower speed of adjustment for $\beta' z_t$ than is estimated from the log linear specification. These results are maintained as the sample period is extended through the 1980s as long as the New Operating Procedures period, defined here as 79:4 - 81:4, is omitted from the regressions. The only substantial difference between the sample periods ending in the late 1970s and those extending into the 1980s is the inference about weak exogeneity. In the samples that include data from the 1980s the inference from this model is consistent with that from the log linear model: real balances appear weakly exogenous and weak exogeneity is rejected for nominal interest rates.

The effect of the 79:4 - 81:4 subsample can be seen in the estimates tabulated in Table 6.8. In these estimations the 79:4 - 81:4 period is included in the samples, but two dummy variables are added to the specification. The first, D79 is zero through 79:3 and one thereafter. The second, D82, is zero through 81:4 and one thereafter. The second and third estimated coefficients under $\beta_0$ indicate the estimated shift in the mean of the cointegrating vector at the points where the values of the two dummy variables change from zero to one. The implication of these estimated coefficients is that there is a large reduction in the mean of the equilibrium demand for real balances at the beginning of the New Operating Procedures period, which is essentially reversed at the beginning of 1982.[12] With the exception of the sample period ending in 91:4, the Johansen trace and maximum eigenvalue statistics are both consistent with a single cointegrating vector among the three variables, even though the New Operating Procedures period is included in the samples. The estimated interest rate semielasticities are not changed in any economically significant amount from the estimates reported in Table 6.7.

The implication of the shift in the mean in the semi-log cointegrating vector during the period of the New Operating Procedures is that the equilibrium demand equation for real balances shifted upward during this period (as conventionally plotted with the nominal interest rate on the vertical axis). Three implied equilibrium velocity functions are plotted in Figure 6.4. The double log specification uses the parameter estimates from the 85:4 sample period in Table 6.3. The semi-log and semi-log with D79 shift specifications use the parameter estimates from the 85:4 sample period in Table 6.8. It is important to remember that both the double log and the semi-log functional forms impose a nonlinear relationship on the equilibrium velocity as a function of the nominal interest rate.

Both functional forms produce a vertical asymptote at zero velocity.[13] There are no degrees of freedom in establishing the curvature of either functional form. Once the slope parameter estimate has been determined, the speed at which $M/Y$ approaches the vertical asymptote is determined. Since the elasticity of

[12]We tested the restriction that the mean of the cointegrating vector is the same after 1981 as it was before 1979:4. In no case was the restriction rejected, and the parameter estimates under the restriction are unchanged from those reported in Table 6.8.

[13]An alternative functional form which has both a vertical asymptote at $M/Y = 0$ and a horizontal intercept is a double log specification with $\ln(1 + .01 \times Rtb)$. This form shares the property of the semilog form that the elasticity of velocity with respect to *Rtb* increases as *Rtb* increases, though it does not quite increase linearly as in the former case. Consequently, the problems that are evident from the semilog specification in fitting the high interest rate observations will be shared by the $\ln(1 + .01 \times Rtb)$ specification.

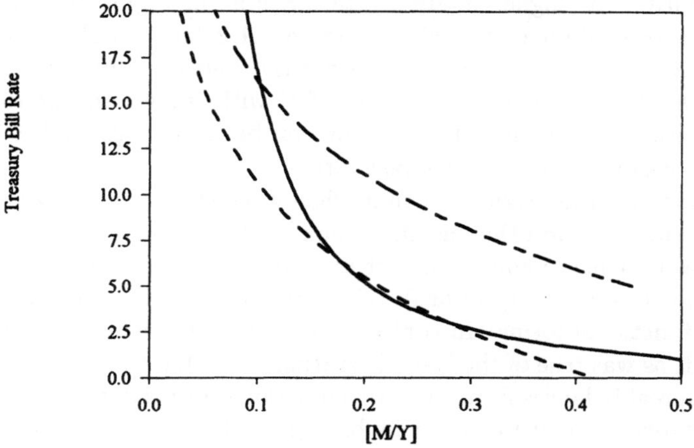


Figure 6.4: Equilibrium Money Demand Functions

Table 6.8: Estimates of Error Correction Parameters, ln(M/P), ln(Y/P), Rtb with D79 and D82(Recursive Estimation with samples that begin in 1956:2)

| End of Sample | Trace Tests r=0 | r≤0 | $\beta_c$ | | | $\beta_0$ | | | $\alpha_c$ | | | I-$\beta$'$\alpha$ |
|---|---|---|---|---|---|---|---|---|---|---|---|---|
| 82:4 | 18.1 | .30 | 1.0 | -1.0 | .135 (.016) | .87 | -.68 | .37 | .013 (.006) | .031 (.008) | 1.75 (.763) | .78 |
| 83:4 | 18.6 | .40 | 1.0 | -1.0 | .134 (.016) | .87 | -.71 | .53 | .012 (.006) | .030 (.008) | 1.66 (.723) | .80 |
| 84:4 | 22.0 | .50 | 1.0 | -1.0 | .136 (.016) | .87 | -.75 | .62 | .010 (.006) | .032 (.007) | 1.60 (.677) | .80 |
| 85:4 | 19.7 | .51 | 1.0 | -1.0 | .134 (.017) | .87 | -.75 | .67 | .012 (.005) | .028 (.007) | 1.42 (.652) | .83 |
| 86:4 | 16.1 | .36 | 1.0 | -1.0 | .130 (.019) | .89 | -.73 | .71 | .016 (.005) | .021 (.007) | 1.08 (.635) | .86 |
| 87:4 | 11.4 | .63 | 1.0 | -1.0 | .126 (.023) | .91 | -.76 | .90 | .010 (.005) | .020 (.007) | .929 (.606) | .89 |
| 88:4 | 14.9 | .64 | 1.0 | -1.0 | .125 (.023) | .91 | -.69 | .77 | .005 (.005) | .019 (.006) | 1.41 (.520) | .84 |
| 89:4 | 17.4 | .75 | 1.0 | -1.0 | .127 (.023) | .91 | -.70 | .76 | .004 (.004) | .019 (.005) | 1.47 (.486) | .83 |
| 90:4 | 16.1 | .78 | 1.0 | -1.0 | .127 (.025) | .91 | -.70 | .77 | .003 (.004) | .016 (.005) | 1.48 (.470) | .83 |
| 91:4 | 13.1 | .73 | 1.0 | -1.0 | .122 (.027) | .93 | -.69 | .83 | .005 (.004) | .013 (.005) | 1.28 (.448) | .85 |

velocity with respect to *Rtb* increases for the semi-log function as *Rtb* increases, when the double log and semi-log functions are very close at low interest rates as in Figure 6.4, the semi-log function will necessarily approach the vertical asymptote faster at higher interest rate levels as in Figure 6.4. Finally, the reciprocal specification discussed in Section 6.1.2 has the characteristic of a horizontal asymptote at $Rtb = 0$ and a positive vertical asymptote at $M/Y = exp(\beta_0)$. On this function the elasticity of $V$ with respect to *Rtb* decreases as *Rtb* increases. Consequently this function can be to the right of the double log function in Figure 6.4 at high interest rates.

It is apparent from Figure 6.4 that when interest rates are low (< nine percent) the double log and the unshifted semi-log functional forms are very close. For samples in which nominal interest rates fluctuate between roughly two and nine percent it will be very difficult, if not impossible, to discriminate between these two functional forms. In contrast, when nominal interest rates go above ten percent, as was true of the New Operating Procedures period, the estimated equilibrium real balances from these two functional forms diverges substantially. Since the implicit curvature in the double log functional form fits the data of the New Operating Procedures period substantially better than that of the semi-log functional form, inclusion of the D79 and D82 dummy variables allows the necessary upward shift in the estimated equilibrium demand for real balances under the semi-log specification to approximate this high interest rate period. This clearly illustrates why the Friedman-Kuttner result is not a rejection of cointegration, but a reflection of the inadequacy of their choice of functional form. As long as the analysis of the U.S. economy is restricted to periods when nominal interest rates are less than 10 percent, either functional form should be adequate. For conditions under which nominal interest rates fluctuate over a wider range than this, inference based on models with a semi-log specification and an assumption of a stable mean of the cointegrating vector is likely to be misleading.

### 6.2.4 Alternative Estimation Techniques

Stock and Watson (1993) have questioned the usefulness of the Johansen reduced rank FIML estimation procedure in small sample situations, and have proposed alternative estimators (see Chapter 3, section 4.1). In order to evaluate the sensitivity or our results to our choice of estimation technique, we have estimated equilibrium demand equations for real balances using the Stock-Watson DOLS estimator. For this analysis we assume that there exists one and only one cointegrating vector among the three variables $ln(M/P)$, $ln(Y/P)$ and *Rtb* or $\ln Rtb$. In all cases we have imposed a unitary long-run income elasticity on the demand for real balances, and have normalized the Stock-Watson estimating equation on velocity. All equations are augmented with leads and lags of up to order 2 in changes in both real income and nominal interest rates. Four lags are used to estimate autocorrelation coefficients for the standard error adjustment.

The recursive DOLS estimates are tabulated in Tables 6.9 and 6.10 for the double log specification.

**Table 6.9: DOLS Estimates, ln(M/P), ln(Y/P), lnRtb (Recursive Estimation with samples that begin in 1956:2)**

| End of Sample | ln*Rtb* | Constant |
|---|---|---|
| 72:4 | 0.40 | 0.80 |
| | (0.04) | (0.06) |
| 73:4 | 0.42 | 0.79 |
| | (0.04) | (0.06) |
| 74:4 | 0.44 | 0.79 |
| | (0.04) | (0.07) |
| 75:4 | 0.45 | 0.77 |
| | (0.04) | (0.07) |
| 76:4 | 0.47 | 0.74 |
| | (0.08) | (0.13) |
| 77:4 | 0.49 | 0.71 |
| | (0.10) | (0.17) |
| 78:4 | 0.51 | 0.68 |
| | (0.08) | (0.15) |
| 79:4 | 0.52 | 0.67 |
| | (0.08) | (0.14) |
| 80:4 | 0.52 | 0.68 |
| | (0.07) | (0.13) |
| 81:4 | 0.51 | 0.68 |
| | (0.06) | (0.12) |
| 82:4 | 0.51 | 0.69 |
| | (0.05) | (0.11) |
| 83:4 | 0.50 | 0.71 |
| | (0.05) | (0.10) |
| 84:4 | 0.50 | 0.70 |
| | (0.05) | (0.09) |
| 85:4 | 0.51 | 0.69 |
| | (0.05) | (0.09) |
| 86:4 | 0.51 | 0.69 |
| | (0.05) | (0.11) |
| 87:4 | 0.52 | 0.69 |
| | (0.05) | (0.11) |
| 88:4 | 0.52 | 0.69 |
| | (0.06) | (0.12) |
| 89:4 | 0.52 | 0.68 |
| | (0.06) | (0.12) |
| 90:4 | 0.53 | 0.70 |
| | (0.07) | (0.15) |

Table 6.10: DOLS Estimates, ln(M/P), ln(Y/P), lnRtb, D82 (Recursive Estimation with samples that begin in 1956:2)

| End of Sample | ln*Rtb* | Constant | D82 |
|---|---|---|---|
| 82:4 | 0.51 | 0.69 | 0.01 |
| | (0.06) | (0.12) | (0.12) |
| 83:4 | 0.51 | 0.70 | -0.02 |
| | (0.06) | (0.11) | (0.10) |
| 84:4 | 0.51 | 0.70 | -0.01 |
| | (0.05) | (0.11) | (0.09) |
| 85:4 | 0.51 | 0.70 | 0.01 |
| | (0.06) | (0.11) | (0.08) |
| 86:4 | 0.50 | 0.72 | 0.05 |
| | (0.06) | (0.12) | (0.08) |
| 87:4 | 0.49 | 0.73 | 0.06 |
| | (0.06) | (0.12) | (0.07) |
| 88:4 | 0.49 | 0.74 | 0.08 |
| | (0.06) | (0.11) | (0.07) |
| 89:4 | 0.48 | 0.74 | 0.08 |
| | (0.06) | (0.11) | (0.06) |
| 90:4 | 0.48 | 0.77 | 0.10 |
| | (0.06) | (0.12) | (0.06) |

In Table 6.10 the estimated equation includes the dummy variable D82. In no case is the estimated coefficient on this dummy variable significant at conventional levels. This is consistent with our conclusion from the Johansen estimates that there is no consistent evidence of a shift in the mean of the cointegrating vector with this functional form. The DOLS estimates of the equilibrium interest elasticity of velocity are always somewhat smaller than those from the Johansen estimator for the comparable sample period (see Figure 6.5).This is the same result as found by Hoffman, Rasche and Tieslau (1995). In most cases the point estimate from the alternative estimator is within a one standard error interval from the point estimate of the estimator under consideration. Regardless of the statistical significance of these differences, there is no difference in the economic implications of the alternative estimates.

The DOLS estimates of the semi-log functional form are included in Tables 6.11 and 6.12. At the top of Table 6.12, the estimating equation is augmented by the two dummy variables, D79 and D82, but in the particular form D79-D82 and D82. The significance of the estimated coefficient on D82 can then be used directly to judge whether any shift in the estimated intercept during the New Operating Procedures period is completely offset at the end of that period. With the exception of the sample period ending in 82:4, where the coefficient on D82 is estimated from four observations, this estimated coefficient is never significantly different from zero. At the bottom of Table 6.12, reestimates of the equation are shown with D82 omitted from the specification. Surprisingly, the substantial point estimates of the shift in the constant term during the period of the New Operating Procedures are never significant.

In contrast to the comparison of the DOLS and Johansen estimates of the

Table 6.11: DOLS Estimates, ln(M/P), ln(Y/P), Rtb (Recursive Estimation with samples that begin in 1956:2)

| End of Sample | ln*Rtb* | Constant |
|---|---|---|
| 72:4 | 0.10 | 0.90 |
| | (0.01) | (0.05) |
| 73:4 | 0.11 | 0.89 |
| | (0.01) | (0.05) |
| 74:4 | 0.11 | 0.89 |
| | (0.01) | (0.05) |
| 75:4 | 0.11 | 0.88 |
| | (0.01) | (0.05) |
| 76:4 | 0.12 | 0.85 |
| | (0.01) | (0.08) |
| 77:4 | 0.12 | 0.83 |
| | (0.02) | (0.11) |
| 78:4 | 0.13 | 0.82 |
| | (0.01) | (0.09) |
| 79:4 | 0.12 | 0.83 |
| | (0.01) | (0.08) |
| 80:4 | 0.11 | 0.87 |
| | (0.02) | (0.11) |
| 81:4 | 0.09 | 0.97 |
| | (0.02) | (0.16) |
| 82:4 | 0.09 | 0.99 |
| | (0.02) | (0.13) |
| 83:4 | 0.09 | 1.01 |
| | (0.01) | (0.12) |
| 84:4 | 0.09 | 1.00 |
| | (0.01) | (0.11) |
| 85:4 | 0.09 | 1.00 |
| | (0.01) | (0.12) |
| 86:4 | 0.09 | 1.00 |
| | (0.02) | (0.14) |
| 87:4 | 0.09 | 1.00 |
| | (0.02) | (0.14) |
| 88:4 | 0.09 | 1.00 |
| | (0.02) | (0.15) |
| 89:4 | 0.09 | 1.00 |
| | (0.02) | (0.15) |
| 90:4 | 0.09 | 1.03 |
| | (0.02) | (0.21) |

Table 6.12: DOLS Estimates, ln(M/P), ln(Y/P), Rtb,D79-D82, D82. (Recursive Estimation with samples that begin in 1956:2)

| End of Sample | *Rtb* | Constant | D79-D82 | D82 |
|---|---|---|---|---|
| 82:4 | 0.114 | 0.868 | -0.283 | -0.292 |
| | (0.01) | (0.09) | (0.11) | (0.11) |
| 83:4 | 0.113 | 0.870 | -0.284 | -0.233 |
| | (0.01) | (0.08) | (0.11) | (0.11) |
| 84:4 | 0.112 | 0.874 | -0.280 | -0.192 |
| | (0.01) | (0.09) | (0.11) | (0.10) |
| 85:4 | 0.108 | 0.898 | -0.252 | -0.125 |
| | (0.02) | (0.10) | (0.14) | (0.12) |
| 86:4 | 0.097 | 0.968 | -0.196 | -0.014 |
| | (0.02) | (0.14) | (0.19) | (0.14) |
| 87:4 | 0.091 | 1.003 | -0.168 | 0.048 |
| | (0.02) | (0.14) | (0.20) | (0.13) |
| 88:4 | 0.090 | 1.017 | -0.162 | 0.074 |
| | (0.02) | (0.13) | (0.19) | (0.11) |
| 89:4 | 0.089 | 1.022 | -0.164 | 0.085 |
| | (0.02) | (0.13) | (0.19) | (0.10) |
| 90:4 | 0.086 | 1.049 | -0.160 | 0.110 |
| | (0.02) | (0.14) | (0.21) | (0.11) |
| | | Excluding D82 | | |
| 82:4 | 0.100 | 0.943 | -0.204 | - |
| | (0.01) | (0.11) | (0.11) | |
| 83:4 | 0.095 | 0.973 | -0.185 | - |
| | (0.01) | (0.11) | (0.11) | |
| 84:4 | 0.094 | 0.979 | -0.180 | - |
| | (0.01) | (0.10) | (0.15) | |
| 85:4 | 0.095 | 0.972 | -0.184 | - |
| | (0.01) | (0.10) | (0.15) | |
| 86:4 | 0.096 | 0.976 | -0.189 | - |
| | (0.01) | (0.11) | (0.17) | |
| 87:4 | 0.097 | 0.975 | -0.197 | - |
| | (0.02) | (0.12) | (0.18) | |
| 88:4 | 0.098 | 0.975 | -0.21 | - |
| | (0.02) | (0.12) | (0.18) | |
| 89:4 | 0.099 | 0.972 | -0.233 | - |
| | (0.01) | (0.11) | (0.17) | |
| 90:4 | 0.100 | 0.989 | -0.257 | - |
| | (0.02) | (0.13) | (0.20) | |

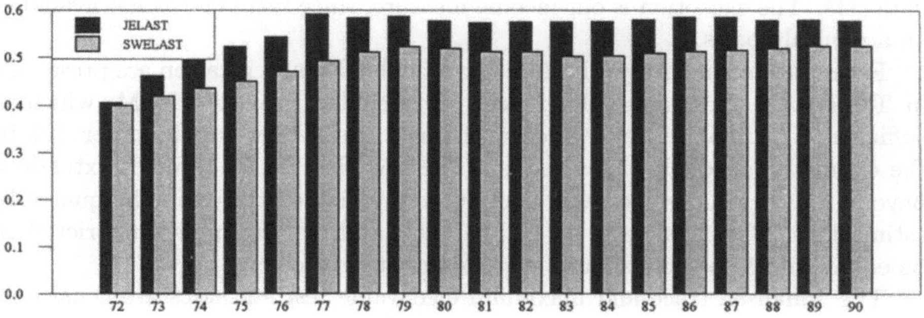


Figure 6.5: Estimated Equilibrium Interest Elasticities

**Note:samples end in fourth quarter of each year**

double log functional form, the differences in the estimated interest semielasticities from the two approaches are substantial for the semi-log specification. For the sample periods ending in the 1980s, the DOLS estimates of the equilibrium semielasticity of velocity (top of Table 6.12) are generally only about 75 percent the size of those obtained from the Johansen estimator (Table 6.8) For the sample periods that end in the 1970s, while the DOLS estimates of the semielasticity of velocity are generally smaller than the estimates from the Johansen procedure, the percentage differences are much smaller than is observed in the longer samples, and are comparable to the percentage differences between the estimates of the elasticity from the double log functional form. Our conclusion from this is that the results from the two estimators are most sensitive when the imposed curvature of the functional form of the estimating equation appears to be inconsistent with the full range of the data.

## 6.3 Time Disaggregation

In Hoffman and Rasche (1991) we estimated cointegrating vectors from monthly observations on a real income measure, an interest rate measure, and either real M1 or the real monetary base. In this section we present a detailed analysis of vector error correction models involving real personal income, real M1 and the Treasury bill rate and examine the consistency of these results with the estimates from quarterly data in the previous section.

In the literature of single equation money demand functions, the degree of time disaggregation presents some of the most confusing results. Estimates of "speeds of adjustment" frequently imply substantially different response patterns when estimated on data sets that are essentially the same except for the frequency of observation. In the results presented here, we have attempted to maintain consistent specifications and samples across quarterly and monthly data sets. The exception is our income measure, since real GDP is not available on a monthly basis.

Estimates of a monthly VECM using a double log specification are presented in Table 6.13. Six lagged differences are included in each VECM, which is sufficient to eliminate any evidence of serial correlation (up to order 12) in the estimated residuals of the model. The specification for samples extending beyond 81:12 includes the same D82 dummy variable utilized in the quarterly estimations. The coefficients on real balances and real income are restricted to be equal but of opposite sign in any cointegrating vector.

The Johansen trace and maximum eigenvalue test statistics are consistent with a single cointegrating vector between the log of velocity and the log of the Treasury bill rate. For samples ending in 75:12 and subsequent years, the estimated equilibrium interest elasticity of velocity ranges from .56 - .68. This compares with a range of .52 - .59 estimated from the quarterly data (Tables 6.3 and 6.5). The estimated AR(1) coefficient in the $\beta' z_t$ process, $[I - \beta'\alpha]$, ranges from .91 - .96 with the most frequent estimate at .94. $(.94)^3 = .83$ that is consistent with the AR(1) parameter of this process in the quarterly data. The estimated shift in the constant term of the cointegrating vector after 81:12 is always small and not significantly different from zero.

The one substantial difference between the estimates based on the monthly observations and those based on the quarterly observations is in the estimated "error correction" vector ($\alpha_c$). In the quarterly based models the coefficients in the real balance equations were always smaller than those in the real GDP equation that in turn were always smaller than those in the interest rate equation. Frequently the coefficients in the real balance equation are not significantly different from zero. In contrast, in the monthly based models, the "error correction" coefficients in the real balance equations and the real income equations are estimated at the same order of magnitude. This may just reflect the substitution of real personal income for real GDP. However, in the monthly based models, there is no evidence to suggest that any of the three variables are weakly exogenous. If the VECM were rewritten as a three variable system in the logs of velocity, real income and the Treasury bill rate, the "error correction" coefficient in the velocity equation would be equal to the difference between the error correction coefficients in the real income and real balance equations. All the other estimated parameters in Table 6.13 would remain unchanged, since this is just a linear transformation of the original structure. Since the estimated "error correction" coefficients in the real balance and real income equations have the same sign, the implied error correction coefficient on velocity is very small in absolute value (the estimates range from -.0019 to .0018). These are not significantly different from zero, implying that velocity is weakly exogenous.

The estimates of the semi-log specification on the monthly data sets are reported in Table 6.14 for samples ending in 72:12 - 79:09 and 82:12 - 91:12. In

Table 6.13: Estimates of Error Correction Parameters, ln(M/P), ln(Y/P), Rtb, D82 (Recursive Estimation with Samples that begin in 1955:8)

| End of Sample | Trace Tests r=0 | r≤0 | $\beta_c$ | | | $\beta_0$ (> 81) | $\alpha_c$ | | | I-$\beta$'$\alpha$ |
|---|---|---|---|---|---|---|---|---|---|---|
| 72:12 | 33.3 | 8.7 | 1.0 | -1.0 | .38 | .70 | .016 | .016 | .110 | .96 |
| | | | | | (.04) | | (.004) | (.005) | (.092) | |
| 73:12 | 26.9 | 4.7 | 1.0 | -1.0 | .440 | .62 | .011 | .013 | .176 | .92 |
| | | | | | (.04) | | (.004) | (.004) | (.030) | |
| 74:12 | 21.7 | .94 | 1.0 | -1.0 | .503 | .53 | .007 | .008 | .189 | .91 |
| | | | | | (.052) | | (.003) | (.004) | (.058) | |
| 75:12 | 17.7 | .25 | 1.0 | -1.0 | .566 | .45 | .005 | .007 | .151 | .92 |
| | | | | | (.072) | | (.003) | (.003) | (.047) | |
| 76:12 | 15.5 | .11 | 1.0 | -1.0 | .642 | .36 | .004 | .006 | .101 | .94 |
| | | | | | (.104) | | (.002) | (.003) | (.037) | |
| 77:12 | 16.5 | .17 | 1.0 | -1.0 | .668 | .33 | .004 | .005 | .095 | .94 |
| | | | | | (1.06) | | (.002) | (.002) | (.033) | |
| 78:12 | 17.5 | .01 | 1.0 | -1.0 | .652 | .35 | .004 | .005 | .100 | .94 |
| | | | | | (.090) | | (.002) | (.002) | (.033) | |
| 79:12 | 18.5 | .33 | 1.0 | -1.0 | .644 | .35 | .005 | .006 | .095 | .94 |
| | | | | | (.081) | | (.002) | (.002) | (.033) | |
| 80:12 | 19.6 | 1.2 | 1.0 | -1.0 | .630 | .36 | .006 | .005 | .091 | .94 |
| | | | | | (.075) | | (.002) | (.002) | (.035) | |
| 81:12 | 21.3 | 1.3 | 1.0 | -1.0 | .610 | .39 | .006 | .005 | .094 | .94 |
| | | | | | (.066) | | (.002) | (.002) | (.054) | |
| 82:12 | 22.2 | 1.3 | 1.0 | -1.0 | .612 | .39 | .007 | .005 | .091 | .94 |
| | | | | | (.065) | .04 | (.002) | (.002) | (.035) | |
| 83:12 | 23.4 | 1.4 | 1.0 | -1.0 | .612 | .39 | .007 | .005 | .091 | .94 |
| | | | | | (.064) | .01 | (.002) | (.002) | (.034) | |
| 84:12 | 24.0 | 1.4 | 1.0 | -1.0 | .615 | .38 | .007 | .006 | .089 | .94 |
| | | | | | (.064) | .02 | (.002) | (.002) | (.033) | |
| 85:12 | 25.1 | 1.4 | 1.0 | -1.0 | .615 | .38 | .007 | .005 | .087 | .94 |
| | | | | | (.063) | .05 | (.002) | (.002) | (.033) | |
| 86:12 | 26.2 | 1.4 | 1.0 | -1.0 | .617 | .38 | .007 | .006 | .085 | .95 |
| | | | | | (.062) | .08 | (.002) | (.002) | (.032) | |
| 87:12 | 23.6 | 1.4 | 1.0 | -1.0 | .605 | .40 | .006 | .006 | .095 | .94 |
| | | | | | (.065) | .11 | (.002) | (.002) | (.032) | |
| 88:12 | 24.2 | 1.3 | 1.0 | -1.0 | .600 | .41 | .005 | .006 | .102 | .94 |
| | | | | | (.064) | .10 | (.002) | (.002) | (.031) | |
| 89:12 | 24.5 | 1.4 | 1.0 | -1.0 | .597 | .41 | .005 | .006 | .105 | .94 |
| | | | | | (.064) | .10 | (.002) | (.002) | (.030) | |
| 90:12 | 24.2 | 1.4 | 1.0 | -1.0 | .596 | .41 | .004 | .005 | .105 | .94 |
| | | | | | (.065) | .11 | (.002) | (.002) | (.029) | |
| 91:12 | 24.4 | 1.5 | 1.0 | -1.0 | .597 | .41 | .005 | .005 | .092 | .95 |
| | | | | | (.071) | .15 | (.002) | (.002) | (.028) | |

Note: Numbers in parentheses denote standard errors

the latter case the VECM models include two dummy variables, D79 that is 1.0 starting in 79:10 and D82 that is 1.0 starting in 82:1.

Again there is considerable similarity with the quarterly estimates in Tables 6.6 and 6.8. The trace and maximum eigenvalue tests for the shortest sample periods suggest two cointegrating vectors that would imply that both velocity and the Treasury bill rate are stationary. We believe that this reflects small sample problems resulting from an inadequate span of data (16-17 years). In the longer sample periods the statistics are consistent with a single cointegrating vector. The range of estimated semielasticities with respect to the Treasury bill rate (.123 - .166) is slightly larger than the range estimated from the quarterly data (.124 - .149), but the economic implications are not substantially different. The estimated coefficients on the dummy variables in the longer samples imply the same type of upward shift in the equilibrium velocity during the high interest rate period of the New Operating Procedures as that pictured in Figure 6.4, but a net shift from the pre 79:10 regime to the post 81 regime that is not significantly different from zero.

The estimated "error correction" coefficients are always significantly different from zero for all three variables, but the implicit "error correction" coefficient on velocity is very close to zero (-.0021 to .0026) and is not significantly different from zero. Again the implication is that velocity is weakly exogenous, in contrast to the quarterly estimates that suggest real balances are weakly exogenous.

## 6.4 Analysis of Dynamic Responses to Permanent Shocks

There are three objectives in this section. First, the decomposition of the various time series' permanent and transitory components is examined using the quarterly double log specification. Such decompositions are not unique, but require some identifying restrictions. We examine alternatives that either specify the permanent shocks as random walks or require that both the permanent and transitory components of each series be linear combinations of all the data series in the vector error correction model. Second, we utilize additional identifying restrictions to determine dynamic response patterns to the two permanent shocks that characterize the data. These analyses are constructed for both quarterly and monthly specifications and the consistency of the system dynamics is checked at different levels of time disaggregation. Finally, we examine the allocation of the forecast variance for each variable among the permanent and transitory shocks.

### 6.4.1 Permanent-Transitory Decompositions of Data Series

The conclusion that there is a single cointegrating vector among the three variables in these VECMs implies that there are two permanent shocks and one

**Table 6.14: Estimates of Error Correction Parameters, ln(M/P), ln(Y/P), Rtb, D79 and D82; (Recursive Estimation with samples that begin in 1955:8)**

| End of Sample | Trace Tests r=0 | r≤0 | $\beta_c$ | | | $\beta_0$ > 79 > 81 | $\alpha_c$ | | | I-$\beta$'$\alpha$ |
|---|---|---|---|---|---|---|---|---|---|---|
| 72:12 | 28.8 | 5.6 | 1.0 | -1.0 | .093 | 0.84 | .015 | .015 | .066 | .99 |
| | | | | | (.01) | | (.004) | (.005) | (.248) | |
| 73:12 | 25.7 | 3.3 | 1.0 | -1.0 | .107 | 0.77 | .014 | .012 | .447 | .95 |
| | | | | | (.011) | | (.004) | (.004) | (.247) | |
| 74:12 | 26.4 | 2.3 | 1.0 | -1.0 | .123 | 0.70 | .012 | .012 | .546 | .93 |
| | | | | | (.011) | | (.003) | (.004) | (.244) | |
| 75:12 | 20.0 | .52 | 1.0 | -1.0 | .144 | 0.63 | .008 | .011 | .414 | .94 |
| | | | | | (.016) | | (.003) | (.003) | (.203) | |
| 76:12 | 17.2 | .47 | 1.0 | -1.0 | .156 | 0.58 | .006 | .009 | .236 | .97 |
| | | | | | (.023) | | (.002) | (.003) | (.159) | |
| 77:12 | 17.6 | .39 | 1.0 | -1.0 | .166 | 0.53 | .005 | .007 | .256 | .96 |
| | | | | | (.026) | | (.002) | (.002) | (.133) | |
| 78:12 | 18.6 | .39 | 1.0 | -1.0 | .155 | 0.57 | .005 | .007 | .286 | .96 |
| | | | | | (.020) | | (.002) | (.002) | (.144) | |
| 79:9 | 17.8 | 1.5 | 1.0 | -1.0 | .149 | 0.58 | .005 | .007 | .200 | .97 |
| | | | | | (.020) | | (.002) | (.002) | (.144) | |
| 82:12 | 19.6 | .92 | 1.0 | -1.0 | .144 | 0.61<br>−.70<br>0.55 | .005 | .005 | .430 | .94 |
| | | | | | (.021) | | (.002) | (.002) | (.201) | |
| 83:12 | 22.6 | .85 | 1.0 | -1.0 | .144 | 0.61<br>−.70<br>0.54 | .006 | .005 | .431 | .94 |
| | | | | | (.020) | | (.002) | (.002) | (.188) | |
| 84:12 | 24.4 | .80 | 1.0 | -1.0 | .145 | 0.61<br>−.70<br>0.54 | .005 | .006 | .438 | .94 |
| | | | | | (.020) | | (.002) | (.002) | (.182) | |
| 85:12 | 24.2 | .74 | 1.0 | -1.0 | .143 | 0.62<br>−.70<br>0.61 | .006 | .005 | .382 | .94 |
| | | | | | (.020) | | (.002) | (.002) | (.178) | |
| 86:12 | 27.4 | .52 | 1.0 | -1.0 | .144 | .61<br>−.70<br>.67 | .007 | .005 | .304 | .95 |
| | | | | | (.019) | | (.002) | (.002) | (.172) | |
| 87:12 | 20.1 | .80 | 1.0 | -1.0 | .137 | .64<br>−.66<br>.73 | .004 | .005 | .395 | .94 |
| | | | | | (.023) | | (.002) | (.002) | (.162) | |
| 88:12 | 21.6 | .77 | 1.0 | -1.0 | .135 | .65<br>−.64<br>.68 | .004 | .004 | .473 | .94 |
| | | | | | (.022) | | (.001) | (.002) | (.153) | |
| 89:12 | 22.3 | .85 | 1.0 | -1.0 | .136 | .65<br>−.64<br>.68 | .003 | .004 | .496 | .94 |
| | | | | | (.023) | | (.001) | (.002) | (.148) | |
| 90:12 | 21.9 | .85 | 1.0 | -1.0 | .137 | .64<br>−.65<br>.70 | .003 | .004 | .498 | .94 |
| | | | | | (.024) | | (.001) | (.002) | (.144) | |
| 91:12 | 19.3 | .86 | 1.0 | -1.0 | .134 | .66<br>−.63<br>.75 | .003 | .003 | .424 | .95 |
| | | | | | (.026) | | (.001) | (.002) | (.139) | |

transitory shock that affect each of the three variables, and a fourth variable, the log of M1 velocity that can be constructed as the difference between the log of real output and the log of real balances. Under these conditions, it is possible to decompose each of these time series into a permanent and transitory component. There are several ways to implement such a decomposition. One technique is to impose the indentifying restriction that the permanent component of each series follows a random walk (King, Plosser, Stock and Watson (1991)) (see Chapter 3). A second technique is to assume that the permanent components are linear combinations of the observable variables in the VECM and that the transitory components are stationary (Gonzalo and Granger (1991), Park (1990)).

In addition, the inclusion of the dummy variable, D82, allows for a one time discrete change in the deterministic trend in the permanent component of each series. Therefore, implicit in our VECM is a permanent-transitory specification of the class considered by Brunner and Meltzer (1993) and Meltzer (1986). Meltzer (1986) has estimated permanent-transitory decompositions of various time series using a univariate multistate Kalman filter model developed by Kool (1989) and Bomhoff and Kool (1983). The differences between the approach used here and that employed by Meltzer are a) these are multivariate, b) the Kalman filter approach specifies that the permanent and transitory components are uncorrelated, and c) we allow only discrete permanent changes in growth rates of the variables in addition to the transitory changes in the growth rates (permanent changes in the levels of the variables), while the multistate Kalman filter approach allows for stochastic permanent shocks to growth rates. In practice, the latter difference probably has little importance, since Meltzer (1985, 1986) finds only a small contribution to the total variances from the variance in growth rates. The first of the three differences is important because it allows for restrictions on the permanent shocks across variables that cannot be recognized by the univariate approach.

An alternative multivariate multistate Kalman filtering approach has been used by Bomhoff (1990, 1991) to estimate a "money demand function". This approach is the same as the univariate approach employed by Meltzer, with the extension that the single variable that is subject to the Kalman filtering is a linear combination of income velocity and an interest rate. In principle this approach can accommodate cancellation of the permanent shocks between velocity and interest rates, so that the resulting linear combination of the two is stationary. However, it has the disadvantage that it does not accommodate differences between the short-run and long-run interest elasticities of the demand for real balances, nor can it accommodate short-run income elasticities of the demand for real balances that differ from unity.

The permanent components of each of the four quarterly series, derived from the King, Plosser, Stock and Watson "common trends" approach, are plotted against the actual data in Figures 6.6-6.9. The shaded portions of these figures are the peak to trough periods of NBER reference cycles. The permanent components are constructed from the estimated cointegrating vector for the 55:2 - 91:4 sample period, with the shift in the intercept of the cointegrating vector at the beginning of 1982 constrained to zero and real balances constrained to

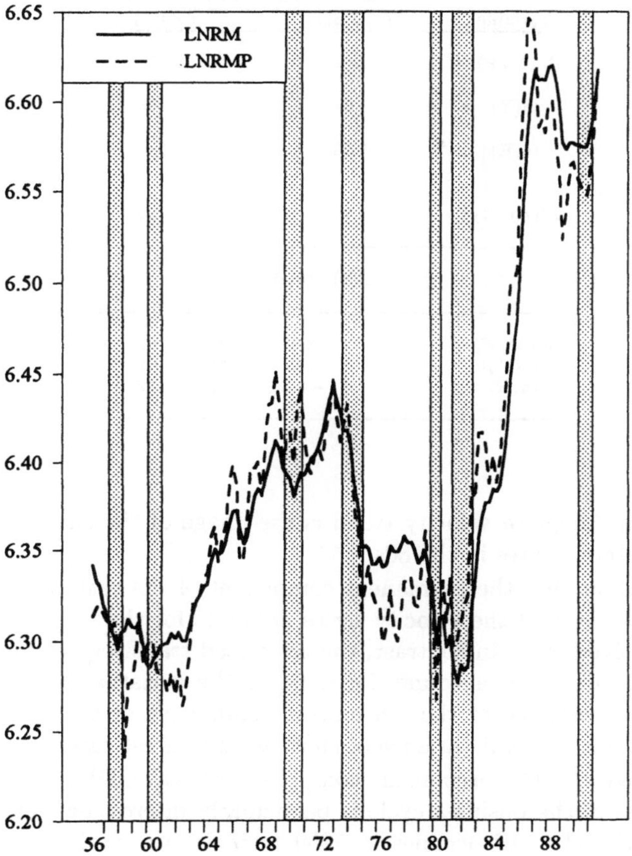


Figure 6.6: Actual and KPSW Permanent Real M1 Balances

be weakly exogenous (Table 6.8). The permanent and transitory components are computed according to the decomposition discussed in Chapter 3 where $z_0$ is estimated by assuming that the sample mean of the stationary (transitory) component of $z$ is zero. The estimated trends in the permanent components of each series ($C(1)\mu t$) and the estimated $C(1)$ matrix for this sample period are reported in Table 6.15. The trends are reported as percentages at annual rates. The real income trend is estimated at 3.07 percent per annum for the 50s through the 70s, but is estimated to decline to 2.58 percent in the 80s. This is quite consistent with conventional univariate estimates of the drift in real GDP. The trend in M1 velocity is estimated at 3.26 percent through the 70s, which is consistent with the Monetarist assumption of that time of a three percent trend in this velocity measure. After 1981 the trend in velocity is estimated at -.95

Table 6.15: Quarterly Double Log Specification 56:2-91:4

| Variable | Trends at Percentage Annual Rates | |
|---|---|---|
| | Thru 81:4 | 82:1-91:4 |
| ln(M/P) | -.19 | 3.53 |
| ln(Y) | 3.07 | 2.58 |
| ln(R) | 5.56 | -1.64 |
| ln(velocity) | 3.26 | -.95 |

C(1) Matrix

| | | | |
|---|---|---|---|
| $\ln(M/P)$ | 2.87 | .20 | −.02 |
| $\ln(Y)$ | .35 | .99 | −0.9 |
| $\ln(R)$ | −4.30 | 1.36 | −.12 |

percent. This change in velocity trend is the image of the change in the trend in nominal interest rates in the 80s.

It is apparent that the permanent component of the real output series, the real balance series and the velocity series accounts for the bulk of the variance in the respective series. In contrast, the estimated transitory component of the Treasury bill rate series accounts for most of the variation with the business cycle, and the variance of the permanent component of this series is only a small fraction of the total variance of short-term interest rates.

The behavior of the permanent component of real GDP during NBER recession phases of the business cycle is particularly interesting. The permanent component of real GDP declines in 1959 (coincidental with the steel strike), during the 1970 recession, and during the oil shock induced recessions of 74-5 and 79-80. In contrast, it continues to rise during the recessions of 58, 60, and 90-91. This suggests that the exogenous shocks that initiated various recessions differ substantially. In 1970, 74-5 and 79-80 actual GDP is substantially above the permanent component of real GDP, which is directly the opposite of the traditional interpretation of an aggregate demand induced recessionary condition with a negative transitory fluctuation in real output.

The permanent component of the Treasury bill rate exhibits a positive trend through 1979. Subsequently it fluctuates without any substantial trend. This is consistent with the interpretation of a positive deterministic trend in expected inflation through the 70s and no deterministic trend (or at most a very small deterministic trend) in expected inflation throughout the 80s. Note that other than the information in the nominal interest rate series, no information on actual or expected inflation is utilized in extracting the permanent component of these time series.

Gonzalo and Granger (1991) suggest an alternative permanent-transitory

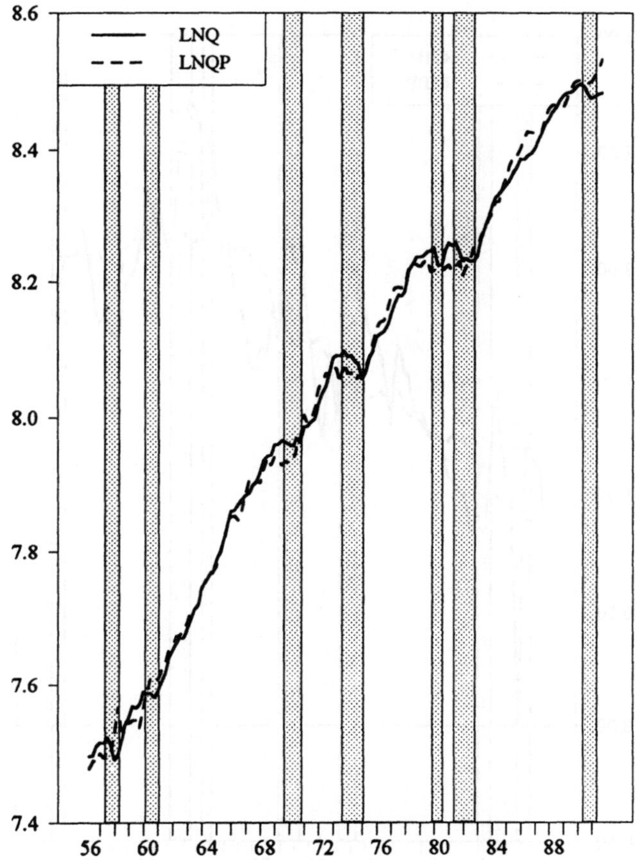


Figure 6.7: Actual and KPSW Permanent GDP

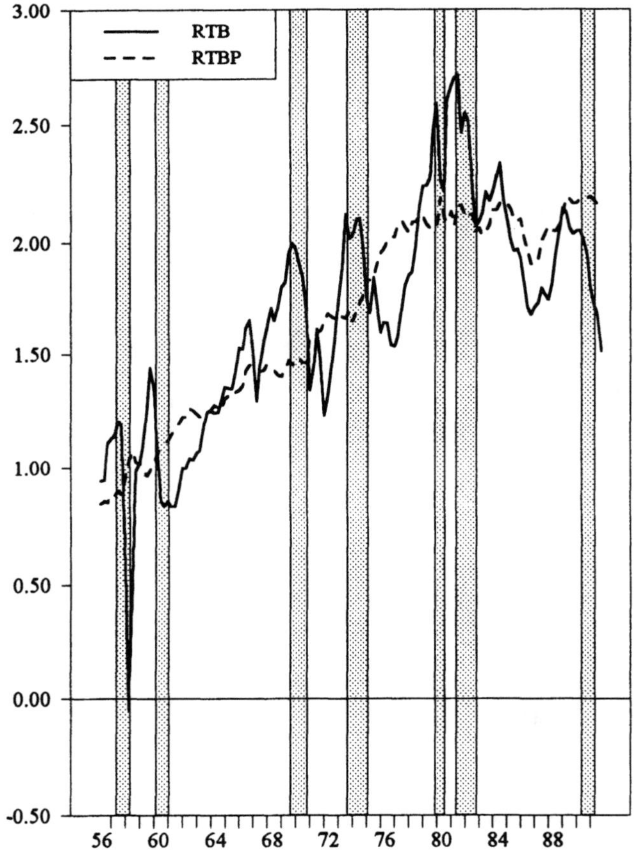


Figure 6.8: Actual and KPSW Permanent Treasury Bill Rate

decomposition of the multivariate process that they call a common factor approach. Their approach is to construct an decomposition such that both the permanent and transitory components are linear combinations of the vector $z_t$. Under their choice of normalization, the transitory component of $z_t$ is just the matrix of cointegrating vectors, $\beta' z_t$, premultiplied by the error correction matrix $\alpha$.[14] Since the $\alpha$ element for $ln(M/P)$ is constrained to zero in the model considered here, the Gonzalo-Granger decomposition attributes all of the behavior of real balances to permanent factors and none to transitory fluctuations. The transitory component of velocity under these conditions reflects only the transitory component in real output.

The Gonzalo-Granger permanent factors for real output and the Treasury bill rate are plotted against the respective time series in Figures 6.10-6.11. The differences between actual real output and the common factor permanent component are very small. This follows from the small estimated error correction coefficient (.0256 in Table 6.6) for this variable. In contrast to the King, Plosser, Stock and Watson decomposition, the Gonzalo-Granger approach attributes almost all of the traditional "business cycle" fluctuation in real output to fluctuations in the permanent component rather than fluctuations in the transitory component of real GDP.

The difference between the KPSW and Gonzalo-Granger permanent and transitory decompositions is even more dramatic in terms of the nominal interest rate behavior (Figure 6.9 versus Figure 6.11). In the former case, little if any of the cyclical fluctuation in the rate is attributed to the permanent component of rates. In the latter case the permanent component of the Treasury bill rate tracks the cyclical fluctuations of the actual series quite closely.

Park (1990) proposes a third alternative permanent-transitory decomposition of the multivariate VECM process. This decomposition shares the Gonzalo-Granger assumption of components that are linear combinations of the elements of the $z_t$ vector, but uses a different normalization . Park (1990, equation 8) constructs the transitory component equal to $\alpha(\beta'\alpha)^{-1}\beta' z_t$, which would only equal the Gonzalo-Granger transitory component if $(\beta'\alpha)$ is an identity matrix. Under this condition the vectors $\beta' z_t$ would not revert to their means and hence the data would not be cointegrated. Thus these two decompositions are distinct.

In the model considered here, the transitory component of real balances is again identically zero under the weak exogeneity restriction. From Table 6.6 we know that $\beta'\alpha$ is estimated at .14, so the Park transitory component is 6.93 times the Gonzalo–Granger transitory component. The Park common factors for real GDP and the Treasury bill rate are plotted against the KPSW permanent components in Figures 6.12 and 6.13 respectively. It is apparent that for the variables modeled here these two decompositions are very highly correlated. The correlations between the KPSW permanent component and the Park common factor are .92, .98 and .98 for real balances, real GDP and the

[14]The VECM that Gonzalo and Granger consider does not include a constant term. In the model under consideration here, we allocate the constant term to the transitory and permanent components using the same decomposition that Gonzalo and Granger apply to $z_t$. Under this assumption our transitory component is constructed as $\alpha(\beta' z_t - \beta_0')$.

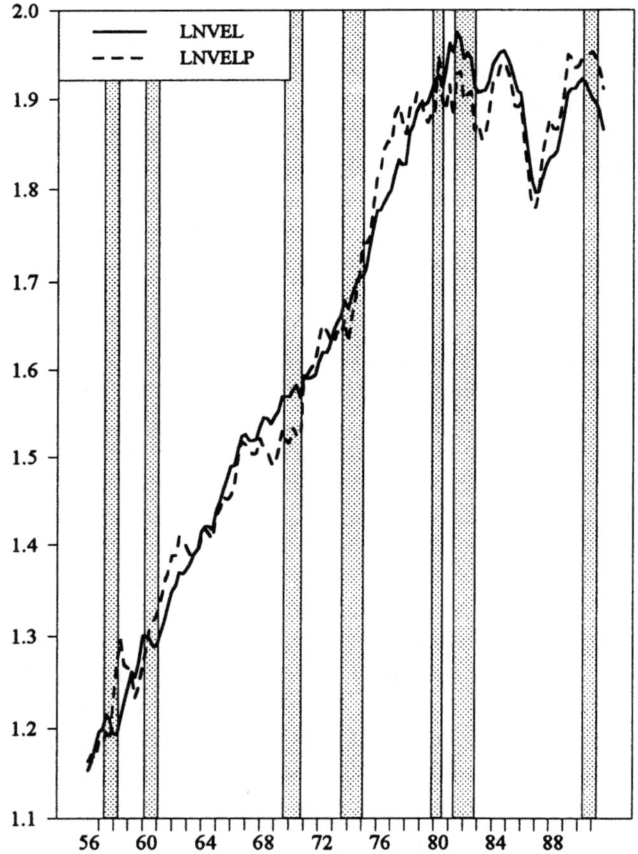


Figure 6.9: Actual and KPSW Permanent Velocity

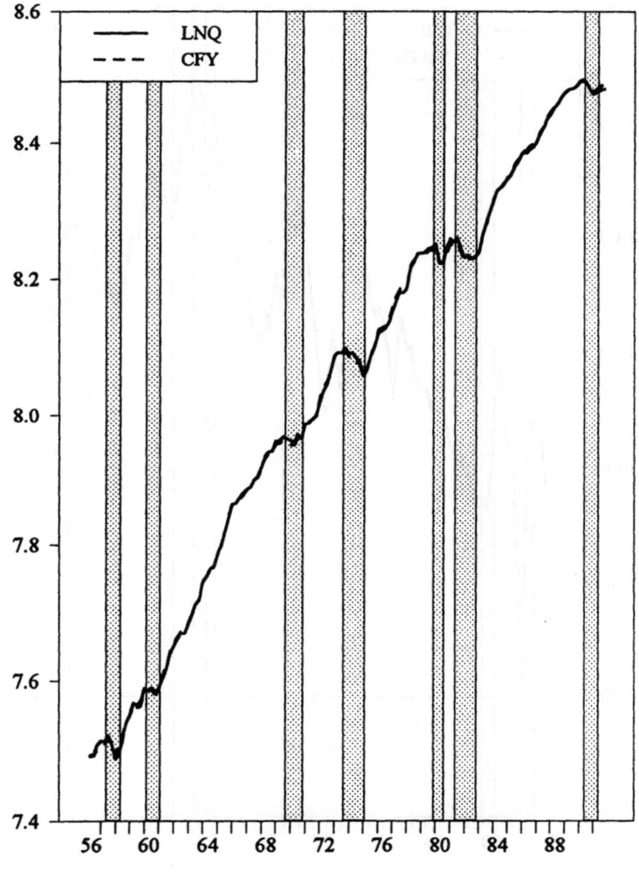


Figure 6.10: Actual and Common Factor Real GDP

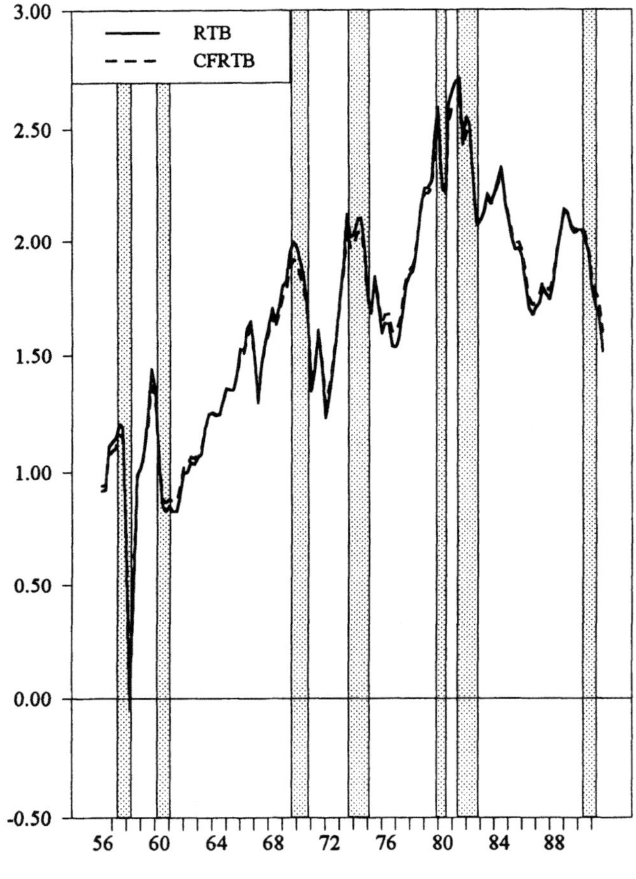


Figure 6.11: Actual and Common Factor Treasury Bill Rate

Treasury bill rate respectively. In particular, the implications for the permanent versus transitory character of "business cycle" fluctuations in real output are the same regardless of which of these two decompositions is examined. The Park common factor for the Treasury bill exhibits even less high frequency fluctuation than the KPSW permanent component.

Our conclusion from this analysis is that the vector error correction models are consistent with established univariate time series results. Variables such as real output, real balances and velocity reflect the dominant influence of permanent shocks. In contrast, a substantial component of short-term nominal interest rate fluctuation reflects the influence of transitory shocks. This latter result is consistent with Mishkin's (1990a, 1990b) analyses of nominal interest rates that conclude that short-term interest rate behavior is dominated by transitory real rate fluctuations.

### 6.4.2 Dynamic Analysis of a Quarterly Three Variable Log-linear VECM

In order to investigate the dynamic responses to individual shocks of the variables in the VECM it is necessary to apply short-run identifying restrictions that determine the economic shocks of interest as linear combinations of the reduced form shocks that are estimated from the VECM. Alternative sets of identifying restrictions have been proposed to construct estimates of the "structural shocks" or "economic shocks" that drive the behavior of the variables under consideration. One such set of identifying restrictions is the "common trends" approach of King, Plosser, Stock and Watson (1991). As discussed in Chapter 3, this approach involves a) defining the permanent shocks in terms of the permanent components of the observable variables in the VECM and b) the application of a Wold causal chain structure under the assumption that the permanent "structural shocks" are ordered prior to the transitory "structural shocks" in the causal chain and c) that all "structural shocks" are uncorrelated. These conditions are sufficient to exactly identify the "structural shocks" as linear combinations of the reduced form shocks.

In our three variable VECM with one cointegrating vector there are two permanent shocks. In the macroeconomic model developed in Chapter 5, one of these shocks, $\varepsilon_{1t}$, is a natural output (or productivity) shock that is a permanent shock to real output. This shock also produces a permanent change in real balances, but no permanent change in nominal interest rates or velocity, since the real interest rate is hypothesized to be a stationary process (see equation 5.50). A permanent inflation shock, $\varepsilon_{2t}$, in that model produces a permanent change in the nominal interest rate, real balances, and velocity, but leaves real output and the real interest rate unchanged. This type of economic structure implies a coefficient matrix on the factor loading that transmits the long-run effects of the permanent shocks of the form of $\beta_\perp^0$ in Table 6.16. Note that the economic structure imposes two zero restrictions on the elements of $\beta_\perp^0$. These restrictions together with the assumption that the permanent and transitory shocks are not correlated are sufficient to identify the two permanent shocks.

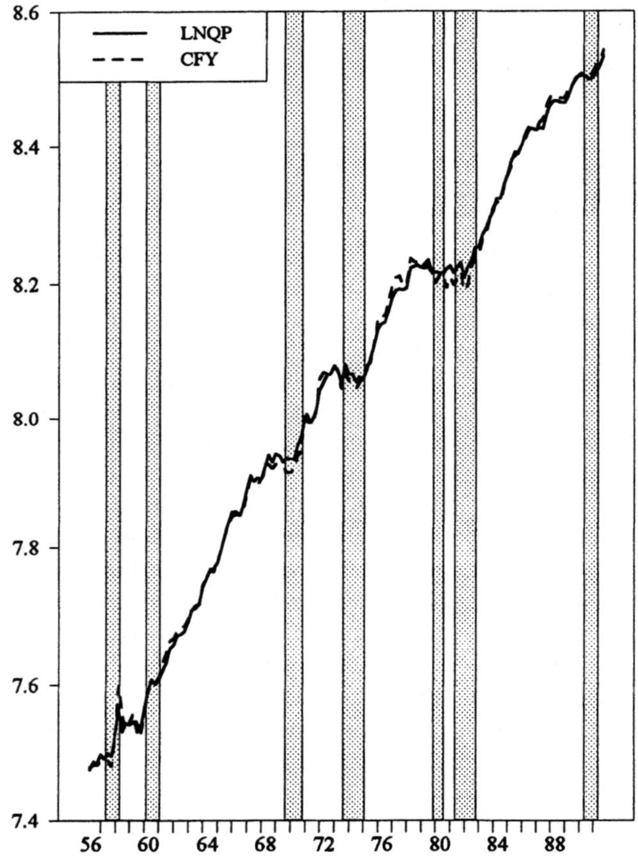


Figure 6.12: KPSW Permanent and Park Common Factor Real GDP

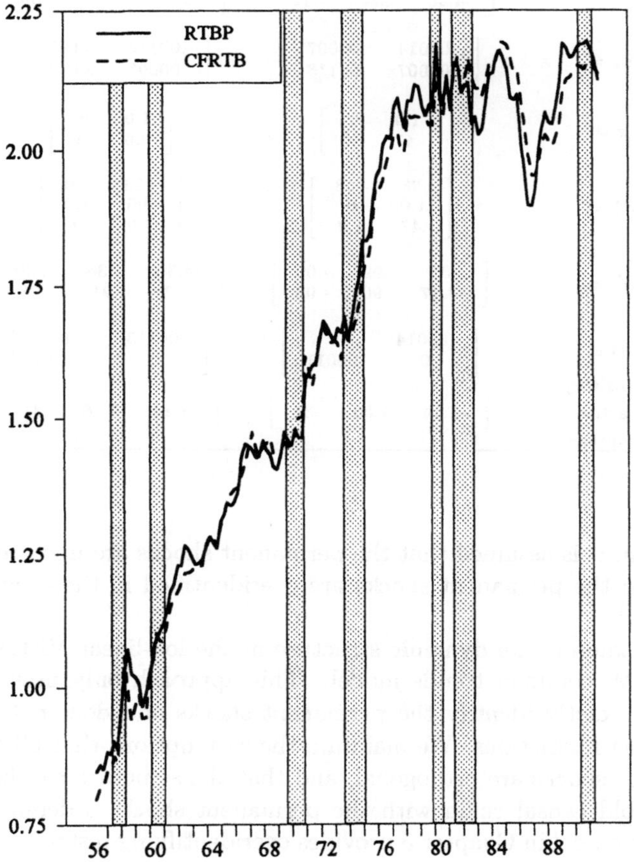


Figure 6.13: KPSW Permanent and Park Common Factor Treasury Bill Rate

Table 6.16: Identification of Permanent Shocks, Quarterly Double Log Specification 56:2-91:4–Weakly Exogenous ln(M/P)

| | Real Output Shock First | Nominal Shock First |
|---|---|---|
| $\beta_{\perp}^{0} =$ | $\begin{bmatrix} 1.0 & -.585 \\ 1.0 & 0.0 \\ 0.0 & 1.0 \end{bmatrix}$ | $\begin{bmatrix} -.585 & 1.0 \\ 0.0 & 1.0 \\ 1.0 & 0.0 \end{bmatrix}$ |
| $\alpha_{\perp}^{0\prime} =$ | $\begin{bmatrix} .35 & .99 & -.09 \\ -4.30 & 1.36 & -.12 \end{bmatrix}$ | $\begin{bmatrix} -4.30 & 1.36 & -.12 \\ .35 & .99 & -.09 \end{bmatrix}$ |
| $\Sigma_{v} =$ | $\begin{bmatrix} .00014 & .00007 \\ .00007 & .00113 \end{bmatrix}$ | $\begin{bmatrix} .00113 & .00007 \\ .00007 & .00014 \end{bmatrix}$ |
| $\pi =$ | $\begin{bmatrix} 1.0 & 0 \\ .47 & 1.0 \end{bmatrix}$ | $\begin{bmatrix} 1.0 & 0 \\ .06 & 1.0 \end{bmatrix}$ |
| $\beta_{\perp}^{*} =$ | $\begin{bmatrix} .73 & -.58 \\ 1.0 & 0 \\ .47 & 1.0 \end{bmatrix}$ | $\begin{bmatrix} -.53 & 1.0 \\ .06 & 1.0 \\ 1.0 & 0 \end{bmatrix}$ |
| $\alpha_{\perp}^{\prime} =$ | $\begin{bmatrix} .35 & .99 & -.09 \\ -4.47 & .90 & -.08 \end{bmatrix}$ | $\begin{bmatrix} -4.30 & 1.36 & -.13 \\ .60 & .91 & -.08 \end{bmatrix}$ |
| D= | $\begin{bmatrix} .00014 & 0 \\ 0 & .00011 \end{bmatrix}$ | $\begin{bmatrix} .00113 & 0 \\ 0 & .00014 \end{bmatrix}$ |
| Transitory Factor Loadings | $\begin{bmatrix} -1.14 & 7.56 & .31 \end{bmatrix}$ | $\begin{bmatrix} -1.14 & 7.56 & .31 \end{bmatrix}$ |

If, in addition, it is assumed that the permanent shocks are uncorrelated (as in KPSW), then the permanent shocks are overidentified in the economic model in Chapter 5.[15]

We first examine the dynamic structure in the log-linear VECM by applying the KPSW common trends model. This approach only uses information necessary to exactly identify the permanent shocks and does not impose any overidentifying restrictions. We maintain the assumptions that all "structural" or "economic" shocks are orthogonal, and that the structure can be characterized by a Wold causal chain with the permanent shocks ordered first. Since the economic model in Chapter 5 provides overidentifying restrictions, there are two possible common trend specifications within which the permanent shocks are exactly identified. These are represented in parts A and B of Table 6.16. In part A, the permanent real output shock is ordered first in the causal chain. In part B, the permanent nominal shock is ordered first. The estimates are from the sample period ending in 91:4 with the constant of the cointegrating vector

[15] In Chapter 4, we note that weak exogeneity can imply zero restrictions on $\alpha_{\perp}$ that are useful in identifying the factor loading matrix for the common trends. In the VECM considered here, only one variable is weakly exogenous and there are two common trends. In this case $\alpha_{\perp}^{\prime}\alpha = 0$ is a set of two homogeneous equations which impose no exclusion restrictions on the $\alpha_{\perp}$ matrix.

constrained to no shift in 82:1 and with $ln(M/P)$ constrained to be weakly exogenous.

Under the first of these two orderings, the estimated correlation of the measured common trends can be interpreted as a test of the hypothesis that the real interest rate is stationary. Under this hypothesis and the assumed identifying restrictions, the correlation of the permanent shocks is zero. The estimated correlation of these shocks in part A of Table 6.16 is 0.16. The significance of this estimated correlation is marginal.[16]

The orthogonalizing decomposition of $\Sigma_v = \pi D \pi'$ is shown in Table 6.16. After orthogonalization of the permanent shocks, the coefficient matrix for the common trends is $\beta_\perp^*$. The zero restriction on the (2,2) element of this matrix is imposed by the causal ordering. The value of the (3,1) element, .47, implies a substantial positive permanent response of nominal (and real) interest rates to the real output shock. If this response is significantly different from zero, it implies that the real interest rate is nonstationary.

In the identifying restrictions on $\beta_\perp^0$ (and $\beta_\perp^*$) it is assumed the second permanent shock has a one unit impact on the log of the Treasury bill rate. This is an arbitrary and inconsequential normalization of the long-run impact of this shock. None of the conclusions about the dynamic response patterns, other that the scale of the responses to the second permanent shock, would be affected by renormalizing the shock to have a unit long-run impact on the log of real balances or the log of velocity.

The factor loading matrix for the common trends is given by the estimated $\alpha_\perp$ matrix. Each permanent shock is measured as a linear combination of the reduced form shocks in the VECM. The largest weight in the first common trend (real output shock) is on the reduced form error in the real output equation (.99), with some positive weight (.35) given to the reduced form error in the real balance equation. The largest weight in the second common trend is a strong negative relationship to the reduced form error in the real balance equation. The reduced form error in the interest rate equation has only a small negative (and almost identical) weight in both common trends. The small weight associated with the reduced form interest rate equation error is not surprising, since the residual variance in this equation is more than 200 times as large as the reduced form errors in the other two equations, which are of the same order of magnitude. Finally, the factor loading vector for the transitory shock that is produced as a byproduct of the KPSW methodology is shown at the bottom of Table 6.16. This loading vector is normalized so that the transitory shock has a unit impact effect on the nominal interest rate.

The alternative set of exactly identifying restrictions is imposed by ordering the permanent nominal (inflation) shock first in the causal chain structure as indicated by the $\beta_\perp^0$ matrix in part B of Table 6.16. The effect of this assumption is to interchange the columns of $\beta_\perp^0$, the rows of $\alpha_\perp^0$, and both rows and columns of $\Sigma_v$. No change in made in the estimated correlation of the permanent shocks.

[16] The test utilized here is that proposed by Baillie (1987) for testing the significance of elements of estimated covariance matrices. The test statistic, that in this case is distributed as $\chi^2$ with one degree of freedom, is 3.76.

However, the effect of ordering the permanent shock with the largest variance first is to greatly reduce the size of the off diagonal element in the $\pi$ matrix.[17] As a result the long-run impact of the nominal common trend on real output is estimated to be quite small (.06). The factor loading matrix for the common trends ($\alpha'_\perp$) indicates that the nominal common trend has a larger weight on the reduced form error for real output and a smaller weight on the reduced form error for real balances than is computed when the real output shock is ordered first. Conversely, the real output common trend is now computed to have a smaller weight on the reduced form real output equation error and a larger weight on the reduced form real balance equation error than is computed when the real output shock is ordered first.

It is possible to construct estimated common trends subject to all the overidentifying restrictions implied by the model in Chapter 5, plus the assumptions that all economic shocks are orthogonal and that the permanent shocks are ordered first in a block causal chain structure. The SVAR program developed by Giannini (1992) can be adapted to this problem. The program provides a likelihood ratio test of the overidentifying restrictions. The test of the overidentifying restrictions is essentially a likelihood ratio test of the restriction that the covariance matrix in Table 6.16 ($\Sigma_v$) is diagonal. The computed value of this test statistic is 3.91. This is distributed as $\chi^2$ with one degree of freedom, which is on the margin of significance like the test for diagonality of the covariance matrix of the permanent shocks that is reported above.

With the imposition of all the identifying restrictions of the economic model and the associated error structure, the estimated $\beta^*_\perp$ matrix is exactly $\beta^0_\perp$ in Table 6.16 and the factor loading matrix for the common trends is exactly $\alpha^{0\prime}_\perp$ in that table. The estimated factor loading vector for the transitory shock (again normalized so that the transitory shock has a unit impact effect on the log of the nominal interest rate is [-1.1304, 7.5315,.3096]. The impulse response functions to the real output common trend in the overidentified model are identical to those when the real output shock is ordered first in a causal chain structure. Similarly, the impulse response functions to a permanent nominal (inflation) shock are identical to those when the nominal shock is ordered first in a causal chain structure.

The $\alpha'_\perp$ matrix, augmented by the vector of factor loadings for the transitory shock, represents the simultaneous structure of the identified "structural VECM" (the $\Gamma_0$ matrix in the notation of KPSW (1991)). The first two equations in this structure are first difference equations, since $\alpha'_\perp \alpha = 0$. The structural error term in one of these equations is the permanent nominal trend and the structural error in the second equation is the permanent real trend.

Consider the structural equation with the permanent nominal trend error. This equation has the same form as the typical first difference single equation

[17] This follows immediately from the Cholesky decomposition of a $2 \times 2$ matrix. In this case $\pi_{12} = \sigma_{12}/\sigma_{11}$ where $\sigma_{12}$ is a covariance of the two variables and $\sigma_{11}$ is the variance of the variable ordered first in the causal chain. Clearly $\pi_{12}$ is smaller when $\sigma_{11} > \sigma_{22}$. If $\sigma_{12}$ is not significantly different from zero, then $\pi_{12}$ is not significantly different from zero, regardless of the ordering chosen.

regression that is interpreted as a "dynamic money demand" function. When this equation of the "structural model" is normalized on real balances, using the estimated factor loadings in part B of Table 6.16, the resulting equation is:[18]

$$\begin{aligned}\Delta\ln(M/P)_t &= .3168\Delta\ln GDP_t - .0290\Delta\ln Rtb_t\\ &+.0462\Delta\ln GDP_{t-1}\\ &-.0221\Delta\ln Rtb_{t-1} + .2772\Delta\ln(M/P)_{t-1}\\ &+.1862\Delta\ln GDP_{t-2} - .0151\Delta\ln Rtb_{t-2}\\ &+.0374\Delta\ln(M/P)_{t-2} - .0317\Delta\ln GDP_{t-3}\\ &-.0037\Delta\ln Rtb_{t-3} + .1678\Delta\ln(M/P)_{t-3} \qquad (6.4)\end{aligned}$$

The estimated coefficients here look like perfectly sensible estimates of a money demand function.

The usual derivation of an "equilibrium money demand function" is to compute the sum of the distributed lag coefficients in the above equation and to renormalize on real balances:

$$\Delta\ln(M/P) = 1.0002\Delta\ln GDP - .1350\Delta\ln Rtb \qquad (6.5)$$

Note that there are no constraints imposed upon the coefficients of the VECM to generate the coefficient of 1.0 on $\Delta\ln GDP$. The conventional interpretation of such a single equation result is that the equilibrium income elasticity of money demand is 1.0 and the equilibrium interest elasticity is -.135. Of course, the equilibrium interest elasticity of the demand for real balances is -.585 from the cointegrating vector. This illustrates the danger of misinterpreting overdifferenced single equation specifications in the presence of cointegrating vectors, and the underidentification of the short-run demand for real balances in this reduced form model. The true money demand shock is transitory and is buried in the one composite transitory shock in the model. The error term in this "dynamic money demand function" is not a money demand shock, but the permanent nominal shock to the economy.

The impulse response functions for real output, velocity, the Treasury bill rate, and the stationary linear combination of velocity and the nominal interest rate are shown in Figures 6.14-6.21 for each of the two common trends. The response of the cointegrating vector to both permanent shocks approaches zero in 3-4 years (12-16 quarters).

[18] The calculated values from this exercise would differ very little if the factor loadings from part A of Table 6.16 were used instead.

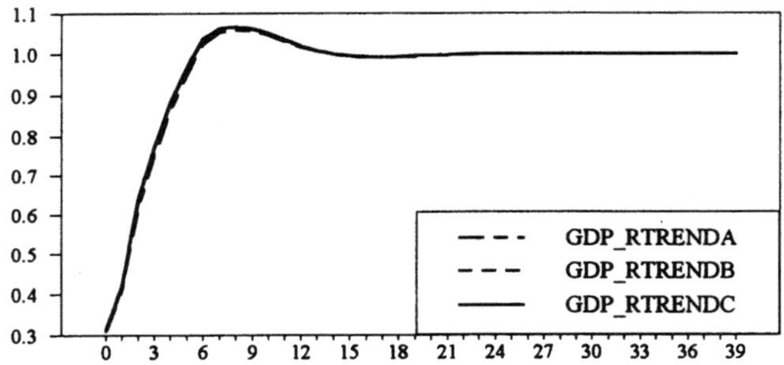


Figure 6.14: I.R.F. for GDP w.r.t. the Permanent Real Shock

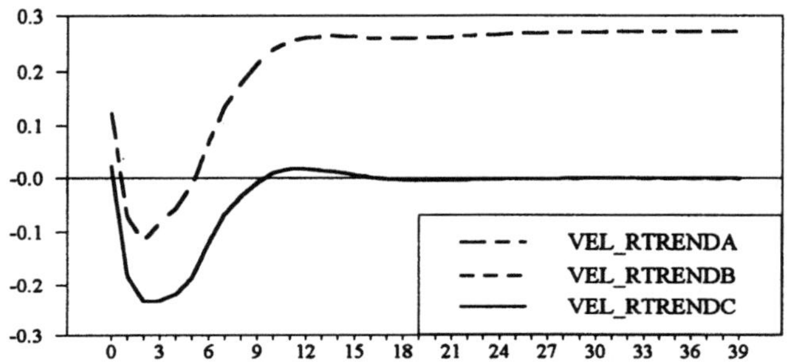


Figure 6.15: I.R.F. for Velocity w.r.t. the Permanent Real Shock

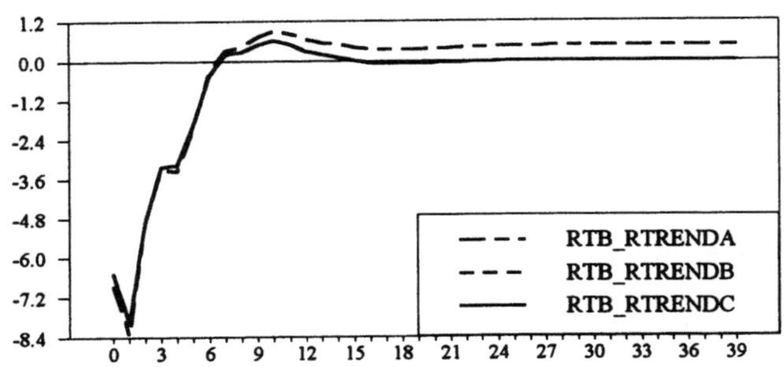


Figure 6.16: I.R.F. for Rtb w.r.t. the Permanent Real Shock

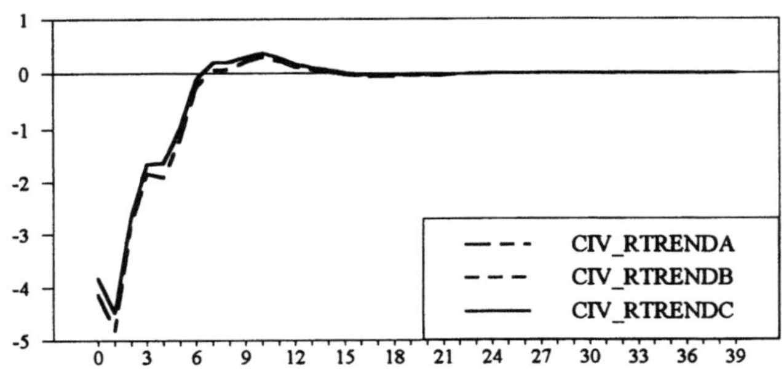


Figure 6.17: I.R.F. for the CIV w.r.t. the Permanent Real Shock

Real GDP exhibits a small impact response to the real output common trend, but this response increases rapidly. In less than two years the real GDP response achieves its steady-state value (1.0), then overshoots slightly and approaches the steady-state value after approximately three years. The response pattern is quite smooth, although no constraints have been imposed on the dynamic structure of the VECM model. The response pattern is almost identical regardless of the ordering of the common trends.

The initial response of the nominal interest rate to the real output common trend is strongly negative, though this response dissipates quickly. The steady-state response is positive when the real output shock is ordered first, contrary to the assumption of a stationary real interest rate in the economic model in Chapter 5. When there is a permanent positive impact of the real output shock on the nominal interest rate, the effect is mirrored in velocity behavior through the cointegrating relationship. Regardless of ordering, the initial impact of the real output shock on "disequilibrium real balances" as measured by the effect on the cointegrating vector is strongly negative (holdings of real balances do not immediately increase to their new higher equilibrium level). This effect dissipates smoothly and quickly, regardless of the ordering of the common trends, so that within a year and a half real balances have reached their new equilibrium levels. After this there is a small overshooting of the equilibrium, which disappears fully after approximately another two years.

The real output response to the permanent nominal shock in Figure 6.18 is not particularly sensitive to the ordering of the trends. In all cases, the real output response pattern starts positive and then goes negative within the first year. It goes to zero by assumption when the real common trend is ordered first, and to a positive value when the nominal trend is ordered first, reflecting the .06 value of $\pi_{21}$ for this ordering. At all time horizons the response of real output to the permanent nominal trend is quite small.

The response of the nominal interest rate to the permanent nominal shock is very similar for the two orderings, with slightly stronger initial effects when the nominal trend is ordered first. The effect is negative for about six quarters, then becomes positive and slowly builds towards 1.0. This is consistent with a substantial liquidity effect, but with a very small transitory output response.

Regardless of the ordering of the common trends, it takes a substantially longer time for the responses of all the variables to the permanent nominal shock to approach their equilibrium values than it does to achieve the equilibrium response to the real output common trend.

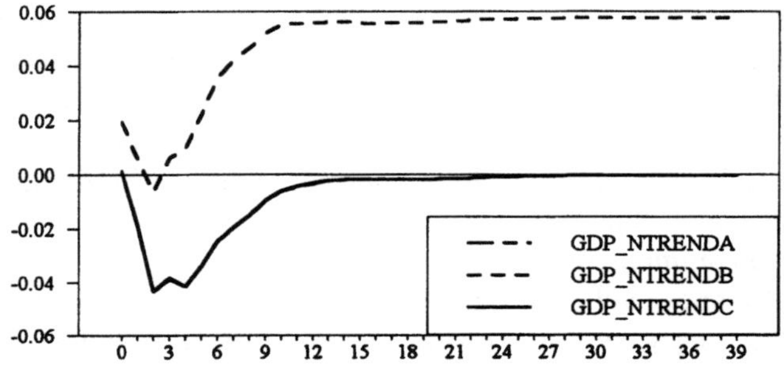


Figure 6.18: I.R.F. for GDP w.r.t. the Permanent Nominal Shock

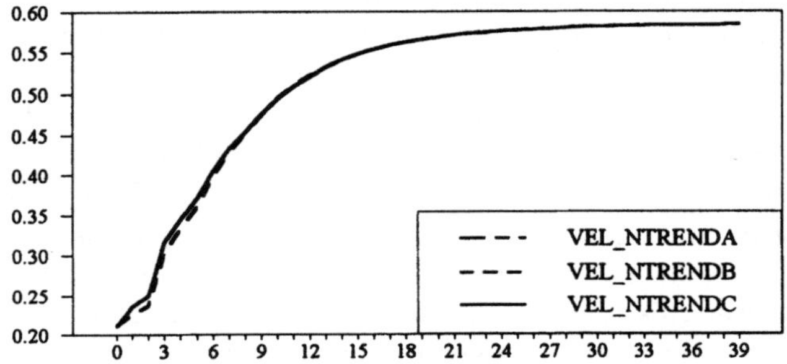


Figure 6.19: I.R.F. for Velocity w.r.t. the Permanent Nominal Shock

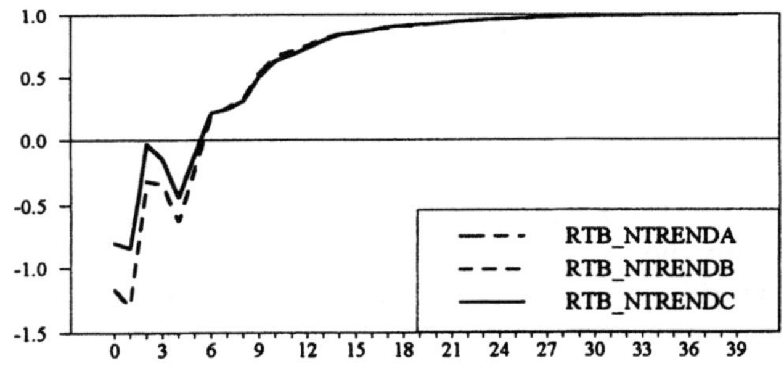


Figure 6.20: I.R.F. for Rtb w.r.t. the Permanent Nominal Shock

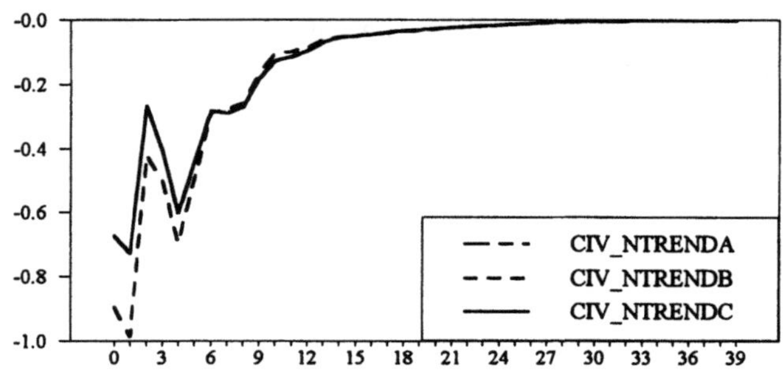


Figure 6.21: I.R.F. for the CIV w.r.t. the Permanent Nominal Shock

The impulse response functions for the third (transitory) shock in the model are graphed in Figures 6.22 through 6.25. This shock represents a weighted average of all the transitory shocks that affect the macroeconomy. In terms of the model developed in Chapter 5, this shock is a weighted average of the $\varepsilon_{3t}$ and $\varepsilon_{4t}$ shocks (see equation 5.48). Therefore it is impossible to give any economic interpretation to the impulse response functions shown in these figures. An economic interpretation of transitory shocks requires a larger menu of variables and identifying restrictions that will separate individual transitory shocks from the average of all such shocks (see Chapter 4 for an analysis of such identifying conditions).

Two characteristics of the impulse response functions for the transitory shock need to be noted, since they are the result of either identifying restrictions or restrictions on the structure of the reduced form VECM. First, the impact (period zero) response of the Treasury bill rate to the transitory shock is 1.0 (Figure 6.24). This results from the normalization used to construct the factor loading vector for the transitory shock as the third shock in the causal chain ordering. Second, the impact effects of this shock on real output and velocity (Figures 6.22 and 6.23) are identical. This follows from the restriction that real balances are weakly exogenous. The latter restriction on the $\alpha$ vector requires that the ratio of the second and third elements in both rows of $\alpha'_{\perp}$ matrix be equal, since $\alpha'_{\perp}\alpha = 0$. This property of the factor loading matrix implies that the (1,3) element in the inverse of the factor loading matrix is zero. Since the inverse of the factor loading matrix measures the impact effects of "structural shocks", the weak exogeneity restriction on real balances requires that the impact effect of the transitory shock on real balances is zero.

### 6.4.3 Variance Decompositions of Forecasts from the Log-Log Model

The decompositions of the forecast variance at various horizons for the five variables that can be constructed from the double log VECM are shown in Table 6.17. Several interesting characteristics are apparent. First, the behavior of real M1 balances is dominated by permanent shocks at all horizons. The composite transitory shock never accounts for as much as 10 percent of the forecast variance. This is the result of the restriction that real balances are weakly exogenous.

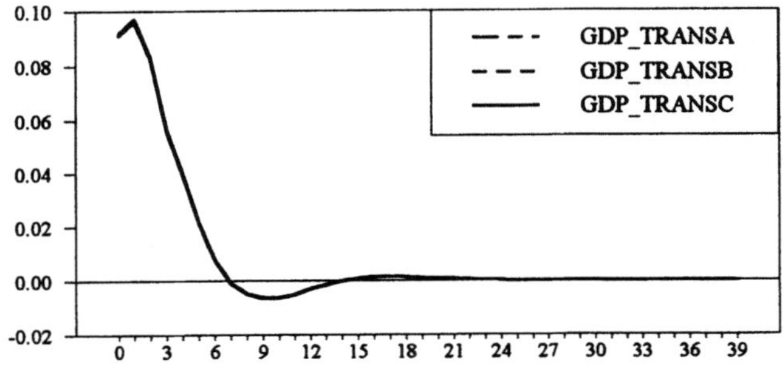


Figure 6.22: I.R.F. for GDP w.r.t. the Transitory Shock

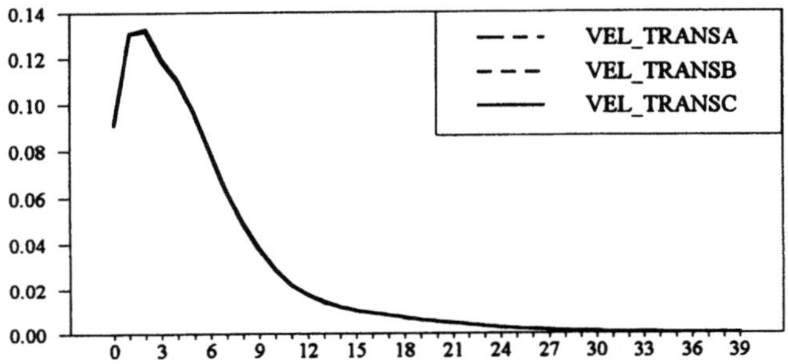


Figure 6.23: I.R.F. for Velocity w.r.t. the Transitory Shock

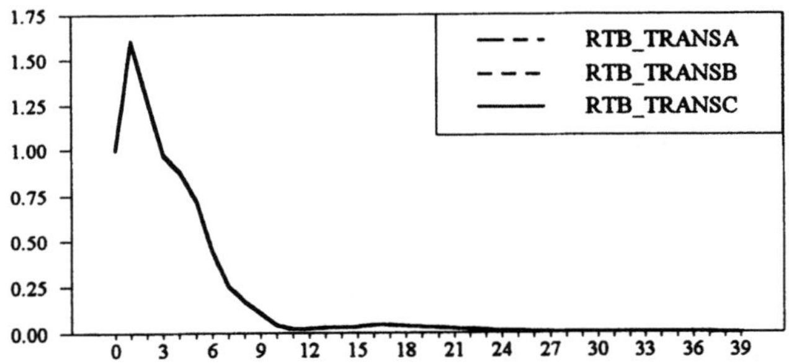


Figure 6.24: I.R.F. for Rtb w.r.t. the Transitory Shock

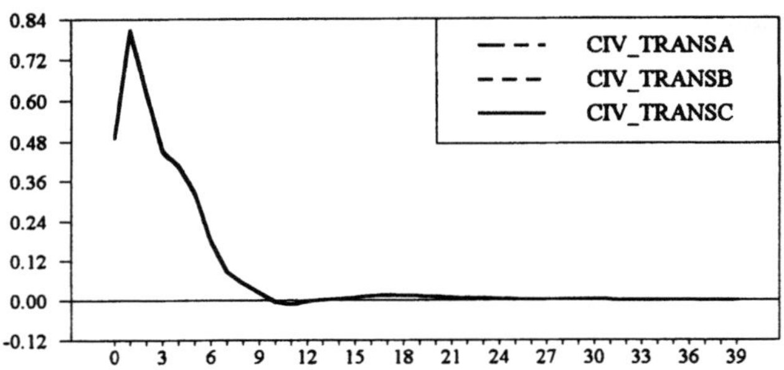


Figure 6.25: I.R.F. for the CIV w.r.t. the Transitory Shock

Table 6.17: Variance Decompositions:Quarterly double Log Specification with ln(M/P) Weakly Exogenous and No Shift in Mean of Equilibrium Demand for Real Balances, Overidentifying Restrictions Maintained

| Variable | Horizon | Permanent Nominal Shock | Permanent Real Shock | Transitory Shock |
|---|---|---|---|---|
| ln(M/P) | | | | |
| | 1 | 81.1 | 18.9 | 0.0 |
| | 4 | 50.5 | 42.9 | 6.6 |
| | 8 | 49.3 | 43.6 | 7.1 |
| | 12 | 54.8 | 40.1 | 5.1 |
| | 16 | 59.6 | 36.8 | 3.6 |
| | 200 | 72.6 | 27.2 | 0.2 |
| ln(GDP) | | | | |
| | 1 | 0.0 | 20.5 | 79.5 |
| | 4 | 1.2 | 50.1 | 48.7 |
| | 8 | 0.9 | 78.8 | 20.3 |
| | 12 | 0.6 | 87.3 | 12.2 |
| | 16 | 0.4 | 90.7 | 8.9 |
| | 200 | 0.0 | 99.3 | 0.3 |
| ln(*Rtb*) | | | | |
| | 1 | 5.5 | 46.0 | 48.4 |
| | 4 | 2.6 | 32.7 | 64.7 |
| | 8 | 2.6 | 29.9 | 67.1 |
| | 12 | 4.4 | 29.4 | 66.2 |
| | 16 | 8.1 | 28.3 | 63.6 |
| | 200 | 75.2 | 7.6 | 17.2 |
| ln(velocity) | | | | |
| | 1 | 48.9 | 0.0 | 51.0 |
| | 4 | 44.2 | 2.9 | 52.9 |
| | 8 | 62.8 | 2.1 | 35.1 |
| | 12 | 76.8 | 1.3 | 21.9 |
| | 16 | 84.3 | 0.9 | 14.8 |
| | 200 | 99.2 | 0.0 | 0.8 |
| CIV | | | | |
| | 1 | 12.6 | 50.2 | 37.1 |
| | 4 | 8.2 | 36.7 | 55.1 |
| | 8 | 10.9 | 33.3 | 55.8 |
| | 12 | 11.6 | 33.1 | 55.3 |
| | 16 | 11.6 | 33.1 | 55.2 |
| | 200 | 11.7 | 33.1 | 55.2 |

Second, the very short-run behavior of real output is dominated by the composite transitory shock, which accounts for approximately 80 percent of the variance of output at a one quarter horizon. At business cycle frequency (16 quarter horizon) about 90 percent of the forecast variance in real GDP is attributable to the permanent real shock. At no horizon does the permanent nominal shock account for as much as three percent of the forecast variance in real GDP. Clearly, to understand the sources of short-run real output fluctuations, more elaborate models are required. If additional cointegrating relationships can be found in higher dimension VECMs, then the composite transitory shock identified here can be separated into components. If, in addition, identifying restrictions can be found to isolate economically meaningful components of the transitory shock, then it may be possible to interpret the sources of the higher frequency real output fluctuations. Identification of such shocks is a distinctly different and additional problem from the identification applied in this chapter.

The variance decomposition of M1 velocity is almost exactly the reverse of that of real GDP. At very short horizons, approximately half of the variance is attributable to the composite transitory shock. At no horizon does the permanent real output shock account for as much as three percent of the forecast variance in velocity.

The distinct character of the real output, real balance, and velocity variance decompositions is particularly interesting.[19] It is very tempting, on the basis of these decompositions, to interpret the permanent nominal shock as the predictable, or anticipated, component of nominal shocks. The variance decompositions of these three variables are consistent with the hypotheses derived from monetary misperceptions models (e.g. Lucas (1972)). However, caution is advisable before making such an association, since rational agents will not, in general, correctly perceive permanent shocks when faced with unknown mixtures of permanent and transitory shocks (Muth (1960); Brunner and Meltzer (1993)).

The variance decomposition of the nominal interest rate is also quite interesting. At shorter and intermediate horizons, including business cycle frequencies, very little of the variance (less than 10 percent) is attributable to the permanent nominal shock. This suggests that very little of the short-run fluctuation in short-term interest rates is attributable to changes in inflation or inflationary expectations. This is consistent with the conclusions of several bivariate investigations of short-term nominal interest rates and inflation by Mishkin (1990a, 1990b). Even at business cycle frequencies (16 quarters) over 60 percent of the forecast variance is attributable to the composite transitory shock. Only at extremely long forecasting horizons does the permanent nominal shock become the dominant source of forecast variance in the short-term nominal rate.

### 6.4.4 Dynamic Analysis of a Quarterly Three Variable Semi-log VECM

In order to facilitate the analysis of larger dimensional VECMs in subsequent chapters, we briefly discuss the dynamic patterns that can be extracted from the semi-log specification. Two sets of identifying restrictions on the dynamic structure are shown in Table 6.18. In both cases, the two permanent shocks are assumed to precede the transitory shock in a causal chain structure and all three shocks are assumed to be independent. In part A of the table, the permanent real output trend is ordered first in the causal chain; in part B the permanent nominal trend is ordered first, as indicated in the respective $\beta_{\perp}^{0}$ matrices. The factor loading matrices ($\alpha_{\perp}^{0}$) implied by the assumed impact matrices generate a correlation between the two permanent shocks of only .01, and as a result the orthogonalizing transformation $\pi$ is very close to a diagonal matrix, particularly when the permanent nominal trend is ordered first. In this

[19] The zero fraction of the one period forecast variance of real balances attributable to the transitory shock follows directly from the weak exogeneity of real balances and the identifying restrictions for the permanent and transitory shocks.

case, the overidentifying restrictions of the model in Chapter 5 are satisfied almost exactly.

Impulse response functions for both causal chain orderings of the permanent shocks are shown in Figures 6.26-6.33. The impulse responses under the overidentifying restrictions are imperceptibly different from those produced when the nominal trend is ordered first. The impulse response functions from the semi-log structure retain all the characteristics of those derived from the double log structure. The scale of the responses to the permanent nominal shock is different. This is consistent with the normalization of this shock. In this case, the nominal shock is normalized to a 100 basis point permanent effect on the nominal rate. In the double log structure the normalization of this shock is to a 100 percent change in the nominal rate.

### 6.4.5 The Dynamic Responses in the Monthly Specifications

The monthly estimates used for the construction of this dynamic analysis are from the sample period ending in 1991:12, subject to the restriction that velocity is weakly exogenous. The restriction is not rejected, and the estimated coefficients of the VECM once the restriction is applied, are virtually unchanged from those reported in Table 6.14.

The factor loading matrices for the common trends model under both orderings of the permanent shocks are reported in Table 6.19. Again the real permanent shock is assumed to ultimately impact on real output and the permanent nominal shock affects nominal interest rate ($\beta_\perp^0$). The estimated covariance matrix of the permanent shocks defined by the factor loadings $\alpha_\perp^0$ is almost diagonal; the correlation between the two shocks is only 0.03. As a result, when the nominal shock with the larger variance is ordered first, the orthogonalizing transformation, $\pi$, is nearly an identity matrix, as is the case with the quarterly data (Table 6.17). When the real shock with the smaller variance is ordered first, the off diagonal element of the $\pi$ matrix is quite large (0.34).

The factor loadings for the orthogonal trends ($a_\perp^{*\prime}$) have many similarities to the corresponding loadings derived from the quarterly data. In both loading vectors, the weight on the reduced form interest rate error is quite small, though in the nominal trend vector the sign on the interest rate reduced form error is the opposite of that in the corresponding factor loading vector derived from the quarterly data. The weight placed on the real balance reduced form error in both common trends derived from the monthly data is also smaller in absolute value than the corresponding weight derived from the quarterly data, and the sign is reversed in the real output trend loading vector.

Table 6.18: Identification of Permanent Shocks, Quarterly Semi–Log Specification, 56:2-91:4–Weakly Exogenous ln(M/P), No Shift in Mean of Equilibrium Real Balances Except During New Operating Procedures Period

| | Real Output Shock First | Nominal Shock First |
|---|---|---|
| $\beta_{\perp}^{0} =$ | $\begin{bmatrix} 1.0 & -.1301 \\ 1.0 & 0.0 \\ 0.0 & 1.0 \end{bmatrix}$ | $\begin{bmatrix} -.1301 & 1.0 \\ 0.0 & 1.0 \\ 1.0 & 0.0 \end{bmatrix}$ |
| $\alpha_{\perp}^{0\prime} =$ | $\begin{bmatrix} .46 & 1.09 & -.01 \\ -19.3 & 5.63 & -.06 \end{bmatrix}$ | $\begin{bmatrix} -19.3 & 5.63 & -.06 \\ .48 & 1.08 & -.01 \end{bmatrix}$ |
| $\Sigma_v =$ | $\begin{bmatrix} 1.1\times10^{-4} & 1.9\times10^{-5} \\ 1.9\times10^{-5} & .02 \end{bmatrix}$ | $\begin{bmatrix} .02 & 1.9\times10^{-5} \\ 1.9\times10^{-5} & 1.1\times10^{-4} \end{bmatrix}$ |
| $\pi =$ | $\begin{bmatrix} 1.0 & 0.0 \\ 0.2 & 1.0 \end{bmatrix}$ | $\begin{bmatrix} 1.0 & 0.0 \\ 1.1\times10^{-3} & 1.0 \end{bmatrix}$ |
| $\beta_{\perp}^{*} =$ | $\begin{bmatrix} .98 & -.13 \\ 1.0 & 0.0 \\ .17 & 1.0 \end{bmatrix}$ | $\begin{bmatrix} -.13 & 1.0 \\ 1.1\times10^{-3} & 1.0 \\ 1.0 & 0.0 \end{bmatrix}$ |
| $\alpha_{\perp}^{\prime} =$ | $\begin{bmatrix} .46 & 1.08 & -.01 \\ -19.3 & 5.45 & -.05 \end{bmatrix}$ | $\begin{bmatrix} -19.3 & 5.63 & -.05 \\ .48 & 1.08 & -.01 \end{bmatrix}$ |
| D= | $\begin{bmatrix} 1.1\times10^{-4} & 0.0 \\ 0.0 & 0.02 \end{bmatrix}$ | $\begin{bmatrix} .02 & 0.0 \\ 0.0 & 1.1\times10^{-4} \end{bmatrix}$ |
| Transitory Factor Loadings | $\begin{bmatrix} 10.5 & -42.7 & -.57 \end{bmatrix}$ | $\begin{bmatrix} 10.5 & -42.7 & -.57 \end{bmatrix}$ |

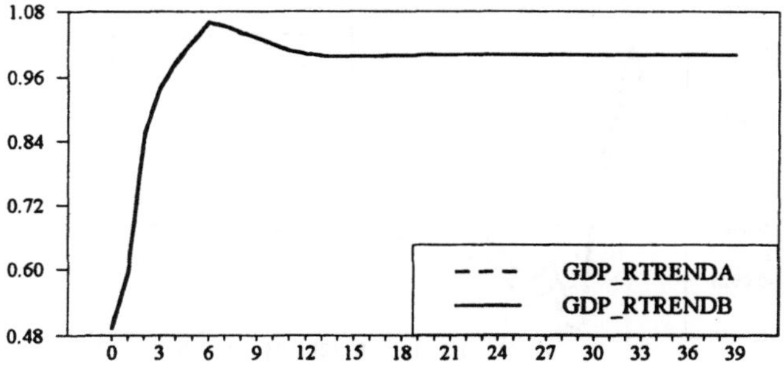


Figure 6.26: I.R.F. for GDP w.r.t. the Permanent Real Shock

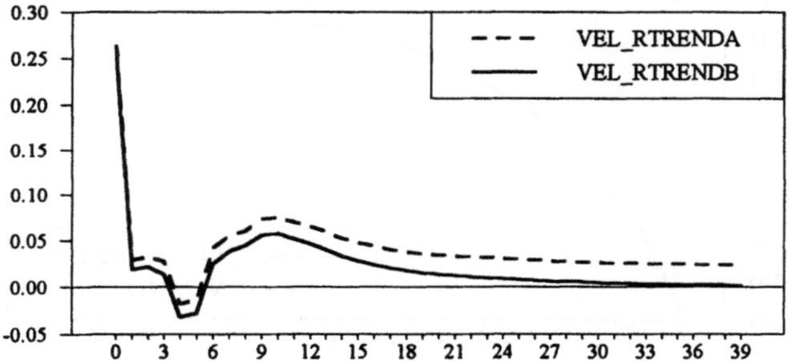


Figure 6.27: I.R.F. for Velocity w.r.t. the Permanent Real Shock

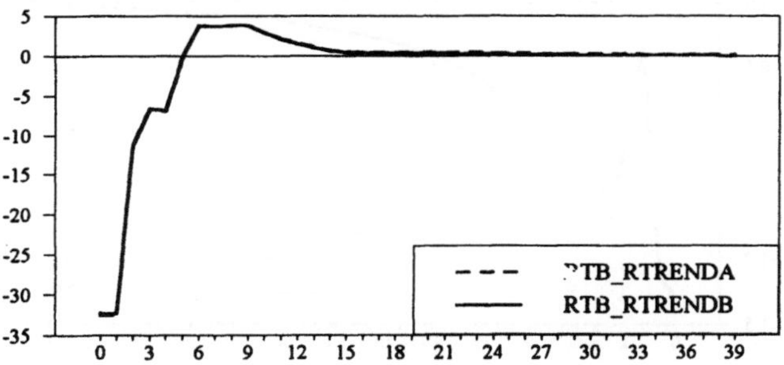


Figure 6.28: I.R.F. for Rtb w.r.t. the Permanent Real Shock

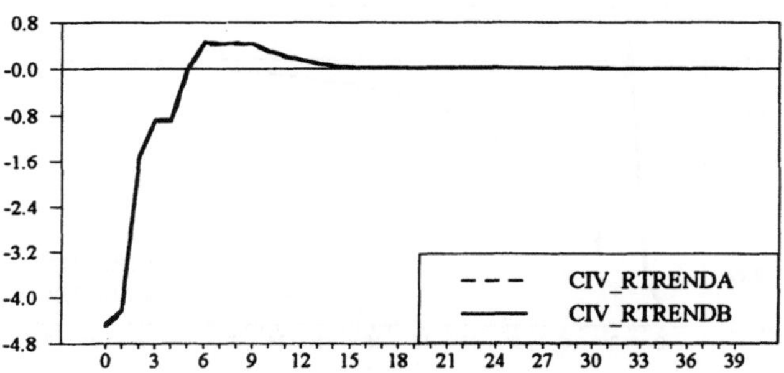


Figure 6.29: I.R.F. for the CIV w.r.t. the Permanent Real Shock

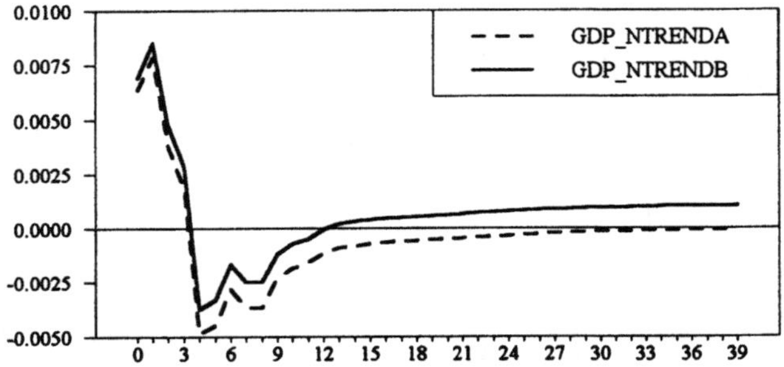


Figure 6.30: I.R.F. for GDP w.r.t. the Permanent Nominal Shock

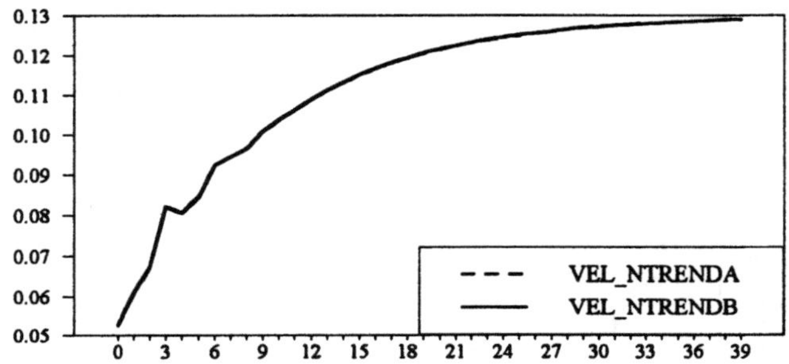


Figure 6.31: I.R.F. for Velocity w.r.t. the Permanent Nominal Shock

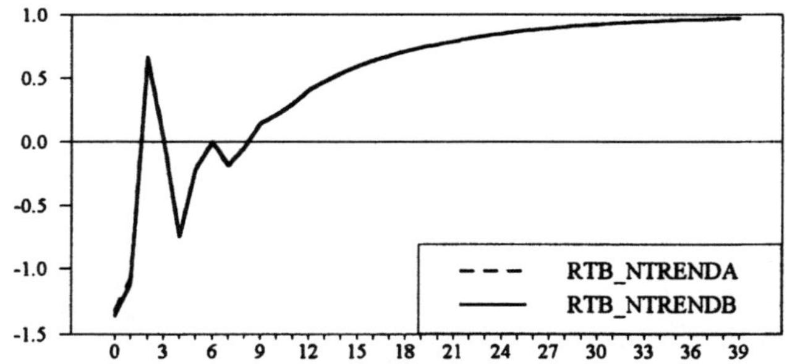


Figure 6.32: I.R.F. for Rtb w.r.t. the Permanent Nominal Shock

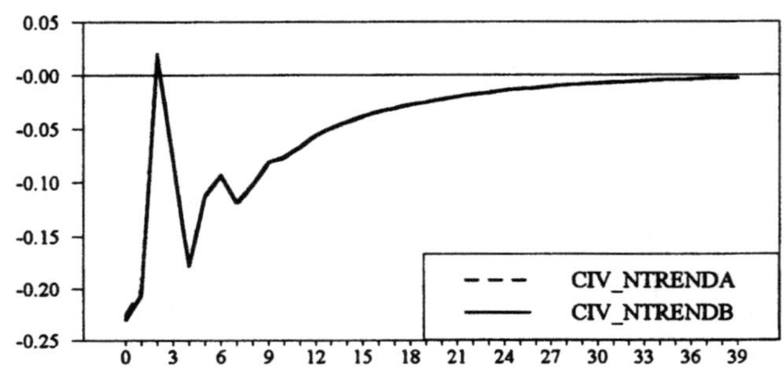


Figure 6.33: I.R.F. for the CIV w.r.t. the Permanent Nominal Shock

Table 6.19: Identification of Permanent Shocks, Monthly Semi–Log Specification, 56:2-91:12–Weakly Exogenous Velocity

| | Real Output Shock First | Nominal Shock First |
|---|---|---|
| $\beta^0_\perp =$ | $\begin{bmatrix} 1.0 & -.13 \\ 1.0 & 0.0 \\ 0.0 & 1.0 \end{bmatrix}$ | $\begin{bmatrix} -.13 & 1.0 \\ 0.0 & 1.0 \\ 1.0 & 0.0 \end{bmatrix}$ |
| $\alpha^{0\prime}_\perp =$ | $\begin{bmatrix} -.13 & .95 & -5.7\times10^{-3} \\ -12.5 & 5.31 & .04 \end{bmatrix}$ | $\begin{bmatrix} -12.4 & 5.31 & .04 \\ -.13 & .95 & -5.7\times10^{-3} \end{bmatrix}$ |
| $\Sigma_v =$ | $\begin{bmatrix} 2.4\times10^{-5} & 8.1\times10^{-6} \\ 8.1\times10^{-6} & 3.5\times10^{-3} \end{bmatrix}$ | $\begin{bmatrix} 3.5\times10^{-3} & 8.1\times10^{-6} \\ 8.1\times10^{-6} & 2.4\times10^{-5} \end{bmatrix}$ |
| $\pi =$ | $\begin{bmatrix} 1.0 & 0.0 \\ .34 & 1.0 \end{bmatrix}$ | $\begin{bmatrix} 1.0 & 0.0 \\ 2.4\times10^{-3} & 1.0 \end{bmatrix}$ |
| $\beta^*_\perp =$ | $\begin{bmatrix} .95 & -.13 \\ 1.0 & 0.0 \\ .33 & 1.0 \end{bmatrix}$ | $\begin{bmatrix} -.12 & 1.0 \\ 2.4\times10^{-3} & 1.0 \\ 1.0 & 0.0 \end{bmatrix}$ |
| $\alpha'_\perp =$ | $\begin{bmatrix} -.13 & .95 & -5.7\times10^{-3} \\ -12.4 & 4.99 & .05 \end{bmatrix}$ | $\begin{bmatrix} -12.5 & 5.31 & .04 \\ -.10 & .94 & -5.8\times10^{-3} \end{bmatrix}$ |
| D= | $\begin{bmatrix} 2.4\times10^{-5} & 0.0 \\ 0.0 & 3.5\times10^{-3} \end{bmatrix}$ | $\begin{bmatrix} 3.5\times10^{-3} & 0.0 \\ 0.0 & 2.4\times10^{-5} \end{bmatrix}$ |
| Transitory Factor Loadings | $\begin{bmatrix} -40.0 & -23.4 & -.56 \end{bmatrix}$ | $\begin{bmatrix} -40.0 & -23.4 & -.56 \end{bmatrix}$ |

Finally, the weights on the reduced form real output error have the same sign and are of the same order of magnitude in the factor loadings derived from the monthly and quarterly data sets. The impulse response functions derived from the monthly based model are shown in Figures 6.34-6.41. The time axis in these graphs covers 120 months, which is exactly the same span as the 40 quarters in Figures 6.26-6.33. There are many consistencies between the quarterly based estimates and the monthly based estimates. In both cases the responses approach their steady-state values in 3-4 years. This supports our conjecture that the AR(1) part of the $\beta' z_t$ process estimated from the monthly data is consistent with the estimate of the same parameter derived from the quarterly data.

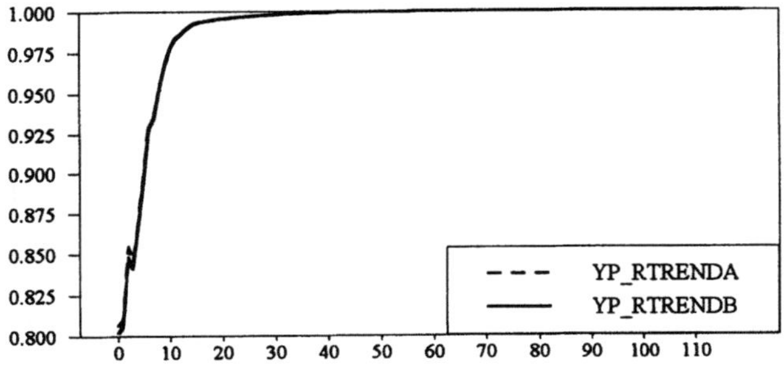


Figure 6.34: I.R.F. for Y/P w.r.t. the Permanent Real Shock

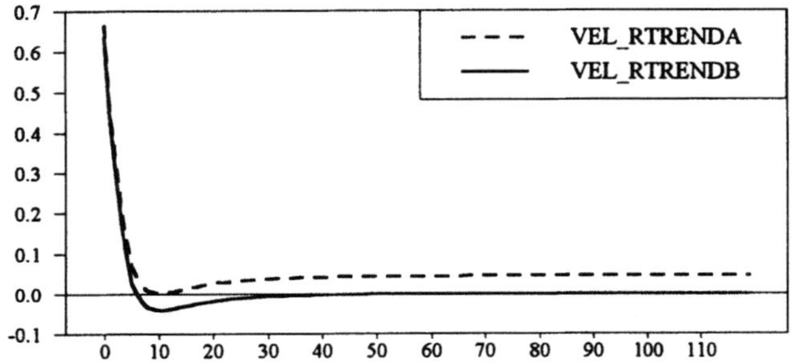


Figure 6.35: I.R.F. for Velocity w.r.t. the Permanent Real Shock

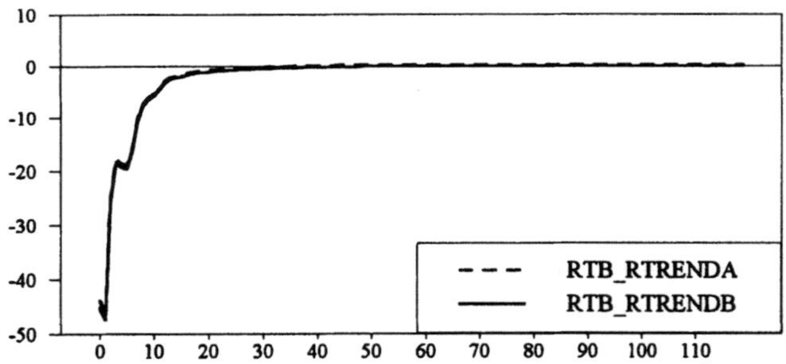


Figure 6.36: I.R.F. for Rtb w.r.t. the Permanent Real Shock

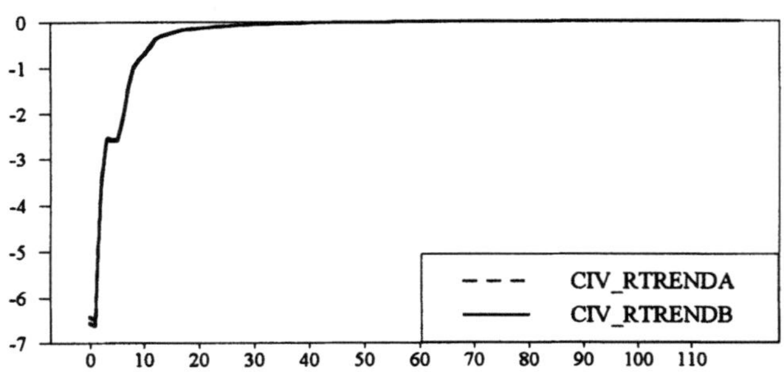


Figure 6.37: I.R.F. for the CIV w.r.t. the Permanent Real Shock

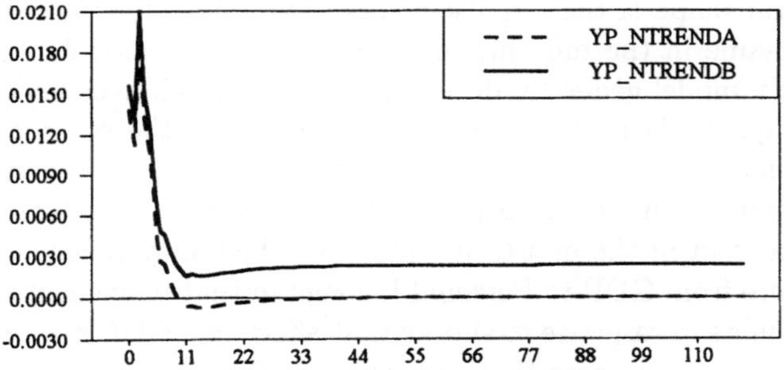


Figure 6.38: I.R.F. for Y/P w.r.t. the Permanent Nominal Shock

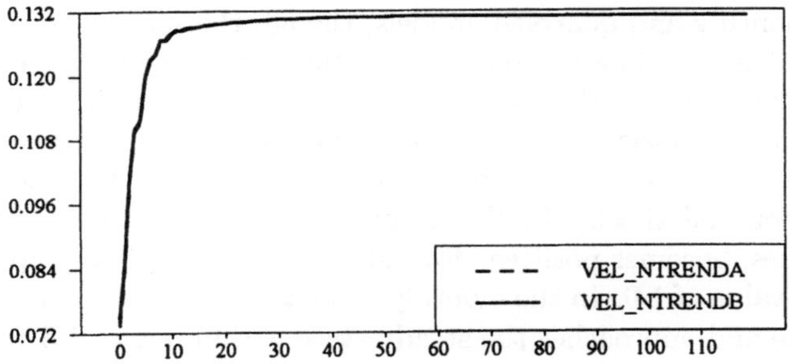


Figure 6.39: I.R.F. for Velocity w.r.t. the Permanent Nominal Shock

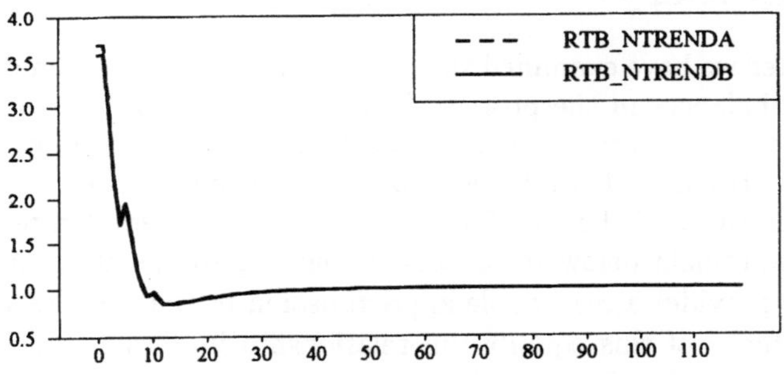


Figure 6.40: I.R.F. for Rtb w.r.t. the Permanent Nominal Shock

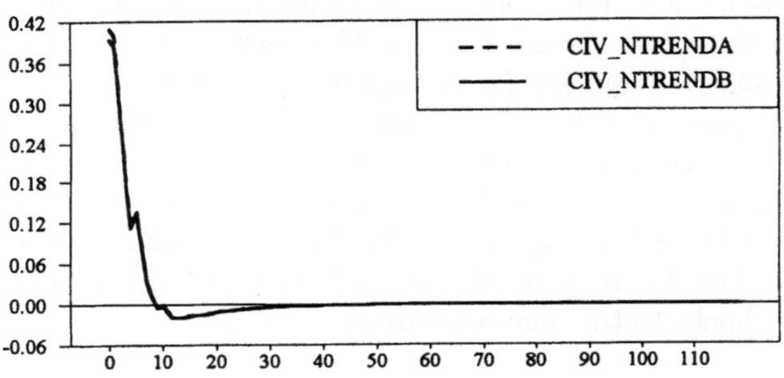


Figure 6.41: I.R.F. for the CIV w.r.t. the Permanent Nominal Shock

The general shape of the impulse response functions for the real permanent shock is the same in the monthly and quarterly based models. The patterns in the monthly model generally do not exhibit the small overshooting patterns noted in the quarterly model. The initial response of the nominal rate to the permanent real shock is the same in both models. Surprisingly, the initial response of real output to the permanent real trend is much larger (.8) in the monthly data than in the quarterly data (.5). This may reflect the change in output measure from GDP to Personal Income, in that movements in taxes and transfer payments in response to shocks that affect real GDP may generate high and low frequency responses that are more similar in magnitude for Personal Income than for real GDP.

The real income response patterns to the permanent nominal trend are similar in the monthly and quarterly models, though the impact effect is larger in the monthly based estimates, and the monthly estimates again do not exhibit the overshooting pattern that is present in the quarterly based estimates.

The obvious inconsistency between the monthly and quarterly estimates of the response patterns is in the response of the nominal interest rate to the permanent nominal shock. In the quarterly estimates, the pattern starts at negative values, becomes positive after 2-3 years, and gradually approaches the steady-state value of 1.0. In the monthly estimates, the pattern starts at a large positive value and approaches the steady-state within one to 1.5 years.

## 6.5 Summary

In this chapter we have examined the evidence for an equilibrium demand function for real balances in the postwar U.S. data and the implications of such a relationship for the sources of shocks affecting the U.S. economy. We conclude that there is strong evidence for a stable equilibrium relationship between the log of M1 velocity and the log of short-term nominal interest rates. As long as nominal rates remain below 10 percent, a semi-log specification in the nominal interest rate provides a reasonable approximation to the basic relationship.

The existence of this equilibrium relationship implies two permanent and one transitory shock affect the three variable structure we investigate in this chapter. We identify the two permanent shocks as real and nominal shocks using the KPSW common trends model. The dynamic responses (impulse response functions) to these two shocks are generally consistent with a macroeconomy that adjusts relatively quickly (2-3 years) to equilibrium.

The structure studied here is too limited to identify a short-run or dynamic demand for real balances. The one transitory shock that is identified in the dynamic analysis is a composite of all the transitory shocks that affect the economy. In subsequent chapters we expand the structure to include additional variables, search for additional permanent shocks, and attempt to identify specific sources of transitory shocks to the macroeconomy.

# Chapter 7

# HIGHER DIMENSIONAL VECM MODELS WITH LONG-RUN MONEY DEMAND FUNCTIONS

In the previous chapter, we analyzed various specifications of vector error correction models that involve three variables: real money balances, real income, and the Treasury bill rate. It was determined that there is one cointegrating vector among these variables, so there are two permanent shocks and one transitory shock that affect these three variables. The size of the model makes it impossible to attribute any economic interpretation to the transitory shock. In this chapter, the dimension of the VECM is increased to four variables. Two different specifications of such models are examined. In one the inflation rate is added to the vector of variables considered in Chapter 6, and questions of stationarity or nonstationarity of the real interest rate and the presence of absence of a long-run Fisher effect in the U.S. data are investigated. In the second model a long-term rate of interest is added to the vector of variables previously examined, and questions of the role of the term structure in affecting the demand for real balances and the elasticities of the demand for real balances with respect to long and short-term rates of interest are investigated. In both cases there is evidence for a second cointegrating vector. Restrictions on the second vector to a real interest rate or an interest rate spread, respectively, are not rejected. The estimated interest semielasticity of the velocity cointegrating vector is robust to this expansion of the model.

With two cointegrating vectors among the four variables there are two permanent and two transitory shocks to the system. The dynamic responses with respect to the permanent shocks are examined for robustness with respect to the size of the model, and identifying restrictions for the transitory shocks are proposed and investigated.

## 7.1 Real Balances, Inflation, Real Output and Interest Rates

### 7.1.1 Specification and Estimation

This selection of variables differs from the traditional four variable VAR that appears in the macroeconomics literature (Sims (1980); Litterman and Weiss (1985)). In those analyses the menu of variables is real output, inflation, nominal balances, and an interest rate. Since the log of the current price level is the lagged log of the price level plus .025 times the inflation rate measured at annual percentage rates, and since the log of nominal balances is equal to the log of real balances plus the log of the current price level, the traditional four variables can be computed from the four variable VECM that we specify here when supplemented by two identities. If the degree of differencing were the same for all the variables in the VAR, the particular selection of the variables that appear explicitly in the VAR estimation is irrelevant; the estimated coefficients of the equations for the excluded variables could be constructed by applying the appropriate identities to the included variables. However, in the VAR investigations that appear in the literature the degree of differencing is not uniform. One additional degree of differencing is applied to the price level compared with real output and nominal money balances. The advantage of including real balances rather than nominal balances in the VECM is that all of the variables that appear in a long-run demand function for real balances appear in the estimated VECM (see Rasche (1993)). The level of the interest rate, rather than the log transformation used in the three variable VECM discussed in Chapter 6 provides the opportunity to test for a long-run Fisher effect in the data.

The four variable VECM is supplemented by three dummy variables; D79 and D82 as utilized in the semi-log models in Chapter 6, and D67 that is defined as zero through 67:3 and 1.0 thereafter. The third dummy variable is included to capture the acceleration of inflation with the Vietnam conflict. These three dummy variables are included to capture shifts in the mean of a stationary *ex post* real interest rate relationship across regimes in which the trend in the expected rate of inflation differs as suggested by the reduced form VECM representation of the economic model discussed in Chapter 5, section 2.

There is substantial single equation evidence that suggests that the level of the *ex ante* real interest rate in the U.S. economy increased at or around the start of the New Operating Procedures, but then declined again sometime in 1982 (Huizinga and Mishkin (1986)). The initial single equation investigations were conditional upon an assumption that inflation expectations are formed rationally, so that the *ex post* one period ahead real interest rate can be assumed to be equal to the *ex ante* one period ahead real interest rate plus an error term that is uncorrelated with all information available at time t. These investigations did not give particular consideration to the stationarity properties of the data series.

Mishkin (1992) supplements the earlier single equation analyses by examining monthly CPI inflation rates and Treasury bill yields for cointegration. He concludes that there is substantial evidence for cointegration between these two series. He further concludes that:

> "cointegration tests for a common trend in interest rates and inflation provides support for the existence of a long-run Fisher effect. Indeed the findings here are more consistent with the views expressed by Fisher (1930) than with the standard characterization of the so-called Fisher effect in the last fifteen years. Fisher did not state that there should be a strong short-run relationship between expected inflation and interest rates. Rather he viewed the positive relationship between inflation and interest rates as a long-run phenomenon." (p. 213)

The VECM that we specify allows testing for the existence of two cointegrating vectors. If there are two cointegrating vectors in these data, one can be identified as a long-run demand for real balances and the second as a long-run relationship between inflation and nominal interest rates, if the former is specified to exclude an impact of inflation on the demand for real balances independent of the effect through the response of nominal interest rates, and the latter is specified to exclude any impact of real balances on the inflation-nominal rate relationship. These exclusions are necessary and sufficient to satisfy the identifying restrictions on two cointegrating vectors as discussed in Chapter 3.[1] Restriction of the income coefficient to be equal in absolute value, but of opposite sign of the coefficient on real balances in both cointegrating vectors is neither necessary nor sufficient to identify the vectors. If the income coefficient restriction is applied together with the identifying restrictions in the presence of two cointegrating vectors, one cointegrating vector is specified as a relationship between velocity and the nominal interest rate and the second is specified to include only the inflation rate and the nominal interest rate. Under the velocity restriction, if two cointegrating vectors are found to be present in the data, and the evidence does not reject the hypothesis that the interest rate coefficient in the inflation-nominal interest rate cointegrating vector is unity, then there is support for the conclusion that the real interest rate is stationary. For a well defined long-run demand for real balances, there should be no shift in the constant of the real balance cointegrating vector associated with the D67 dummy variable, nor should there be any net shift after 1982. We expect a shift in the constant of this cointegrating vector associated with the D79 dummy variable because of the restricted curvature of the semi-log functional form. We expect shifts in the constant of the real interest rate cointegrating vector in 1979 and 82 based on the implications of the theoretical model in Chapter 5 and previous single equation analyses.

[1] The exclusion of the inflation rate from the demand for real balances is necessary here to identify the equilibrium demand function, in contrast to the identification problem for partial adjustment models discussed in Goldfeld and Sichel (1987).

We pursue the following testing strategy. It is determined from the results in Chapter 6 that there is at least one cointegrating vector among the four variables: $lnM/P$, $\Delta p, lnY/P$, *and* $Rtb$ with coefficients (1.0, 0.0, $\beta_1$,$\beta_2$), where estimates of $\beta_1$are not significantly different from 1.0. We seek to determine if on the margin there is a second cointegrating vector among these four variables, and if it is of the form (0.0, 1.0, 0.0, -1.0). We utilize two tests to examine the evidence on the marginal cointegrating vector. First, we construct Johansen trace and maximum eigenvalue tests under the restriction that the coefficients on $lnM/P$ and $lnY/P$ are equal in absolute value, but of opposite sign in both cointegrating vectors. Under our identifying restrictions the first cointegrating vector is the velocity vector and the potential second cointegrating vector is a stationary linear combination of the inflation rate and the Treasury bill rate. This is a test of the dimension of the cointegration space spanned by the restricted(overidentified) cointegration vectors. The maximum eigenvalue test, which tests the alternative hypothesis of $r+1$ (2) cointegrating vectors against the null hypothesis of $r$ (1) cointegrating vectors is most relevant here. If there is evidence in favor of two cointegrating vectors of this form, then we examine the stationarity of the real rate (the Fisher effect) with a Wald test on the interest rate coefficient in the second cointegrating vector and with the likelihood ratio test proposed by Johansen and Juselius (1992).

Our second approach is based upon the test developed by Horvath and Watson (1993) for a marginal cointegrating vector with coefficients that are known *a priori* from economic theory in the presence of one cointegrating vector. The test is also designed for cases where some coefficients do not have values predetermined by economic theory ("unknown coefficient") . The prespecified coefficient values in the second cointegrating vector are (0.0, 1.0, 0.0, -1.0) of the Fisher equation. Horvath and Watson (1993) show that for this configuration of vectors, their test statistic is just the standard test that all the error correction coefficients on the marginal ("known") cointegrating vector are zero in the VECM. The Horvath-Watson (HW) test statistic establishes stationarity (cointegration) as the null hypothesis. It has the advantage of higher power in small sample applications.

Recursive estimates of the long-run parameters of the four variable VECM including the rate of inflation are given in Table 7.1. The estimator is the Johansen FIML procedure.[2] The cointegration test statistics (maximum eigenvalue) consistently support the conclusion that there are two cointegrating vectors among the four variables.[3]

---

[2]In this case the additional variable that we are adding to the VECM (the inflation rate) is the variable on which we are normalizing the additional cointegrating vector. Under these conditions, the Stock-Watson DOLS estimating equation for the velocity cointegrating vector is unchanged from the estimating equation that is used in Chapter 6. If the interest rate coefficient in the second cointegrating is constrained to -1.0, then there are no coefficients to be estimated in this vector.

[3]If the D67 dummy variable is omitted from the VECM model, the significance of the second cointegrating vector is reduced. For example, with D67 omitted from the specification for the 56:2 - 90:4 sample period, the trace test statistic for the hypothesis $r \preceq 1$ is 17.44 compared with 20.15 reported in Table 7.1. The maximum eigenvalue test for the hypothesis

Table 7.1: Recursive Estimates of Error Correction Coefficients.

| end: | 72:4 | T=67 |
|---|---|---|
| $H_0$ | *trace* | $\lambda$ |
| $r = 0$ | 47.4 | 0.3 |
| $r \leq 1$ | 24.3 | 0.3 |
| $r \leq 2$ | 4.3 | 0.1 |

| $\beta_c$ | |
|---|---|
| 1.0 | 0.0 |
| 0.0 | 1.0 |
| -1.0 | 0.0 |
| .09 | -0.7 |
| (0.01) | (0.21) |

| | $\beta_{01}$ | $\beta_{02}$ |
|---|---|---|
| <67:4 | -1.06 | .11 |
| >67:3 | -0.04 | 1.48 |

| $\alpha_c$ | |
|---|---|
| 0.05 | $1.0\text{x}10^{-3}$ |
| (4.5) | (1.4) |
| -4.78 | 0.34 |
| (1.46) | (1.6) |
| 0.05 | $-1.7\text{x}10^{-4}$ |
| (2.9) | (1.5) |
| $-4.7\text{x}10^{-4}$ | -0.2 |
| (-0.01) | (-3.2) |

| end: | 73:4 | T=71 |
|---|---|---|
| $H_0$ | *trace* | $\lambda$ |
| $r = 0$ | 45.3 | 0.28 |
| $r \leq 1$ | 22.1 | 0.23 |
| $r \leq 2$ | 3.2 | 0.04 |

| $\beta_c$ | |
|---|---|
| 1.0 | 0.0 |
| 0.0 | 1.0 |
| -1.0 | 0.0 |
| 0.1 | -0.84 |
| (0.02) | (0.27) |

| | $\beta_{01}$ | $\beta_{02}$ |
|---|---|---|
| <67:4 | -1.02 | -.50 |
| >67:3 | 0.01 | 1.41 |

| $\alpha_c$ | |
|---|---|
| 0.05 | $1.3\text{x}10^{-3}$ |
| (4.3) | (1.9) |
| -1.25 | 0.27 |
| (.41) | (1.4) |
| .05 | $-1.1\text{x}10^{-3}$ |
| (2.9) | (-1.04) |
| .06 | -0.2 |
| (4.1) | (-3.3) |

| end: | 74:4 | T=75 |
|---|---|---|
| $H_0$ | *trace* | $\lambda$ |
| $r = 0$ | 44.5 | 0.28 |
| $r \leq 1$ | 19.5 | 0.22 |
| $r \leq 2$ | .43 | 0.01 |

| $\beta_c$ | |
|---|---|
| 1.0 | 0.0 |
| 0.0 | 1.0 |
| -1.0 | 0.0 |
| 0.13 | -1.03 |
| (0.02) | (0.31) |

| | $\beta_{01}$ | $\beta_{02}$ |
|---|---|---|
| <67:4 | -0.92 | -1.25 |
| >67:3 | 0.09 | 1.63 |

| $\alpha_c$ | |
|---|---|
| 0.04 | $2.0\text{x}10^{-3}$ |
| (4.5) | (3.0) |
| -1.46 | 0.2 |
| (0.52) | (1.0) |
| 0.04 | $-2.8\text{x}10^{-4}$ |
| (2.53) | (-0.3) |
| 0.14 | -0.17 |
| (0.17) | (-2.9) |

| end: | 751:4 | T=79 |
|---|---|---|
| $H_0$ | *trace* | $\lambda$ |
| $r = 0$ | 53.4 | 0.34 |
| $r \leq 1$ | 21.0 | 0.21 |
| $r \leq 2$ | 2.7 | 0.03 |

| $\beta_c$ | |
|---|---|
| 1.0 | 0.0 |
| 0.0 | 1.0 |
| -1.0 | 0.0 |
| 0.13 | -0.8 |
| (0.02) | (0.2) |

| | $\beta_{01}$ | $\beta_{02}$ |
|---|---|---|
| <67:4 | -0.93 | -0.26 |
| >67:3 | 0.02 | 1.88 |

| $\alpha_c$ | |
|---|---|
| 0.04 | $2.4\text{x}10^{-3}$ |
| (4.0) | (3.2) |
| -2.56 | 0.2 |
| (-0.9) | (0.92) |
| 0.04 | $-1.4\text{x}10^{-3}$ |
| (2.97) | (-1.3) |
| 0.24 | -0.19 |
| (0.27) | (-2.8) |

| end: | 76:4 | T=83 |
|---|---|---|
| $H_0$ | *trace* | $\lambda$ |
| $r = 0$ | 52.9 | 0.33 |
| $r \leq 1$ | 19.4 | 0.18 |
| $r \leq 2$ | 3.1 | 0.04 |

| $\beta_c$ | |
|---|---|
| 1.0 | 0.0 |
| 0.0 | 1.0 |
| -1.0 | 0.0 |
| 0.12 | -0.8 |
| (0.02) | (0.18) |

| | $\beta_{01}$ | $\beta_{02}$ |
|---|---|---|
| <67:4 | -0.93 | -0.22 |
| >67:3 | -0.02 | 2.0 |

| $\alpha_c$ | |
|---|---|
| 0.03 | $1.9\text{x}10^{-3}$ |
| (3.3) | (2.6) |
| -0.67 | 0.29 |
| (-0.3) | (1.40) |
| 0.04 | $-1.8\text{x}10^{-3}$ |
| (3.1) | (-1.7) |
| 0.16 | -0.2 |
| (0.2) | (-3.1) |

| end: | 77:4 | T=87 |
|---|---|---|
| $H_0$ | *trace* | $\lambda$ |
| $r = 0$ | 51.4 | 0.32 |
| $r \leq 1$ | 17.8 | 0.16 |
| $r \leq 2$ | 2.6 | 0.03 |

| $\beta_c$ | |
|---|---|
| 1.0 | 0.0 |
| 0.0 | 1.0 |
| -1.0 | 0.0 |
| 0.14 | -0.85 |
| (0.03) | (0.22) |

| | $\beta_{01}$ | $\beta_{02}$ |
|---|---|---|
| <67:4 | -0.88 | -0.55 |
| >67:3 | -0.01 | 2.03 |

| $\alpha_c$ | |
|---|---|
| 0.03 | $1.9\text{x}10^{-3}$ |
| (3.3) | (2.6) |
| 0.32 | 0.29 |
| (0.2) | (1.4) |
| 0.03 | $-1.6\text{x}10^{-3}$ |
| (2.4) | (-1.5) |
| -0.03 | -0.19 |
| (-0.04) | (-3.2) |

Table 7.1: Recursive Estimates of Error Correction Coefficients.(continued)

| end: | 78:4 | T=91 |
|---|---|---|
| $H_0$ | *trace* | $\lambda$ |
| $r=0$ | 57.4 | 0.33 |
| $r\leq 1$ | 21.6 | 0.19 |
| $r\leq 2$ | 2.3 | 0.02 |

| $\beta_c$ | |
|---|---|
| 1.0 | 0.0 |
| 0.0 | 1.0 |
| -1.0 | 0.0 |
| 0.13 | -0.79 |
| (0.03) | (0.19) |

| | $\beta_{01}$ | $\beta_{02}$ |
|---|---|---|
| <67:4 | -0.91 | -0.36 |
| >67:3 | -0.01 | 2.22 |

| $\alpha_c$ | |
|---|---|
| 0.03 | $1.9\text{x}10^{-3}$ |
| (3.6) | (2.7) |
| 0.39 | 0.27 |
| (0.2) | (1.4) |
| 0.03 | $-1.7\text{x}10^{-3}$ |
| (2.8) | (-1.67) |
| $-1.7\text{x}10^{-3}$ | -0.2 |
| (-0.01) | (-3.23) |

| end: | 79:3 | T=94 |
|---|---|---|
| $H_0$ | *trace* | $\lambda$ |
| $r=0$ | 55.5 | 0.31 |
| $r\leq 1$ | 20.3 | 0.19 |
| $r\leq 2$ | 0.6 | 0.01 |

| $\beta_c$ | |
|---|---|
| 1.0 | 0.0 |
| 0.0 | 1.0 |
| -1.0 | 0.0 |
| 0.11 | -0.78 |
| (0.03) | (0.17) |

| | $\beta_{01}$ | $\beta_{02}$ |
|---|---|---|
| <67:4 | -0.97 | -0.33 |
| >67:3 | -0.02 | 2.18 |

| $\alpha_c$ | |
|---|---|
| 0.03 | $1.8\text{x}10^{-3}$ |
| (3.5) | (2.5) |
| 0.61 | 0.28 |
| (1.3) | (1.43) |
| 0.03 | $-1.8\text{x}10^{-3}$ |
| (2.8) | (-1.7) |
| -0.05 | -0.2 |
| (-0.1) | (-3.3) |

| end: | 80:4 | T=99 |
|---|---|---|
| $H_0$ | *trace* | $\lambda$ |
| $r=0$ | 58.7 | 0.33 |
| $r\leq 1$ | 19.3 | 0.17 |
| $r\leq 2$ | 0.8 | 0.01 |

| $\beta_c$ | |
|---|---|
| 1.0 | 0.0 |
| 0.0 | 1.0 |
| -1.0 | 0.0 |
| 0.12 | -0.79 |
| (0.02) | (0.17) |

| | $\beta_{01}$ | $\beta_{02}$ |
|---|---|---|
| <67:4 | -0.96 | -0.36 |
| >67:3 | -0.01 | 2.16 |

| $\alpha_c$ | |
|---|---|
| 0.03 | $2.0\text{x}10^{-3}$ |
| (3.7) | (2.7) |
| 0.59 | 0.31 |
| (0.3) | (1.63) |
| 0.03 | $1.8\text{x}10^{-3}$ |
| (2.8) | (-1.7) |
| 0.21 | -0.23 |
| (0.27) | (-3.0) |

| end: | 81:4 | T=103 |
|---|---|---|
| $H_0$ | *trace* | $\lambda$ |
| $r=0$ | 66.9 | 0.39 |
| $r\leq 1$ | 16.4 | 0.14 |
| $r\leq 2$ | 0.4 | 0.0 |

| $\beta_c$ | |
|---|---|
| 1.0 | 0.0 |
| 0.0 | 1.0 |
| -1.0 | 0.0 |
| 0.1 | -0.8 |
| (0.02) | (0.14) |

| | $\beta_{01}$ | $\beta_{02}$ |
|---|---|---|
| <67:4 | -1.01 | -0.34 |
| >67:3 | -0.05 | 2.16 |

| $\alpha_c$ | |
|---|---|
| 0.02 | $1.8\text{x}10^{-3}$ |
| (2.9) | (2.3) |
| 2.24 | 0.36 |
| (1.2) | (2.0) |
| 0.03 | $-2\text{x}10^{-3}$ |
| (2.5) | (-1.9) |
| 0.49 | -0.34 |
| (0.6) | (-4.0) |

| end: | 82:4 | T=107 |
|---|---|---|
| $H_0$ | *trace* | $\lambda$ |
| $r=0$ | 67.2 | 0.37 |
| $r\leq 1$ | 18.4 | 0.16 |
| $r\leq 2$ | 0.3 | 0.0 |

| $\beta_c$ | |
|---|---|
| 1.0 | 0.0 |
| 0.0 | 1.0 |
| -1.0 | 0.0 |
| 0.1 | -0.72 |
| (0.02) | (0.15) |

| | $\beta_{01}$ | $\beta_{02}$ |
|---|---|---|
| <67:4 | -1.02 | -0.13 |
| >67:3 | -0.05 | 2.3 |

| $\alpha_c$ | |
|---|---|
| 0.03 | $1.9\text{x}10^{-3}$ |
| (3.3) | (2.5) |
| 2.02 | 0.34 |
| (1.1) | (1.9) |
| 0.03 | $-1.9\text{x}10^{-3}$ |
| (2.6) | (-1.9) |
| -0.15 | -0.4 |
| (-0.2) | (-4.4) |

| end: | 83:4 | T=111 |
|---|---|---|
| $H_0$ | *trace* | $\lambda$ |
| $r=0$ | 69.4 | 0.37 |
| $r\leq 1$ | 19.0 | 0.16 |
| $r\leq 2$ | 0.05 | 0.0 |

| $\beta_c$ | |
|---|---|
| 1.0 | 0.0 |
| 0.0 | 1.0 |
| -1.0 | 0.0 |
| 0.10 | -0.69 |
| (0.02) | (0.14) |

| | $\beta_{01}$ | $\beta_{02}$ |
|---|---|---|
| <67:4 | -1.03 | -0.003 |
| >67:3 | -0.06 | 2.39 |

| $\alpha_c$ | |
|---|---|
| 0.03 | $1.8\text{x}10^{-3}$ |
| (3.2) | (2.4) |
| 2.15 | 0.34 |
| (1.2) | (2.0) |
| 0.03 | $-2\text{x}10^{-3}$ |
| (2.7) | (-2.0) |
| -0.26 | -0.39 |
| (-0.3) | (-4.5) |

Table 7.1: Recursive Estimates of Error Correction Coefficients.(continued)

| end: | 84:4 | T=115 |
|---|---|---|
| $H_0$ | *trace* | $\lambda$ |
| $r = 0$ | 69.1 | 0.33 |
| $r \leq 1$ | 22.6 | 0.18 |
| $r \leq 2$ | 0.2 | 0.002 |

| $\beta_c$ | |
|---|---|
| 1.0 | 0.0 |
| 0.0 | 1.0 |
| -1.0 | 0.0 |
| 0.1 | -0.8 |
| (0.02) | (0.15) |

| | $\beta_{01}$ | $\beta_{02}$ |
|---|---|---|
| <67:4 | -1.01 | -0.43 |
| >67:3 | -0.04 | 2.0 |
| >79:3 | 0.5 | -3.5 |
| >82:1 | -0.55 | -1.52 |

| $\alpha$ | |
|---|---|
| 0.02 | 1.6x10$^{-3}$ |
| (3.02) | (2.3) |
| 2.5 | -0.35 |
| (1.5) | (2.1) |
| 0.03 | -1.5x10$^{-3}$ |
| (3.3) | (-1.6) |
| -0.1 | -0.36 |
| (-0.11) | (-4.1) |

| end: | 85:4 | T=119 |
|---|---|---|
| $H_0$ | *trace* | $\lambda$ |
| $r = 0$ | 69.3 | 0.33 |
| $r \leq 1$ | 22.5 | 0.17 |
| $r \leq 2$ | 0.2 | 0.002 |

| $\beta_c$ | |
|---|---|
| 1.0 | 0.0 |
| 0.0 | 1.0 |
| -1.0 | 0.0 |
| 0.1 | -0.78 |
| (0.02) | (0.16) |

| | $\beta_{01}$ | $\beta_{02}$ |
|---|---|---|
| <67:4 | -1.01 | -0.3 |
| >67:3 | -0.04 | 2.1 |
| >79:3 | 0.49 | -3.36 |
| >82:1 | -0.51 | -1.3 |

| $\alpha$ | |
|---|---|
| 0.02 | 1.8x10$^{-3}$ |
| (3.4) | (2.4) |
| 2.6 | 0.37 |
| (1.6) | (2.3) |
| 0.03 | -1.3x10$^{-3}$ |
| (3.2) | (-1.5) |
| -0.17 | -0.35 |
| (-0.2) | (-4.3) |

| end: | 86:4 | T=123 |
|---|---|---|
| $H_0$ | *trace* | $\lambda$ |
| $r = 0$ | 55.0 | 0.27 |
| $r \leq 1$ | 16.1 | 0.12 |
| $r \leq 2$ | 0.11 | 0.001 |

| $\beta_c$ | |
|---|---|
| 1.0 | 0.0 |
| 0.0 | 1.0 |
| -1.0 | 0.0 |
| 0.1 | -0.69 |
| (0.02) | (-0.22) |

| | $\beta_{01}$ | $\beta_{02}$ |
|---|---|---|
| <67:4 | -1.03 | 0.02 |
| >67:3 | -0.06 | 2.36 |
| >79:3 | 0.46 | -2.82 |
| >82:1 | -0.48 | -1.54 |

| $\alpha$ | |
|---|---|
| 0.03 | 1.3x10$^{-3}$ |
| (3.7) | (1.8) |
| 2.21 | 0.43 |
| (1.4) | (2.7) |
| 0.03 | -3.5x10$^{-4}$ |
| (2.6) | (-0.4) |
| -0.36 | -0.3 |
| (-0.44) | (-3.7) |

| end: | 87:4 | T=127 |
|---|---|---|
| $H_0$ | *trace* | $\lambda$ |
| $r = 0$ | 55.6 | 0.29 |
| $r \leq 1$ | 12.2 | 0.09 |
| $r \leq 2$ | 0.3 | 0.002 |

| $\beta_c$ | |
|---|---|
| 1.0 | 0.0 |
| 0.0 | 1.0 |
| -1.0 | 0.0 |
| 0.09 | -0.68 |
| (0.03) | (0.23) |

| | $\beta_{01}$ | $\beta_{02}$ |
|---|---|---|
| <67:4 | -1.06 | 0.08 |
| >67:3 | -0.07 | 2.35 |
| >79:3 | 0.46 | -2.95 |
| >81:4 | -0.63 | -0.77 |

| $\alpha_c$ | |
|---|---|
| 0.02 | 1.7x10$^{-3}$ |
| (3.2) | (2.5) |
| 2.66 | 0.46 |
| (1.7) | (3.1) |
| 0.03 | 1.3x10$^{-4}$ |
| (2.9) | (0.14) |
| -0.33 | -0.26 |
| (-0.4) | (-3.4) |

| end: | 88:4 | T=131 |
|---|---|---|
| $H_0$ | *trace* | $\lambda$ |
| $r = 0$ | 59.8 | 0.27 |
| $r \leq 1$ | 18.0 | 0.11 |
| $r \leq 2$ | 2.5 | 0.02 |

| $\beta_c$ | |
|---|---|
| 1.0 | 0.0 |
| 0.0 | 1.0 |
| -1.0 | 0.0 |
| 0.1 | -0.82 |
| (0.03) | (0.27) |

| | $\beta_{01}$ | $\beta_{02}$ |
|---|---|---|
| <67:4 | -1.02 | -0.43 |
| >67:3 | -0.04 | 1.91 |
| >79:3 | 0.47 | -4.01 |
| >81:4 | -0.59 | 0.36 |

| $\alpha_c$ | |
|---|---|
| 0.02 | 1.6x10$^{-3}$ |
| (2.5) | (2.3) |
| 3.94 | 0.47 |
| (2.9) | (3.3) |
| 0.03 | 1.5x10$^{-4}$ |
| (3.0) | (0.2) |
| 0.13 | -0.24 |
| (0.2) | (-3.2) |

| end: | 89:4 | T=135 |
|---|---|---|
| $H_0$ | *trace* | $\lambda$ |
| $r = 0$ | 61.9 | 0.26 |
| $r \leq 1$ | 21.1 | 0.13 |
| $r \leq 2$ | 3.0 | 0.02 |

| $\beta_c$ | |
|---|---|
| 1.0 | 0.0 |
| 0.0 | 1.0 |
| -1.0 | 0.0 |
| 0.11 | -0.89 |
| (0.03) | (0.23) |

| | $\beta_{01}$ | $\beta_{02}$ |
|---|---|---|
| <67:4 | -1.0 | -0.67 |
| >67:3 | -0.02 | 1.7 |
| >79:3 | 0.5 | -4.38 |
| >81:4 | -0.6 | 0.57 |

| $\alpha_c$ | |
|---|---|
| 0.01 | 1.5x10$^{-3}$ |
| (2.2) | (2.3) |
| 4.09 | 0.46 |
| (3.3) | (3.4) |
| 0.02 | 1.9x10$^{-4}$ |
| (3.2) | (0.23) |
| 0.31 | -0.22 |
| (0.5) | (-3.1) |

Table 7.1: Recursive Estimates of Error Correction Coefficients.(continued)

| end: | 90:4 | T=139 | end: | 91:4 | T=143 |
|---|---|---|---|---|---|
| $H_0$ | *trace* | $\lambda$ | $H_0$ | *trace* | $\lambda$ |
| $r = 0$ | 60.8 | 0.25 | $r = 0$ | 58.2 | 0.25 |
| $r \leq 1$ | 20.2 | 0.12 | $r \leq 1$ | 16.4 | 0.09 |
| $r \leq 2$ | 3.1 | 0.02 | $r \leq 2$ | 3.1 | 0.02 |

| $\beta_c$ | | $\beta_c$ | |
|---|---|---|---|
| 1.0 | 0.0 | 1.0 | 0.0 |
| 0.0 | 1.0 | 0.0 | 1.0 |
| -1.0 | 0.0 | -1.0 | 0.0 |
| 0.12 | -0.94 | 0.11 | -0.9 |
| (0.04) | (0.26) | (0.04) | (0.29) |

| | $\beta_{01}$ | $\beta_{02}$ | | $\beta_{01}$ | $\beta_{02}$ |
|---|---|---|---|---|---|
| <67:4 | -0.97 | -0.84 | <67:4 | -0.99 | -0.7 |
| >67:3 | 0.01 | 1.55 | >67:3 | -0.01 | 1.67 |
| >79:3 | 0.55 | -4.77 | >79:3 | 0.55 | -4.6 |
| >81:4 | -0.65 | 1.2 | >81:4 | -0.7 | 1.3 |

| $\alpha_c$ | | $\alpha_c$ | |
|---|---|---|---|
| 0.01 | $1.4x10^{-3}$ | 0.01 | $1.4x10^{-3}$ |
| (1.9) | (2.1) | (2.3) | (2.0) |
| 4.18 | 0.48 | 3.8 | 0.48 |
| (3.7) | (3.5) | (3.4) | (3.6) |
| 0.02 | $1.6x10^{-5}$ | 0.02 | $3.7x10^{-6}$ |
| (2.7) | (0.02) | (2.3) | (0.01) |
| 0.28 | -0.22 | 0.06 | -0.22 |
| (0.5) | (3.1) | (0.1) | (-3.1) |

**Note:Recursive Samples indicated by the end of the sample period. Trace and $\lambda$ statistics refer to Johansen tests. $\beta_c$ is the estimate of the normalized cointegration vectors. $\beta_{01}$ and $\beta_{02}$ are the constant terms(that can change with intervention dummies) in the cointegrating relations. $\alpha$ is the matrix of error correction coefficients at each recursive sample.**

The estimated interest rate semielasticity in the cointegrating vector that is identified as the long-run money demand function by excluding the inflation rate and normalizing on velocity is quite precise. In contrast, the estimated coefficient on the nominal interest rate is relatively imprecise in the cointegrating vector that is identified by excluding real balances (and real income). In almost all of the samples, the absolute value of this estimated coefficient is substantially less than 1.0, but not significantly so, when judged by a Wald test (Johansen (1991)).[4] Therefore in general with these data it is impossible to discriminate between the hypothesis of a traditional "Fisher effect" and the alternative hypothesis that the coefficient on the nominal interest rate should be greater than -1.0 (alternatively that the coefficient on the inflation rate should be less -1.0 when the cointegrating vector is normalized on the nominal interest rate) to reflect the absence of indexing of interest income in the tax system (Darby (1975)). The estimated constants in the real balance cointegrating vector exhibit a pattern that is quite similar to that found for the semi-log specification in Chapter 6. The implied shift in this constant associated with the D67 dummy is always close to zero. There is a substantial shift in the constant at the beginning of the New Operating Procedures period, but once the high interest rate period ends, the net shift in the constant of this vector is very small.

The constant of the inflation-nominal rate cointegrating vector varies substantially with the dummy variables. In these unrestricted estimations, the constant shifts down substantially after 1967, then shifts up in 1979. The shift associated with D82 varies considerably as the sample period is extended through the 1980s. Interpretation of these shifts in the constant of the inflation-nominal rate cointegrating vector is not straightforward in the absence of (1.0, -1.0) coefficients on the two variables. Therefore we postpone interpretation of the constant term in this vector until after restricted estimates have been constructed.

In contrast to the robust results that emerge for the coefficients of the cointegrating vectors, there is mixed evidence in the estimated error correction coefficients across sample periods with the error correction coefficients in the inflation equation exhibiting instabilities.[5] Before the 1980s, the estimates of these coefficients are very small in absolute value and have very small "$t$"-ratios. In the samples extending beyond the New Operating Procedures period the estimates of these coefficients become large and positive, and the samples incorporating

---

r = 1 is more robust. For the 56:2 - 90:4 sample period, this statistic is 16.89 when D67 is omitted, compared with a value of 17.06 reported in Table 7.1

[4]The omission of D67 affects the estimated size of the interest rate coefficient in the "Fisher equation". The estimate is substantially less than 1.0 when this dummy variable is excluded, though not significantly so (judged by a Wald test) in the longer sample periods.

[5]The "$t$" ratios for the error correction coefficients were obtained using an Engle-Granger two step estimation procedure in which the coefficients of the cointegrating vectors were estimated in a first stage using the Johansen FIML estimator. In the second step the estimated cointegrating vectors are introduced as additional regressors in a VECM specification. The estimates of the remaining VECM coefficients in the second stage are identical to those produced by the Johansen algorithm. The estimated "$t$" ratios from the second stage on the error correction coefficients are identical to those produced by the Juselius/Hansen CATS program.

information from the late 1980s the "$t$"-ratios are quite large. In the samples that do not incorporate data from the 1980s, the estimates suggest that inflation is weakly exogenous. When information from the 1980s is included the weak exogeneity hypothesis is rejected.

The remaining estimated error correction coefficients are quite robust. The error correction coefficient associated with the real balance cointegrating vector is always insignificant in the Treasury bill rate equation (that is exactly the opposite result from the three variable models in Chapter 6). The error correction coefficients for this vector in the real balance and real income equations always have large "$t$"-ratios and are usually almost the same size. This suggests that the growth rate of velocity is not affected by deviations from equilibrium real balances.

The error correction coefficients for real balances and the Treasury bill rate with respect to the inflation-nominal interest rate cointegrating vector are also quite robust. Except for the shortest sample periods, these estimated coefficients exhibit large "$t$"-ratios. The error correction coefficient in the real balance equation is always positive; that in the nominal interest rate equation is always negative. The error correction coefficient in the real output equation for the inflation-nominal interest rate cointegrating vector is always small in absolute value and generally has a small "$t$"-ratio, suggesting that real output growth does not adjust to deviations of inflation and nominal rates.

In the absence of systematic evidence against the traditional "Fisher equation", the overidentifying restriction that the *ex post* real interest rate is stationary has been imposed. In no sample period is the overidentifying restriction rejected by the likelihood ratio test proposed by Johansen and Juselius (1992). In addition the Horvath-Watson $HW$ statistic fails to reject the stationarity of the *ex post* real rate given the velocity cointegrating vector at the one percent level in all samples. Recursive estimates of the long-run parameters of the overidentified model are presented in Table 7.2. To facilitate investigation of the hypothesis that velocity is weakly exogenous the four variable model reported in Table 7.2 is an algebraic transformation of the model in Table 7.1. In Table 7.2 the four equations are $\Delta \ln Vel$, $\Delta p$, $\Delta \ln Y/P$, and $\Delta Rtb$. The estimates of the coefficients for the three equations for $\Delta p$, $\Delta \ln Y/P$, and $\Delta Rtb$ are invariant to this transformation of the model. Once the overidentifying restriction for the "Fisher effect" is imposed, the estimated interest semielasticity of the demand for real balances is extremely stable in the recursive estimation and is very similar to the estimated coefficient found in the corresponding sample period using the three variable model reported in Chapter 6.

A comparison of the estimated interest rate semielasticities from the three (COEF3) and four (COEF4) variable models is shown in Figure 7.1.[6] The results of these estimations are consistent with the implication of the economic model in Chapter 5 that expansion of the dimension of the model should not affect the inference about the interest semielasticity of the demand for real balances.

[6]The estimated interest semielasticities are from Table 6.7 and 6.8 for the three variable models and from Table 7.2 for the four variable model.

Table 7.2: Recursive Estimates of Error Correction Coefficients.

| end: | 72:4 |
|---|---|
| $H_0$ | statistic |
| $\chi^2_1$ | 1.38 |
| $HW_{12}$ | 23.1 |

| $\beta_c$ | |
|---|---|
| 1.0 | 0.0 |
| 0.0 | 1.0 |
| -1.0 | 0.0 |
| 0.09 | -1.0 |
| (0.02) | |

| | $\beta_{01}$ | $\beta_{02}$ |
|---|---|---|
| <67:4 | -1.06 | -1.17 |
| >67:3 | -0.02 | 0.88 |

| $\alpha_c$ | |
|---|---|
| 0.002 | -0.002 |
| (0.12) | (-2.12) |
| 4.34 | 0.19 |
| (1.32) | (1.1) |
| -0.05 | -0.001 |
| (2.8) | (1.4) |
| 0.13 | -0.17 |
| (0.2) | (-3.5) |

| end: | 73:4 |
|---|---|
| $H_0$ | statistic |
| $\chi^2_1$ | 0.25 |
| $HW_{12}$ | 25.6 |

| $\beta_c$ | |
|---|---|
| 1.0 | 0.0 |
| 0.0 | 1.0 |
| -1.0 | 0.0 |
| 0.10 | -1.0 |
| (0.02) | |

| | $\beta_{01}$ | $\beta_{02}$ |
|---|---|---|
| <67:4 | -1.01 | -1.1 |
| >67:3 | 0.02 | 1.13 |

| $\alpha_c$ | |
|---|---|
| -0.002 | -0.002 |
| (0.1) | (-2.02) |
| 1.04 | 0.22 |
| (0.34) | (1.2) |
| -0.05 | -0.001 |
| (-2.8) | (-0.9) |
| 0.03 | -0.18 |
| (0.03) | (-3.4) |

| end: | 74:4 |
|---|---|
| $H_0$ | statistic |
| $\chi^2_1$ | 0.004 |
| $HW_{12}$ | 28.5 |

| $\beta_c$ | |
|---|---|
| 1.0 | 0.0 |
| 0.0 | 1.0 |
| -1.0 | 0.0 |
| 0.13 | -1.0 |
| (0.02) | |

| | $\beta_{01}$ | $\beta_{02}$ |
|---|---|---|
| <67:4 | -0.92 | -1.15 |
| >67:3 | 0.09 | 1.69 |

| $\alpha_c$ | |
|---|---|
| 0.005 | -0.002 |
| (0.32) | (2.01) |
| 1.5 | 0.2 |
| (0.53) | (0.96) |
| -0.04 | -0.0003 |
| (-2.6) | (-0.3) |
| -0.16 | -0.17 |
| (-0.2) | (-2.9) |

| end: | 75:4 |
|---|---|
| $H_0$ | statistic |
| $\chi^2_1$ | 1.01 |
| $HW_{12}$ | 37.7 |

| $\beta_c$ | |
|---|---|
| 1.0 | 0.0 |
| 0.0 | 1.0 |
| -1.0 | 0.0 |
| 0.14 | -1.0 |
| (0.02) | |

| | $\beta_{01}$ | $\beta_{02}$ |
|---|---|---|
| <67:4 | -0.88 | -1.03 |
| >67:3 | 0.05 | 1.32 |

| $\alpha_c$ | |
|---|---|
| 0.002 | -0.003 |
| (0.11) | (-2.9) |
| 2.17 | 0.2 |
| (0.8) | (0.9) |
| -0.04 | -0.001 |
| (-2.6) | (-1.0) |
| -0.02 | -0.19 |
| (-0.02) | (-2.9) |

| end: | 76:4 |
|---|---|
| $H_0$ | statistic |
| $\chi^2_1$ | 1.2 |
| $HW_{12}$ | 38.2 |

| $\beta_c$ | |
|---|---|
| 1.0 | 0.0 |
| 0.0 | 1.0 |
| -1.0 | 0.0 |
| 0.14 | -1.0 |
| (0.02) | |

| | $\beta_{01}$ | $\beta_{02}$ |
|---|---|---|
| <67:4 | -0.88 | -1.03 |
| >67:3 | 0.02 | 1.40 |

| $\alpha_c$ | |
|---|---|
| -0.004 | -0.003 |
| (-0.31) | (-2.9) |
| 0.36 | 0.28 |
| (0.14) | (1.5) |
| -0.03 | -0.001 |
| (-2.7) | (-1.3) |
| 0.04 | -0.19 |
| (0.1) | (-3.2) |

| end: | 77:4 |
|---|---|
| $H_0$ | statistic |
| $\chi^2_1$ | 0.36 |
| $HW_{12}$ | 39.5 |

| $\beta_c$ | |
|---|---|
| 1.0 | 0.0 |
| 0.0 | 1.0 |
| -1.0 | 0.0 |
| 0.15 | -1.0 |
| (0.03) | |

| | $\beta_{01}$ | $\beta_{02}$ |
|---|---|---|
| <67:4 | -0.83 | -1.07 |
| >67:3 | -0.03 | 1.65 |

| $\alpha_c$ | |
|---|---|
| 0.001 | -0.003 |
| (0.11) | (-2.9) |
| -0.42 | 0.29 |
| (-0.2) | (1.5) |
| -0.02 | -0.001 |
| (-2.2) | (-1.3) |
| 0.13 | -0.19 |
| (0.2) | (-3.2) |

Table 7.2: Recursive Estimates of Error Correction Coefficients.(continued)

| end: | 78:4 |
|---|---|
| $H_0$ | statistic |
| $\chi^2_1$ | 0.9 |
| $HW_{12}$ | 40.8 |

| $\beta_c$ | |
|---|---|
| 1.0 | 0.0 |
| 0.0 | 1.0 |
| -1.0 | 0.0 |
| 0.15 | -1.0 |
| (0.03) | |

| | $\beta_{01}$ | $\beta_{02}$ |
|---|---|---|
| <67:4 | 0.84 | -1.07 |
| >67:3 | -0.04 | 1.65 |

| $\alpha_c$ | |
|---|---|
| -0.0004 | -0.003 |
| (-0.04) | (-2.9) |
| -0.48 | 0.28 |
| (0.25) | (1.42) |
| -0.03 | -0.002 |
| (-2.4) | (-1.3) |
| 0.13 | -0.19 |
| (0.22) | (3.2) |

| end: | 79:3 |
|---|---|
| $H_0$ | statistic |
| $\chi^2_1$ | 1.4 |
| $HW_{12}$ | 39.5 |

| $\beta_c$ | |
|---|---|
| 1.0 | 0.0 |
| 0.0 | 1.0 |
| -1.0 | 0.0 |
| 0.13 | -1.0 |
| (0.02) | |

| | $\beta_{01}$ | $\beta_{02}$ |
|---|---|---|
| <67:4 | 0.05 | 15.3 |
| >67:3 | 0.48 | -10.6 |

| $\alpha_c$ | |
|---|---|
| -0.003 | -0.003 |
| (0.21) | (-2.9) |
| 0.66 | -0.28 |
| (0.33) | (1.5) |
| 0.03 | -0.002 |
| (2.6) | (1.4) |
| -0.15 | -0.19 |
| (-0.3) | (3.2) |

| end: | 80:4 |
|---|---|
| $H_0$ | statistic |
| $\chi^2_1$ | 1.3 |
| $HW_{12}$ | 45.4 |

| $\beta_c$ | |
|---|---|
| 1.0 | 0.0 |
| 0.0 | 1.0 |
| -1.0 | 0.0 |
| 0.13 | -1.0 |
| (0.02) | |

| | $\beta_{01}$ | $\beta_{02}$ |
|---|---|---|
| <67:4 | -0.9 | -1.06 |
| >67:3 | 0.04 | 1.54 |

| $\alpha_c$ | |
|---|---|
| 0.002 | -0.004 |
| (0.14) | (-3.2) |
| 0.65 | 0.31 |
| (0.33) | (1.7) |
| 0.03 | -0.002 |
| (2.6) | (-1.4) |
| 0.08 | -0.22 |
| (0.1) | (-2.9) |

| end: | 81:4 |
|---|---|
| $H_0$ | statistic |
| $\chi^2_1$ | 1.71 |
| $HW_{12}$ | 56.4 |

| $\beta_c$ | |
|---|---|
| 1.0 | 0.0 |
| 0.0 | 1.0 |
| -1.0 | 0.0 |
| 0.12 | -1.0 |
| (0.02) | |

| | $\beta_{01}$ | $\beta_{02}$ |
|---|---|---|
| <67:4 | -0.94 | -1.1 |
| >67:3 | 0.01 | 1.5 |
| >79:3 | 0.54 | -4.34 |

| $\alpha_c$ | |
|---|---|
| -0.001 | -0.003 |
| (-0.05) | (-3.2) |
| 2.29 | -0.35 |
| (1.24) | (-2.0) |
| 0.02 | -0.002 |
| (2.24) | (-1.6) |
| 0.3 | -0.32 |
| (0.4) | (-3.8) |

| end: | 82:4 |
|---|---|
| $H_0$ | statistic |
| $\chi^2_1$ | 2.55 |
| $HW_{12}$ | 57.5 |

| $\beta_c$ | |
|---|---|
| 1.0 | 0.0 |
| 0.0 | 1.0 |
| -1.0 | 0.0 |
| 0.13 | -1.0 |
| (0.02) | |

| | $\beta_{01}$ | $\beta_{02}$ |
|---|---|---|
| <67:4 | -0.91 | -1.08 |
| >67:3 | 0.04 | 1.52 |
| >79:3 | 0.62 | -4.38 |
| >81:4 | -0.32 | -3.42 |

| $\alpha_c$ | |
|---|---|
| 0.004 | -0.004 |
| (0.34) | (-3.3) |
| -2.07 | 0.33 |
| (-1.2) | (1.9) |
| -0.02 | -0.002 |
| (-2.2) | (-1.53) |
| 0.49 | -0.37 |
| (0.6) | (-4.2) |

| end: | 83:4 |
|---|---|
| $H_0$ | statistic |
| $\chi^2_1$ | 3.3 |
| $HW_{12}$ | 58.9 |

| $\beta_c$ | |
|---|---|
| 1.0 | 0.0 |
| 0.0 | 1.0 |
| -1.0 | 0.0 |
| 0.13 | -1.0 |
| (0.02) | |

| | $\beta_{01}$ | $\beta_{02}$ |
|---|---|---|
| <67:4 | -0.91 | -1.07 |
| >67:3 | 0.05 | 1.47 |
| >79:3 | 0.65 | -4.6 |
| >81:4 | -0.57 | -1.42 |

| $\alpha_c$ | |
|---|---|
| 0.003 | -0.003 |
| (0.3) | (-3.3) |
| -2.25 | 0.34 |
| (-1.3) | (2.0) |
| -0.02 | -0.002 |
| (-2.2) | (-1.6) |
| 0.67 | -0.36 |
| (0.8) | (-4.2) |

Table 7.2: Recursive Estimates of Error Correction Coefficients.(continued)

| end: | 84:4 |
|---|---|
| $H_0$ | statistic |
| $\chi_1^2$ | 1.13 |
| $HW_{12}$ | 54.5 |

| $\beta_c$ | |
|---|---|
| 1.0 | 0.0 |
| 0.0 | 1.0 |
| -1.0 | 0.0 |
| 0.12 | -1.0 |
| (0.02) | |

| | $\beta_{01}$ | $\beta_{02}$ |
|---|---|---|
| <67:4 | -0.95 | -1.06 |
| >67:3 | 0.01 | 1.46 |
| >79:3 | 0.6 | -4.68 |
| >81:4 | -0.61 | -0.88 |

| $\alpha_c$ | |
|---|---|
| -0.006 | -0.003 |
| (-0.6) | (-3.0) |
| -2.64 | 0.34 |
| (-1.6) | (2.1) |
| -0.03 | -0.001 |
| (-3.0) | (1.4) |
| 0.37 | -0.34 |
| (0.5) | (4.2) |

| end: | 85:4 |
|---|---|
| $H_0$ | statistic |
| $\chi_1^2$ | 1.43 |
| $HW_{12}$ | 56.4 |

| $\beta_c$ | |
|---|---|
| 1.0 | 0.0 |
| 0.0 | 1.0 |
| -1.0 | 0.0 |
| 0.12 | -1.0 |
| (0.02) | |

| | $\beta_{01}$ | $\beta_{02}$ |
|---|---|---|
| <67:4 | -0.94 | -1.06 |
| >67:3 | 0.02 | 1.44 |
| >79:3 | 0.62 | -4.76 |
| >81:4 | -0.59 | -0.46 |

| $\alpha_c$ | |
|---|---|
| -0.002 | -0.003 |
| (-0.2) | (-2.9) |
| -2.77 | 0.35 |
| (-1.8) | (2.2) |
| -0.02 | 0.001 |
| (-2.8) | (-1.24) |
| 0.52 | -0.34 |
| (0.7) | (-4.2) |

| end: | 86:4 |
|---|---|
| $H_0$ | statistic |
| $\chi_1^2$ | 1.43 |
| $HW_{12}$ | 42.0 |

| $\beta_c$ | |
|---|---|
| 1.0 | 0.0 |
| 0.0 | 1.0 |
| -1.0 | 0.0 |
| 0.13 | -1.0 |
| (0.02) | |

| | $\beta_{01}$ | $\beta_{02}$ |
|---|---|---|
| <67:4 | -0.93 | -1.07 |
| >67:3 | 0.03 | 1.43 |
| >79:3 | 0.64 | -4.83 |
| >81:4 | -0.61 | 0.09 |

| $\alpha_c$ | |
|---|---|
| 0.003 | -0.002 |
| (0.31) | (-1.4) |
| -2.58 | 0.41 |
| (-1.7) | (2.7) |
| -0.02 | -0.0002 |
| (-2.3) | (-0.2) |
| 0.75 | -0.28 |
| (1.0) | (-3.6) |

| end: | 87:4 |
|---|---|
| $H_0$ | statistic |
| $\chi_1^2$ | 1.3 |
| $HW_{02}$ | 62.8 |
| $HW_{12}$ | 49.8 |

| $\beta_c$ | |
|---|---|
| 1.0 | 0.0 |
| 0.0 | 1.0 |
| -1.0 | 0.0 |
| 0.13 | -1.0 |
| (0.02) | |

| | $\beta_{01}$ | $\beta_{02}$ |
|---|---|---|
| <67:4 | -0.94 | -1.05 |
| >67:3 | 0.03 | 1.38 |
| >79:3 | 0.67 | -5.1 |
| >81:4 | -0.83 | 1.2 |

| $\alpha_c$ | |
|---|---|
| -0.001 | -0.002 |
| (-0.1) | (-1.5) |
| -3.05 | 0.44 |
| (-2.12) | (3.0) |
| -0.02 | 0.0003 |
| (-2.6) | (0.33) |
| 0.69 | -0.24 |
| (0.93) | (-3.2) |

| end: | 88:4 |
|---|---|
| $H_0$ | statistic |
| $\chi_1^2$ | 0.4 |
| $HW_{02}$ | 65.2 |
| $HW_{12}$ | 48.0 |

| $\beta_c$ | |
|---|---|
| 1.0 | 0.0 |
| 0.0 | 1.0 |
| -1.0 | 0.0 |
| 0.12 | -1.0 |
| (0.02) | |

| | $\beta_{01}$ | $\beta_{02}$ |
|---|---|---|
| <67:4 | -0.96 | -1.06 |
| >67:3 | 0.02 | 1.38 |
| >79:3 | 0.59 | -5.19 |
| >81:4 | -0.7 | 1.43 |

| $\alpha_c$ | |
|---|---|
| -0.006 | -0.001 |
| (-0.6) | (-1.4) |
| -4.1 | 0.46 |
| (-3.14) | (3.2) |
| -0.02 | 0.0003 |
| (-2.8) | (0.3) |
| 0.15 | -0.23 |
| (0.2) | (-3.1) |

| end: | 89:4 |
|---|---|
| $H_0$ | statistic |
| $\chi_1^2$ | 0.13 |
| $HW_{02}$ | 66.8 |
| $HW_{12}$ | 46.3 |

| $\beta_c$ | |
|---|---|
| 1.0 | 0.0 |
| 0.0 | 1.0 |
| -1.0 | 0.0 |
| 0.12 | -1.0 |
| (0.02) | |

| | $\beta_{01}$ | $\beta_{02}$ |
|---|---|---|
| <67:4 | -0.96 | -1.05 |
| >67:3 | 0.02 | 1.38 |
| >79:3 | 0.57 | -5.08 |
| >81:4 | -0.66 | 1.18 |

| $\alpha_c$ | |
|---|---|
| -0.01 | -0.001 |
| (-1.0) | (-1.3) |
| -4.16 | 0.45 |
| (-3.5) | (3.3) |
| -0.02 | 0.0002 |
| (-3.1) | (0.3) |
| -0.13 | -0.22 |
| (-0.2) | (-3.1) |

Table 7.2: Recursive Estimates of Error Correction Coefficients.(continued)

| end: | 90:4 | end: | 91:4 |
|---|---|---|---|
| $H_0$ | statistic | $H_0$ | statistic |
| $\chi_1^2$ | 0.03 | $\chi_1^2$ | 0.03 |
| $HW_{12}$ | 46.3 | $HW_{12}$ | 47.1 |

| $\beta_c$ (90:4) | | $\beta_c$ (91:4) | |
|---|---|---|---|
| 1.0 | 0.0 | 1.0 | 0.0 |
| 0.0 | 1.0 | 0.0 | 1.0 |
| -1.0 | 0.0 | -1.0 | 0.0 |
| 0.12 | -1.0 | 0.12 | -1.0 |
| (0.02) | | (0.02) | |

| | $\beta_{01}$ | $\beta_{02}$ | | $\beta_{01}$ | $\beta_{02}$ |
|---|---|---|---|---|---|
| <67:4 | -0.95 | -1.06 | <67:4 | -0.94 | -1.07 |
| >67:3 | 0.03 | 1.37 | >67:3 | 0.03 | 1.37 |
| >79:3 | 0.6 | -5.18 | >79:3 | 0.63 | -5.32 |
| >81:4 | -0.69 | 1.57 | >81:4 | -0.77 | 1.95 |

| $\alpha_c$ (90:4) | | $\alpha_c$ (91:4) | |
|---|---|---|---|
| -0.007 | -0.001 | -0.002 | -0.001 |
| (-0.9) | (-1.4) | (-0.3) | (-1.34) |
| -4.2 | 0.47 | -3.85 | 0.48 |
| (-3.8) | (3.5) | (-3.6) | (-3.6) |
| -0.02 | 0.0 | -0.01 | -0.0 |
| (-2.6) | (0.06) | (-2.2) | (-0.1) |
| -0.17 | 0.21 | 0.1 | -0.21 |
| (-0.3) | (-3.0) | (0.1) | (-3.0) |

Note:Recursive Samples indicated by the end of the sample period. HW statistics refer to Horvath and Watson tests. $\beta_c$ is the estimate of the normalized cointegration vectors. $\beta_{01}$ and $\beta_{02}$ are the constant terms(that can change with intervention dummies) in the cointegrating relations. $\alpha_c$ is the matrix of error correction coefficients at each recursive sample.

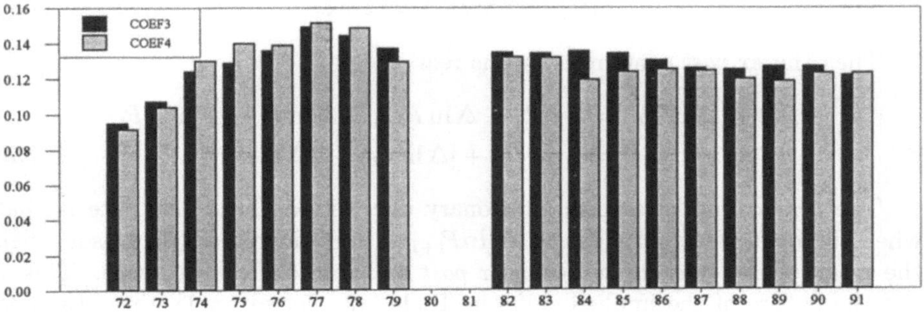


Figure 7.1: Estimated Interest Semielasticities

Regardless of the sample size, the error correction coefficients in the velocity equation have small absolute value. In the longer sample periods (those extending beyond the mid 1980s) neither of these error correction coefficients is significantly different from zero that is consistent with weak exogeneity of velocity. The error correction coefficients in the inflation equation are measured very imprecisely in the shorter sample periods. In the longer sample periods the precision of these two estimated coefficients improves and their estimated values become more robust in the recursive estimation. The estimated error correction coefficients on real output and the Treasury bill rate are robust and are estimated with considerable precision regardless of the length of the sample period. These estimates suggest that real output responds significantly to deviations from equilibrium velocity, but not to deviations from the equilibrium real rate. Conversely the Treasury bill rate appears to respond significantly to deviations from the equilibrium real rate, but not to deviations from equilibrium velocity.

The estimated constant of the real balance cointegrating vector is consistent with the results reported for the semi-log models estimated in Chapter 6 and with the results reported in Table 7.1. The only measured change in this constant is during the New Operating Procedures period. In contrast, there appear to be at least three breaks in the *ex post* real rate cointegrating vector. Therefore it seems most appropriate to characterize the contemporaneous *ex post* real rate (the nominal rate less the current rate of inflation) as a stationary series subject to discrete breaks.

The inference from the economic model in Chapter 5 is that the contemporaneous *ex post* real rate can be characterized by breaks (changes in the mean) even if the *ex ante* and *ex post* one period ahead real interest rates (nominal rates minus the future expected or actual inflation rate) are mean stationary series. In a rational expectations world this occurs because changes in the drift of the inflation (and expected inflation) process affect the mean of the contemporaneous *ex post* real rate. Assume that the one period ahead *ex post* real interest rate is stationary about a constant mean,

$$Rtb_t - \Delta \ln P_{t+1} = \alpha + \varepsilon_t \tag{7.1}$$

Then the *ex post* contemporaneous real rate is :

$$\begin{aligned} Rtb_t - \Delta \ln P_t &= Rtb_t - \Delta \ln P_{t+1} + \Delta \ln P_{t+1} - \Delta \ln P_t \\ &= \alpha + \varepsilon_t + [\Delta \ln P_{t+1} - \Delta \ln P_t] \end{aligned} \tag{7.2}$$

The implication of a mean stationary one period ahead real rate is that when the drift of actual inflation $\Delta(lnP_{t+1} - lnP_t)$ increases (decreases) then the mean of the contemporaneous *ex post* real rate shifts up (down). This is not the nature of the implied shifts in Table 7.2. For example, the estimated contemporaneous *ex post* real rate for the sample period ending in 1991:4 is

$$Rtb_t - \Delta \ln P_t = 1.07 - 1.37D67 + 5.32D79 - 1.95D82 + \varepsilon_t \tag{7.3}$$

The values of $\varepsilon_t$ from this relationship are plotted in Figure 7.2. The interpretation of the effect of the dummy variables on the estimated mean of the contemporaneous *ex post* real rate is that the mean shifted down during the period 68-79, shifted up during 79-81 and shifted back down after 1981. This is not consistent with the hypothesis that the one period ahead *ex post* (or *ex ante*) real rate is stationary around a constant mean, since the shifts in the mean of the contemporaneous *ex post* real rate are opposite to the shifts implied by equation 7.2 for these periods. Hence it is appropriate to conclude that the estimates presented here support the hypothesis that there were shifts in the mean of the *ex post* and *ex ante* one period ahead real rates with the onset of the Vietnam inflation and also at the beginning and end of the New Operating Procedures period. This is consistent with conclusions of the univariate analysis of real rate behavior in the US at these times. The particular point estimates of the mean of the contemporaneous real rate from the sample ending in 91:4 are about 1.0 percent prior to the Vietnam inflation, around zero in the late 60s through the 70s, around five percent in the 81-2 recession, and around three percent subsequently.

### 7.1.2 Dynamics

The evidence for two cointegrating vectors among the four variables, $lnM/P$, $\Delta p$, $lnY$, and $Rtb$ implies that there are two permanent and two transitory shocks responsible for the observed behavior of the time series. The VECM structure that we have estimated in Table 7.2, like all such VECM structures is a reduced form model. Analysis of the dynamic responses of the various series to the permanent and transitory shocks requires additional identifying restrictions.

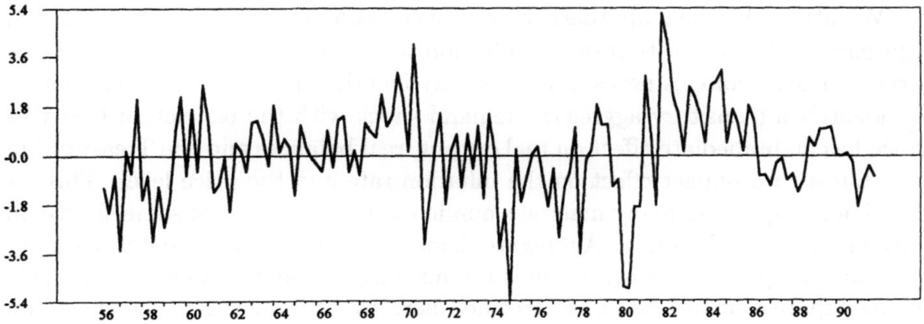


Figure 7.2: Deviations from the Equilibrium Real Interest Rate

The identifying restrictions that are utilized here are an extension of those that are applied to the three variable models in Chapter 6. We maintain the assumption that the two permanent shocks are a nominal shock and a real shock. Both are assumed to be random walks with drift. The first is identified by the restriction that it has a permanent effect on both the nominal variables, the Treasury bill rate and the inflation rate, and through the permanent effect on the bill rate and the cointegrating vector for money demand, a permanent effect on the log of real balances and the log of velocity. As long as the *ex post* real rate is assumed to be stationary about a mean that is unaffected by this permanent shock, the equilibrium impact of this shock on inflation and the nominal rate is equal. The normalizing assumption for the permanent nominal shock is that it has a unit (100 basis point) impact on inflation and the Treasury bill rate in equilibrium.

The second identifying restriction for the permanent shocks is that they are uncorrelated. The third identifying restriction is that the permanent real shock has a unit impact on real output in equilibrium, and has no effect on the nominal variables (or velocity) in equilibrium. The two permanent shocks form a Wold causal chain (recursive structure), with the nominal shock ordered first. An additional overidentifying (testable) restriction is that the nominal shock has no equilibrium impact on real output. Evidence in support of this overidentifying restriction is discussed below.

In the analysis in Chapter 6, the single transitory shock was identified by the assumption that it is uncorrelated with the permanent shocks and follows those shocks in a Wold causal chain structure. That assumption, together with the identifying restrictions on the permanent shocks complete the KPSW "common trends" model. No economic interpretation can be assigned to the single transitory shock in the models in Chapter 6. It represents the reduced form of all transitory shocks that affect the time series.

In the current VECM there is the possibility of identifying one of the transitory economic shocks. Warne (1993) has proposed an approach to identify transitory shocks that extends the KPSW common trends model (see Chapter 4). We utilize Warne's approach here. Since there are two transitory shocks, only one identifying restriction, in addition to the normalizations and zero covariance restrictions, is necessary to exactly identify the two transitory shocks. We identify a transitory aggregate demand shock with the restriction that this shock has an immediate effect on real output, real balances and the Treasury bill rate, but a zero impact effect on the inflation rate and the price level. This restriction is implicit in many macroeconomic models that assume some short-run price or wage "stickiness".[7] Aggregate demand shocks in the model in Chapter 5 satisfy this condition when there is no indexing of nominal wages. Effectively the aggregate demand shock is identified here by assuming that the short-run aggregate supply function (or instantaneous Phillips curve) is perfectly horizontal.

The relevant information for the structure of the identified shocks is presented in Table 7.3. The data in part A of that table refer to the model that is exactly identified. Data in part B refer to the model subject to the overidentifying restriction that the permanent nominal shock has no permanent impact on real output. When the model is exactly identified, the estimated correlation between the two permanent shocks is .073. This is not significantly different from zero under the $\chi^2$ test developed by Baillie (1987) ($\chi^2_{(1)}$ = .76, p = .38). The orthogonalizing decomposition of the covariance matrix of the permanent shocks, $\Sigma = \pi D \pi'$ is shown in Table 7.3. Since the variance of the permanent nominal shock is greater than that of the permanent real shock and the correlation between the two permanent shocks is small, $\pi$ is close to an identity matrix under the exact identification restrictions. After orthogonalization, the coefficient matrix for the common trends is $\beta^*_\perp$. The zero restrictions in the second column of this matrix are imposed by the causal ordering of the shocks. The small value of the (3,1) element in this matrix implies a very small equilibrium response of real output to the permanent nominal shock.

The factor loading matrix for the two common trends is given by $\alpha'_\perp$. This indicates each permanent shock as a linear combination of the reduced form errors from the VECM. The largest weight in the nominal common trend (permanent nominal shock) is on the reduced form error in the real balance equation (-15.45) with some positive weight (6.76) given to the reduced form error in the real output equation. The largest weight in the second common trend (permanent real shock) is on the reduced form error in the real output equation with some negative weight (-.13) to the reduced form error in the real balance equation. The reduced form errors in the inflation and Treasury bill rate equations

[7] see for example Hall and Taylor (1993) Chapter 17.

Table 7.3: Identification of Permanent and Transitory Shocks: Quarterly Semi–Log Specification, ln(M/P), 400*(lnP-lnP(-1)), ln(Y/P), Rtb.

| | Exactly Identified Model | Overidentified Model |
|---|---|---|
| $\beta_{\perp}^{0} =$ | $\begin{bmatrix} -0.12 & 1.0 \\ 1.0 & 0 \\ 0 & 1.0 \\ 1.0 & 0 \end{bmatrix}$ | $\begin{bmatrix} -0.12 & 1.0 \\ 1.0 & 0 \\ 0 & 1.0 \\ 1.0 & 0.0 \end{bmatrix}$ |
| $\alpha_{\perp}^{0\prime} =$ | $\begin{bmatrix} -15.4 & 0.02 & 6.76 & -0.05 \\ -0.03 & -0.004 & 1.15 & -0.01 \end{bmatrix}$ | $\begin{bmatrix} -15.45 & 0.02 & 6.76 & -0.05 \\ -0.03 & -0.004 & 1.15 & -0.01 \end{bmatrix}$ |
| $\Sigma_{v} =$ | $\begin{bmatrix} 0.02 & 0.0001 \\ 0.0001 & 0.0001 \end{bmatrix}$ | $\begin{bmatrix} 0.02 & 0.0001 \\ 0.0001 & 0.0001 \end{bmatrix}$ |
| $\pi =$ | $\begin{bmatrix} 1.0 & 0 \\ 0.007 & 1.0 \end{bmatrix}$ | $\begin{bmatrix} 1.0 & 0 \\ 0 & 1.0 \end{bmatrix}$ |
| $\beta_{\perp}^{*} =$ | $\begin{bmatrix} -0.12 & 1.0 \\ 1.0 & 0 \\ 0.007 & 1.0 \\ 1.0 & 0 \end{bmatrix}$ | $\begin{bmatrix} -0.12 & 1.0 \\ 1.0 & 0 \\ 0 & 1.0 \\ 1.0 & 0 \end{bmatrix}$ |
| $\alpha_{\perp}^{\prime} =$ | $\begin{bmatrix} -15.45 & 0.02 & 6.76 & -0.05 \\ -0.13 & -0.004 & 1.19 & -0.01 \end{bmatrix}$ | $\begin{bmatrix} -15.45 & 0.02 & 6.76 & -0.05 \\ -0.13 & -0.004 & 1.19 & -0.01 \end{bmatrix}$ |
| Transitory Factor Loadings | $\begin{bmatrix} 99.19 & 0.59 & 24.05 & -0.26 \\ -0.10 & -0.001 & 0.28 & 0.01 \end{bmatrix}$ | $\begin{bmatrix} 99.19 & 0.59 & 24.05 & -0.26 \\ -0.1 & -0.001 & 0.28 & 0.01 \end{bmatrix}$ |

Note: Derived from estimates of 91:4 sample period in Table 7.2

are assigned very small weight in both common trends. The weights assigned to real balances, real output and the nominal interest rate in the nominal common trend are quite similar to the corresponding weights assigned to this trend in the three variable semi-log model (Table 6.18, Part B). The weight assigned to the reduced form real output error in the real common trend is also similar to that in the three variable model, but here the real balance equation reduced form error is assigned a negative weight in contrast to the positive weight on this error in the three variable semi-log model.

The factor loadings for the two transitory shocks are shown at the bottom of Table 7.3. The second row of this matrix reflects the shock that is identified as the transitory aggregate demand shock. The only substantial difference between the weights assigned to this shock and those assigned to the real output common trend is the smaller weight on the reduced form error in the real output equation.

The analogous information is presented in Part B of Table 7.3 with the overidentifying restriction of orthogonality imposed on the permanent real output and permanent nominal shocks. Here the two permanent shocks are identical to the KPSW common trends. The factor loadings under the overidentifying restriction are estimated using the SVAR program in Gianinni (1992). The overidentifying restriction is not rejected ($\chi^2_{(1)}$ =.77 , $p = .40$ ). The estimated factor loadings are very similar to those in Part A of the table, which is not surprising given the small correlation in $\Sigma_v$.

The impulse response functions for the three identified shocks are shown in Figures 7.3-7.20. The solid lines in the graphs represent the response functions from the overidentified model and the broken lines are the impulse response functions from the exactly identified model. The two sets of restrictions imply exactly the same response functions to the permanent real output shock, so only one line is graphed in Figures 7.3-7.8. In the remaining figures the two impulse response functions are almost identical, which follows from the similarity of the factor loadings in Parts A and B of Table 7.3.

The graphs are arranged so that the responses to the permanent shocks can be compared conveniently with the impulse response functions generated by the three variable semi-log model shown in Figures 6.26-6.33. It can be seen that the responses to the permanent real shock are almost identical to those derived from the three variable model, with respect to the time path of the response and the amplitude of the response during the adjustment to the steady state. The pattern of the response to the permanent nominal shock, shown in Figures 7.9-7.14 is quite similar to the response to this shock derived from the three variable model (Figures 6.30-6.33). However, the magnitude of the response of real output and the Treasury bill rate during the transition to the steady state in the four variable model is somewhat larger than indicated by the three variable model. Our general conclusion is that the dynamic response paths that are common to the two specifications are comparable.

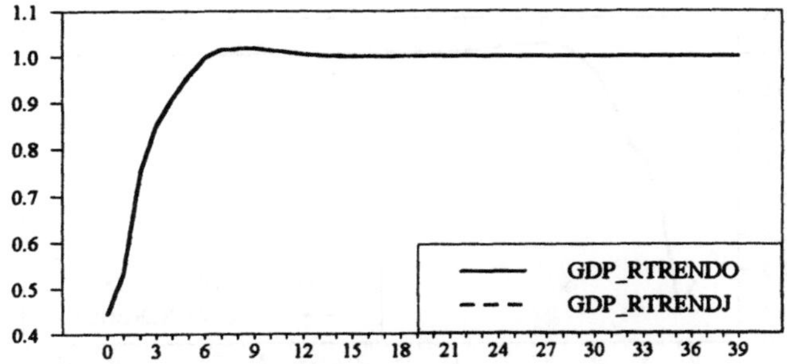


Figure 7.3: I.R.F. for GDP w.r.t. the Permanent Real Shock

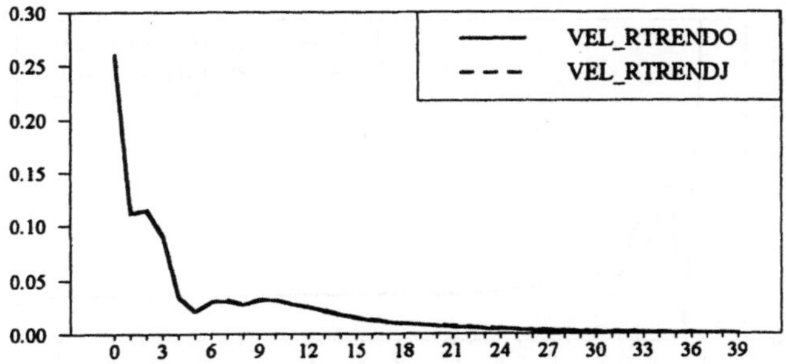


Figure 7.4: I.R.F. for Velocity w.r.t. the Permanent Real Shock

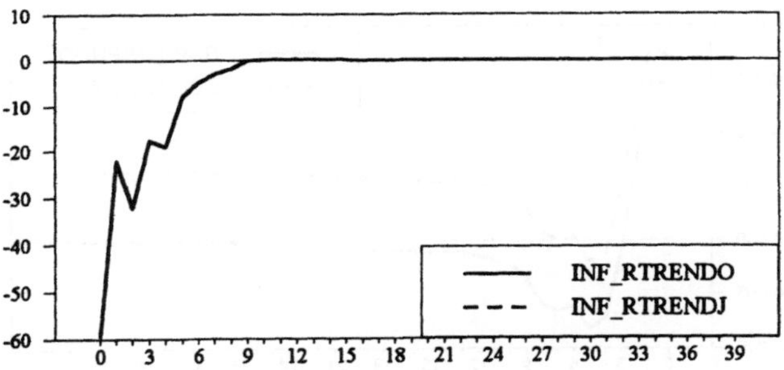


Figure 7.5: I.R.F. for Inflation w.r.t. the Permanent Real Shock

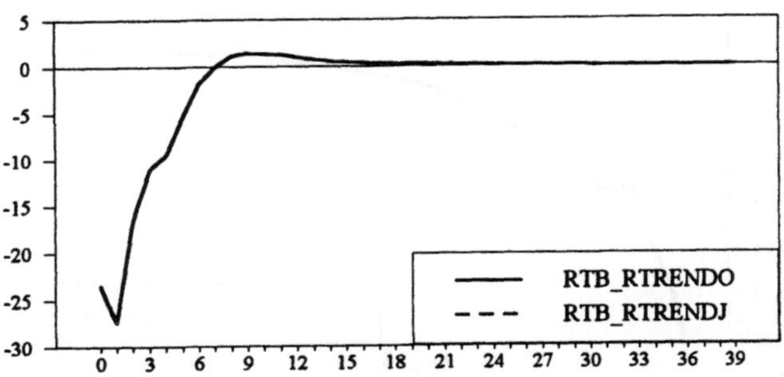


Figure 7.6: I.R.F. for Rtb w.r.t. the Permanent Real Shock

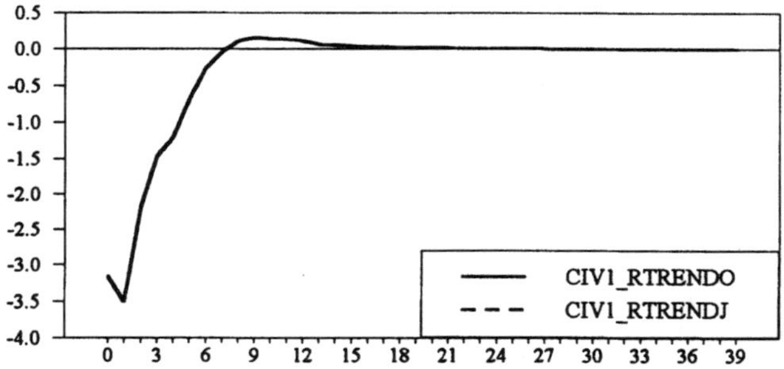


Figure 7.7: I.R.F. for CIV1 w.r.t. the Permanent Real Shock

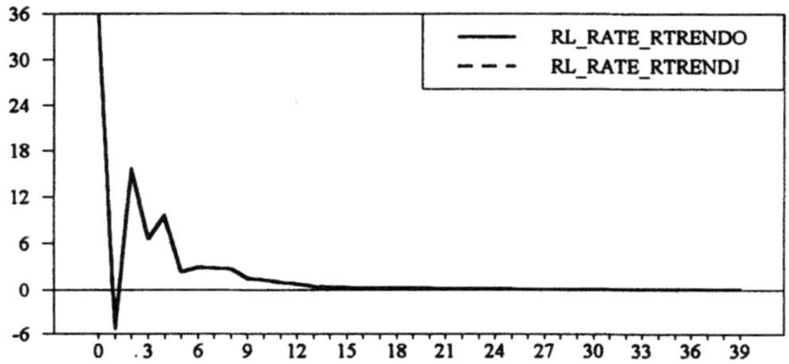


Figure 7.8: I.R.F. for the Real Rate w.r.t. the Permanent Real Shock

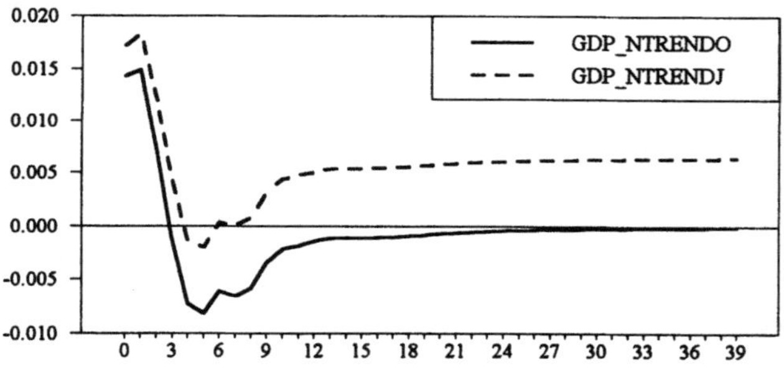


Figure 7.9: I.R.F. for GDP w.r.t. the Permanent Nominal Shock

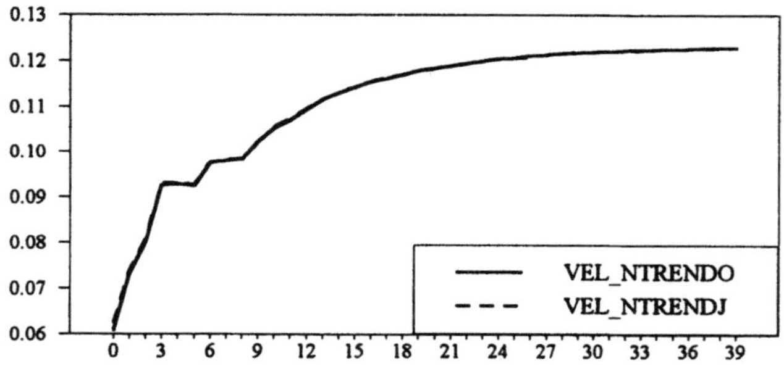


Figure 7.10: I.R.F. for Velocity w.r.t. the Permanent Nominal Shock

The advantage of the four variable model over the model developed in Chapter 6 is that more information is available. The initial inflation response to the permanent real shock is clearly negative (Figure 7.5). This is reflected in the initial response of the nominal interest rate (Figure 7.6), which was the evidence available from the three variable model from which we inferred a negative inflation response. In terms of a textbook macromodel, the real permanent shock is analogous to a rightward shift in a long-run Phillips (aggregate supply) curve and a downward shift in a short-run Phillips (aggregate supply) curve. The transitory effects of the permanent real shock on the inflation rate are larger in absolute value than the nominal interest rate responses, so the transitory effect of this shock on the *ex post* real interest rate is positive (Figure 7.8). The transitory responses of all the variables have effectively gone to zero after about three years.

The permanent nominal shock is clearly a permanent inflation shock (Figure 7.11). The response path of inflation is particularly interesting. There is a strong positive impact effect on inflation, but then the inflation response moves quite quickly toward the steady-state response, and subsequently shows only small fluctuations around that level. In contrast, the initial response of the nominal interest rate to this shock is negative and the response path approaches the steady-state level quite slowly over five or more years (Figure 7.12). hence the permanent inflation shock generates a negative transitory response on the *ex post* real interest rate that approaches zero very slowly (Figure 7.14). The real output response to this shock is initially positive, becomes negative after about one year and then approaches zero after three to four years.

The impulse response functions for the transitory shock identified by the restriction that it has a zero impact effect on inflation (the aggregate demand shock) are shown in Figures 7.15-7.20. The pattern of these responses is quite consistent with the effect of an aggregate demand shock in an economy where prices and inflation do not instantaneously adjust to steady-state levels. The real output response is a maximum in the first quarter after the shock and declines quite rapidly towards zero over a year and one half (Figure 7.15). The nominal interest rate response to this shock is positive, achieves a maximum one quarter after the shock coincident with the maximum output response, then gradually and smoothly approaches zero after three to four years. The initial inflation response is zero by construction. Subsequently the inflation response is generally positive, though the pattern exhibits considerable high frequency fluctuation, and approaches zero after three years. The response of the inflation rate is smaller than that of the nominal interest rate, so the effect of this transitory aggregate demand shock on the *ex post* real interest rate is positive and gradually approaches zero after three to four years.

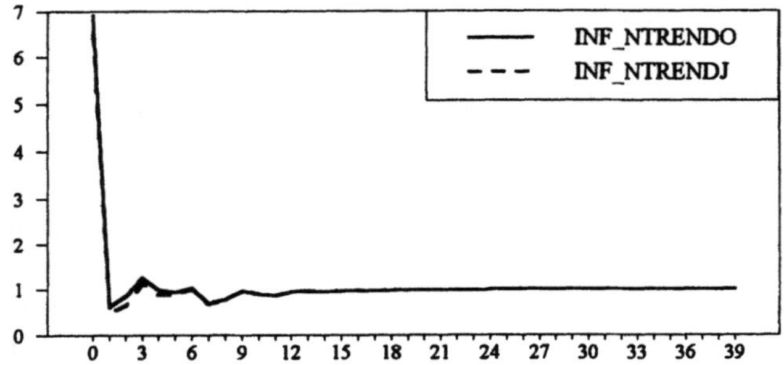


Figure 7.11: I.R.F. for Inflation w.r.t. the Permanent Nominal Shock

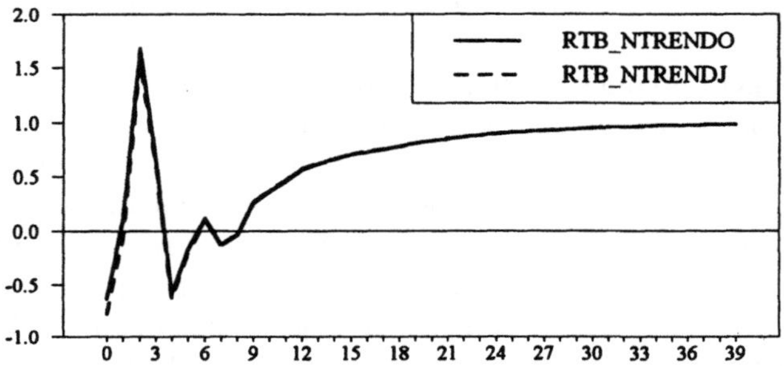


Figure 7.12: I.R.F. for Rtb w.r.t. the Permanent Nominal Shock

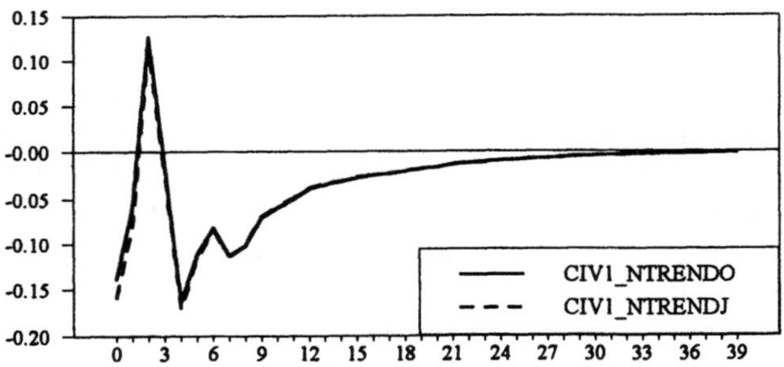


Figure 7.13: I.R.F. for CIV1 w.r.t. the Permanent Nominal Shock

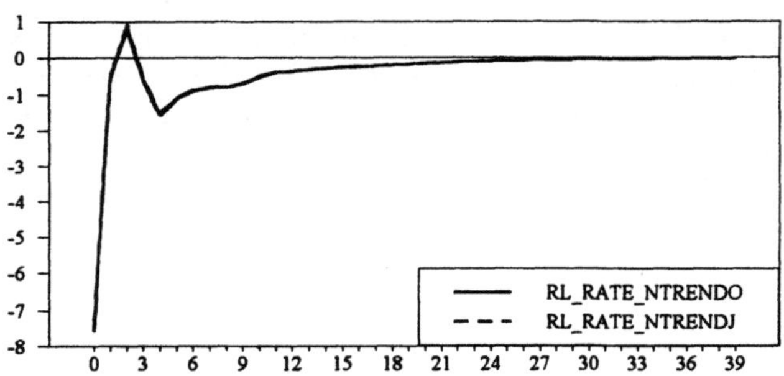


Figure 7.14: I.R.F. for the Real Rate w.r.t. the Permanent Nominal Shock

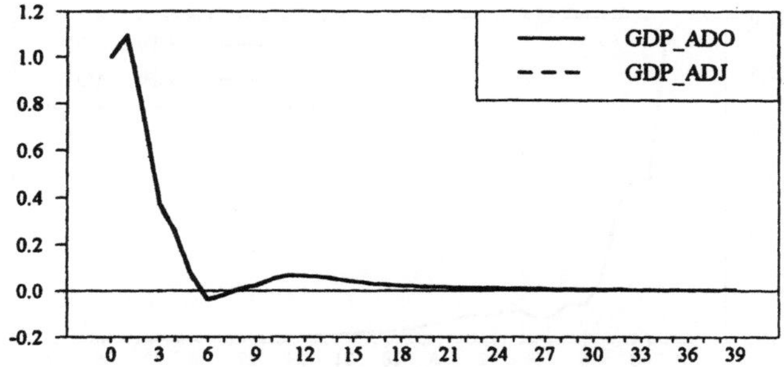


Figure 7.15: I.R.F. for GDP w.r.t. the Transitory AD Shock

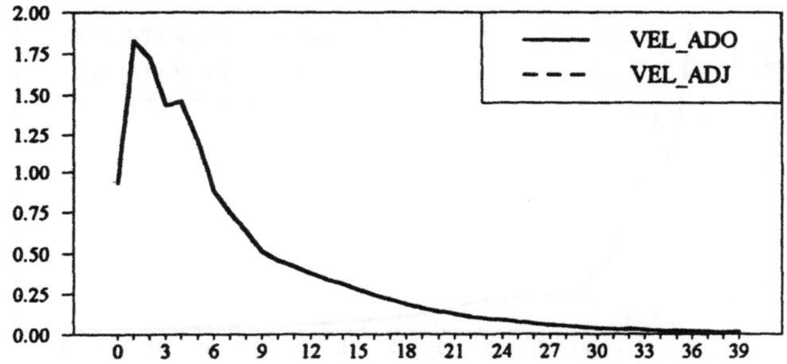


Figure 7.16: I.R.F. for Velocity w.r.t. the Transitory AD Shock

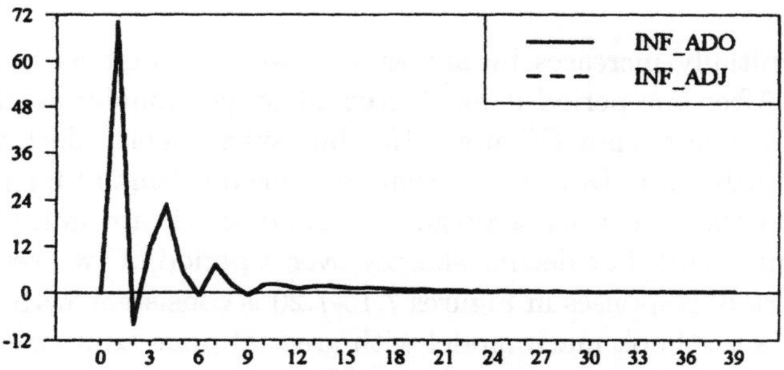


Figure 7.17: I.R.F. for Inflation w.r.t. the Transitory AD Shock

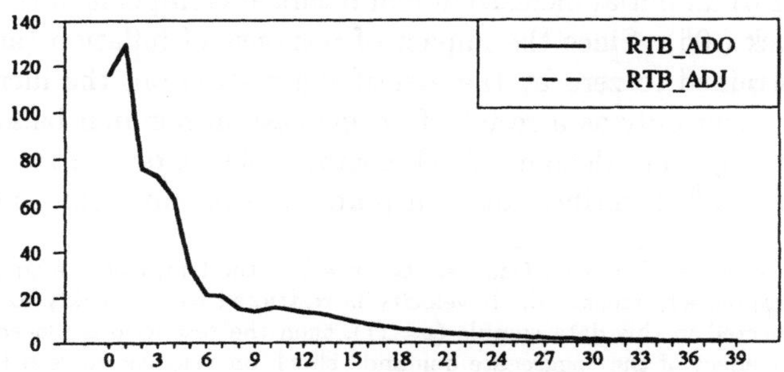


Figure 7.18: I.R.F. for Rtb w.r.t. the Transitory AD Shock

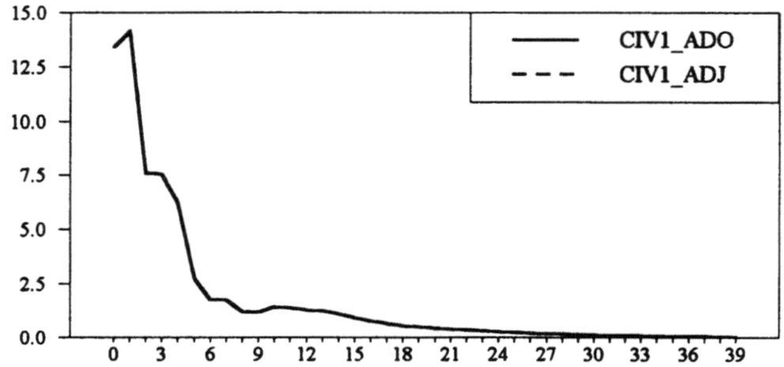


Figure 7.19: I.R.F. for CIV1 w.r.t. the Transitory AD Shock

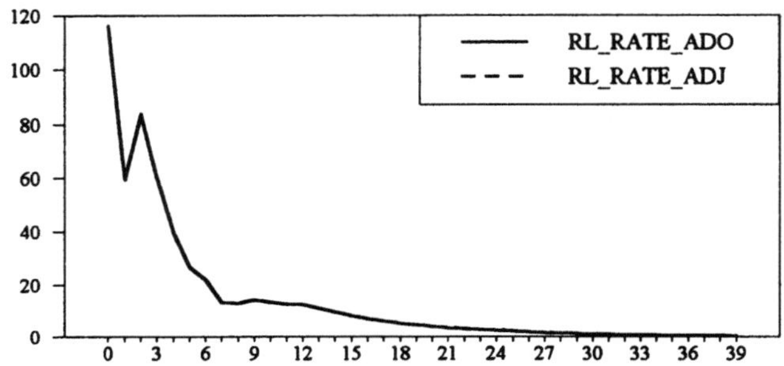


Figure 7.20: I.R.F. for the Real Rate w.r.t. the Transitory AD Shock

Velocity initially increases by almost the same amount as the increase in real output. After one period it has increased proportionally much more than the increase in real output (Figure 7.16), but subsequently declines relatively smoothly towards zero. Deviations from equilibrium demand for real balances in response to the transitory aggregate demand shock are initially large and positive (Figure 7.19), but decline sharply over a period of two years.

The pattern of responses in Figures 7.15-7.20 is consistent with the response pattern from a textbook macromodel with gradual price adjustment to a fiscal shock or autonomous expenditure shock. However, the analogy is not perfect. Since the impact response of velocity is less than proportional (.94) to that of real output (1.0) an initial increase in real balances is implicit in the "aggregate demand" shock (.06). Since the impact of response of inflation (and the price level) is constrained to zero by the identifying restriction, the increase in real balances can occur only as a result of an increase in nominal balances. Hence the identified aggregate demand shock contains elements of a transitory nominal money shock.[8] Identification of a pure fiscal or autonomous expenditure

[8]The initial response of velocity (and real balances) to the transitory "aggregate demand" shock is very imprecisely measured. If velocity is restricted to be weakly exogenous, a restriction not rejected in this data sample ($p$=.11), then the restrictions placed on $\alpha$ require that the impact effect of the "aggregate demand" shock on velocity be zero (in addition to the restriction that the impact effect of this shock on inflation is zero). Thus under the weak exogeniety of velocity the impact effect of the transitory "aggregate demand" shock on real

shock requires the additional restriction that the response of the growth rate of real balances at all points in time be the negative of the observed inflation response, so that nominal balances are unchanged at all horizons as a result of the transitory "aggregate demand" shock.

### 7.1.3 Variance Decompositions

The decompositions of the forecast variance at various horizons are shown in Table 7.4 for seven variables that can be constructed from this VECM, including the variables that are common with the three variable VECM in Chapter 6. The decompositions of real balances, real output and velocity with respect to the permanent shocks are quite similar to those obtained from the three variable VECM (see Table 6.17) Very little of the forecast variance of real output at any horizon is attributable to the permanent nominal shock, and very little of the forecast variance of velocity at any horizon is attributable to the permanent real output shock. More than 80 percent of the forecast variance of real balances is attributable to the two permanent shocks at all horizons, so the effects of the transitory shocks on velocity and real output in large part cancel out.

The interesting additional information in Table 7.4 is the decomposition of the forecast variance between the two transitory shocks. The "aggregate demand" transitory shock is responsible for a major portion of the forecast variance of velocity and real output at the shorter horizons. The remaining composite transitory shock never accounts for more than three percent of the forecast variance of velocity at any horizon. Since, with the exception of the one period forecast variance, the permanent real shock does not account for more than two percent of the forecast variance of velocity, velocity is approximately determined by two shocks: the permanent nominal shock and the transitory "aggregate demand" shock. The effect of the transitory "aggregate demand' shock on velocity presumably is transmitted through nominal interest rates. The short horizon forecast variance of the latter is dominated by the transitory "aggregate demand" shock.

Much of the transitory variance of real GDP at the shorter forecasting horizons is also attributable to the "aggregate demand' shock, though in contrast to velocity, 10 - 15 percent of the forecast variance of real GDP is attributable to the composite transitory shock. The "aggregate demand" shock also accounts for more than 60 percent of the deviations from equilibrium velocity (CIV1).

In contrast to the decompositions for the other variables , the "aggregate demand" shock is a relatively unimportant component of the forecast variance for real balances and inflation, at any forecast horizon. For one period ahead forecasts the contribution of this shock to the inflation variance is zero by construction of the identifying restriction. At all other tabulated horizons the contribution to the inflation forecast variance is less than seven percent. The remaining composite transitory error is a major factor in the short horizon forecast variance of inflation, accounting for roughly one third of the forecast

and nominal money balances is proportional to the impact response of real output.

Table 7.4: Variance Decompositions:Overidentifying Restrictions on Permanent Shocks

| Variable | Horizon | Perm. Nominal Shock | Perm. Real Shock | A.D. Shock | Comp. Trans. Shock |
|---|---|---|---|---|---|
| ln(M/P) | | | | | |
| | 1 | 75.9 | 9.8 | 0.3 | 14.0 |
| | 4 | 53.3 | 27.9 | 14.6 | 4.2 |
| | 8 | 51.3 | 34.7 | 11.8 | 2.2 |
| | 16 | 55.0 | 38.0 | 5.8 | 1.2 |
| | 200 | 63.1 | 36.4 | 0.4 | 0.1 |
| ln(GDP) | | | | | |
| | 1 | 7.0 | 36.1 | 43.4 | 13.5 |
| | 4 | 3.6 | 60.9 | 23.6 | 12.0 |
| | 8 | 1.5 | 82.0 | 10.3 | 6.1 |
| | 16 | 0.8 | 91.7 | 4.7 | 2.7 |
| | 200 | 0.6 | 98.9 | 0.4 | 0.2 |
| Rtb | | | | | |
| | 1 | 2.1 | 14.5 | 83.4 | 0.0 |
| | 4 | 3.2 | 12.3 | 70.3 | 14.2 |
| | 8 | 3.0 | 11.6 | 67.4 | 18.5 |
| | 12 | 3.3 | 11.0 | 67.3 | 10.9 |
| | 16 | 4.5 | 10.7 | 66.7 | 18.2 |
| | 200 | 59.1 | 4.6 | 28.6 | 7.8 |
| Inflation | | | | | |
| | 1 | 39.5 | 25.2 | 0.0 | 35.3 |
| | 4 | 30.9 | 28.8 | 6.5 | 33.8 |
| | 8 | 30.7 | 29.2 | 6.8 | 33.3 |
| | 16 | 33.6 | 28.0 | 6.5 | 31.9 |
| | 200 | 68.9 | 13.1 | 3.1 | 15.0 |
| ln(velocity) | | | | | |
| | 1 | 64.5 | 8.6 | 26.5 | 0.3 |
| | 4 | 57.3 | 1.8 | 39.7 | 1.2 |
| | 8 | 67.3 | 0.9 | 28.8 | 3.0 |
| | 16 | 82.3 | 0.5 | 15.4 | 1.8 |
| | 200 | 98.9 | 0.0 | 1.0 | 0.1 |
| CIV1 | | | | | |
| | 1 | 5.9 | 18.0 | 76.2 | 0.0 |
| | 4 | 3.2 | 16.2 | 65.2 | 15.4 |
| | 8 | 6.5 | 14.5 | 60.3 | 18.8 |
| | 16 | 7.8 | 14.1 | 59.7 | 18.4 |
| | 200 | 7.9 | 14.0 | 59.7 | 18.4 |
| Real Rate | | | | | |
| | 1 | 42.2 | 7.8 | 19.6 | 30.5 |
| | 4 | 34.5 | 7.8 | 31.9 | 25.9 |
| | 8 | 34.7 | 7.7 | 32.6 | 25.0 |
| | 16 | 34.9 | 7.6 | 33.0 | 24.5 |
| | 200 | 34.9 | 7.6 | 33.1 | 24.5 |

variance at all horizons up to four years. An interpretation of these forecast variance decompositions in terms of a textbook long-run, short-run Phillips curve analysis is that very little of observed inflation behavior is attributable to movements along a stable short-run Phillips curve (the "aggregate demand" shock). Almost 95 percent of inflation variance is attributable to permanent and transitory shocks that cause the hypothesized short-run Phillips curve to shift up and down.

## 7.2 Real Balances, Output, Short and Long Term Rates

The question of which interest rate to use in analyses of the demand for real balances is the subject of long-standing discussion in the literature. Some theoretical analyses (Friedman (1956, 1977) and Saving(1971)) suggest that a whole range of rates of return are appropriate arguments of such a demand function, while another perspective is that only short-term nominal rates are appropriate (Ando and Shell (1975)). Since the mid 1960s, empirical analyses have attempted to deal with this question. Early on it became apparent that the correlations among nominal interest rates along the maturity spectrum were so high that the effort to introduce more than one nominal rate into a regression equation for real balances was futile. A compromise approach involved estimation of separate regressions each with a single, but different interest rate argument. Typically a conclusion was reached on the "best" interest rate based on some overall measure of the goodness-of-fit of these regressions (see, for example, Laidler (1966)). The general preference that appears to emerge from these analyses is that short-term nominal interest rates are "superior" to long-term rates. Dissenting arguments to this view exist (Meltzer (1963), Hamberger (1977), Poole (1988)), but by the 1970s analyses using U.S. data focused almost exclusively on short-term interest rates.

Milton Friedman's analysis (1977) rekindled the argument about multiple rates of return, and generated a number of attempts to parameterize the term structure in a parsimonious fashion that would allow the implicit introduction of a whole spectrum of interest rates into the demand function for real balances. The initial analysis by Heller and Khan (1979) approximated each quarterly term structure in the U.S. data by a quadratic in maturity, and used the three time series of the estimated parameters of the quadratic polynomial in place of the interest rate variable in a standard "real partial adjustment" model of the short-run demand for money. Subsequently Friedman and Schwartz (1982) applied the same technique to cycle-average data for a century of U.S. experience in an equilibrium specification of the demand for real balances. Both studies found that the higher order coefficients of the polynomial approximation were significant regressors, which the authors interpret to indicate an effect on the shape of the term structure beyond that generated by parallel shifts in the term structure (as measured by the time series of estimated zero order coefficients of the polynomial).

Subsequently Heller and Khan's conclusion was challenged as subject to specification error. Allan and Hafer (1983) argue that the stability of the Heller and Khan specification during the 1970s is an artifact of their adjustment for serial correlation in the residuals of their regression equation. Hwang (1985) argues that both the Heller and Khan and Allen and Hafer analyses impose restrictions on the coefficients of the money demand function (the "real partial adjustment model") that are rejected by the data. He concludes that when the partial adjustment model is estimated subject to restrictions that are not rejected by the data, the only variable generated by the polynomial approximation to the term structure that has a significant estimated coefficient is the zero order coefficients term. Hence he argues the appropriate conclusion is that only shifts in the level of the term structure affect the demand for real balances in the U.S. Interpreted literally, this conclusion implies that the demand for real balances is affected only when all rates of interest across the maturity spectrum move together. Equivalently, what affects the demand for real balances is the average nominal rate of interest across the maturity spectrum.[9]

Poole (1988) questions all of the single interest rate analyses that show differential estimates of interest elasticities or semielasticities with differing maturity nominal interest rates. He argues:

> "these regressions yield a much higher estimate of the interest elasticity for the long rate than for the short rate. Many others have found this same result but, strangely, no one seems to have been puzzled by it. Under the expectations theory of the term structure of interest rates, the long rate is a weighted average of expected future short rates, and consequently the full-adjustment (or long-run) elasticity with respect to the long rate ought to be equal to that with respect to the short rate.
>
> To understand this point, suppose an economy operates for a long time with zero inflation and short and long rates in the neighborhood of 3 percent, and then adjusts to a long-lasting inflationary equilibrium with an inflation rate of 10 percent and short and long rates in the neighborhood of 13 percent. Using these hypothetical data, estimates of the interest elasticity from short rates and long rates should be identical because both rates have risen by the same amount." (p. 80-81)

The purpose of this analysis is to investigate the joint hypothesis of a stable long-run (equilibrium) demand for real balances and the expectations theory of

[9]This follows since the maturity spectrum of interest rates can always be rewritten in terms of such an average and deviations from that average. In this case polynomials fitted by OLS to the deviations from the average rate as functions of deviations from average maturity would have a zero constant term and the same estimated higher order coefficients as produced by the Heller and Khan technique. Since the estimated coefficients of these higher order coefficients are insignificant in the Hwang regressions, the only interest rate argument remaining in his demand for money specifications would be the average rate across the maturity spectrum.

the term structure. Section 2.1 discusses estimation in the context of nonstationary data generating processes and the problem of identification under the joint maintained hypotheses and nonstationary data. It is shown there that under the joint maintained hypotheses, effects of the term structure on the equilibrium demand for real balances cannot be identified. Equilibrium demand functions for real balances are estimated in section 2.2 and overidentifying restrictions on the term structure are tested. Some results on the differential effect of permanent and transitory shocks on real balances and the term structure are discussed in section 2.3.

### 7.2.1 Identification of Term Structure Effects on the Equilibrium Demand for Real Balances

Research on the structure of interest rates derives the prediction from the rational expectations theory of the term structure that when individual rates of different maturities are nonstationary, the spreads (differences) of these rates are stationary (Campbell and Shiller (1987, 1988)). Empirical tests of this hypothesis generally support the conclusion that there exists a stationary linear combination of the long-term and short-term interest rates in the U.S. and the specific conclusion that the spread between these two rates is stationary. If there exists an equilibrium demand for real balances in the logs of real balances, real income and the levels of interest rates as found in the three variable VECMs estimated in Chapter 6, and if linear combinations of interest rates are stationary, then there are at least two cointegrating vectors among real balances, real income and short-term and long-term interest rates.

The necessary and sufficient conditions for identification of a unique matrix of cointegrating vectors, $\beta$, in terms of linear restrictions on the columns of $\beta$ are analogous to the classical identification problem in simultaneous equation models, as discussed in Chapter 3. In the problem under consideration here, if there are two cointegrating vectors among the four data series, then identification requires at least one linear restriction on each cointegrating vector. Let $z_t = [\ln(M/P)_t, r_{Lt}, \ln(Y/P)_t, r_{St}]$. Identification of the term structure is straightforward, Assume that the equilibrium term structure relationship is not affected by either real balances or real output. Then there are two restrictions on the first cointegrating vector, and the order condition for identification is satisfied. In fact exclusion of both $\ln(M/P)_t$ and $\ln(Y/P)_t$ from the equilibrium term structure vector overidentifies this relationship. Identification of the second cointegrating vector as a money demand function requires at least one restriction on the elements of this vector. At first glance, it seems that identification of this equation can be achieved by restricting the long-run income elasticity of the demand for real balances to unity, consistent with the results in Chapter 6 and in Hoffman, Rasche and Tieslau (1995). This restriction satisfies the order condition, but fails the rank condition, given the overidentifying restrictions on the term structure relationship. To illustrate this underidentification consider the restricted matrix of cointegrating vectors:

$$\beta' = \begin{bmatrix} 0.0 & 1.0 & 0.0 & \beta_{14} \\ 1.0 & \beta_{22} & -1.0 & \beta_{24} \end{bmatrix}$$

and transform this matrix by:

$$R = \begin{bmatrix} 1.0 & 0.0 \\ r_{21} & 1.0 \end{bmatrix}.$$

Then:

$$\begin{aligned} \beta^{*\prime} &= R\beta' = \begin{bmatrix} 1.0 & 0.0 \\ r_{21} & 1.0 \end{bmatrix} \begin{bmatrix} 0.0 & 1.0 & 0.0 & \beta_{14} \\ 1.0 & \beta_{22} & -1.0 & \beta_{24} \end{bmatrix} \\ &= \begin{bmatrix} 0.0 & 1.0 & 0.0 & \beta_{14} \\ 1.0 & r_{21} + \beta_{22} & -1.0 & r_{21} + \beta_{24} \end{bmatrix} \end{aligned}$$

is an admissible alternative matrix of cointegrating vectors which satisfies the restrictions on both vectors for any arbitrary choice of $r_{21}$. Clearly the set of restrictions does not produce unique long-run interest semielasticities of velocity.

There are only two valid alternatives that achieve identification of both vectors: 1) relax the overidentifying restriction on the equilibrium term structure and allow it to be affected by either real balances or real output (but not both) while maintaining the velocity restriction on the equilibrium demand for real balances, or 2) restrict one of the interest rate coefficients in the equilibrium money demand relationship. The former choice of identifying restriction is at variance with the established term structure literature; the second appears to assume away the problem under investigation.

The choice of an exclusion restriction on one interest rate in the money demand equation is arbitrary when the interest rate spread is stationary. Under these conditions the term structure vector is (0.0, 1.0, 0.0, -1.0), which has two overidentifying restrictions. The exclusion of the long rate from the money demand vector gives:

$$\beta' = \begin{bmatrix} 0.0 & 1.0 & 0.0 & -1.0 \\ 1.0 & 0.0 & -1.0 & \beta_{24} \end{bmatrix}.$$

Now consider the transformation matrix:

$$R = \begin{bmatrix} 1.0 & 0.0 \\ \beta_{24} & 1.0 \end{bmatrix}.$$

Then

$$\beta^{*\prime} = R\beta' = \begin{bmatrix} 0.0 & 1.0 & 0.0 & -1.0 \\ 1.0 & \beta_{24} & -1.0 & 0.0 \end{bmatrix},$$

$\beta^{*\prime}$ still admits one interest rate exclusion, and the equilibrium interest semielasticity of the same value as in $\beta'$, but the equilibrium semielasticity has been transferred to the long rate from the short rate. In general under stationarity of the interest rate spread, equilibrium long-rate and short-rate semielasticities are not individually identified. Only the sum of the semielasticities is identified, since any shock which has a permanent impact on real balances and interest rates will always produce equal permanent changes in both long rates and short rates and an equal permanent change in any weighted average of the two rates. This lack of identification of the individual equilibrium semielasticities can be seen by considering a matrix of cointegrating vectors of the form:

$$\beta' = \begin{bmatrix} 0.0 & 1.0 & 0.0 & -1.0 \\ 1.0 & \beta_{22} & -1.0 & \beta_{24} \end{bmatrix}.$$

The second cointegrating vector is not identified. Consider a transformation matrix of the form:

$$R = \begin{bmatrix} 1.0 & 0.0 \\ -\beta_{22} & 1.0 \end{bmatrix}.$$

Then:

$$\beta^{*\prime} = R\beta' = \begin{bmatrix} 0.0 & 1.0 & 0.0 & -1.0 \\ 1.0 & 0.0 & -1.0 & \beta_{22}+\beta_{24} \end{bmatrix}.$$

Here both cointegrating vectors are identified (there are no nondiagonal transformations that preserve the zero restrictions) and the coefficient on the short rate in the second cointegrating vector is properly interpreted as the sum of the equilibrium long-rate and short-rate semielasticities. Alternatively, if the chosen transformation matrix is:

$$R = \begin{bmatrix} 1.0 & 0.0 \\ -\beta_{24} & 1.0 \end{bmatrix},$$

then:

$$\beta^{*\prime} = R\beta' = \begin{bmatrix} 0.0 & 1.0 & 0.0 & -1.0 \\ 1.0 & \beta_{22}+\beta_{24} & -1.0 & 0.0 \end{bmatrix},$$

and the coefficient on the long-term rate measures the sum of the equilibrium interest semielasticities. Thus, given stationarity of the interest rate spread when both rates are nonstationary, identification of the equilibrium effects of the term structure on the demand for real balances is impossible.

### 7.2.2 Estimation of VECMs with Term Structure Relations and Tests for Cointegration

The data used in this analysis are quarterly geometric average observations on M1, quarterly arithmetic averages on the Treasury bill rate and the 10 year government bond rate, plus quarterly series on real GDP and the GDP deflator from 55:2 - 91:4. The vector error correction models are estimated with $k$=4 lags. This lag length is sufficient to remove autocorrelation from the estimated residuals in all equations. The estimates of recursive regressions from 72:4 - 91:4 are reported in Table 7.5 with the coefficients on real balances and real income constrained to be equal but of opposite sign, and with no restriction on the

Treasury bill rate coefficients in either cointegrating vector. The samples which extend beyond 1979:3 include the D79 dummy variable, and those extending beyond 1981:4 include the D82 dummy variable.

Our testing strategy is similar to that for the Fisher effect. We are interested in the evidence, on the margin, for cointegration between the long rate and the short rate, given the velocity - nominal interest rate cointegrating vector that we have found in Chapter 6. Given evidence for such a marginal relationship in the data, we utilize a variety of tests to verify the stationarity of the interest rate spread.

The results in Table 7.5 are quite mixed. In the samples ending before the New Operating Procedures period, there is very weak evidence for two cointegrating vectors. In about half the samples the hypothesis of one or fewer cointegrating vectors is rejected; in the other samples this hypothesis is not rejected at conventional significance levels. This may reflect low power of the Johansen maximum eigenvalue test in small samples, since the two vectors(associated with the largest eigenvalues) may be normalized to obtain an interest semielasticity of the assumed cointegrating vector with real balances that is very similar to the corresponding estimate in Chapter 6, and the unrestricted coefficient on the short-term interest rate in the assumed second vector is very close to -1.0 in all but the shortest sample periods.

At first glance, the evidence for two cointegrating vectors in the longer sample periods is even less supportive of the term structure hypothesis. However, since these VECMs include the two dummy variables D79 and D82, the correct critical values for the maximum eigenvalue test may be considerably lower than those tabulated in Osterwald-Lenum (1992).[10] In most of the samples which include D79 and D82, the implied constants of the cointegrating vectors under the assumption of two vectors indicate a shift during the New Operating Procedures period, but a return to the pre 1979 levels after 1981. Therefore we have reestimated the 82:4 - 91:4 samples without the dummy variables and omitting the observations 79:4 - 81:4 inclusive. Table 7.6 contains the results of these reestimations. The revised estimates contain much stronger evidence for a second cointegrating vector. The Johansen maximum eigenvalue tests always reject the hypothesis of one cointegrating vector in favor of two cointegrating vectors at the 10 percent level, and frequently at the five percent level.

There is considerable evidence that the second cointegrating vector is a stationary interest rate spread. The Wald test never rejects the hypothesis that the coefficient on the Treasury bill rate is -1.0 in the vector that is normalized on the long-term rate. The VECMs are reestimated subject to the interest rate spread restriction in Table 7.7 utilizing the restricted maximum likelihood procedure proposed by Johansen and Juselius (1992). The likelihood ratio test of this restriction only rejects the restriction at the five percent level in the shortest (72:4) and longest (91:4) samples of the recursive estimations. Finally we constructed the Horvath/Watson $W$ test for the presence of a second cointegrating vector with known coefficients (the interest rate spread) given a cointegrating vector

[10] see Hansen and Johansen (1993)

Table 7.5: Recursive Estimates of Error Correction Coefficients.(No D67)

| end: | 72:4 | T=67 |
|---|---|---|
| $H_0$ | *trace* | $\lambda$ |
| $r=0$ | 35.1** | 0.26 |
| $r\leq 1$ | 14.9* | 0.18 |
| $r\leq 2$ | 1.6 | 0.02 |

| $\beta_c$ | |
|---|---|
| 1.0 | 0.0 |
| 0.0 | 1.0 |
| -1.0 | 0.0 |
| 0.17 | -2.35 |
| (0.03) | (1.83) |

| $\beta_{01}$ | $\beta_{02}$ |
|---|---|
| -.78 | -7.02 |

| $\alpha_c$ | |
|---|---|
| 0.06 | 0.003 |
| (4.4) | (4.4) |
| -0.06 | -0.02 |
| (−0.1) | (−0.7) |
| 0.04 | 0.001 |
| (2.2) | (0.5) |
| -0.29 | -0.07 |
| (−0.3) | (−1.7) |

| end: | 73:4 | T=71 |
|---|---|---|
| $H_0$ | *trace* | $\lambda$ |
| $r=0$ | 33.6** | 0.25 |
| $r\leq 1$ | 18.0** | 0.16 |
| $r\leq 2$ | 5.5 | 0.07 |

| $\beta_c$ | |
|---|---|
| 1.0 | 0.0 |
| 0.0 | 1.0 |
| -1.0 | 0.0 |
| 0.12 | -1.5 |
| (0.02) | (0.4) |

| $\beta_{01}$ | $\beta_{02}$ |
|---|---|
| -.92 | -2.10 |

| $\alpha_c$ | |
|---|---|
| 0.06 | 0.003 |
| (2.3) | (0.3) |
| -0.11 | -0.04 |
| (−0.1) | (−1.8) |
| 0.05 | -0.0004 |
| (2.3) | (0.3) |
| -0.16 | -0.13 |
| (−0.2) | (−1.8) |

| end: | 74:4 | T=75 |
|---|---|---|
| $H_0$ | *trace* | $\lambda$ |
| $r=0$ | 34.1** | 0.24 |
| $r\leq 1$ | 13.3* | 0.12 |
| $r\leq 2$ | 4.0 | 0.1 |

| $\beta_c$ | |
|---|---|
| 1.0 | 0.0 |
| 0.0 | 1.0 |
| -1.0 | 0.0 |
| 0.12 | -1.12 |
| (0.01) | (0.16) |

| $\beta_{01}$ | $\beta_{02}$ |
|---|---|
| -.92 | .24 |

| $\alpha_c$ | |
|---|---|
| 0.05 | 0.002 |
| (3.4) | (1.7) |
| 0.30 | 0.04 |
| (0.5) | (0.6) |
| 0.05 | -0.0004 |
| (2.6) | (0.2) |
| 0.06 | -0.12 |
| (−0.1) | (−1.1) |

| end: | 75:4 | T=79 |
|---|---|---|
| $H_0$ | *trace* | $\lambda$ |
| $r=0$ | 32.3** | 0.24 |
| $r\leq 1$ | 10.5 | 0.12 |
| $r\leq 2$ | 0.13 | 0.002 |

| $\beta_c$ | |
|---|---|
| 1.0 | 0.0 |
| 0.0 | 1.0 |
| -1.0 | 0.0 |
| 0.13 | -1.08 |
| (0.01) | (0.12) |

| $\beta_{01}$ | $\beta_{02}$ |
|---|---|
| -.89 | .53 |

| $\alpha_c$ | |
|---|---|
| 0.03 | 0.001 |
| (2.3) | (0.9) |
| 0.91 | 0.08 |
| (1.6) | (1.2) |
| 0.05 | -0.0003 |
| (3.2) | (−0.1) |
| 0.58 | -0.12 |
| (0.6) | (−1.0) |

| end: | 76:4 | T=83 |
|---|---|---|
| $H_0$ | *trace* | $\lambda$ |
| $r=0$ | 33.7** | 0.22 |
| $r\leq 1$ | 12.7 | 0.14 |
| $r\leq 2$ | 0.1 | 0.001 |

| $\beta_c$ | |
|---|---|
| 1.0 | 0.0 |
| 0.0 | 1.0 |
| -1.0 | 0.0 |
| 0.14 | -1.1 |
| (0.012) | (0.11) |

| $\beta_{01}$ | $\beta_{02}$ |
|---|---|
| -.87 | .49 |

| $\alpha_c$ | |
|---|---|
| 0.03 | 0.002 |
| (2.4) | (1.3) |
| 0.79 | 0.1 |
| (1.5) | (1.6) |
| 0.05 | 0.003 |
| (3.1) | (0.1) |
| 0.46 | -0.09 |
| (0.5) | (−0.7) |

| end: | 77:4 | T=87 |
|---|---|---|
| $H_0$ | *trace* | $\lambda$ |
| $r=0$ | 34.2** | 0.21 |
| $r\leq 1$ | 13.6* | 0.14 |
| $r\leq 2$ | 0.1 | 0.001 |

| $\beta_c$ | |
|---|---|
| 1.0 | 0.0 |
| 0.0 | 1.0 |
| -1.0 | 0.0 |
| 0.15 | -1.14 |
| (0.01) | (0.11) |

| $\beta_{01}$ | $\beta_{02}$ |
|---|---|
| -.83 | .35 |

| $\alpha_c$ | |
|---|---|
| 0.03 | 0.002 |
| (2.4) | (1.5) |
| 0.94 | 0.12 |
| (1.9) | (1.8) |
| 0.04 | -0.0001 |
| (2.6) | (−0.0) |
| 0.66 | -0.06 |
| (0.8) | (−0.5) |

Table 7.5: Recursive Estimates of Error Correction Coefficients.(No D67),(Continued)

| end: | 78:4 | T=91 |
|---|---|---|
| $H_0$ | *trace* | $\lambda$ |
| $r=0$ | 36.6** | 0.23 |
| $r\leq 1$ | 13.1 | 0.13 |
| $r\leq 2$ | 0.3 | 0.003 |

| $\beta_c$ | |
|---|---|
| 1.0 | 0.0 |
| 0.0 | 1.0 |
| -1.0 | 0.0 |
| 0.15 | -1.14 |
| (0.01) | (0.1) |

| $\beta_{01}$ | $\beta_{02}$ |
|---|---|
| -.84 | .35 |

| $\alpha_c$ | |
|---|---|
| 0.03 | 0.002 |
| (2.5) | (1.6) |
| 1.04 | 0.12 |
| (2.1) | (1.8) |
| 0.04 | -0.0004 |
| (2.5) | (−0.2) |
| 0.73 | -0.04 |
| (0.8) | (−0.3) |

| end: | 79:3 | T=94 |
|---|---|---|
| $H_0$ | *trace* | $\lambda$ |
| $r=0$ | 36.2** | 0.21 |
| $r\leq 1$ | 14.2* | 0.13 |
| $r\leq 2$ | 0.8 | 0.009 |

| $\beta_c$ | |
|---|---|
| 1.0 | 0.0 |
| 0.0 | 1.0 |
| -1.0 | 0.0 |
| 0.14 | -1.09 |
| (0.01) | (0.1) |

| $\beta_{01}$ | $\beta_{02}$ |
|---|---|
| -.85 | .50 |

| $\alpha_c$ | |
|---|---|
| 0.02 | 0.002 |
| (2.2) | (1.3) |
| 1.07 | 0.13 |
| (2.2) | (1.9) |
| 0.04 | -0.001 |
| (2.5) | (−0.2) |
| 0.59 | -0.05 |
| (0.7) | (−0.4) |

| end: | 80:4 | T=99 |
|---|---|---|
| $H_0$ | *trace* | $\lambda$ |
| $r=0$ | 38.4** | 0.21 |
| $r\leq 1$ | 15.2* | 0.14 |
| $r\leq 2$ | 0.7 | 0.01 |

| $\beta_c$ | |
|---|---|
| 1.0 | 0.0 |
| 0.0 | 1.0 |
| -1.0 | 0.0 |
| 0.14 | -1.11 |
| (0.01) | (0.1) |

| | $\beta_{01}$ | $\beta_{02}$ |
|---|---|---|
| <79:4 | -.85 | .30 |
| >79:3 | .39 | 1.03 |

| $\alpha_c$ | |
|---|---|
| 0.03 | 0.002 |
| (2.5) | (1.5) |
| 1.75 | 0.23 |
| (2.9) | (2.8) |
| 0.04 | -0.0001 |
| (2.9) | (−0.0) |
| 2.06 | 0.14 |
| (1.7) | (0.9) |

| end: | 81:4 | T=103 |
|---|---|---|
| $H_0$ | *trace* | $\lambda$ |
| $r=0$ | 30.4** | 0.19 |
| $r\leq 1$ | 8.3 | 0.07 |
| $r\leq 2$ | 0.3 | 0.003 |

| $\beta_c$ | |
|---|---|
| 1.0 | 0.0 |
| 0.0 | 1.0 |
| -1.0 | 0.0 |
| 0.14 | -1.15 |
| (-0.01) | (0.11) |

| | $\beta_{01}$ | $\beta_{02}$ |
|---|---|---|
| <79:4 | -0.86 | 0.22 |
| >79:3 | 0.19 | 2.6 |

| $\alpha_c$ | |
|---|---|
| 0.01 | 0.001 |
| (1.2) | (0.7) |
| 1.4 | 0.18 |
| (2.7) | (2.4) |
| 0.03 | -0.002 |
| (2.2) | (−1.1) |
| 3.17 | 0.27 |
| (3.0) | (1.8) |

| end: | 82:4 | T=107 |
|---|---|---|
| $H_0$ | *trace* | $\lambda$ |
| $r=0$ | 34.5** | 0.2 |
| $r\leq 1$ | 10.6 | 0.1 |
| $r\leq 2$ | 0.3 | 0.003 |

| $\beta_c$ | |
|---|---|
| 1.0 | 0.0 |
| 0.0 | 1.0 |
| -1.0 | 0.0 |
| 0.14 | -1.13 |
| (0.014) | (0.1) |

| | $\beta_{01}$ | $\beta_{02}$ |
|---|---|---|
| <79:4 | -0.87 | 0.31 |
| >79:3 | 0.35 | 0.87 |
| >81:4 | 0.4 | -5.05 |

| $\alpha_c$ | |
|---|---|
| 0.01 | 0.001 |
| (1.2) | (0.4) |
| 1.63 | 0.26 |
| (2.7) | (3.1) |
| 0.03 | -0.002 |
| (2.3) | (−1.0) |
| 3.49 | 0.35 |
| (3.0) | (2.2) |

| end: | 83:4 | T=111 |
|---|---|---|
| $H_0$ | *trace* | $\lambda$ |
| $r=0$ | 34.3** | 0.18 |
| $r\leq 1$ | 11.7 | 0.1 |
| $r\leq 2$ | 0.4 | 0.004 |

| $\beta_c$ | |
|---|---|
| 1.0 | 0.0 |
| 0.0 | 1.0 |
| -1.0 | 0.0 |
| 0.14 | -1.12 |
| (0.02) | (0.1) |

| | $\beta_{01}$ | $\beta_{02}$ |
|---|---|---|
| <79:4 | -0.87 | 0.32 |
| >79:3 | 0.32 | 1.2 |
| >81:4 | -0.02 | -1.5 |

| $\alpha_c$ | |
|---|---|
| 0.01 | 0.004 |
| (1.2) | (0.3) |
| 1.83 | 0.28 |
| (3.0) | (3.1) |
| 0.03 | -0.002 |
| (2.3) | (−1.1) |
| 3.3 | 0.34 |
| (3.1) | (2.1) |

Table 7.5: Recursive Estimates of Error Correction Coefficients.(No D67),(Continued)

| end: | 84:4 | T=115 |
|---|---|---|
| $H_0$ | *trace* | $\lambda$ |
| $r=0$ | 40.7** | 0.21 |
| $r\leq 1$ | 14.2* | 0.11 |
| $r\leq 2$ | 0.6 | 0.01 |

| $\beta_c$ | |
|---|---|
| 1.0 | 0.0 |
| 0.0 | 1.0 |
| -1.0 | 0.0 |
| 0.14 | -1.17 |
| (0.01) | (0.1) |

| | $\beta_{01}$ | $\beta_{02}$ |
|---|---|---|
| <79:4 | -0.86 | 0.33 |
| >79:3 | 0.4 | 0.55 |
| >81:4 | -0.18 | 0.25 |

| $\alpha_c$ | |
|---|---|
| 0.01 | 0.0003 |
| (1.1) | (0.2) |
| 2.1 | 0.31 |
| (3.6) | (3.4) |
| 0.03 | -0.002 |
| (2.5) | (−1.0) |
| 3.3 | 0.34 |
| (3.2) | (2.2) |

| end: | 85:4 | T=119 |
|---|---|---|
| $H_0$ | *trace* | $\lambda$ |
| $r=0$ | 37.5** | 0.18 |
| $r\leq 1$ | 13.3* | 0.1 |
| $r\leq 2$ | 0.6 | 0.01 |

| $\beta_c$ | |
|---|---|
| 1.0 | 0.0 |
| 0.0 | 1.0 |
| -1.0 | 0.0 |
| 0.13 | -1.1 |
| (0.02) | (0.1) |

| | $\beta_{01}$ | $\beta_{02}$ |
|---|---|---|
| <79:4 | -0.37 | 0.36 |
| >79:3 | 0.4 | 0.53 |
| >81:4 | -0.2 | 0.04 |

| $\alpha_c$ | |
|---|---|
| 0.01 | 0.0003 |
| (1.2) | (0.2) |
| 1.93 | 0.3 |
| (3.3) | (3.3) |
| 0.02 | -0.002 |
| (2.1) | (−1.1) |
| 3.13 | 0.34 |
| (3.1) | (2.2) |

| end: | 86:4 | T=123 |
|---|---|---|
| $H_0$ | *trace* | $\lambda$ |
| $r=0$ | 37.4** | 0.19 |
| $r\leq 1$ | 11.1 | 0.08 |
| $r\leq 2$ | 0.4 | 0.003 |

| $\beta_c$ | |
|---|---|
| 1.0 | 0.0 |
| 0.0 | 1.0 |
| -1.0 | 0.0 |
| 0.13 | -1.1 |
| (0.02) | (0.09) |

| | $\beta_{01}$ | $\beta_{02}$ |
|---|---|---|
| <79:4 | -0.9 | 0.44 |
| >79:3 | 0.41 | 0.56 |
| >81:4 | -0.26 | -0.53 |

| $\alpha_c$ | |
|---|---|
| 0.02 | 0.001 |
| (2.1) | (1.0) |
| 1.34 | 0.23 |
| (2.3) | (2.6) |
| 0.01 | -0.004 |
| (0.9) | (−2.4) |
| 2.28 | 0.22 |
| (2.4) | (1.5) |

| end: | 87:4 | T=127 |
|---|---|---|
| $H_0$ | *trace* | $\lambda$ |
| $r=0$ | 37.7** | 0.2 |
| $r\leq 1$ | 10.1 | 0.07 |
| $r\leq 2$ | 1.0 | 0.01 |

| $\beta_c$ | |
|---|---|
| 1.0 | 0.0 |
| 0.0 | 1.0 |
| -1.0 | 0.0 |
| 0.13 | -1.1 |
| (0.03) | (0.1) |

| | $\beta_{01}$ | $\beta_{02}$ |
|---|---|---|
| <79:4 | -0.88 | 0.46 |
| >79:3 | 0.72 | -1.33 |
| >81:4 | -0.84 | 3.14 |

| $\alpha_c$ | |
|---|---|
| 0.01 | 0.0004 |
| (1.1) | (0.4) |
| 1.5 | 0.25 |
| (3.0) | (2.9) |
| 0.004 | -0.0004 |
| (0.5) | (−2.9) |
| 1.6 | 0.16 |
| (2.0) | (1.1) |

| end: | 88:4 | T=131 |
|---|---|---|
| $H_0$ | *trace* | $\lambda$ |
| $r=0$ | 40.5** | 0.2 |
| $r\leq 1$ | 12.0 | 0.8 |
| $r\leq 2$ | 0.8 | 0.01 |

| $\beta_c$ | |
|---|---|
| 1.0 | 0.0 |
| 0.0 | 1.0 |
| -1.0 | 0.0 |
| 0.13 | -1.1 |
| (0.02) | (0.1) |

| | $\beta_{01}$ | $\beta_{02}$ |
|---|---|---|
| <79:4 | -0.9 | 0.47 |
| >79:3 | 0.59 | -0.37 |
| >81:4 | -0.63 | 1.37 |

| $\alpha_c$ | |
|---|---|
| 0.003 | 0.0001 |
| (0.4) | (0.1) |
| 1.43 | 0.24 |
| (3.3) | (2.9) |
| 0.004 | -0.004 |
| (0.5) | (−3.1) |
| 2.04 | 0.18 |
| (2.9) | (1.3) |

| end: | 89:4 | T=135 |
|---|---|---|
| $H_0$ | *trace* | $\lambda$ |
| $r=0$ | 36.1** | 0.16 |
| $r\leq 1$ | 12.3 | 0.08 |
| $r\leq 2$ | 1.0 | 0.001 |

| $\beta_c$ | |
|---|---|
| 1.0 | 0.0 |
| 0.0 | 1.0 |
| -1.0 | 0.0 |
| 0.13 | -1.1 |
| (0.02) | (0.1) |

| | $\beta_{01}$ | $\beta_{02}$ |
|---|---|---|
| <79:4 | -0.9 | 0.44 |
| >79:3 | 0.6 | 1.0 |
| >81:4 | -0.62 | -1.0 |

| $\alpha_c$ | |
|---|---|
| -0.002 | -0.001 |
| (0.3) | (0.5) |
| 1.19 | 0.2 |
| (3.2) | (2.6) |
| 0.01 | -0.003 |
| (1.5) | (−2.4) |
| 1.9 | 0.15 |
| (3.1) | (1.2) |

Table 7.5: Recursive Estimates of Error Correction Coefficients.(No D67),(Continued)

| end: | 90:4 | T=139 |
|---|---|---|
| $H_0$ | *trace* | $\lambda$ |
| $r = 0$ | 41.4** | 0.17 |
| $r \leq 1$ | 14.9* | 0.1 |
| $r \leq 2$ | 1.1 | 0.01 |

| $\beta_c$ | |
|---|---|
| 1.0 | 0.0 |
| 0.0 | 1.0 |
| -1.0 | 0.0 |
| 0.13 | -1.1 |
| (0.03) | (0.1) |

| | $\beta_{01}$ | $\beta_{02}$ |
|---|---|---|
| <79:4 | -0.88 | 0.45 |
| >79:3 | 0.69 | 0.48 |
| >81:4 | -0.75 | -0.18 |

| $\alpha_c$ | |
|---|---|
| -0.002 | -0.001 |
| (0.5) | (0.7) |
| 1.19 | 0.21 |
| (3.6) | (3.2) |
| 0.008 | -0.003 |
| (1.4) | (−2.9) |
| 1.78 | 0.14 |
| (3.4) | (1.3) |

| end: | 91:4 | T=143 |
|---|---|---|
| $H_0$ | *trace* | $\lambda$ |
| $r = 0$ | 38.7* | 0.17 |
| $r \leq 1$ | 11.7 | 0.07 |
| $r \leq 2$ | 1.0 | 0.01 |

| $\beta_c$ | |
|---|---|
| 1.0 | 0.0 |
| 0.0 | 1.0 |
| -1.0 | 0.0 |
| 0.13 | -1.1 |
| (0.03) | (0.1) |

| | $\beta_{01}$ | $\beta_{02}$ |
|---|---|---|
| <79:4 | -0.91 | 0.47 |
| >79:3 | 0.76 | 0.05 |
| >81:4 | -0.91 | 0.6 |

| $\alpha_c$ | |
|---|---|
| 0.001 | -0.001 |
| (0.2) | (0.5) |
| 1.05 | 0.2 |
| (3.3) | (3.0) |
| 0.004 | -0.004 |
| (0.8) | (−3.2) |
| 1.5 | 0.12 |
| (3.0) | (1.1) |

Note:Recursive Samples indicated by the end of the sample period. Trace and $\lambda$ statistics refer to Johansen tests. $\beta_c$ is the estimate of the normalized cointegration vectors. $\beta_{01}$ and $\beta_{02}$ are the constant terms(that can change with intervention dummies) in the cointegrating relations. $\alpha$ is the matrix of error correction coefficients at each recursive sample.

Table 7.6: Recursive Estimates of Error Correction Coefficients, (omitting 79:4-81:4 and there are no Dummies)

| end: | 82:4 | T=98 |
|---|---|---|
| $H_0$ | *trace* | $\lambda$ |
| $r=0$ | 62.3** | 0.31 |
| $r\leq 1$ | 26.7** | 0.23 |
| $r\leq 2$ | 1.3 | 0.01 |

| $\beta_c$ | |
|---|---|
| 1.0 | 0.0 |
| 0.0 | 1.0 |
| -1.0 | 0.0 |
| 0.14 | -1.08 |
| (0.01) | (0.08) |

| $\beta_{01}$ | $\beta_{02}$ |
|---|---|
| -0.8 | 0.46 |

| $\alpha_c$ | |
|---|---|
| -0.004 | -0.01 |
| (0.6) | (1.1) |
| 1.51 | 0.23 |
| (4.9) | (3.9) |
| 0.03 | -0.002 |
| (3.8) | (−1.1) |
| 0.89 | -0.01 |
| (1.8) | (−0.1) |

| end: | 83:4 | T=102 |
|---|---|---|
| $H_0$ | *trace* | $\lambda$ |
| $r=0$ | 41.4** | 0.24 |
| $r\leq 1$ | 14.1* | 0.12 |
| $r\leq 2$ | 1.4 | 0.01 |

| $\beta_c$ | |
|---|---|
| 1.0 | 0.0 |
| 0.0 | 1.0 |
| -1.0 | 0.0 |
| 0.13 | -1.13 |
| (0.02) | (0.09) |

| $\beta_{01}$ | $\beta_{02}$ |
|---|---|
| -0.85 | 0.23 |

| $\alpha_c$ | |
|---|---|
| -0.001 | -0.001 |
| (−0.2) | (−0.7) |
| 1.05 | 0.2 |
| (3.3) | (3.2) |
| 0.02 | -0.002 |
| (3.4) | (−1.2) |
| 1.07 | 0.11 |
| (2.1) | (1.1) |

| end: | 84:4 | T=106 |
|---|---|---|
| $H_0$ | *trace* | $\lambda$ |
| $r=0$ | 42.2** | 0.24 |
| $r\leq 1$ | 13.8* | 0.11 |
| $r\leq 2$ | 1.5 | 0.01 |

| $\beta_c$ | |
|---|---|
| 1.0 | 0.0 |
| 0.0 | 1.0 |
| -1.0 | 0.0 |
| 0.13 | -1.14 |
| (0.02) | (0.1) |

| $\beta_{01}$ | $\beta_{02}$ |
|---|---|
| -0.86 | 0.22 |

| $\alpha_c$ | |
|---|---|
| -0.003 | -0.001 |
| (−0.6) | (−1.3) |
| 1.02 | 0.19 |
| (3.2) | (3.2) |
| 0.02 | -0.002 |
| (3.6) | (−1.7) |
| 1.31 | 0.16 |
| (2.8) | (1.8) |

| end: | 85:4 | T=110 |
|---|---|---|
| $H_0$ | *trace* | $\lambda$ |
| $r=0$ | 45.3** | 0.23 |
| $r\leq 1$ | 17.1** | 0.13 |
| $r\leq 2$ | 1.8 | 0.02 |

| $\beta_c$ | |
|---|---|
| 1.0 | 0.0 |
| 0.0 | 1.0 |
| -1.0 | 0.0 |
| 0.14 | -1.14 |
| (0.02) | (0.11) |

| $\beta_{01}$ | $\beta_{02}$ |
|---|---|
| -0.83 | 0.24 |

| $\alpha_c$ | |
|---|---|
| -0.005 | -0.001 |
| (−1.0) | (−1.7) |
| 1.0 | 0.2 |
| (3.5) | (3.5) |
| 0.02 | -0.002 |
| (3.8) | (−1.4) |
| 1.38 | 0.17 |
| (3.3) | (2.2) |

| end: | 86:4 | T=114 |
|---|---|---|
| $H_0$ | *trace* | $\lambda$ |
| $r=0$ | 41.1** | 0.19 |
| $r\leq 1$ | 17.7** | 0.13 |
| $r\leq 2$ | 2.5 | 0.02 |

| $\beta_c$ | |
|---|---|
| 1.0 | 0.0 |
| 0.0 | 1.0 |
| -1.0 | 0.0 |
| 0.14 | -1.15 |
| (0.02) | (0.11) |

| $\beta_{01}$ | $\beta_{02}$ |
|---|---|
| -0.8 | 0.14 |

| $\alpha_c$ | |
|---|---|
| -0.003 | -0.001 |
| (−0.7) | (−1.3) |
| 0.92 | 0.2 |
| (3.3) | (3.5) |
| 0.02 | -0.002 |
| (3.1) | (−1.9) |
| 1.16 | 0.45 |
| (3.0) | (1.9) |

| end: | 87:4 | T=118 |
|---|---|---|
| $H_0$ | *trace* | $\lambda$ |
| $r=0$ | 39.4** | 0.15 |
| $r\leq 1$ | 19.8** | 0.14 |
| $r\leq 2$ | 2.0 | 0.02 |

| $\beta_c$ | |
|---|---|
| 1.0 | 0.0 |
| 0.0 | 1.0 |
| -1.0 | 0.0 |
| 0.15 | -1.2 |
| (0.03) | (0.13) |

| $\beta_{01}$ | $\beta_{02}$ |
|---|---|
| -0.77 | 0.08 |

| $\alpha_c$ | |
|---|---|
| -0.01 | -0.001 |
| (−1.4) | (−1.4) |
| 1.01 | 0.21 |
| (4.1) | (3.6) |
| 0.01 | -0.003 |
| (1.9) | (−2.3) |
| 0.92 | 0.16 |
| (2.7) | (2.0) |

Table 7.6: Recursive Estimates of Error Correction Coefficients.(No Dummies),(Continued)

| end: | 88:4 | T=122 |
|---|---|---|
| $H_0$ | *trace* | $\lambda$ |
| $r=0$ | 37.7** | 0.14 |
| $r \leq 1$ | 18.9** | 0.13 |
| $r \leq 2$ | 2.4 | 0.02 |

| $\beta_c$ | |
|---|---|
| 1.0 | 0.0 |
| 0.0 | 1.0 |
| -1.0 | 0.0 |
| 0.16 | -1.23 |
| (0.03) | (0.14) |

| $\beta_{01}$ | $\beta_{02}$ |
|---|---|
| -0.74 | -0.14 |

| $\alpha_c$ | |
|---|---|
| -0.005 | -0.001 |
| (−1.3) | (−1.3) |
| 1.01 | 0.2 |
| (4.0) | (3.6) |
| 0.01 | -0.002 |
| (1.7) | (−2.1) |
| 0.84 | 0.11 |
| (2.5) | (1.4) |

| end: | 89:4 | T=126 |
|---|---|---|
| $H_0$ | *trace* | $\lambda$ |
| $r=0$ | 37.9** | 0.14 |
| $r \leq 1$ | 18.9** | 0.13 |
| $r \leq 2$ | 1.4 | 0.01 |

| $\beta_c$ | |
|---|---|
| 1.0 | 0.0 |
| 0.0 | 1.0 |
| -1.0 | 0.0 |
| 0.15 | -1.17 |
| (0.03) | (0.12) |

| $\beta_{01}$ | $\beta_{02}$ |
|---|---|
| -0.79 | 0.15 |

| $\alpha_c$ | |
|---|---|
| -0.003 | -0.001 |
| (−0.8) | (−0.9) |
| 0.99 | 0.2 |
| (4.0) | (3.6) |
| 0.01 | -0.002 |
| (2.2) | (2.0) |
| 0.84 | 0.1 |
| (2.5) | (1.2) |

| end: | 90:4 | T=130 |
|---|---|---|
| $H_0$ | *trace* | $\lambda$ |
| $r=0$ | 38.9** | 0.16 |
| $r \leq 1$ | 16.5** | 0.11 |
| $r \leq 2$ | 1.1 | 0.01 |

| $\beta_c$ | |
|---|---|
| 1.0 | 0.0 |
| 0.0 | 1.0 |
| -1.0 | 0.0 |
| 0.17 | -1.24 |
| (0.04) | (0.14) |

| $\beta_{01}$ | $\beta_{02}$ |
|---|---|
| -0.71 | -0.17 |

| $\alpha_c$ | |
|---|---|
| -0.003 | -0.001 |
| (−1.0) | (−0.9) |
| 0.93 | 0.2 |
| (4.2) | (3.7) |
| 0.01 | -0.003 |
| (1.3) | (−2.4) |
| 0.71 | -0.08 |
| (2.3) | (1.1) |

| end: | 91:4 | T=134 |
|---|---|---|
| $H_0$ | *trace* | $\lambda$ |
| $r=0$ | 37.4** | 0.16 |
| $r \leq 1$ | 14.3* | 0.09 |
| $r \leq 2$ | 2.3 | 0.02 |

| $\beta_c$ | |
|---|---|
| 1.0 | 0.0 |
| 0.0 | 1.0 |
| -1.0 | 0.0 |
| 0.21 | -1.37 |
| (0.1) | (0.27) |

| $\beta_{01}$ | $\beta_{02}$ |
|---|---|
| -0.47 | -0.8 |

| $\alpha_c$ | |
|---|---|
| -0.002 | -0.001 |
| (−0.9) | (−0.9) |
| 0.76 | 0.2 |
| (4.3) | (3.6) |
| 0.0002 | -0.003 |
| (0.0) | (−2.6) |
| 0.48 | 0.08 |
| (2.0) | (1.1) |

**Note:Recursive Samples indicated by the end of the sample period. Trace and $\lambda$ statistics refer to Johansen tests. $\beta_c$ is the estimate of the normalized cointegration vectors. $\beta_{01}$ and $\beta_{02}$ are the constant terms in the cointegrating relations. $\alpha$ is the matrix of error correction coefficients at each recursive sample.**

between velocity and a nominal interest rate with an estimated (unknown) interest rate semielasticity. In all but the shortest sample periods the hypothesis that all the error correction coefficients on the interest rate spread are zero is rejected.

Once the interest rate spread constraint is imposed, the estimates of the interest rate semielasticity are 1) quite precise, 2) robust in recursive estimation, and 3) very similar to the estimated values from the three variable VECM discussed in Chapter 6. The comparison of the interest rate semielasticities from the model in Chapter 6 with those estimated from this model is shown in Figure 7.1. There seems to be some instability of the estimate of this coefficient for the sample periods that end in 90:4 and 91:4. This may reflect atypical behavior of interest rate spreads during the 90-91 recession. Friedman and Kuttner (1992) note that the spread between the Treasury bill rate and the commercial paper rate does not provide the historical contribution toward predicting the behavior of real GDP during this recession.

The estimated error correction coefficients exhibit some variation in the recursive estimation. In the sample periods that terminate in the 1970s, the error correction coefficient for real balances on the velocity cointegrating vector is significantly different from zero. In the longer sample periods the absolute value of this estimated coefficient is small and it is measured imprecisely. In these samples weak exogeneity of real balances is not rejected.

The error correction coefficients for real output are consistent across the recursive samples. The real output coefficient on the velocity cointegrating vector is always significant, while that on the interest rate spread vector is never significant and is always extremely small in absolute value. The error correction coefficients on the interest rate variables for the velocity cointegrating vector become quite stable after the shortest sample periods, with the exception of the sample period ending in 91:4. These error correction coefficients have the same sign and are approximately the same size. The error correction coefficient on the short-term interest rate for the spread cointegrating vector is generally measured with less precision than the corresponding error correction coefficient on the long-term nominal rate.

### 7.2.3 Dynamics

The identifying restrictions for the dynamic analysis of the VECM are analogous to those used with the Fisher equation model in the first part of this chapter. The two cointegrating vectors among the four variables imply two permanent and two transitory shocks. Following KPSW (1991) the permanent shocks are ordered first in a Wold causal chain structure. The permanent shocks are identified in the same fashion as in previous models; a real shock that is assumed to have a long-run impact on real output but no long-run effect on the nominal variables in the economy and a permanent nominal shock that is normalized to have a 100 basis point long-run effect on both of the nominal interest rates. The third identifying restriction is that the two permanent shocks are orthogonal. Finally an overidentifying restriction is that the nominal shock has no long-run

Table 7.7: Recursive Estimates of Error Correction Coefficients.(Spread Constraint-Omitting 79-81)

**end: 72:4**

| $H_0$ | statistic |
|---|---|
| $\chi_1^2$ | 7.2 |
| $HW_{02}$ | 9.3 |

| $\beta_c$ | |
|---|---|
| 1.0 | 0.0 |
| 0.0 | 1.0 |
| -1.0 | 0.0 |
| 0.1 | -1.0 |
| (0.01) | |

| $\beta_{01}$ | $\beta_{02}$ |
|---|---|
| -1.1 | 0.78 |

| $\alpha_c$ | |
|---|---|
| 0.06 | 0.003 |
| (4.6) | (1.9) |
| -0.23 | 0.004 |
| (0.35) | (0.05) |
| 0.03 | -0.002 |
| (1.6) | (-1.13) |
| -0.83 | -0.13 |
| (-0.83) | (-1.3) |

**end: 73:4**

| $H_0$ | statistic |
|---|---|
| $\chi_1^2$ | 3.1 |
| $HW_{02}$ | 12.0 |

| $\beta_c$ | |
|---|---|
| 1.0 | 0.0 |
| 0.0 | 1.0 |
| -1.0 | 0.0 |
| 0.1 | -1.0 |
| (0.01) | |

| $\beta_{01}$ | $\beta_{02}$ |
|---|---|
| -1.0 | 0.73 |

| $\alpha_c$ | |
|---|---|
| 0.06 | 0.003 |
| (4.6) | (2.4) |
| -0.09 | -0.0004 |
| (-0.12) | (0.01) |
| 0.04 | -0.001 |
| (2.12) | (-0.4) |
| -0.32 | -0.2 |
| (-0.3) | (-1.6) |

**end: 74:4**

| $H_0$ | statistic |
|---|---|
| $\chi_1^2$ | 0.5 |
| $HW_{02}$ | 9.4 |

| $\beta_c$ | |
|---|---|
| 1.0 | 0.0 |
| 0.0 | 1.0 |
| -1.0 | 0.0 |
| 0.12 | -1.0 |
| (0.01) | |

| $\beta_{01}$ | $\beta_{02}$ |
|---|---|
| -0.94 | 0.81 |

| $\alpha_c$ | |
|---|---|
| 0.04 | 0.002 |
| (3.3) | (1.3) |
| 0.36 | 0.07 |
| (0.59) | (0.9) |
| 0.05 | 0.00 |
| (3.0) | (0.00) |
| 0.26 | -0.11 |
| (0.25) | (-0.93) |

**end: 75:4**

| $H_0$ | statistic |
|---|---|
| $\chi_1^2$ | 0.55 |
| $HW_{12}$ | 10.6 |

| $\beta_c$ | |
|---|---|
| 1.0 | 0.0 |
| 0.0 | 1.0 |
| -1.0 | 0.0 |
| 0.13 | -1.0 |
| (0.01) | |

| $\beta_{01}$ | $\beta_{02}$ |
|---|---|
| -0.91 | 0.89 |

| $\alpha_c$ | |
|---|---|
| 0.03 | 0.001 |
| (2.4) | (0.8) |
| 0.88 | 0.08 |
| (1.6) | (1.2) |
| 0.05 | -0.0003 |
| (3.3) | (-0.2) |
| 0.66 | -0.13 |
| (0.7) | (-1.05) |

**end: 76:4**

| $H_0$ | statistic |
|---|---|
| $\chi_1^2$ | 0.86 |
| $HW_{02}$ | 12.9 |

| $\beta_c$ | |
|---|---|
| 1.0 | 0.0 |
| 0.0 | 1.0 |
| -1.0 | 0.0 |
| 0.13 | -1.0 |
| (0.01) | |

| $\beta_{01}$ | $\beta_{02}$ |
|---|---|
| -0.9 | 0.92 |

| $\alpha_c$ | |
|---|---|
| 0.03 | 0.002 |
| (2.5) | (1.3) |
| 0.74 | 0.1 |
| (1.4) | (1.6) |
| 0.05 | 0.0003 |
| (3.4) | (0.2) |
| 0.6 | -0.07 |
| (0.7) | (-0.7) |

**end: 77:4**

| $H_0$ | statistic |
|---|---|
| $\chi_1^2$ | 1.7 |
| $HW_{02}$ | 13.6 |

| $\beta_c$ | |
|---|---|
| 1.0 | 0.0 |
| 0.0 | 1.0 |
| -1.0 | 0.0 |
| 0.14 | -1.0 |
| (0.01) | |

| $\beta_{01}$ | $\beta_{02}$ |
|---|---|
| -0.88 | 0.98 |

| $\alpha_c$ | |
|---|---|
| 0.03 | 0.002 |
| (2.5) | (1.6) |
| 0.9 | 0.11 |
| (1.8) | (1.7) |
| 0.04 | -0.0003 |
| (3.0) | (-0.14) |
| 0.82 | -0.05 |
| (1.0) | (-0.5) |

Table 7.7: Recursive Estimates of Error Correction Coefficients.(Spread Constraint-Omitting 79-81),(Continued)

| end: | 78:4 | end: | 79:3 | end: | 82:4 |
|---|---|---|---|---|---|
| $H_0$ | statistic | $H_0$ | statistic | $H_0$ | statistic |
| $\chi^2_1$ | 1.7 | $\chi^2_1$ | 0.8 | $\chi^2_1$ | 1.0 |
| $HW_{12}$ | 12.7 | $HW_{12}$ | 13.9 | $HW_{12}$ | 32.7 |

| $\beta_c$ | | $\beta_c$ | | $\beta_c$ | |
|---|---|---|---|---|---|
| 1.0 | 0.0 | 1.0 | 0.0 | 1.0 | 0.0 |
| 0.0 | 1.0 | 0.0 | 1.0 | 0.0 | 1.0 |
| -1.0 | 0.0 | -1.0 | 0.0 | -1.0 | 0.0 |
| 0.14 | -1.0 | 0.13 | -1.0 | 0.13 | -1.0 |
| (0.01) | | (0.01) | | (0.01) | |

| $\beta_{01}$ | $\beta_{02}$ | $\beta_{01}$ | $\beta_{02}$ | $\beta_{01}$ | $\beta_{02}$ |
|---|---|---|---|---|---|
| -0.89 | 1.0 | -0.89 | 0.93 | -0.88 | 0.86 |

| $\alpha_c$ | | $\alpha_c$ | | $\alpha_c$ | |
|---|---|---|---|---|---|
| 0.03 | 0.002 | 0.02 | 0.002 | -0.003 | -0.001 |
| (2.6) | (1.7) | (2.2) | (1.3) | (-0.5) | (-1.3) |
| 0.97 | 0.11 | 1.03 | 0.11 | 1.42 | 0.22 |
| (2.0) | (1.7) | (2.12) | (1.3) | (4.6) | (3.9) |
| 0.04 | -0.00 | 0.04 | -0.0002 | 0.03 | -0.001 |
| (2.8) | (-0.01) | (2.8) | (-0.1) | (4.4) | (-0.9) |
| 0.81 | -0.04 | 0.62 | -0.06 | 0.99 | -0.01 |
| (1.0) | (-0.32) | (0.7) | (0.5) | (2.1) | (-0.11) |

| end: | 83:4 | end: | 84:4 | end: | 85:4 |
|---|---|---|---|---|---|
| $H_0$ | statistic | $H_0$ | statistic | $H_0$ | statistic |
| $\chi^2_1$ | 1.7 | $\chi^2_1$ | 1.5 | $\chi^2_1$ | 1.2 |
| $HW_{12}$ | 12.9 | $HW_{12}$ | 12.7 | $HW_{12}$ | 15.0 |

| $\beta_c$ | | $\beta_c$ | | $\beta_c$ | |
|---|---|---|---|---|---|
| 1.0 | 0.0 | 1.0 | 0.0 | 1.0 | 0.0 |
| 0.0 | 1.0 | 0.0 | 1.0 | 0.0 | 1.0 |
| -1.0 | 0.0 | -1.0 | 0.0 | -1.0 | 0.0 |
| 0.13 | -1.0 | 0.13 | -1.0 | 0.14 | -1.0 |
| (0.02) | | (0.02) | | (0.02) | |

| $\beta_{01}$ | $\beta_{02}$ | $\beta_{01}$ | $\beta_{02}$ | $\beta_{01}$ | $\beta_{02}$ |
|---|---|---|---|---|---|
| -0.86 | 0.94 | -0.85 | 1.02 | -0.84 | 1.01 |

| $\alpha_c$ | | $\alpha_c$ | | $\alpha_c$ | |
|---|---|---|---|---|---|
| -0.004 | -0.001 | -0.001 | -0.001 | -0.002 | -0.002 |
| (-0.08) | (-1.0) | (-0.3) | (-1.6) | (-0.6) | (-2.0) |
| 0.72 | 0.17 | 0.64 | 0.15 | 0.69 | 0.17 |
| (2.6) | (3.0) | (2.3) | (2.9) | (2.6) | (3.3) |
| 0.03 | -0.001 | 0.03 | -0.002 | 0.03 | -0.001 |
| (4.5) | (-1.1) | (4.8) | (-1.7) | (4.8) | (1.3) |
| 0.87 | 0.07 | 0.98 | 0.12 | 1.09 | 0.14 |
| (2.0) | (0.8) | (2.5) | (1.5) | (2.9) | (1.9) |

Table 7.7: Recursive Estimates of Error Correction Coefficients.(Spread Constraint-Omitting 79-81),(Continued)

| end: | 86:4 |
|---|---|
| $H_0$ | statistic |
| $\chi^2_1$ | 1.4 |
| $HW_{12}$ | 17.18 |

| $\beta_c$ | |
|---|---|
| 1.0 | 0.0 |
| 0.0 | 1.0 |
| -1.0 | 0.0 |
| 0.15 | -1.0 |
| (0.03) | |

| $\beta_{01}$ | $\beta_{02}$ |
|---|---|
| -0.78 | 0.97 |

| $\alpha_c$ | |
|---|---|
| -0.001 | -0.001 |
| (-0.32) | (-1.7) |
| 0.52 | 0.17 |
| (2.2) | (3.2) |
| 0.02 | -0.002 |
| (4.3) | (-1.9) |
| 0.82 | 0.11 |
| (2.6) | (1.6) |

| end: | 87:4 |
|---|---|
| $H_0$ | statistic |
| $\chi^2_1$ | 2.3 |
| $HW_{12}$ | 18.5 |

| $\beta_c$ | |
|---|---|
| 1.0 | 0.0 |
| 0.0 | 1.0 |
| -1.0 | 0.0 |
| 0.15 | -1.0 |
| (0.04) | |

| $\beta_{01}$ | $\beta_{02}$ |
|---|---|
| -0.79 | 1.15 |

| $\alpha_c$ | |
|---|---|
| -0.003 | -0.001 |
| (-0.9) | (-1.8) |
| 0.57 | 0.17 |
| (2.7) | (3.3) |
| 0.02 | -0.002 |
| (3.7) | (-2.2) |
| 0.6 | 0.12 |
| (2.1) | (1.8) |

| end: | 88:4 |
|---|---|
| $H_0$ | statistic |
| $\chi^2_1$ | 2.5 |
| $HW_{12}$ | 17.1 |

| $\beta_c$ | |
|---|---|
| 1.0 | 0.0 |
| 0.0 | 1.0 |
| -1.0 | 0.0 |
| 0.16 | -1.0 |
| (0.04) | |

| $\beta_{01}$ | $\beta_{02}$ |
|---|---|
| -0.76 | 1.12 |

| $\alpha_c$ | |
|---|---|
| -0.003 | -0.001 |
| (-0.8) | (-1.7) |
| 0.53 | 0.15 |
| (2.6) | (3.2) |
| 0.01 | -0.002 |
| (3.5) | (-1.9) |
| 0.6 | 0.07 |
| (2.2) | (1.1) |

| end: | 89:4 |
|---|---|
| $H_0$ | statistic |
| $\chi^2_1$ | 1.7 |
| $HW_{12}$ | 18.6 |

| $\beta_c$ | |
|---|---|
| 1.0 | 0.0 |
| 0.0 | 1.0 |
| -1.0 | 0.0 |
| 0.14 | -1.0 |
| (0.03) | |

| $\beta_{01}$ | $\beta_{02}$ |
|---|---|
| -0.82 | 1.05 |

| $\alpha_c$ | |
|---|---|
| -0.002 | -0.001 |
| (-0.6) | (-1.13) |
| 0.7 | 0.16 |
| (2.9) | (3.5) |
| 0.02 | -0.002 |
| (3.5) | (-1.8) |
| 0.71 | 0.07 |
| (2.3) | (1.0) |

| end: | 90:4 |
|---|---|
| $H_0$ | statistic |
| $\chi^2_1$ | 3.5 |
| $HW_{12}$ | 20.1 |

| $\beta_c$ | |
|---|---|
| 1.0 | 0.0 |
| 0.0 | 1.0 |
| -1.0 | 0.0 |
| 0.17 | -1.0 |
| (0.05) | |

| $\beta_{01}$ | $\beta_{02}$ |
|---|---|
| -0.69 | 1.12 |

| $\alpha_c$ | |
|---|---|
| -0.002 | -0.001 |
| (-0.6) | (-1.13) |
| 0.44 | -0.15 |
| (2.5) | (3.3) |
| 0.01 | -0.002 |
| (3.4) | (-2.3) |
| 0.5 | 0.05 |
| (2.1) | (0.8) |

| end: | 91:4 |
|---|---|
| $H_0$ | statistic |
| $\chi^2_1$ | 4.1 |
| $HW_{12}$ | 20.5 |

| $\beta_c$ | |
|---|---|
| 1.0 | 0.0 |
| 0.0 | 1.0 |
| -1.0 | 0.0 |
| 0.27 | -1.0 |
| (0.21) | |

| $\beta_{01}$ | $\beta_{02}$ |
|---|---|
| -0.16 | 1.21 |

| $\alpha_c$ | |
|---|---|
| -0.0003 | -0.001 |
| (-0.3) | (-1.4) |
| 0.17 | 0.14 |
| (2.0) | (3.1) |
| 0.005 | -0.002 |
| (3.2) | (-2.5) |
| 0.19 | 0.04 |
| (1.7) | (0.6) |

Note:Recursive Samples indicated by the end of the sample period. $\beta_c$ is the estimate of the normalized cointegration vectors. $\beta_{01}$ and $\beta_{02}$ are the constant terms in the cointegrating relations. $\alpha$ is the matrix of error correction coefficients at each recursive sample.

effect on real output.

We wish to identify one of the transitory shocks as a term structure or "time varying risk premium" shock. The identifying restrictions for such a shock are not well defined theoretically, and may not be unique. The approach that we implement here uses the Warne (1993) methodology, and defines the term structure shock as a transitory shock that affects the long-term rate, but has a zero impact effect on the short-term interest rate. Thus the rate spread is initially changed absent any initial shock to the short-term interest rate. An alternative definition of a term structure shock could be identified as one that affects both long and short rates, but with a greater effect on the long-term rate. We have not investigated this alternative here. Our term structure shock is normalized to a 100 basis point initial response of the long-term rate.

The relevant information for the structure of the identified shocks is presented in Table 7.8. The analysis is constructed using the estimated coefficients from the sample period ending in 90:4. The data in Part A of that table refer to the structure in which the permanent nominal shock is ordered first in the Wold causal chain structure. Data in Part B of the table reflect the assumption that the permanent real shock is ordered first. The sample correlation between the two computed permanent shocks is .30, which is considerably larger than in our previously constructed models, and is significantly different from zero by the test proposed by Baillie (1987) ($\chi^2_{(1)} = 11.0$). Therefore the overidentifying restriction of the KPSW "common trends" model is rejected for this VECM in contrast to the models discussed earlier. In comparison to the Fisher equation model (Table 7.3) the variance of the permanent nominal shock is considerably reduced by the substitution of the long-term interest rate for the inflation rate (.0102 in Table 7.8 compared with .0149 in Table 7.3), while the variance of the permanent real shock is approximately the same size in both models.

Since the variance of the permanent nominal shock is larger than that of the permanent real shock, the orthogonalizing Cholesky factor, $\pi$, will be closest to an identity matrix when the permanent nominal shock is ordered first in the Wold causal chain structure. This is evident from Table 7.8 where $\pi_{21}$ is only .03 when the permanent nominal shock is ordered first (Part A), but is 3.04 when the permanent real shock is ordered first (Part B). Consequently in this case the long-run effects of the two shocks differ substantially between the two orderings of the permanent shocks (compare $\beta^*_\perp$ in Parts A and B of Table 7.8).

The factor loading matrix for the permanent shocks in Part A of Table 7.8 ($\alpha'_\perp$) has some characteristics in common with the factor loadings of the permanent shocks in the Fisher equation model. In both cases the permanent nominal shock has a large negative weight for the residuals of the reduced form real balance equation, a large positive weight for the residuals of the reduced form real output equation, and a small negative weight for the residuals of the reduced form Treasury bill rate equation. The factor loadings for the permanent real shock in the two models both contain a positive weight of .3 to .4 for the residuals of the reduced form real output equation, and a negative weight on the order of -.01 to -.02 for the residuals of the reduced form Treasury bill rate equation, but weights that differ in sign and magnitude for the residuals of the

Table 7.8: Identification of Permanent and Transitory Shocks in Term Structure Model 56:2-90:4, Quarterly Semi–Log Specification, ln(M/P), RL, ln(Y/P), Rtb.

| | Nominal Shock First | Real Output Shock First |
|---|---|---|
| $\beta_{\perp}^{0} =$ | $\begin{bmatrix} -0.17 & 1.0 \\ 1.0 & 0.0 \\ 0.0 & 1.0 \\ 1.0 & 0.0 \end{bmatrix}$ | $\begin{bmatrix} -0.17 & 1.0 \\ 1.0 & 0.0 \\ 0.0 & 1.0 \\ 1.0 & 0.0 \end{bmatrix}$ |
| $\alpha_{\perp}^{0\prime} =$ | $\begin{bmatrix} -16.57 & -0.02 & 2.62 & -0.09 \\ 0.13 & 0.01 & 0.46 & -0.02 \end{bmatrix}$ | $\begin{bmatrix} -16.57 & -0.02 & 2.62 & -0.09 \\ 0.13 & 0.01 & 0.46 & -0.02 \end{bmatrix}$ |
| $\Sigma_{v} =$ | $\begin{bmatrix} 0.01 & \\ 3.1\text{x}10^{-4} & 1\text{x}10^{-4} \end{bmatrix}$ | $\begin{bmatrix} 1\text{x}10^{-4} & \\ 3.1\text{x}10^{-4} & 0.01 \end{bmatrix}$ |
| $\pi =$ | $\begin{bmatrix} 1.0 & 0.0 \\ 0.03 & 1.0 \end{bmatrix}$ | $\begin{bmatrix} 1.0 & \\ 3.1\text{x}10^{-4} & 0.01 \end{bmatrix}$ |
| $\beta_{\perp}^{*} =$ | $\begin{bmatrix} -0.14 & 1.0 \\ 1.0 & 0.0 \\ 0.03 & 1.0 \\ 1.0 & 0.0 \end{bmatrix}$ | $\begin{bmatrix} 0.48 & -0.17 \\ 3.0 & 1.0 \\ 1.0 & 0.0 \\ 3.0 & 1.0 \end{bmatrix}$ |
| $\alpha'_{\perp} =$ | $\begin{bmatrix} -16.57 & -0.02 & 2.62 & -0.09 \\ 0.63 & 0.02 & 0.39 & -0.02 \end{bmatrix}$ | $\begin{bmatrix} 0.13 & 0.01 & 0.46 & -0.02 \\ -17.0 & -0.07 & 1.2 & -0.02 \end{bmatrix}$ |
| Transitory Factor Loadings | $\begin{bmatrix} -7.12 & 0.55 & 20.54 & 0.01 \\ 0.63 & 0.42 & -20.19 & -0.15 \end{bmatrix}$ | $\begin{bmatrix} -7.12 & 0.55 & 20.54 & 0.01 \\ 0.63 & 0.42 & -20.19 & -0.15 \end{bmatrix}$ |

Note: The specification is based upon no shift in mean of equilibrium real balances except during New Operating Procedures.

real balance equation.

The factor loadings for the "term structure" shock (the second transitory shock in Table 7.8) place positive weight on the residuals of the reduced form real balance and long-term interest rate equations and negative weights on the residuals of the reduced form real output and Treasury bill rate equations.

The impulse response functions for the three identified shocks and the composite transitory shock are shown in Figures 7.21 through 7.38 with the permanent nominal shock ordered first. The response of real output to the permanent real output shock corresponds quite closely to the patterns that are observed in the previous models. Initially there is a small positive response in real output that increases for about two years, overshoots the equilibrium response and returns to equilibrium after about four years.

The Treasury bill rate response also conforms to the patterns observed in the previously discussed models.(Figure 7.24) The initial response is around 40 basis points for a one percent permanent real output shock. This goes to zero after about three years. There is basically no long-term rate response to a permanent real output shock. The initial response of the long-term rate is less than five basis points for a one percent permanent real output shock and after two quarters the maximum response is less than two basis points.(Figure 7.23) Consequently the response of the interest rate spread is essentially the mirror image of the Treasury bill rate response function. In contrast to the result shown in Figure 7.4, the initial response of velocity in this model to a permanent real output shock is negative. This effect dies out quickly and after six quarters velocity has returned to its initial value.

The observed impulse response function of real output to the permanent nominal shock in this model appears different from that in the Fisher equation model (Figure 7.4) but the results have a consistent interpretation. An examination of the magnitude of the responses at all horizons suggests that real output fundamentally is not affected at any horizon by the permanent nominal shock in either model. The initial response of the Treasury bill rate to the permanent nominal shock in this model is negative and remains so for almost three years.(Figure 7.30) The absolute value of the response for this rate during the first two years is much larger than in the Fisher equation model, around 200 basis points compared to about 75 basis points in the Figure 7.12. The response function for the long-term rate to the permanent nominal shock has the same general pattern as that of the Treasury bill rate, but has a much smaller amplitude in the first two years.(Figure 7.29) It then approaches the equilibrium response more quickly than does the Treasury bill rate. Consequently there is an initial strong positive response of the interest rate spread to this shock that goes to zero after about two years, becomes negative, and slowly returns to zero.(Figure 7.32) The initial velocity response to the permanent nominal shock is positive and increases monotonically to the equilibrium level.(Figure 7.28) The pattern here is almost identical to that in the Fisher equation model.(Figure 7.10)

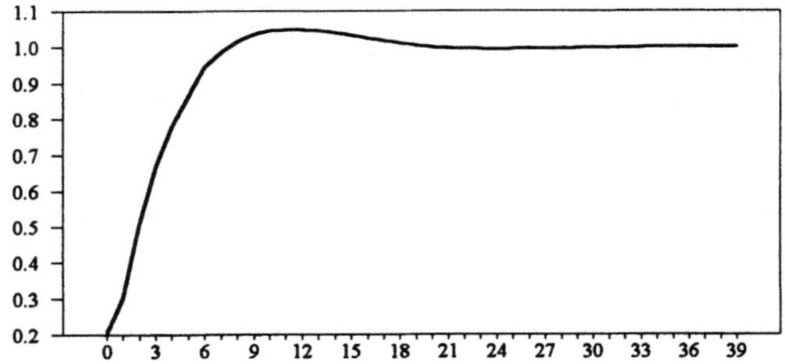


Figure 7.21: I.R.F. for GDP w.r.t. the Permanent Real Shock

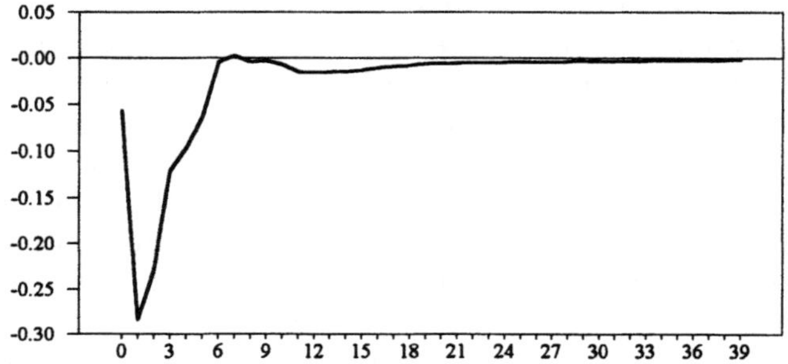


Figure 7.22: I.R.F. for Velocity w.r.t. the Permanent Real Shock

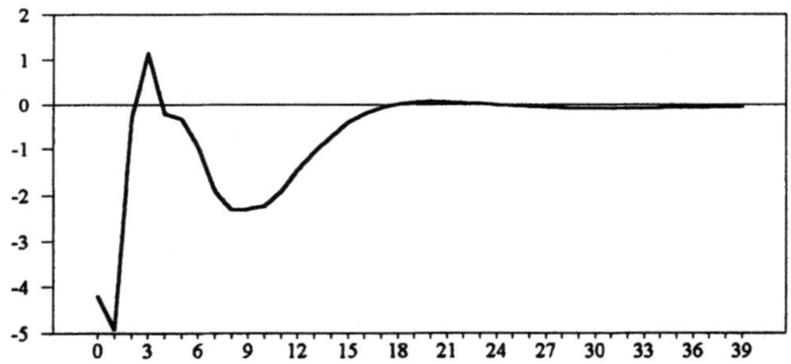


Figure 7.23: I.R.F. of RL w.r.t. the Permanent Real Shock

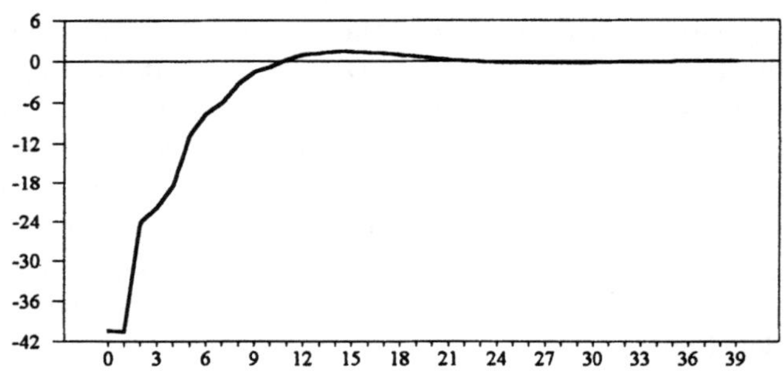


Figure 7.24: I.R.F. for Rtb w.r.t. the Permanent Real Shock

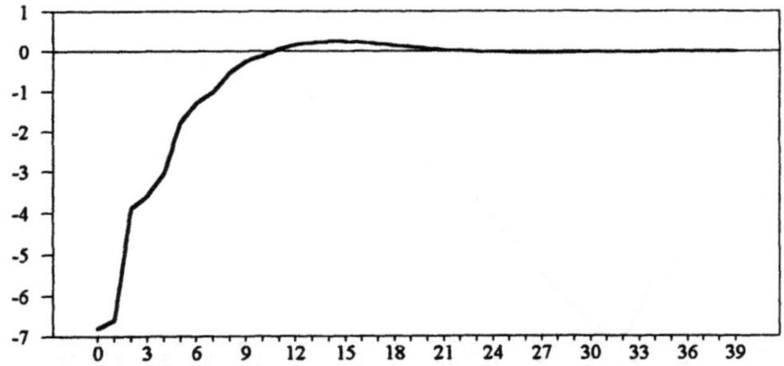


Figure 7.25: I.R.F. for CIV1 w.r.t. the Permanent Real Shock

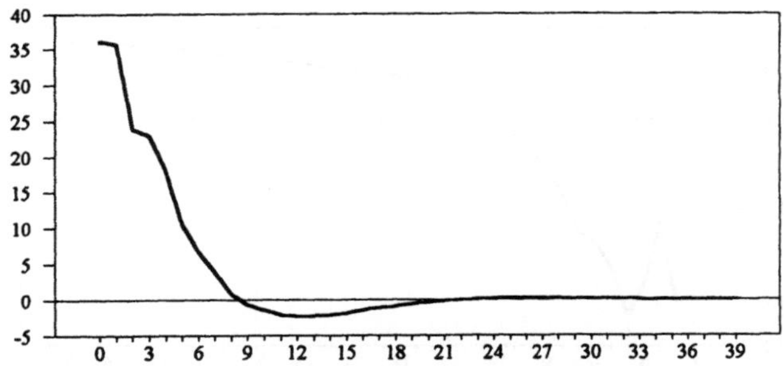


Figure 7.26: I.R.F. for the Rate Spread w.r.t. the Permanent Real Shock

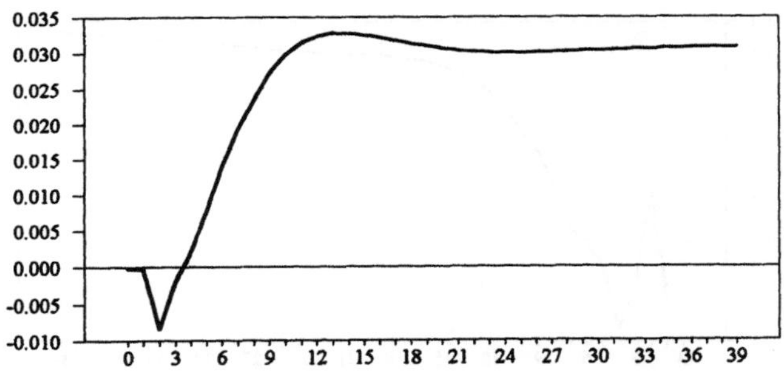


Figure 7.27: I.R.F. for GDP w.r.t. the Permanent Nominal Shock

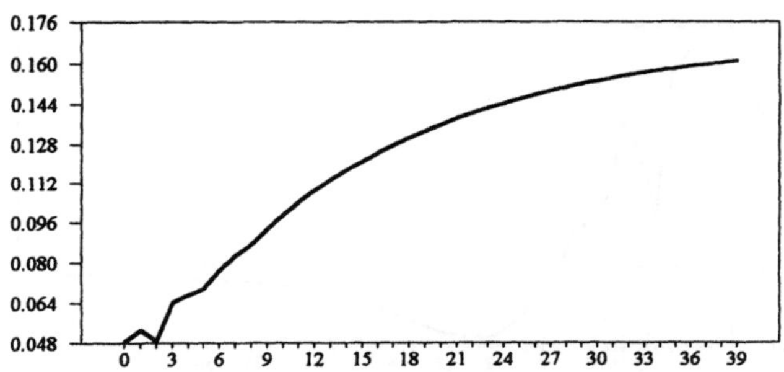


Figure 7.28: I.R.F. for Velocity w.r.t. the Permanent Nominal Shock

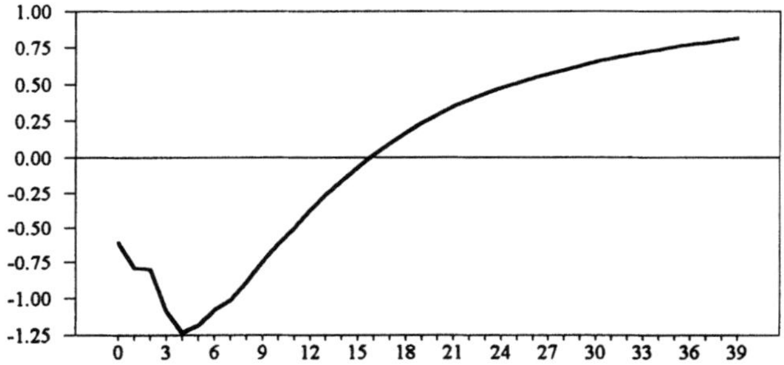


Figure 7.29: I.R.F. for RL w.r.t. the Permanent Nominal Shock

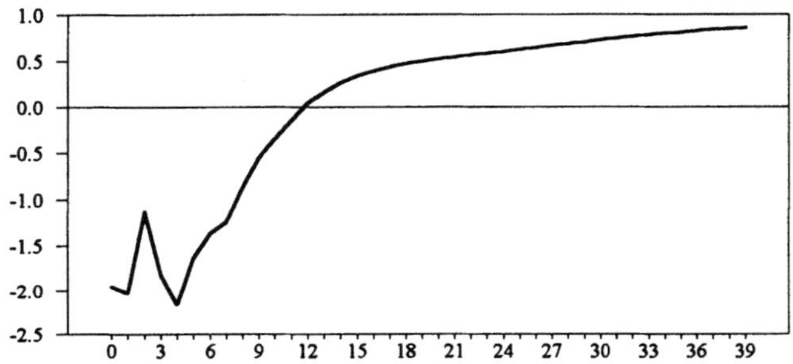


Figure 7.30: I.R.F. for Rtb w.r.t. the Permanent Nominal Shock

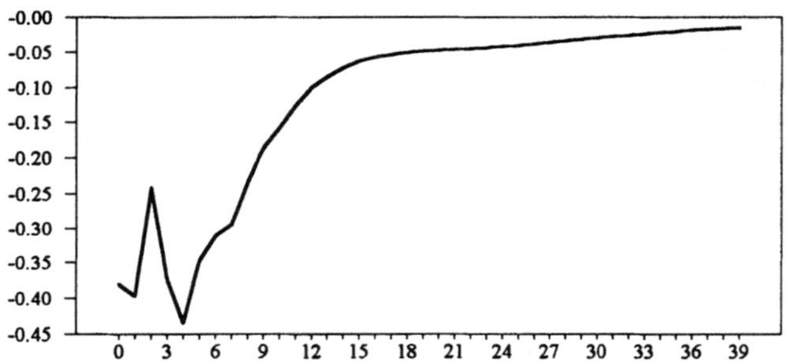


Figure 7.31: I.R.F. for CIV1 w.r.t. the Permanent Nominal Shock

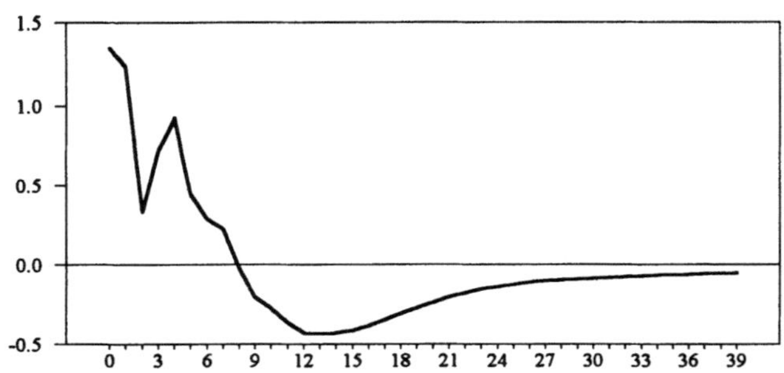


Figure 7.32: I.R.F. for the Rate Spread w.r.t. the Permanent Nominal Shock

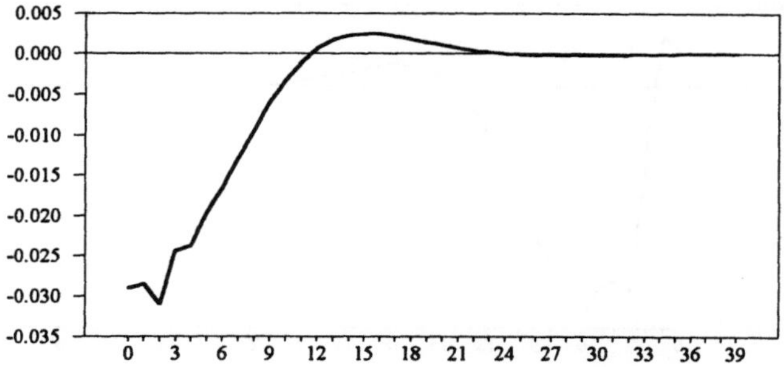


Figure 7.33: I.R.F. for GDP w.r.t. the Transitory Term Structure Shock

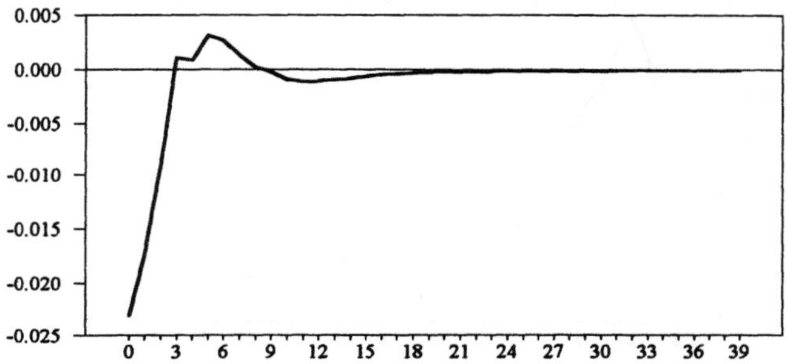


Figure 7.34: I.R.F. for Velocity w.r.t. the Transitory Term Structure Shock

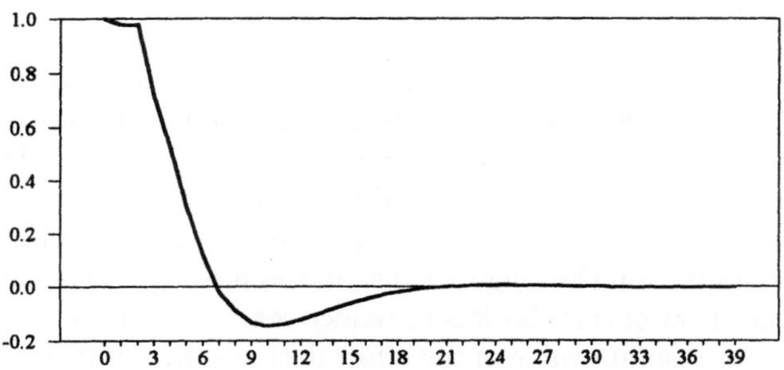


Figure 7.35: I.R.F. for RL w.r.t. the Transitory Term Structure Shock

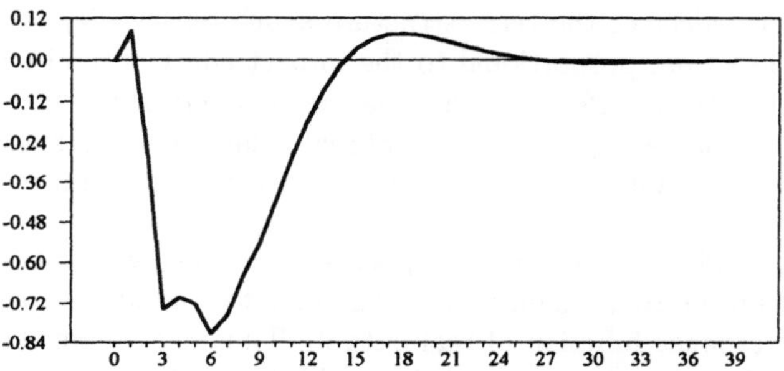


Figure 7.36: I.R.F. for Rtb w.r.t. the Transitory Term Structure Shock

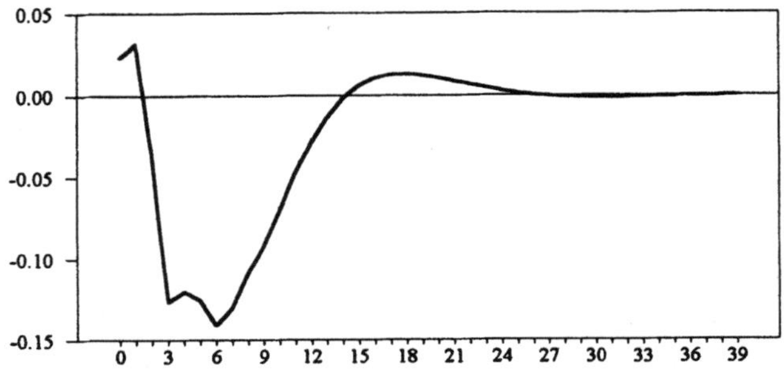


Figure 7.37: I.R.F. for CIV1 w.r.t. the Transitory Term Structure Shock

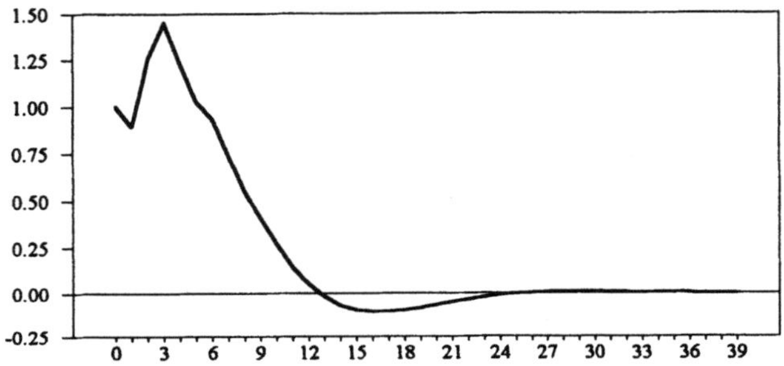


Figure 7.38: I.R.F. for the Rate Spread w.r.t. the Transitory Term Structure Shock

The impulse response function of the interest rate spread to the term structure shock starts at 100 basis points by construction and increases for about one year as the short rate decreases.(Figure 7.38) Subsequently the rate spread returns to zero as the long rate falls and the short rate increases.(Figures 7.35 and 7.36) After the initial period the shock operates on both ends of the yield curve, but the impact on the long rate disappears more quickly than that on the short rate. The effect of this shock is to reduce real output for about three years, during which the absolute value of the effect declines monotonically. After three years there is a small overshooting of the equilibrium before real output returns to the initial level.(Figure 7.33)

The impact effect of the term structure shock on velocity is also negative and slightly less than proportional to the impact effect on real output.(Figure 7.34) Thus the impact effect on real balances is a very small positive amount. This suggests that the impact elasticity of real balances with respect to the term structure spread, holding the short-term interest rate constant is very close to zero.

The initial effect on velocity disappears very quickly and the impulse response function for real balances after the first two or three quarters mirrors the impulse response function of real output. Thus it appears that during the transition of the interest rates to their equilibrium values any negative impact on velocity of the lower short-term rates is fully offset by a positive impact of

Table 7.9: Variance Decompositions:Term Structure Model

| Variable | Horizon | Permanent Nominal Shock | Permanent Real Shock | Composite Shock | Transitory Shock |
|---|---|---|---|---|---|
| ln(M/P) | | | | | |
| | 1 | 72.3 | 18.8 | 5.1 | 3.8 |
| | 4 | 28.5 | 31.2 | 30.4 | 10.0 |
| | 8 | 21.3 | 33.0 | 38.0 | 7.7 |
| | 16 | 25.3 | 41.5 | 29.5 | 3.7 |
| | 200 | 64.9 | 33.0 | 1.9 | 0.2 |
| ln(GDP) | | | | | |
| | 1 | 0.0 | 7.4 | 39.5 | 53.1 |
| | 4 | 0.3 | 28.5 | 31.9 | 39.3 |
| | 8 | 1.0 | 59.1 | 15.0 | 24.9 |
| | 16 | 5.1 | 77.4 | 6.5 | 11.0 |
| | 200 | 8.8 | 89.9 | 0.5 | 0.8 |
| *Rtb* | | | | | |
| | 1 | 14.7 | 54.7 | 30.8 | 0.0 |
| | 4 | 10.4 | 31.6 | 56.2 | 1.8 |
| | 8 | 13.6 | 24.7 | 55.9 | 5.7 |
| | 16 | 13.7 | 23.4 | 55.5 | 7.4 |
| | 200 | 54.5 | 12.2 | 29.5 | 3.8 |
| RL | | | | | |
| | 1 | 2.5 | 1.0 | 72.2 | 24.2 |
| | 4 | 4.0 | 0.5 | 78.2 | 17.3 |
| | 8 | 7.9 | 0.4 | 78.4 | 13.3 |
| | 16 | 8.6 | 0.5 | 79.2 | 11.7 |
| | 200 | 60.0 | 0.2 | 34.9 | 4.9 |
| CIV1 | | | | | |
| | 1 | 19.6 | 55.7 | 24.4 | 0.30 |
| | 4 | 16.5 | 34.2 | 47.1 | 2.1 |
| | 8 | 22.8 | 26.5 | 43.9 | 6.8 |
| | 16 | 24.8 | 24.9 | 41.9 | 8.5 |
| | 200 | 25.2 | 24.6 | 41.8 | 8.4 |
| Spread | | | | | |
| | 1 | 10.6 | 68.0 | 0.9 | 20.6 |
| | 4 | 7.0 | 57.1 | 2.3 | 33.6 |
| | 8 | 6.8 | 47.8 | 2.4 | 43.0 |
| | 16 | 7.4 | 44.7 | 5.5 | 42.4 |
| | 200 | 8.1 | 44.0 | 6.0 | 42.0 |

the increased interest rate spread.

### 7.2.4 Variance Decompositions

The variance decompositions for several variables that can be constructed from this VECM are shown in Table 7.9. The forecast variance decomposition of real output with respect to the permanent shocks is quite similar to the decomposition in the Fisher equation model. Very little of the forecast variance at any horizon is attributable to the permanent nominal shock. At horizons greater than two years, the majority of the forecast variance is attributable to the permanent real shock. The fraction of the forecast variance of real output attributable to the composite transitory shock in this model closely mirrors the pattern attributable to the "aggregate demand shock" in the Fisher equation model. Finally, the majority of the forecast variance of real output at horizons of less than two years is attributable to the "term structure" shock.

Very little, if any, of the forecast variance of the Treasury bill rate at any horizon is attributable to the "term structure" shock (the fraction at one quarter is zero by construction). At horizons of up to four years the composite transitory shock in this model is allocated a substantial portion of the Treasury bill rate forecast variance. Again the composite transitory shock in this model appears to mirror the role of the "aggregate demand" shock in the Fisher equation model. Here, however, permanent real shocks account for a larger portion of the forecast variance of the Treasury bill rate than is observed in the Fisher equation model.

At horizons of up to four years, both permanent shocks together account for less than 10 percent of the forecast variance of the long-term rate. This forecast variance is even more strongly dominated by the composite transitory shock at horizons of up to four years than is that of the Treasury bill rate. In contrast, however, the fraction of the forecast variance of the rate spread attributable to the composite transitory shock is virtually zero. Approximately 90 percent of the forecast variance of the rate spread at horizons of up to four years is attributable to either the permanent real shock or the transitory term structure shock.

Finally, the term structure shock accounts for less than 10 percent of the forecast variance of real balances at horizons of up to four years. This together with the impulse response functions, suggests that any short-run effects of interest rate spreads on the demand for real balances are likely to be very small.

## 7.3 Conclusions

In this chapter we have investigated two different VECMs, in each case it is possible to identify one distinct transitory shock in addition to two permanent shocks. The effects of the two permanent shocks are quite robust across the two models and in comparison to the results from the three variable model in Chapter 6. Transitory shocks identified as "aggregate demand" and "term structure" shock appear to account for a substantial fraction of the short run forecast variance in variables such as real output and nominal interest rates, and seem to be complimentary, in that the composite transitory shock in the Fisher equation model has similar effects to the "term structure" shock in the interest rate spread model, and the composite transitory shock in the interest rate spread model has similar effects to the "aggregate demand" shock in the Fisher equation model. In the following Chapter we investigate a larger model in which two types of "aggregate demand" shocks can be identified and examined simultaneously.

# Chapter 8

# COMBINING TERM STRUCTURE AND FISHER EFFECTS

In the previous chapter we investigated two four variable vector error correction models that include either the rate of inflation or a long-term nominal interest rate in addition to the three variables that appear in the equilibrium specification of the demand for real balances. In each of these cases we found evidence for a second cointegrating vector in the form of a Fisher equation (stationary real interest rate) or a term structure relationship (stationary interest rate spread). The purpose of the analysis in this chapter is to integrate these two separate results into a five variable framework. First we examine recursive estimates of the interest semielasticity of velocity conditional on stationarity of the real rate and the interest rate spread. In section 2 we impose a causal chain structure that follows the King, Plosser, Stock and Watson (1991) "common trends" model and orders the permanent shocks prior to the transitory shocks. We then discuss identifying restrictions that provide economic interpretations for two of the three transitory shocks. These identifying restrictions allow us to make tentative inferences on the values of the short-run elasticities of the demand for real balances. Finally, we examine the implied dynamic response patterns to the identified shocks and analyze the robustness of these patterns to the generalization of the specification of the VECM from the smaller models in Chapter 7.

## 8.1 Recursive Estimates of Five Variable VECMs

The results reported in Table 8.1 follow the approach that we have used in both Chapters 6 and 7. We have constructed recursive estimates of the vector error correction model using the Johansen FIML estimation procedure and assume that there are three cointegrating vectors among the five variables in the model: real M1, inflation, the 10 year U.S. government bond rate, real GDP and the Treasury bill rate in that order. With the exception of 1979, we have updated the sample with four quarterly observations, starting with a sample period that ends in 72:4. In 1979 the sample period is updated only through the third quarter to avoid the beginning of the New Operating Procedures period. In the sample periods that extend into the 1980s, the observations from 1979:4 through 1981:4 initially are omitted from the regressions. No dummy variables are included in any of these estimations.

We have identified the three cointegrating vectors as 1) a demand for real balances, identified by the restrictions that this vector includes only one interest rate, and excludes the rate of inflation; 2) a Fisher equation that is identified by the restrictions that it excludes real balances and includes only one rate of interest; and 3) a term structure equation identified by the exclusion of real balances and the rate of inflation. In fact the latter two vectors are overidentified, since we impose the restriction on all vectors that the coefficients on real balances and real GDP are equal but of opposite sign. This, together with the identifying exclusion restrictions imposes a zero restriction on real GDP in the second and third cointegrating vectors. In addition, we impose the overidentifying restrictions that the nominal interest rate coefficients are -1.0 in both the second and third vectors, since these restrictions are not rejected in the models that are estimated in Chapter 7. Under these restrictions, the estimates of the interest semielasticity of the demand for real balances are invariant to which interest rate is included in any of the three cointegrating vectors. Again, as discussed in Chapter 7, the individual equilibrium interest elasticities of the demand for real balances with respect to long- and short-term interest rates are underidentified when the interest rate spread is stationary as assumed here.

In addition to the estimated interest rate semielasticities, estimates of the matrix of vector error correction coefficients are reported in Table 8.1, together with the estimated "$t$"- ratios for the individual elements of these matrices. The HW statistic reported for each sample period is the Horvath/Watson (1993) test statistic for the significance on the margin of two cointegrating vectors with coefficients that are known *a priori* given one cointegrating vector with unknown (estimated) coefficients. This test statistic is constructed as the usual exclusion test for these cointegrating vectors (i.e. the test that all of the elements of the matrix of error correction coefficients corresponding to these vectors are jointly not significantly different from zero), but has a nonstandard distribution. The critical values of this test statistic as determined by Horvath and Watson are 28.62, 23.41, and 21.10 at the one percent, five percent and ten percent levels respectively.[1] With the exception of the shortest sample periods the Horvath/Watson test statistic significantly rejects the null of no cointegration at the one percent level. When the sample period is extended beyond the end

[1]These critical values are from Horvath and Watson (1993) Table 2.1, Case 3 for $r_{ou} = 4$, $r_{0k} = 0$, $r_{ak} = 2$, and $r_{au} = 0$.

Table 8.1: Recursive Estimates of Error Correction Coefficients

| end-t<br>$\beta_{15}(se)$<br>$HW$ | $\alpha$ | | | end-t<br>$\beta_{15}(se)$<br>$HW$ | $\alpha$ | | |
|---|---|---|---|---|---|---|---|
| | 0.05 | 0.0 | 0.0 | | 0.05 | 0.0 | 0.0 |
| | (4.5) | (0.7) | (0.8) | | (4.2) | (1.7) | (0.4) |
| 72:4 | 0.06 | 0.06 | −0.08 | 73:4 | 0.36 | 0.1 | −0.08 |
| | (0.1) | (0.9) | (−2.3) | | (0.5) | (1.3) | (−2.4) |
| .09(.01) | −4.67 | −0.34 | 0.25 | .11(.01) | −2.7 | −0.34 | 0.3 |
| | (−1.3) | (−0.8) | (1.3) | | (−0.7) | (−0.7) | (1.4) |
| 20.2 | 0.02 | −0.0 | 0.0 | 23.2 | 0.04 | −0.00 | 0.00 |
| | (1.2) | (−1.5) | (0.5) | | (2.1) | (−0.3) | (0.2) |
| | −0.77 | −0.03 | −0.11 | | 0.19 | −0.05 | −0.1 |
| | (−0.9) | (−0.3) | (−2.1) | | (0.1) | (−0.4) | (−2.0) |
| | 0.04 | 0.00 | 0.00 | | 0.03 | −0.00 | 0.00 |
| | (3.1) | (0.3) | (1.5) | | (2.5) | (−0.1) | (2.2) |
| 74:4 | 0.54 | 0.12 | −0.07 | 75:4 | 0.78 | 0.15 | −0.09 |
| | (0.8) | (1.7) | (−2.3) | | (1.5) | (2.1) | (−3.3) |
| .12(.01) | −0.78 | 0.29 | 0.07 | .12(.01) | −1.38 | 0.29 | 0.11 |
| | (−0.2) | (0.6) | (0.4) | | (−0.4) | (0.6) | (0.6) |
| 20.9 | 0.05 | −0.00 | 0.00 | 31.2 | 0.05 | −0.00 | 0.00 |
| | (2.7) | (−0.3) | (0.6) | | (3.2) | (−0.2) | (0.0) |
| | 0.55 | −0.02 | −0.06 | | 0.46 | −0.05 | −0.11 |
| | (0.5) | (−0.2) | (−1.9) | | (0.5) | (−0.4) | (−2.2) |
| | 0.03 | 0.00 | 0.00 | | 0.03 | 0.00 | 0.00 |
| | (2.4) | (0.3) | (1.9) | | (2.4) | (0.6) | (1.8) |
| 76:4 | 0.76 | 0.18 | −0.10 | 77:4 | 0.83 | 0.20 | −0.10 |
| | (1.6) | (2.7) | −3.7) | | (1.9) | (3.1) | (−3.8) |
| .13(.01) | −1.49 | −0.03 | 0.15 | .14(.01) | −1.22 | −0.12 | 0.14 |
| | (−0.5) | (−0.1) | (0.9) | | (−0.4) | (−0.3) | (0.8) |
| 34.3 | 0.05 | 0.00 | −0.00 | 35.7 | 0.04 | 0.00 | −0.00 |
| | (3.4) | (0.4) | (−0.5) | | (2.9) | (0.3) | (−0.2) |
| | 0.58 | 0.01 | −0.12 | | 0.73 | 0.05 | −0.13 |
| | (0.7) | (0.1) | (−2.5) | | (1.0) | (0.4) | (−2.6) |
| | 0.03 | 0.00 | 0.00 | | 0.03 | 0.00 | 0.00 |
| | (2.6) | (0.7) | (2.9) | | (2.3) | (0.5) | (1.9) |
| 78:4 | 0.85 | 0.20 | −0.10 | 79:3 | 0.84 | 0.20 | −0.10 |
| | (1,9) | (3.0) | (−3.8) | | (1.8) | (3.0) | (−3.7) |
| .13(.01) | −0.57 | −0.12 | 0.13 | .13(.01) | −0.10 | −0.07 | 0.13 |
| | (−0.2) | (−0.3) | (0.7) | | (−0.0) | (−0.2) | (0.8) |
| 35.8 | −.043 | 0.00 | −0.00 | 36.5 | 0.04 | 0.00 | −0.00 |
| | (2.8) | (0.2) | (−0.1) | | (2.7) | (0.0) | (−0.0) |
| | 0.57 | 0.06 | −0.12 | | 0.28 | 0.03 | −0.13. |
| | (0.7) | (0.5) | (−2.6) | | (0.3) | (0.2) | (−2.6) |

Table 8.1: Recursive Estimates of Error Correction Coefficients(Continued)

| end-t<br>$\beta_{15}(se)$<br>$HW$ | $\alpha$ | | | end-t<br>$\beta_{15}(se)$<br>$HW$ | $\alpha$ | | |
|---|---|---|---|---|---|---|---|
| | 0.01 | −0.00 | 0.00 | | 0.02 | −0.00 | 0.00 |
| | (1.7) | (−1.5) | (3.1) | | (2.1) | (−1.0) | (3.1) |
| 82:4 | 0.61 | 0.23 | −0.10 | 83:4 | −0.20 | 0.16 | −0.12 |
| | (1.4) | (4.0) | (−3.0) | | (−0.4) | (2.8) | (−3.2) |
| .12(.01) | 3.74 | 0.40 | 0.06 | .12(.01) | 4.65 | 0.49 | 0.06 |
| | (1.7) | (1.4) | (0.3) | | (2.3) | (1.9) | (0.4) |
| 57.0 | 0.04 | −0.00 | 0.00 | 44.2 | 0.03 | −0.00 | −0.00 |
| | (3.3) | (−0.3) | (0.3) | | (2.9) | (−0.3) | (−0.2) |
| | −0.24 | −0.12 | −0.14 | | −0.67 | 0.05 | −0.18 |
| | (−0.3) | (−0.2) | (−2.5) | | (−0.9) | (0.6) | (−3.2) |
| | 0.02 | −0.00 | 0.00 | | 0.02 | −0.00 | 0.00 |
| | (2.3) | (−0.7) | (3.2) | | (2.3) | (−0.8) | (3.5) |
| 84:4 | −0.10 | 0.12 | −0.09 | 85:4 | 0.01 | 0.14 | −0.08 |
| | (−0.2) | (2.2) | (−2.4) | | (0.0) | (2.5) | (−2.3) |
| .11(.01) | 4.42 | 0.49 | 0.05 | .11(.01) | 4.66 | 0.48 | 0.07 |
| | (2.2) | (2.3) | (0.4) | | (2.3) | (2.3) | (0.5) |
| 46.1 | 0.03 | −0.00 | 0.00 | 54.9 | 0.03 | −0.00 | −0.00 |
| | (2.9) | (−0.7) | (0.0) | | (2.8) | (−0.4) | (−0.0) |
| | −0.70 | 0.05 | −0.18 | | −0.56 | 0.06 | −0.18 |
| | (−1.0) | (0.6) | (−3.5) | | (−0.8) | (0.9) | (−3.6) |
| | 0.02 | −0.00 | 0.00 | | 0.02 | −0.00 | 0.00 |
| | (2.6) | (−3.3) | (3.3) | | (2.4) | (−0.4) | (3.5) |
| 86:4 | −0.10 | 0.14 | −0.08 | 87:4 | 0.06 | 0.15 | −0.08 |
| | (−0.2) | (2.4) | (−2.2) | | (0.1) | (2.5) | (−2.2) |
| .11.01) | 4.34 | 0.47 | 0.08 | .11(.01) | 3.92 | 0.42 | 0.12 |
| | (2.1) | (2.2) | (0.6) | | (2.0) | (2.0) | (0.9) |
| 50.9 | 0.03 | −0.00 | 0.00 | 57.5 | 0.02 | −0.00 | 0.00 |
| | (2.5) | (−0.7) | (0.2) | | (2.2) | (−0.9) | (0.4) |
| | −0.69 | 0.04 | −0.17 | | −1.03 | 0.02 | −0.17 |
| | (−0.9) | (0.6) | (−3.4) | | (−1.5) | (0.3) | (−3.5) |
| | 0.01 | −0.00 | 0.00 | | +0.00 | −0.00 | +0.00 |
| | (1.9) | (−0.1) | (2.9) | | (0.7) | (−0.6) | (1.6) |
| 88:4 | 0.31 | 0.14 | −0.06 | 89:4 | 0.26 | 0.13 | −0.06 |
| | (0.6) | (2.3) | (−1.7) | | (0.7) | (2.5) | (−2.0) |
| .11(.01) | 4.05 | 0.43 | 0.13 | .13(.02) | 3.04 | 0.31 | 0.11 |
| | (2.2) | (2.1) | (1.1) | | (2.4) | (1.8) | (1.1) |
| 42.6 | 0.02 | 0.00 | −0.00 | 29.9 | 0.02 | −0.00 | 0.00 |
| | (1.7) | (−0.8) | (−0.2) | | (2.7) | (−1.1) | (0.4) |
| | −0.25 | −0.01 | −0.11 | | 0.12 | −0.00 | −0.07 |
| | (−0.4) | (−0.1) | (−2.4) | | (0.2) | (−0.0) | (−1.9) |
| | +0.00 | −0.00 | +0.00 | | 0.01 | −0.00 | 0.00 |
| | (0.4) | (−0.9) | (1.2) | | (1.1) | (−0.7) | (1.6) |
| 90:4 | 0.32 | 0.14 | −0.04 | 91:4 | 0.31 | 0.14 | −0.05 |
| | (1.0) | (2.8) | (−1.7) | | (0.9) | (2.9) | (−1.9) |
| .14(.02) | 2.76 | 0.29 | 0.10 | .12(.02) | 2.30 | 0.33 | 0.06 |
| | (2.5) | (1.7) | (1.2) | | (2.0) | (1.9) | (0.7) |
| 29.9 | 0.01 | −0.00 | −0.00 | 35.0 | 0.01 | −0.00 | −0.00 |
| | (2.1) | (−1.6) | (−0.5) | | (0.9) | (−1.6) | (−1.5) |
| | 0.11 | 0.00 | −0.07 | | −0.00 | +0.00 | −0.07 |
| | (0.3) | (0.0) | (−2.0) | | (−0.0) | (0.0) | (−2.3) |

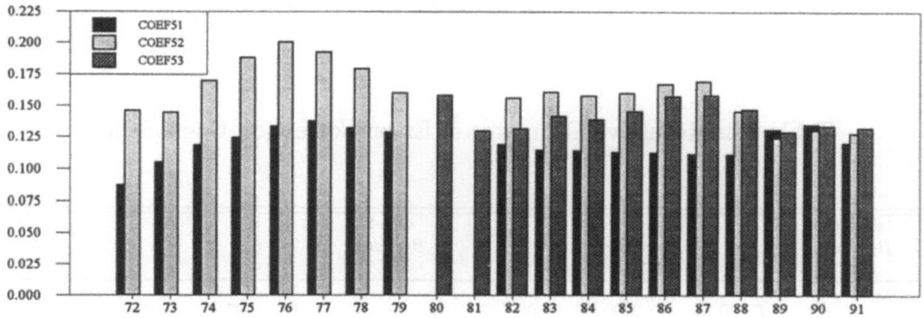


Figure 8.1: Estimated Interest Rate Semi-Elasticities(Recursive Samples)

of 1974 the estimated interest rate semielasticity becomes quite stable around .12 as indicated by the series COEF51 in Figure 8.1.

A second question is how robust are the results in Table 8.1 to the inclusion of various dummy variables. Recall from the results in Chapter 6 and 7 that there was no evidence of changes in the constant term of the either the cointegrating vector for real balances or the interest rate spread outside of the period of the New Operating Procedures, but that there was substantial evidence for shifts in the *ex post* short term real rate of interest in both 1967 and again after 1981. To investigate this question we have reestimated the vector error correction model adding both the D67 and D82 dummy variables as constructed in Chapter 7. The results of the recursive estimation of this model are reported in Table 8.2. With the addition of the two dummy variables to the specification, the Horwath/Watson test statistic for the addition of the two cointegrating vectors with known coefficients is always significant at the one percent level. The inclusion of the two dummy variables has a substantial impact on the estimated equilibrium interest semielasticities of velocity.

The estimated coefficients from this specification are plotted in Figure 8.1 as the series COEF52. For the sample periods that end in the 1970s and the early 1980s the estimated interest semielasticity of the demand for real balances is much larger when the two dummy variables are included in the vector error correction model and the deterministic trends in the nonstationary processes as well as the constant in the real interest rate cointegrating vector are allowed to shift among the various subsamples. However, in the longest sample periods that are estimated (the samples ending in 89:4 - 91:4) the differences in the estimated interest semielasticities of money demand that result from the inclusion of the dummy variables in the VECM are negligible. Finally, we have included the 79:4 - 81:4 subperiod of the New Operating Procedures in the samples extending beyond 79:3, introduced the D79 dummy variable that we included in the estimations in Chapters 6 and 7 and reestimated the VECM. The results of these estimations are presented in Table 8.3. The Horvath/Watson test statis-

Table 8.2: Recursive Estimates of Error Correction Coefficients

| end-t<br>$\beta_{15}(se)$<br>$HW$ | $\alpha$ | | | end-t<br>$\beta_{15}(se)$<br>$HW$ | $\alpha$ | | |
|---|---|---|---|---|---|---|---|
| | 0.05 | 0.00 | 0.00 | | 0.05 | 0.00 | 0.00 |
| | (4.2) | (2.2) | (2.3) | | (4.4) | (2.5) | (2.1) |
| 72:4 | 0.60 | 0.14 | −0.10 | 73:4 | 0.62 | 0.14 | −0.11 |
| | (1.1) | (1.6) | (−2.7) | | (1.1) | (1.7) | (−2.9) |
| .15(.03) | −0.07 | −0.15 | 0.16 | .15(.02) | −0.95 | −0.28 | 0.28 |
| | (−0.0) | (−0.3) | (0.7) | | (−0.3) | (−0.5) | (1.2) |
| 35.4 | 0.03 | −0.00 | −0.00 | 40.8 | 0.03 | −0.00 | −0.00 |
| | (1.6) | (−0.2) | (−0.1) | | (1.7) | (−0.1) | (−0.1) |
| | 0.69 | 0.09 | −0.17 | | 0.51 | −0.01 | −0.16 |
| | (0.8) | (0.7) | (−3.0) | | (0.5) | (−0.1) | (−2.5) |
| | 0.05 | 0.00 | 0.00 | | 0.04 | 0.00 | 0.00 |
| | (4.1) | (1.8) | (3.1) | | (3.9) | (1.7) | (3.5) |
| 74:4 | 0.65 | 0.18 | −0.09 | 75:4 | 0.75 | 0.21 | −0.10 |
| | (1.2) | (2.1) | (−2.4) | | (1.5) | (2.3) | (−2.9) |
| .17(.02) | −0.24 | 0.27 | 0.14 | .19(.02) | −0.51 | 0.28 | 0.17 |
| | (−0.1) | (0.5) | (0.6) | | (−0.2) | (0.5) | (0.7) |
| 43.1 | 0.02 | −0.00 | −0.00 | 58.8 | 0.02 | −0.00 | −0.00 |
| | (1.3) | (−0.3) | (−0.1) | | (1.1) | (−0.4) | (−1.0) |
| | 0.64 | 0.03 | −0.13 | | 0.54 | 0.01 | −0.13 |
| | (0.7) | (0.2) | (−2.1) | | (0.6) | (0.1) | (2.2) |
| | 0.04 | 0.00 | 0.00 | | 0.04 | 0.00 | 0.00 |
| | (3.8) | (2.2) | (3.2) | | (3.9) | (2.4) | (3.1) |
| 76:4 | 0.69 | 0.22 | −0.10 | 77:4 | 0.79 | 0.23 | −0.10 |
| | (1.5) | (2.6) | (−3.1) | | (1.7) | (2.7) | (−3.1) |
| .20(.02) | −0.37 | 0.04 | 0.25 | .19(.02) | −0.05 | 0.01 | 0.26 |
| | (−0.1) | (0.1) | (1.2) | | (−0.0) | (0.0) | (1.2) |
| 64.8 | 0.01 | −0.00 | −0.00 | 66.2 | 0.01 | −0.00 | −0.00 |
| | (0.8) | (−0.6) | (−1.2) | | (0.7) | (−0.7) | (−1.1) |
| | 0.54 | 0.04 | −0.14 | | 0.63 | 0.07 | −0.15 |
| | (0.7) | (0.3) | (−2.4) | | (0.8) | (0.5) | (−2.5) |
| | 0.04 | 0.00 | 0.00 | | 0.03 | 0.00 | 0.00 |
| | (3.9) | (2.3) | (3.0) | | (3.0) | (1.4) | (2.7) |
| 78:4 | 0.83 | 0.23 | −0.11 | 79:3 | 0.82 | 0.21 | −0.11 |
| | (1.7) | (2.7) | (−3.2) | | (1.7) | (2.8) | (−3.3) |
| .18(.02) | −0.10 | −0.06 | 0.26 | .16(.01) | 0.87 | 0.06 | 0.27 |
| | (−0.3) | (−0.1) | (1.2) | | (0.3) | (0.1) | (1.3) |
| 65.7 | 0.01 | −0.00 | −0.00 | 60.8 | 0.02 | −0.00 | −0.00 |
| | (0.8) | (−0.8) | (−1.1) | | (1.1) | (−0.7) | (−1.1) |
| | 0.44 | 0.06 | −0.15 | | −0.15 | −0.02 | −0.16 |
| | (0.5) | (0.4) | (−2.5) | | (−0.2) | (−0.1) | (−2.6) |

Table 8.2: Recursive Estimates of Error Correction Coefficients(Continued)

| end-t<br>$\beta_{15}(se)$<br>*HW* | $\alpha$ | | | end-t<br>$\beta_{15}(se)$<br>*HW* | $\alpha$ | | |
|---|---|---|---|---|---|---|---|
| | 0.04 | 0.00 | 0.00 | | 0.03 | 0.00 | 0.00 |
| | (3.1) | (1.3) | (2.8) | | (2.6) | (0.8) | (3.0) |
| | 0.97 | 0.31 | −0.13 | | 1.03 | 0.36 | −0.15 |
| 82:4 | (1.5) | (3.1) | (−3.0) | 83:4 | (1.6) | (3.6) | (−3.6) |
| | 0.79 | 0.01 | 0.26 | | 1.17 | 0.07 | 0.25 |
| .16(.01) | (0.3) | (0.0) | (1.3) | .16(.01) | (0.4) | (0.2) | (1.3) |
| | 0.02 | −0.00 | −0.00 | | 0.01 | −0.00 | −0.00 |
| 59.5 | (1.3) | (−0.6) | (−1.0) | 72.9 | (0.9) | (−0.7) | (−1.6) |
| | +0.13 | 0.05 | −0.20 | | −0.63 | 0.06 | −0.25 |
| | (0.1) | (0.3) | (−3.0) | | (−0.6) | (0.4) | (−3.6) |
| | 0.02 | 0.00 | 0.00 | | 0.02 | 0.00 | 0.00 |
| | (2.3) | (0.7) | (2.7) | | (2.4) | (0.7) | (2.8) |
| | 1.65 | 0.45 | −0.15 | | 1.41 | 0.42 | −0.14 |
| 84:4 | (2.6) | (4.3) | (−3.4) | 85:4 | (2.3) | (4.0) | (−3.2) |
| | 1.94 | 0.17 | 0.26 | | 2.66 | 0.25 | 0.28 |
| .16(.01) | (0.8) | (0.4) | (1.5) | .16(.01) | (1.1) | (0.6) | (1.6) |
| | 0.02 | −0.00 | −0.00 | | 0.01 | −0.00 | −0.00 |
| 78.3 | (1.5) | (−0.5) | (−1.6) | 80.7 | (1.0) | (−0.9) | (−1.2) |
| | −0.53 | 0.08 | −0.24 | | −0.38 | 0.11 | −0.24 |
| | (−0.6) | (0.5) | (−3.8) | | (−0.4) | (0.7) | (−3.8) |
| | 0.03 | 0.00 | 0.00 | | 0.02 | 0.00 | 0.00 |
| | (3.6) | (2.0) | (2.6) | | (2.8) | (1.0) | (2.9) |
| | 0.27 | 0.21 | −0.10 | | 0.36 | 0.23 | −0.10 |
| 86:4 | (0.5) | (2.2) | (−2.2) | 87:4 | (0.8) | (2.6) | (−2.3) |
| | 1.24 | −0.00 | 0.33 | | 1.70 | 0.02 | 0.40 |
| .17(.02) | (0.6) | (−0.0) | (2.0) | .17(.02) | (1.0) | (0.1) | (2.5) |
| | −0.01 | −0.01 | −0.00 | | −0.00 | −0.01 | −0.00 |
| 82.0 | (−0.6) | (−3.0) | (−0.7) | 91.8 | (−0.5) | (−3.4) | (−0.0) |
| | −1.36 | −0.10 | −0.21 | | −1.54 | −0.14 | −0.18 |
| | (−1.9) | (−0.8) | (−3.4) | | (−2.5) | (−1.3) | (−3.1) |
| | 0.01 | 0.00 | 0.00 | | +0.01 | −0.00 | +0.00 |
| | (1.7) | (0.1) | (2.4) | | (0.8) | (−0.9) | (2.1) |
| | 0.39 | 0.23 | −0.10 | | 0.29 | 0.20 | −0.11 |
| 88:4 | (0.9) | (2.9) | (−2.3) | 89:4 | (0.7) | (3.0) | (−2.7) |
| | 3.68 | 0.20 | 0.45 | | 4.23 | 0.20 | 0.43 |
| .15(.03) | (2.5) | (0.7) | (2.9) | .13(.03) | (3.0) | (0.8) | (3.0) |
| | 0.00 | −0.01 | 0.00 | | 0.02 | −0.00 | 0.00 |
| 68.9 | (0.3) | (−3.3) | (0.4) | 53.5 | (2.0) | (−2.4) | (1.1) |
| | −0.19 | 0.02 | −0.13 | | 0.16 | 0.08 | −0.12 |
| | (−0.3) | (0.2) | (−2.3) | | (0.3) | (0.8) | (−2.2) |
| | 0.00 | −0.00 | 0.00 | | 0.01 | −0.00 | 0.00 |
| | (0.6) | (−1.4) | (2.1) | | (1.4) | (−1.2) | (1.9) |
| | 0.27 | 0.21 | −0.11 | | 0.10 | 0.20 | −0.11 |
| 90:4 | (0.8) | (3.5) | (−2.7) | 91:4 | (0.3) | (3.4) | (−2.6) |
| | 4.12 | 0.22 | 0.44 | | 3.68 | 0.19 | 0.45 |
| .13(.03) | (3.4) | (1.1) | (3.1) | .13(.03) | (3.2) | (0.9) | (3.2) |
| | 0.01 | −0.00 | 0.00 | | 0.01 | −0.00 | 0.00 |
| 64.4 | (1.7) | (−3.0) | (0.9) | 66.6 | (1.3) | (−3.3) | (1.0) |
| | +0.05 | 0.06 | −0.13 | | −0.16 | 0.05 | −0.13 |
| | (0.1) | (0.8) | (−2.3) | | (−0.4) | (0.6) | (−2.3) |

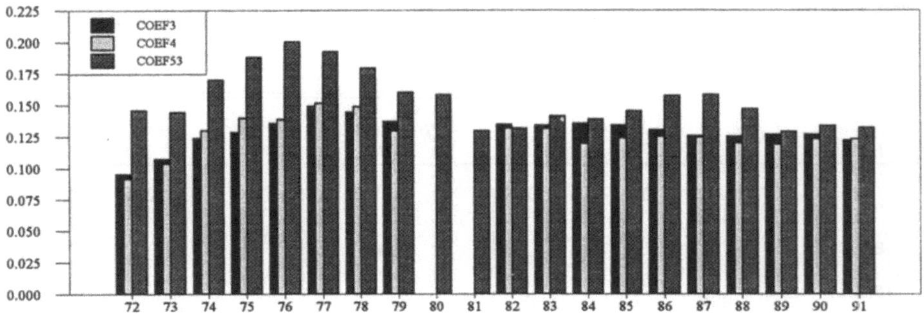


Figure 8.2: Comparing Estimated Interest Rate Semi-Elasticities(Recursive Samples)

tic for the inclusion of two cointegrating vectors with known coefficients given a single cointegrating vector with estimated coefficients is significant at the one percent level in all of the sample periods. It can be seen in Figure 8.1 that the inclusion of the subsample of the New Operating Procedures period has little effect on the estimated semielasticity of the demand for real balances. For the sample periods that end in the early 1980s the estimate of this parameter is intermediate between that obtained from the model excluding all dummy variables and that obtained from the model with the dummy variables but excluding the observations from 79:4 - 81:4. For the samples ending in 89:4 - 91:4 the estimates for this parameter from the three specifications of the model are virtually identical.

In Figure 8.2, the estimates of the interest rate semielasticities of money demand are compared for models of different dimensions. In this figure, COEF3 are the estimates from the three variable model in Chapter 6; COEF4 are the estimates from the four variable Fisher equation model in Chapter 7; and COEF53 are the estimates from Table 8.3. It is apparent from this figure that in the longer sample periods the estimates of this parameter are extremely robust to changes in the dimension of the VECM, consistent with the predictions from the economic model in Chapter 5.

The estimates of the error correction coefficients in Table 8.3 do not provide any consistent evidence that any of the five variables that explicitly appear in the VECM are weakly exogenous. The first column of the matrix of error correction coefficients in Tables 8.1 -8.3 corresponds the real balance cointegrating vector, the second column to the interest rate spread vector, and the third column corresponds to the real interest rate cointegrating vector. The rows of the matrix of error correction coefficients in these tables correspond from first to last to: real balances, the long-term nominal rate, the inflation rate, real output and the Treasury bill rate. The three error correction coefficients for real balances consistently have small absolute values in Table 8.3, and the coefficient for the real rate vector is always significant. In the shorter sample periods, the coefficient for the real balance vector is also significant. The error correction coefficient for the interest rate spread is never significantly different from zero in the real balance equation.

The error correction coefficient for the interest rate spread vector and the real rate vector are always significantly different from zero in the long-term interest rate equation. The former is always positive and the latter is always negative. With the exception of the sample period ending in 80:4, the error correction coefficient for the real balance vector is not significantly different from zero in the long-term interest rate equation.

The error correction coefficient for the interest rate spread vector is never significant in the inflation equation, though the inflation rate responds significantly to both the real balance cointegrating vector and the real rate cointegrating vector in the sample periods extending into the late 1980s. The pattern of the error correction coefficients in the real output equation is exactly the opposite of that in the inflation equation. In the samples that extend into the late 1980s, the error correction coefficient for the interest rate spread vector is significantly different from zero in this equation, but neither the error correction coefficient for the real balance vector nor that for the real rate vector are significant in this equation. In the samples that end in the early 1980s all of the individual error correction coefficients in the inflation and real output equations are at best marginally significant.

Finally, neither the error correction coefficient on the real balance vector nor that on the interest rate spread vector are significant in the Treasury bill rate equation. In contrast, the error correction coefficient on the real rate vector is always strongly significant in the bill rate equation.

At first glance, at least in short samples in Table 8.3, the pattern of error correction coefficients suggests that the long-term interest rate does not affect the long-term behavior of the other four variables in the system. This follows since the error correction coefficient of the interest rate spread does not enter significantly in the matrix of error correction coefficients for the remaining four variables of the system. Further examination of the error correction coefficients suggests that the long-run behavior of the other four variables in the system does affect the long-run behavior of the long-term rate since the error correction coefficient on the real rate vector enters the long-term rate equation significantly. This suggests a block recursive long-run structure of the economy with the long-term rate the single variable in the second block. But, this interpretation does not withstand closer examination. Recall that as long as the interest rate coefficients in the real rate and the term structure vectors are restricted to 1.0 (overidentified), the long-term and short-term interest rates can be used interchangeably in the VECM and the estimated coefficients will not be affected, except for a change in sign on the interest rate spread vector. Thus a more appropriate interpretation of the equilibrium structure implied by the estimated error correction coefficients is that only one interest rate is relevant but the model fails to distinguish between the two rates.

Table 8.3: Recursive Estimates of Error Correction Coefficients

| end-t<br>$\beta_{15}(se)$<br>*HW* | $\alpha$ | | | end-t<br>$\beta_{15}(se)$<br>*HW* | $\alpha$ | | |
|---|---|---|---|---|---|---|---|
| | 0.04 | 0.00 | 0.00 | | 0.02 | 0.00 | 0.00 |
| | (3.5) | (1.9) | (2.8) | | (2.2) | (0.3) | (2.5) |
| 80:4 | 1.39 | 0.32 | −0.12 | 81:4 | 0.38 | 0.21 | −0.17 |
| | (2.3) | (3.6) | (−3.0) | | (0.7) | (2.9) | (−4.2) |
| .16(.02) | 0.37 | −0.14 | 0.31 | .13(.02) | 4.02 | 0.26 | 0.33 |
| | (0.1) | (−0.3) | (1.6) | | (1.7) | (0.8) | (1.8) |
| 68.5 | 0.03 | −0.00 | −0.00 | 68.0 | 0.02 | −0.00 | −0.00 |
| | (1.6) | (−0.4) | (−1.1) | | (1.5) | (−1.4) | (−1.0) |
| | 0.96 | 0.19 | −0.21 | | 1.16 | 0.29 | −0.31 |
| | (0.8) | (1.0) | (−2.6) | | (1.1) | (1.9) | (−3.7) |
| | 0.02 | 0.00 | 0.00 | | 0.02 | 0.00 | 0.00 |
| | (2.2) | (0.1) | (2.6) | | (2.3) | (0.0) | (2.8) |
| 82:4 | 0.34 | 0.29 | −0.20 | 83:4 | 0.42 | 0.31 | −0.22 |
| | (0.5) | (3.4) | (−4.2) | | (0.7) | (3.4) | (−4.4) |
| .13(.02) | 3.71 | 0.23 | 0.33 | .14(.02) | 3.74 | 0.27 | 0.33 |
| | (1.6) | (0.7) | (1.8) | | (1.7) | (0.8) | (1.8) |
| 72.3 | 0.02 | −0.00 | −0.00 | 78.9 | 0.01 | −0.00 | −0.00 |
| | (1.4) | (−1.3) | (−1.2) | | (1.0) | (−1.4) | (−1.5) |
| | 0.90 | 0.36 | −0.39 | | 0.68 | 0.34 | −0.38 |
| | (0.8) | (2.2) | (−4.3) | | (0.6) | (2.1) | (−4.2) |
| | 0.02 | −0.00 | 0.00 | | 0.02 | −0.00 | 0.00 |
| | (2.1) | (−0.0) | (2.8) | | (2.0) | (−0.1) | (2.8) |
| 84:4 | 0.95 | 0.34 | −0.20 | 85:4 | 0.81 | 0.34 | −0.19 |
| | (1.6) | (3.6) | (−4.0) | | (1.4) | (3.5) | (−3.8) |
| .14(.02) | 4.04 | 0.31 | 0.32 | .15(.02) | 4.39 | 0.36 | 0.35 |
| | (2.0) | (1.0) | (1.9) | | (2.3) | (1.1) | (2.1) |
| 78.6 | 0.02 | −0.00 | −0.00 | 82.3 | 0.01 | −0.00 | −0.00 |
| | (1.4) | (−1.4) | (−1.6) | | (0.9) | (−1.6) | (−1.4) |
| | 1.06 | 0.33 | −0.35 | | 0.85 | 0.33 | −0.35 |
| | (1.1) | (2.1) | (−4.1) | | (0.9) | (2.0) | (−4.2) |
| | 0.02 | 0.00 | 0.00 | | 0.12 | 0.00 | 0.00 |
| | (2.9) | (1.1) | (2.4) | | (2.4) | (0.5) | (2.7) |
| 86:4 | 0.20 | 0.22 | −0.15 | 87:4 | 0.28 | 0.22 | −0.14 |
| | (0.4) | (2.2) | (−2.8) | | (0.6) | (2.4) | (−2.9) |
| .16(.02) | 3.60 | 0.24 | 0.42 | .16(.03) | 3.48 | 0.19 | 0.48 |
| | (2.1) | (0.8) | (2.6) | | (2.3) | (0.7) | (3.1) |
| 76.4 | −0.00 | −0.01 | −0.00 | 84.8 | 0.00 | −0.00 | −0.00 |
| | (−0.1) | (−3.1) | (−0.8) | | (0.0) | (−3.4) | (−0.2) |
| | −0.17 | 0.11 | −0.30 | | −0.44 | 0.04 | −0.25 |
| | (−0.2) | (0.7) | (−3.6) | | (−0.6) | (0.2) | (−3.1) |

Table 8.3: Recursive Estimates of Error Correction Coefficients(Continued)

| end-t<br>$\beta_{15}(se)$<br>*HW* | $\alpha$ | | | end-t<br>$\beta_{15}(se)$<br>*HW* | $\alpha$ | | |
|---|---|---|---|---|---|---|---|
| | +0.01 | −0.00 | +0.00 | | +0.01 | −0.00 | +0.00 |
| | (1.6) | (−0.1) | (2.4) | | (0.8) | (−0.9) | (2.1) |
| 88:4 | 0.20 | 0.22 | −0.14 | 89:4 | 0.20 | 0.20 | −0.15 |
| | (0.7) | (2.6) | (−2.9) | | (0.5) | (2.7) | (−3.2) |
| .15(.03) | 4.58 | 0.27 | 0.50 | .13(.03) | 5.07 | 0.24 | 0.49 |
| | (3.5) | (1.0) | (3.4) | | (4.0) | (1.1) | (3.5) |
| 80.8 | 0.00 | −0.01 | −0.00 | 66.6 | 0.02 | −0.00 | 0.00 |
| | (0.4) | (−3.5) | (−0.1) | | (2.0) | (−2.6) | (0.6) |
| | 0.13 | 0.09 | −0.23 | | 0.44 | 0.24 | −0.22 |
| | (0.2) | (0.6) | (−2.9) | | (0.7) | (1.0) | (−2.9) |
| | +0.00 | −0.00 | +0.00 | | +0.01 | −0.00 | +0.00 |
| | (0.7) | (−1.3) | (2.0) | | (1.3) | (−1.1) | (1.9) |
| 90:4 | 0.26 | 0.22 | −0.15 | 91:4 | 0.10 | 0.21 | −0.14 |
| | (0.7) | (3.4) | (−3.2) | | (0.3) | (3.2) | (−3.1) |
| .13(.03) | 4.81 | 0.23 | 0.49 | .13(.03) | 4.31 | 0.20 | 0.50 |
| | (4.4) | (1.2) | (3.5) | | (4.1) | (1.0) | (3.6) |
| 77.4 | 0.01 | −0.00 | 0.00 | 79.8 | 0.01 | −0.00 | 0.00 |
| | (1.8) | (−3.1) | (0.5) | | (1.4) | (−3.4) | (0.5) |
| | 0.39 | 0.13 | −0.22 | | 0.08 | 0.10 | −0.22 |
| | (0.7) | (1.2) | (−3.0) | | (0.1) | (1.0) | (−3.0) |

## 8.2 Dynamic Analysis

The analysis of the dynamic responses of the five variables in this VECM plus the additional variables that can be constructed using identities involving these five variables requires 20 identifying restrictions, (in addition to normalizations) as discussed in Chapter 4. Ten of these restrictions are provided by the standard assumptions that covariance matrix of the "structural shocks" is diagonal. Six additional identifying restrictions are provided by the assumption of the KPSW "common trends" model that the permanent and transitory shocks have a block causal chain structure with the two permanent shocks ordered first in the chain. One additional identifying restriction is provided by the causal ordering of the two permanent shocks. This leaves three identifying restrictions required on the structure of the transitory shocks to exactly identify the full model.

The identifying restrictions that we apply to the transitory shocks are analogous to those used in Chapter 7, and are consistent with the methodology of Warne (1993). We restrict the impact effects of various transitory shocks to zero on particular variables. One restriction is the same as that applied to Fisher equation model in Chapter 7, namely that one transitory shock has a zero impact effect on the inflation rate and the price level. We label the shock identified by this restiriction an "aggregate demand" shock, consistent with a model in which the short-run aggregate supply curve is perfectly elastic. We identify a second transitory shock as a subset of these aggregate demand shocks. The two identifying restrictions on this shock are 1) that the impact effect on the inflation rate and the price level is zero and 2) that the impact effect on real balances is zero. The combination of these two restrictions implies that the shock has a zero impact effect on nominal money balances. Therefore this second shock can be interpreted as an aggregate demand shock in the absence of any immediate monetary accommodation (though as will be seen in the computed impulse response functions there is a lagged response of nominal money balances implied by these identifying restrictions). This set of restrictions is sufficient to exactly identify the two permanent shocks and the three transitory shocks. The third transitory shock is a composite of all the remaining transitory shocks that affect the economy is not given any particular economic interpretation.

The details of the identified shocks are presented in Table 8.4. The estimates used in this analysis are from Table 8.3 for the sample period ending in 1991:4. The data in that table refer to the model that is exactly identified, with the nominal permanent shock ordered first in the causal chain, so that by construction the permanent real shock does not have any permanent effect on the nominal variables in the model. The estimated correlation between the two permanent shocks under the identifying restrictions is .12, which is not significantly different from zero under the test developed by Baillie (1987) ($\chi^2_{(1)} = 2.03, p = .15$). This test fails to reject the overidentifying restriction of the "common trends" model that the permanent nominal common trend has no permanent effect on real output. The orthogonalizing decomposition of this covariance matrix, $\Sigma = \pi D \pi'$, is shown in Table 8.4. Since the variance of the permanent nominal shock in this model is larger than the variance of the permanent real shock as in all the models considered in the previous chapters and the correlation between the two shocks is small, $\pi$ is close to an identity matrix ($\pi_{21} = .0133$). Thus, even under the exactly identifying restrictions, the permanent effect of the permanent nominal shock on real output is very small. After orthogonalization, the coefficient matrix for the common trends is $\beta^*_{\perp}$. The zeros and ones in this matrix are imposed by the identifying restrictions on the permanent shocks and the structure of the three cointegrating vector. The nonzero entry in the (4,1) column reflects the deviation of the orthogonalizing transformation matrix from an identity matrix and, correspondingly, the absolute value of the (1,1) element that measures the permanent effect of the permanent nominal shock is slightly smaller than the semielasticity of the equilibrium velocity.

The factor loading matrix for the nominal and real common trends is $\alpha'_{\perp}$. The weights of the reduced form errors in the real balance, inflation, real output and Treasury bill rate equations for the nominal common trend are very similar to the weights assigned to this trend in the four variable Fisher equation model (Table 7.3). The weight assigned to the reduced form error of the long-term nominal rate equation is smaller in absolute value than that assigned to the error of the short-term nominal rate equation. Since the variance of the reduced form error of long rates is considerably smaller than the corresponding variance for short-term nominal rates this implies that the expansion of the model to include the long rate equation has relatively little effect on the measurement of the nominal common trend.

In contrast, the weights assigned to the reduced form errors on real bal-

Table 8.4: Identification of Permanent and Transitory Shocks: Five Variables Model. ln(M/P, Inflation, RL, ln(Y/P) and Rtb

$$\beta_{\perp}^{0} = \begin{bmatrix} -.13 & 1.0 \\ 1.0 & 0.0 \\ 1.0 & 0.0 \\ 0.0 & 1.0 \\ 1.0 & 0.0 \end{bmatrix}$$

$$\alpha_{\perp}^{0\prime} = \begin{bmatrix} -13.78 & .07 & .01 & -5.98 & -.10 \\ .51 & .03 & -.00 & .69 & -.02 \end{bmatrix}$$

$$\Sigma_{v} = \begin{bmatrix} .01 & 1.5\times10^{-4} \\ 1.5\times10^{-4} & 1.4\times10^{-4} \end{bmatrix}$$

$$\pi = \begin{bmatrix} 1.0 & 0.0 \\ .01 & 1.0 \end{bmatrix}$$

$$\beta_{\perp}^{*} = \begin{bmatrix} -.12 & 1.0 \\ 1.0 & 0.0 \\ 1.0 & 0.0 \\ .01 & 0.0 \\ 1.0 & 0.0 \end{bmatrix}$$

$$\alpha_{\perp}^{\prime} = \begin{bmatrix} -13.73 & .07 & .01 & 5.48 & -.10 \\ .69 & .03 & -.00 & .61 & -.02 \end{bmatrix}$$

$$\text{Transitory Factor Loadings} \quad \begin{bmatrix} 112.09 & .72 & .83 & -5.41 & -.21 \\ .05 & -.00 & .00 & .13 & -.00 \\ -18.96 & -.28 & -.09 & 47.35 & .51 \end{bmatrix}$$

Note: Derived From Estimates for Sample Ending in 91:4 in Table 8.3.The specification is based upon no shift in mean of equilibrium real balances except during New Operating Procedures.

ances and real output in this five variable model for the real common trend are considerably different from those assigned for this trend in the four variable Fisher equation model in Table 7.3. Here the weight on the reduced form error for real output is roughly fifty percent of the corresponding weight in the four equation model, and the weight on the reduced form error for real balances is now positive and larger than the weight assigned to real output, in contrast to the Fisher equation model where this weight is negative and much smaller in absolute value than the weight on the real output errors.

The factor loadings for the transitory errors are ordered such that the composite transitory shock is first, the aggregate demand shock with monetary accommodation is second and the aggregate demand shock without monetary accommodation is last. The principle effects of the addition of the long-term nominal rate and the identification of the second transitory aggregate demand shock is to reduce the weight on the reduced form error in the real output equation and to change the sign of the weight on the reduced form error in the real balance equation in the construction of the aggregate demand shock with monetary accommodation.

The impulse response functions of various variables in this model to the four identified shocks are shown in Figures 8.3 through 8.30. In these figures the impulse responses are plotted for real output, velocity, inflation,the Treasury Bill rate, the long-term rate, real balances, and the growth rate of the nominal money stock. The variables in addition to the five that appear in the VECM are all obtained as identity transformations of the original five variables.

The impulse responses to the real common trend in most cases are quite robust to the increase in the dimension of the VECM with the addition of the long-term interest rate. Real GDP approaches the equilibrium response over a period of 2-3 years and exhibits a very small overshooting of the equilibrium almost identical to that in Figure 7.3. The patterns of the response functions for inflation and the Treasury bill rate are very similar to the corresponding response patterns in Figures 7.5-7.6. The only notable difference is that the variables approach their equilibrium values somewhat more slowly in the expanded model, and the interest rates and velocity deviation exhibit somewhat more overshooting of their respective equilibrium values than is characteristic of the results from the Fisher equation model. The one major difference between the two models is in the response pattern of velocity. In the Fisher equation model the initial response of velocity to the real common trend is positive and declines monotonically to zero. In the larger model, the initial response of velocity is near zero, increases to a maximum after about six quarters, and then declines monotonically to zero. The response pattern of the interest rate spread in this model is similar to that for the term structure model in Figure 7.26.

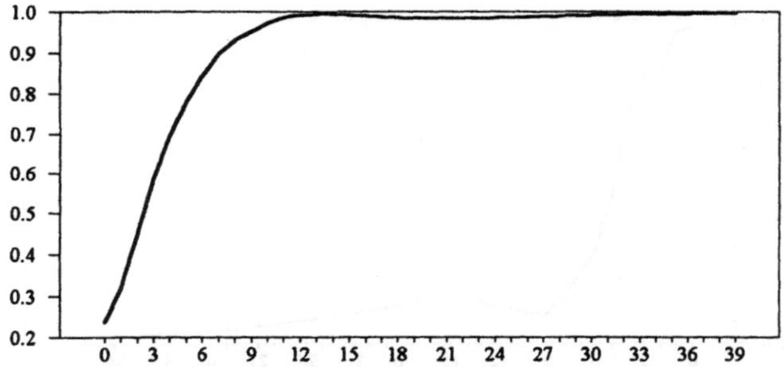


Figure 8.3: I.R.F. for GDP w.r.t. the Permanent Real Shock

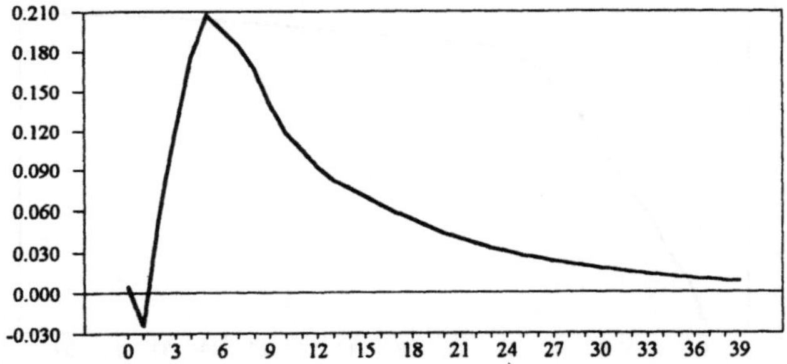


Figure 8.4: I.R.F. for Velocity w.r.t. the Permanent Real Shock

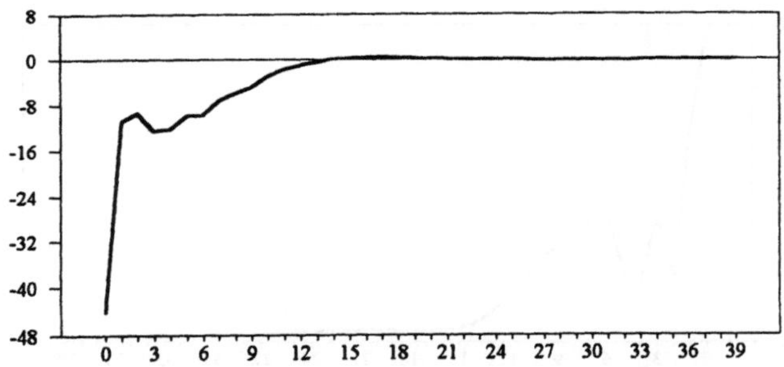


Figure 8.5: I.R.F. for Inflation w.r.t. the Permanent Real Shock

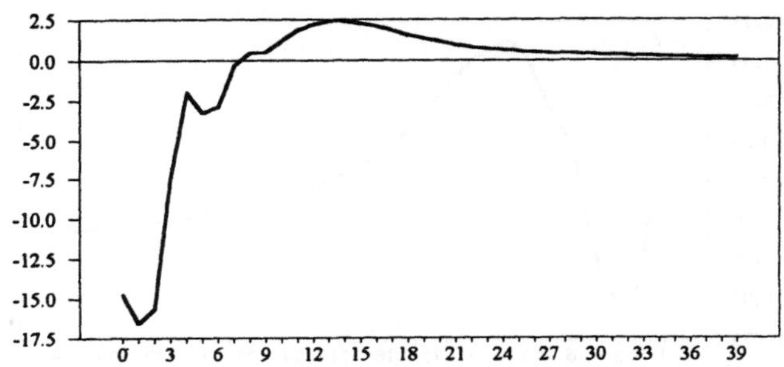


Figure 8.6: I.R.F. for Rtb w.r.t. the Permanent Real Shock

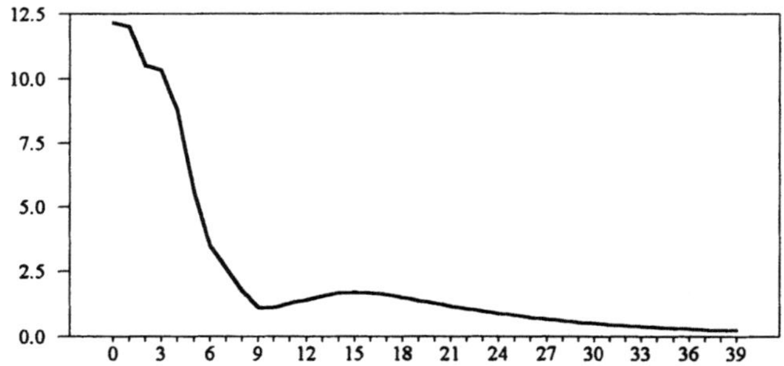


Figure 8.7: I.R.F. for RL w.r.t. the Permanent Real Shock

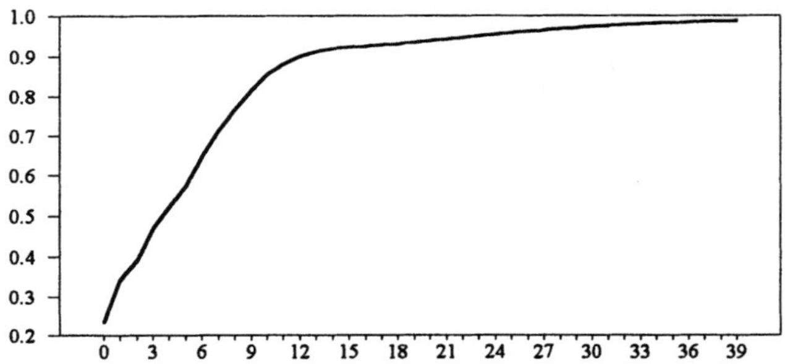


Figure 8.8: I.R.F. for Real Balances w.r.t. the Permanent Real Shock

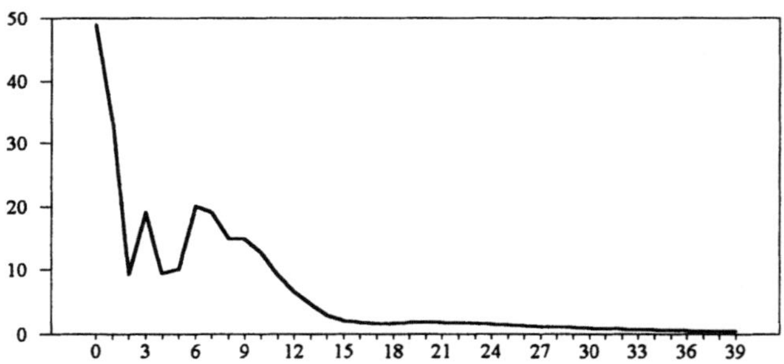


Figure 8.9: I.R.F. for Money Growth w.r.t. the Permanent Real Shock

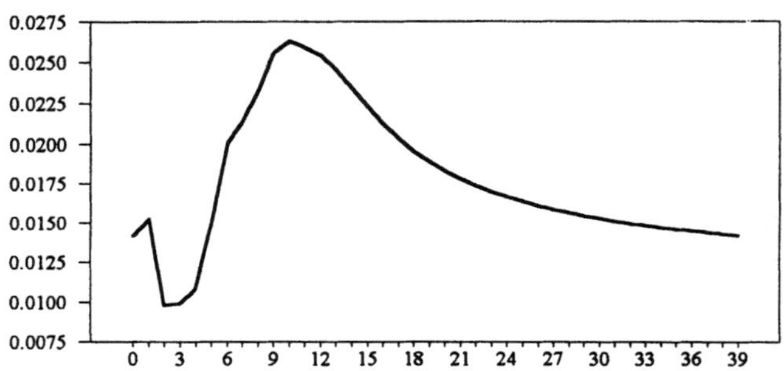


Figure 8.10: I.R.F. for GDP w.r.t. the Permanent Nominal Shock

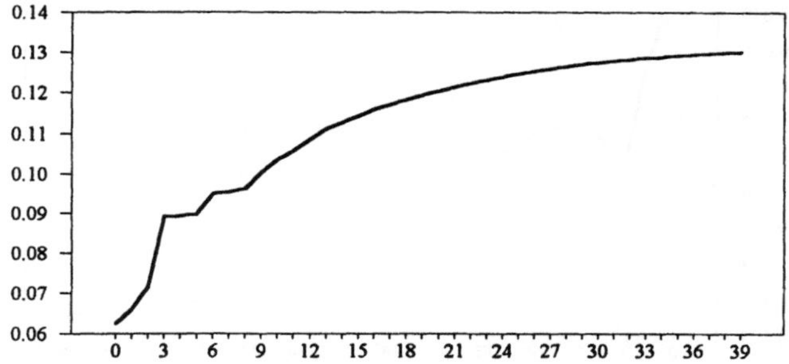


Figure 8.11: I.R.F. for Velocity w.r.t. the Permanent Nominal Shock

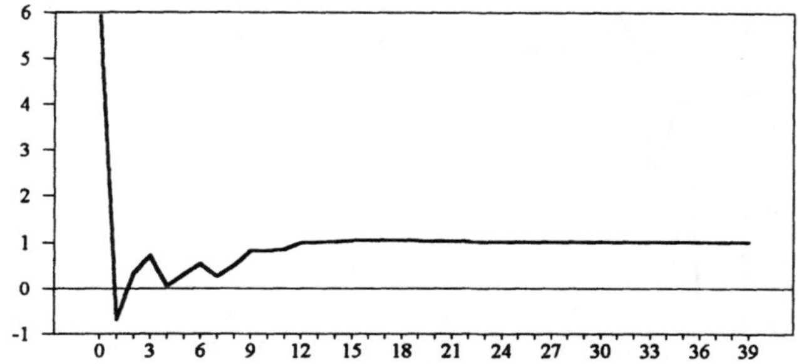


Figure 8.12: I.R.F. for Inflation w.r.t. the Permanent Nominal Shock

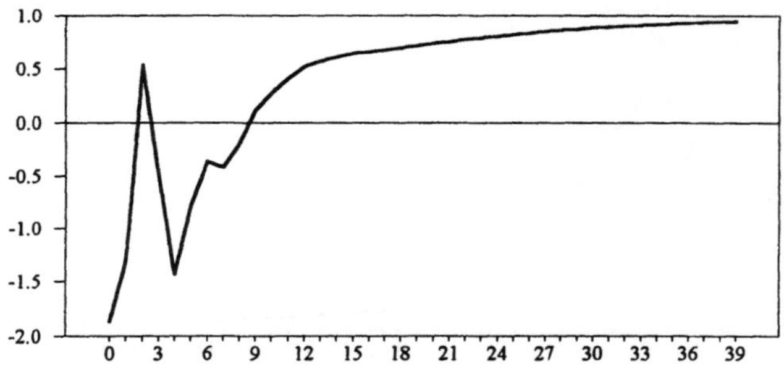


Figure 8.13: I.R.F. for Rtb w.r.t. the Permanent Nominal Shock

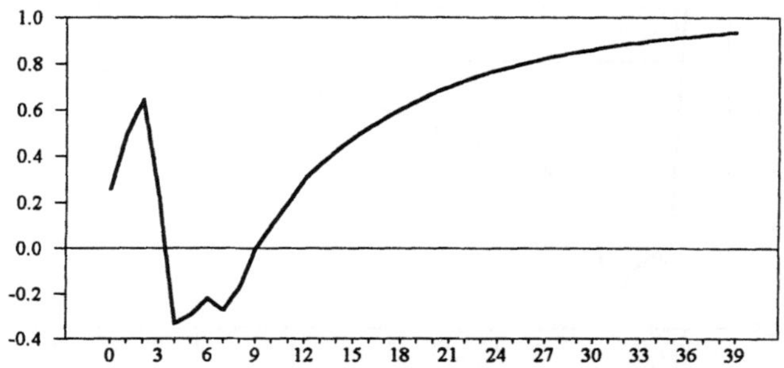


Figure 8.14: I.R.F. for RL w.r.t. the Permanent Nominal Shock

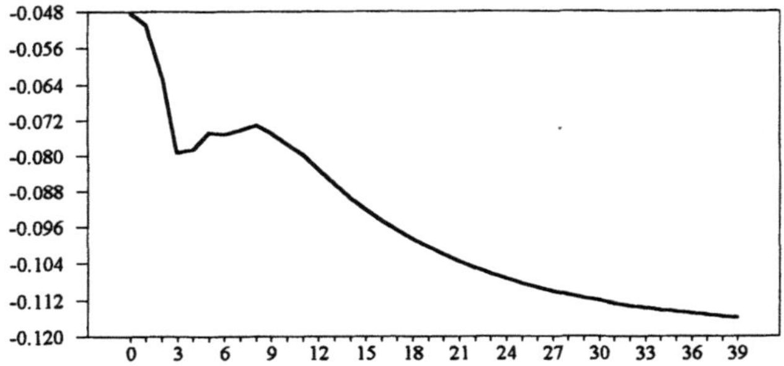


Figure 8.15: I.R.F. for Real Balances w.r.t. the Permanent Nominal Shock

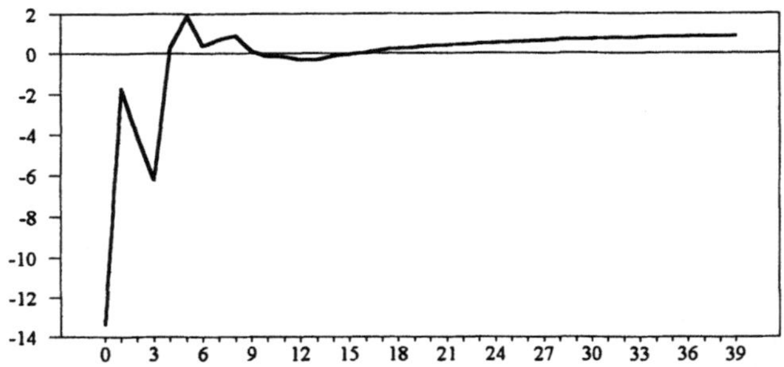


Figure 8.16: I.R.F. for Money Growth w.r.t. the Permanent Nominal Shock

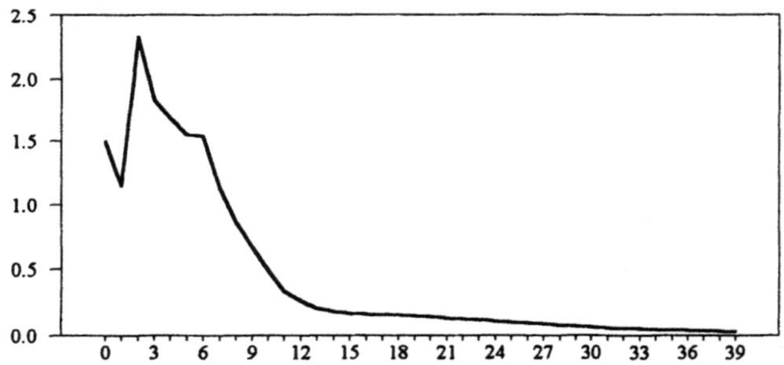


Figure 8.17: I.R.F. for GDP w.r.t. the Trans. AD (w/ money) Shock

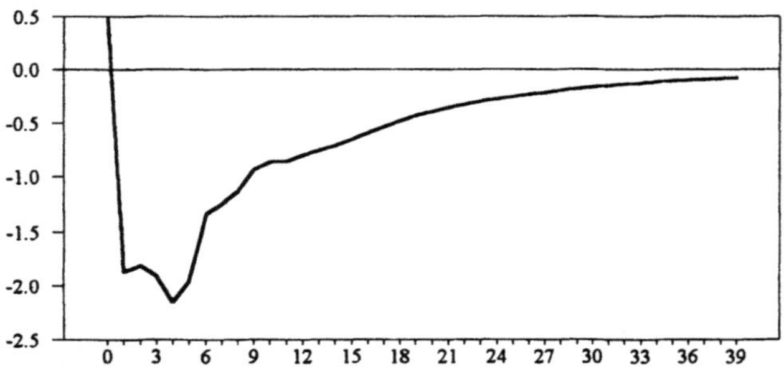


Figure 8.18: I.R.F. for Velocity w.r.t. the Trans. AD (w/ money) Shock

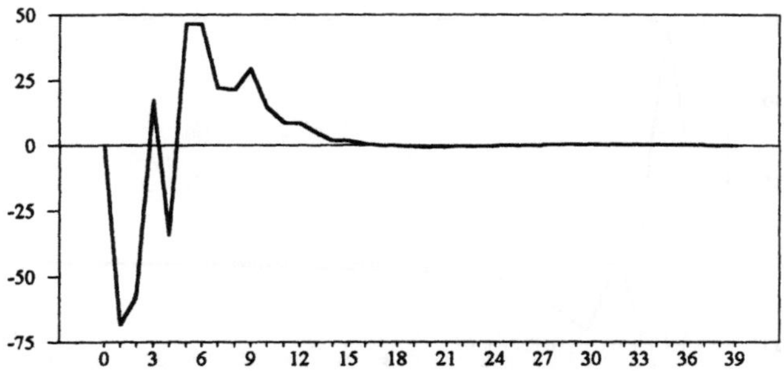


Figure 8.19: I.R.F. for Inflation w.r.t. the Trans. AD (w/ money) Shock

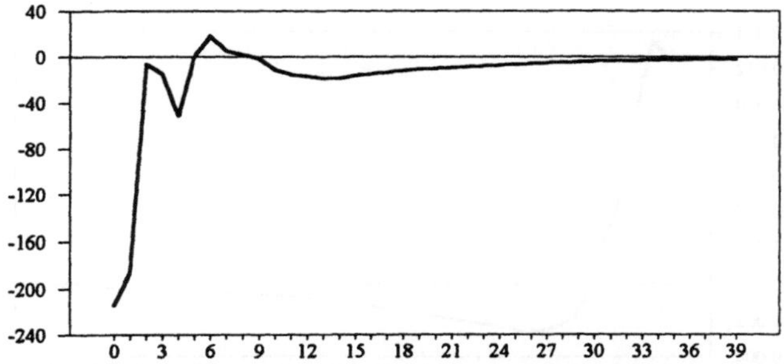


Figure 8.20: I.R.F. for Rtb w.r.t. the Trans. AD (w/ money) Shock

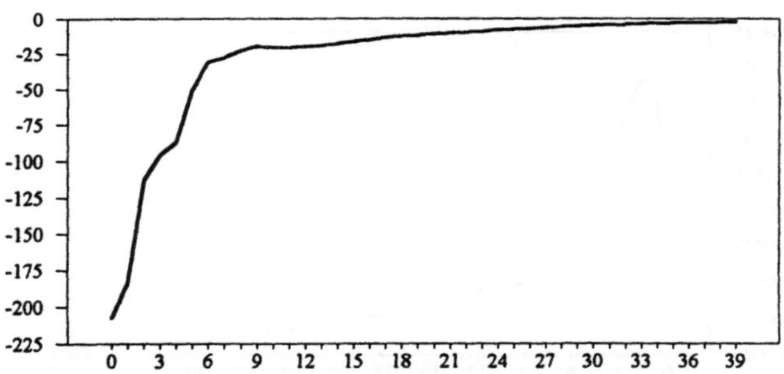


Figure 8.21: I.R.F. for RL w.r.t. the Trans. AD (w/ money) Shock

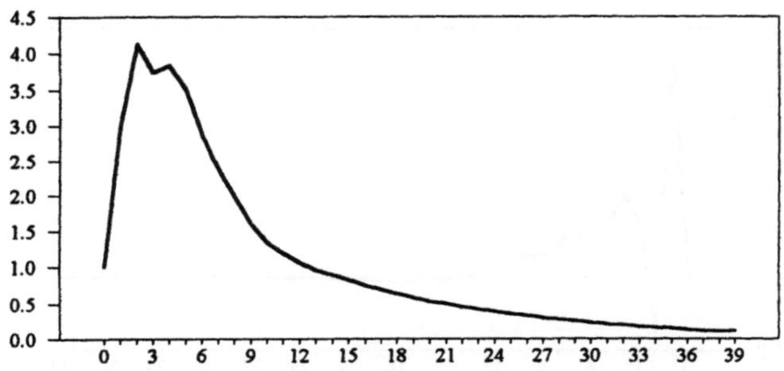


Figure 8.22: I.R.F. for Real Balances w.r.t. the Trans. AD (w/ money) Shock

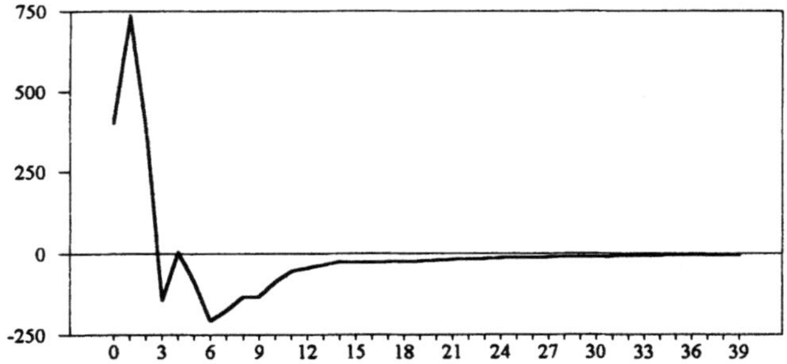


Figure 8.23: I.R.F. for Money Growth w.r.t. the Trans. AD (w/ money) Shock

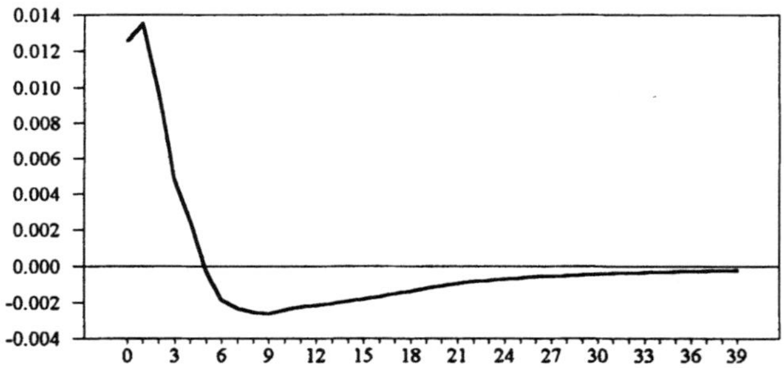


Figure 8.24: I.R.F. for GDP w.r.t. the Trans. AD (w/o money) Shock

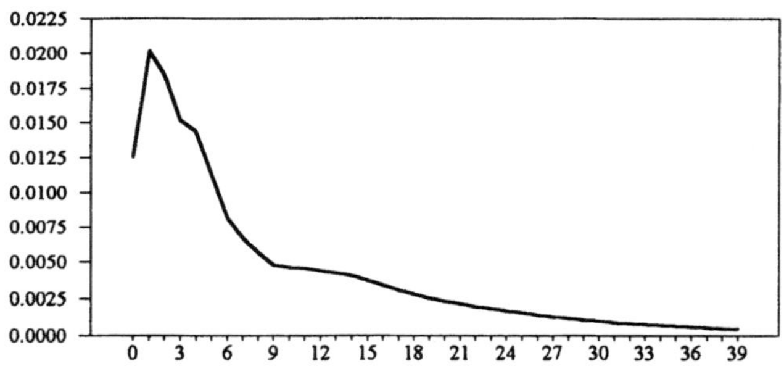


Figure 8.25: I.R.F. for Velocity w.r.t. the Trans. AD (w/o money) Shock

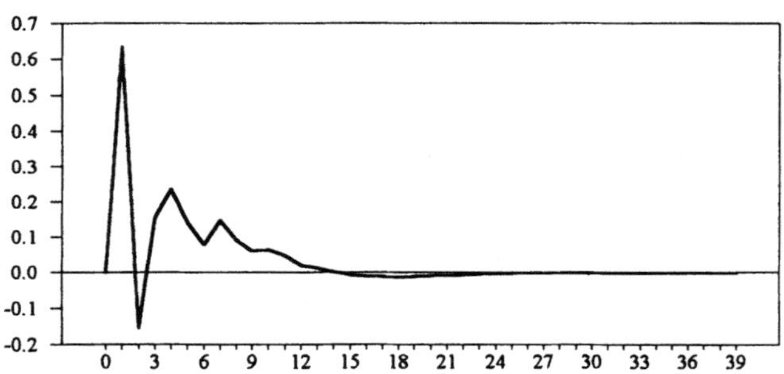


Figure 8.26: I.R.F. for Inflation w.r.t. the Trans. AD (w/o money) Shock

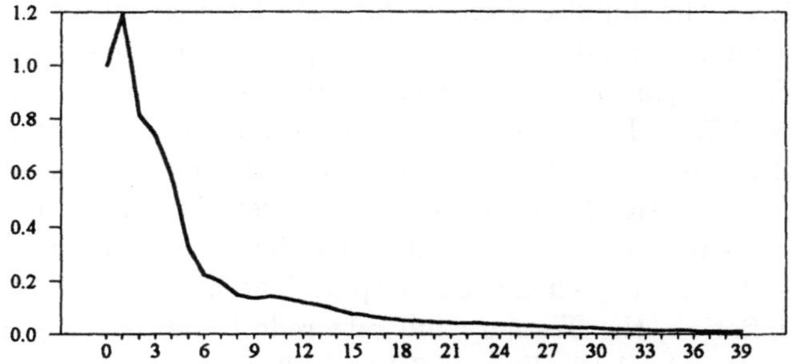


Figure 8.27: I.R.F. for Rtb w.r.t. the Trans. AD (w/o money) Shock

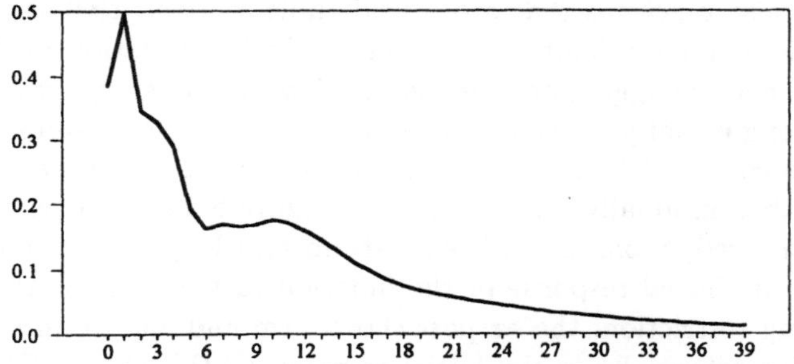


Figure 8.28: I.R.F. for RL w.r.t. the Trans. AD (w/o money) Shock

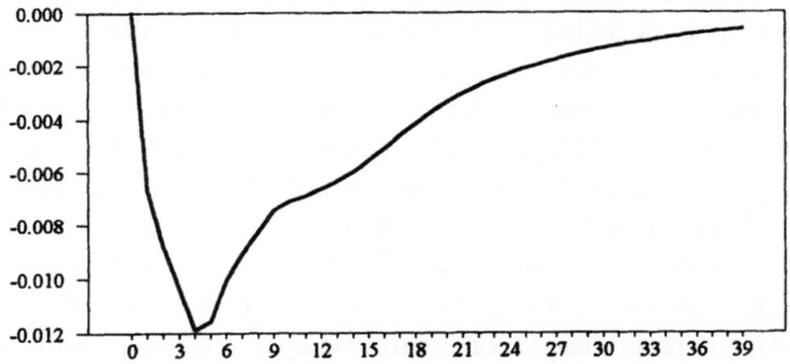


Figure 8.29: I.R.F. for Real Balances w.r.t. the Trans. AD (w/o money) Shock

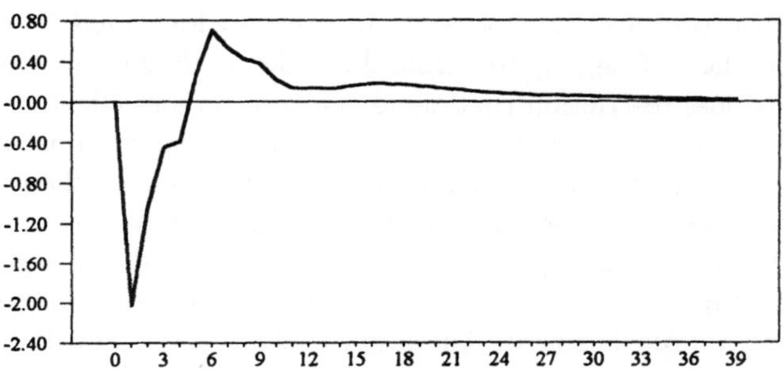


Figure 8.30: I.R.F. for Mon. Growth w.r.t. the Trans. AD (w/o money) Shock

At first glance the impulse response function for real output in response to the nominal common trend in this model appears to differ considerably from that in the Fisher equation model (Figure 7.9) and that in the term structure model (Figure 7.27). It is important, however, to observe the scale of this response function. At all forecast horizons, the estimated response of real output to this shock is very small. A consistent interpretation of all three models is that there is no strong evidence to contradict the conclusion that the nominal common trend has no impact on real output. The impulse response functions for velocity, inflation, the Treasury bill rate reflect the patterns derived from the Fisher equation model in Figures 7.10 - 7.12.

The identification of a second transitory aggregate demand shock results in impulse response functions that are considerable different that those observed for the single aggregate demand shock in the Fisher equation model (Figures 7.15 - 7.20). For the aggregate demand shock with monetary accommodation, there is a strong initial positive growth in the nominal money stock that goes to zero over the course of four quarters, becomes negative for approximately two more years, then gradually returns to zero (Figure 8.23). This is accompanied by large initial reductions in both short-term and long-term nominal interest rates. Since the initial response of the inflation rate is constrained to zero by the identifying restriction, the *ex post* short-term and long-term real rates are also reduced substantially in the initial response to this shock. The effects on short-term rates, both nominal and real, dissipate quite quickly. The effects on the long-term rates are more persistent. After the initial period, the inflation response function is negative for two quarters, then oscillates around zero for several more quarters, reaches a (positive) maximum after about six quarters and declines relatively smoothly to zero after about four years (Figure 8.19). The real output response (Figure 8.17) starts positive, reaches a maximum after about three quarters and then declines to zero after about three years. The response of real balances increases to a maximum after approximately one year, and then declines slowly towards zero.(Figure 8.22) With the exception of the two quarters of negative responses of inflation, these response patterns are quite consistent with the response patterns implied by a textbook model with a highly elastic short-run aggregate supply function to an aggregate demand shock that is initially accompanied by a monetary expansion.

The impulse response functions for the second identified transitory shock that is in the class of aggregate demand shocks as defined in Chapter 7, but with the additional restriction that there is a zero impact effect on the nominal money stock are shown in Figures 8.24- 8.30. The initial response of the growth rate of nominal money to this shock is zero by construction, then goes negative for about one year, then becomes positive and gradually declines toward zero (Figure 8.30). The initial response of real output to this shock is positive(Figure 8.24), but quickly goes to zero, overshoots and becomes slightly negative and then gradually approaches zero. The impact effect of this shock on both short- and long-term nominal interest rates is positive (the normalization of this shock is a 100 basis point shock to the Treasury bill rate), but the effect on the long-term rate is smaller than that on the short-term rate. The responses of both rates reach a maximum after two quarters, and then decline relatively smoothly towards zero. The approach of the long-term rate towards zero is slower than that of the short-term rate, so that the effect of the shock on the interest rate spread that is initially negative overshoots zero and eventually has a small positive value before returning to zero. However, the overshooting effect on the spread is so small that it has effectively gone to zero after two years.

The effect of this aggregate demand shock on inflation is positive after one period, reverses and becomes a small negative in the second period, then reverses again and has small positive values that decline to zero after three years (Figure 8.26). Both short- and long-term *ex post* real interest rates exhibit initial positive responses, but both of these responses have declined to only a few basis points after about six quarters. Again, the response patterns are quite consistent with the implications of a textbook model with a highly elastic short-run aggregate supply curve when there is an aggregate demand shock that is initially not accompanied by a monetary expansion.

The information in the response functions for the two types of aggregate demand shock can be used to construct inferences about the size of the parameters of a short-run demand function for real balances under fairly restrictive identifying restrictions on the structure of that function. Assume that the specification of the short-run demand function for real balances is of the form:

$$\ln M_t - \ln P_t = \alpha + \beta_1 \ln Y/P_t + \beta_2 R$$

where $M_t$ is nominal money balances, $P_t$ is the price level, $Y_t$ is real output and $R_t$ is a single nominal interest rate. This specification restricts the short-run demand function for real balances to be of the same form as the long-run demand with the exception that the income elasticity is not constrained to unity. Under this specification it is possible to measure the values of the parameters $\beta_1$ and $\beta_2$ using information from the impulse response functions. When a shock occurs to the economy (that is not a shock to the money demand function) the impact response of real balances, real output, and the nominal interest rate must satisfy the restriction:

$$\Delta \ln(M_t/P)_t = \alpha + \beta_1 \Delta \ln(Y/P)_t + \beta_2 \Delta R.$$

Two values for each of the variables $\Delta ln(M/P)$, $\Delta ln(Y/P)$ and $\Delta R$ can be obtained from the impulse response functions for each of the aggregate demand shocks. These observations generate a set of two equations in the two unknown parameter values $\beta_1$ and $\beta_2$. As long as these equations are linearly independent, they can be solved for the two parameters. When the impulse response data from the Treasury bill rate are used in this computation, the computed short-run elasticity with respect to real output is .24 and the computed short-run semielasticity with respect to the Treasury bill rate is -.003. When the impulse response data from the long-term interest rate is used in this computation, the computed short-run income elasticity is .12 and the computed short-run semielasticity with respect to the long-term rate is -.004.[2] These estimates are considerably smaller in absolute value than the estimated parameters of the long-run demand for real balances, but do not seem implausible.

Finally, the variance decompositions with respect to the two identified permanent shocks, the two identified transitory shocks and the residual composite shock are shown for selected forecast horizons in Table 8.5. The first observation from the variance decompositions is that almost all of the forecast variance in real output at all horizons is attributable to two shocks: the permanent real output shock and the transitory aggregate demand shock with no immediate monetary accommodation. The majority of the one period ahead forecast variance of real output is attributable to the transitory shock, but the importance of this shock declines rapidly so that on a three year horizon only ten percent of the forecast variance is attributable to this shock. Over the same horizon the fraction of the forecast variance attributable to the real permanent shock increases rapidly. The remaining three shocks, the permanent nominal shock, the transitory aggregate demand shock with monetary accommodation and the residual composite transitory shock individually account for less than twelve percent of the forecast variation at any horizon, and in most instances individually account for less than five percent of the forecast variation. Thus most of the short- and long-run behavior of real output appears to result from a very small number of exogenous influences on the economy.

Similarly, the forecast variance of inflation is also principally attributable to only two shocks, but in contrast to the case of real output the influential shocks for inflation variability are the permanent nominal shock and the residual composite transitory shock. Neither of the identified aggregate demand shock individually accounts for more than ten percent of the forecast variance of inflation at any horizon. Consequently the short-run variability of inflation is largely not identified in this model.

The variance decompositions for long- and short-term nominal interest rates are particularly interesting. At short and intermediate forecasting horizons very little of the forecast variance for either variable is associated with the two permanent shocks. However, the decomposition of the short-horizon forecast variance differs markedly between the two rates. The majority of the forecast variance of the Treasury bill rate at short forecast horizons is attributable to aggregate demand shocks without immediate monetary accommodation. In contrast, the majority of the forecast variance for the long-term rate at the same horizons is attributable to the aggregate demand shock with immediate monetary accommodation. At intermediate forecast horizons of one year or more the composite residual transitory shock accounts for a substantial fraction of the variance of both nominal interest rates. However there is considerable cancellation of influences on the interest rate spread. The most important shocks in the forecast variance of this variable are the permanent real shock and the aggregate demand

[2]Unfortunately it is not possible to assume that both interest rates enter the short-run specification for purposes of this computation. If the short-run specification were generalized to include both interest rates, then there would be three unknown parameters but only two equations.

Table 8.5: Variance Decompositions: Five Variable VECM

| Variable | Horizon | Permanent Real | Permanent Nominal | AD Shock $\Delta M \neq 0$ | AD Shock $\Delta M = 0$ | Composite Transitory |
|---|---|---|---|---|---|---|
| ln(Q) | | | | | | |
| | 1 | 13.4 | 4.0 | 9.3 | 68.5 | 4.7 |
| | 4 | 37.6 | 2.8 | 11.6 | 44.4 | 3.7 |
| | 8 | 68.1 | 3.1 | 7.7 | 17.7 | 3.4 |
| | 16 | 83.1 | 4.2 | 3.1 | 7.1 | 2.5 |
| | 200 | 97.4 | 1.7 | 0.2 | 0.5 | 0.2 |
| Inflation | | | | | | |
| | 1 | 16.7 | 25.0 | 0.0 | 0.0 | 58.4 |
| | 4 | 15.3 | 20.0 | 0.9 | 5.4 | 58.4 |
| | 8 | 16.5 | 18.8 | 1.5 | 6.2 | 57.1 |
| | 16 | 16.2 | 21.2 | 1.6 | 6.1 | 54.8 |
| | 200 | 8.5 | 58.6 | 0.9 | 3.2 | 28.8 |
| *Rtb* | | | | | | |
| | 1 | 6.7 | 8.9 | 24.9 | 56.0 | 3.6 |
| | 4 | 6.5 | 4.0 | 11.7 | 54.7 | 23.1 |
| | 8 | 5.6 | 5.1 | 10.2 | 52.9 | 26.2 |
| | 16 | 5.6 | 5.8 | 10.1 | 52.7 | 25.8 |
| | 200 | 2.9 | 52.3 | 5.1 | 26.6 | 13.1 |
| $R_L$ | | | | | | |
| | 1 | 11.6 | 0.4 | 59.4 | 21.2 | 7.3 |
| | 4 | 10.6 | 1.4 | 36.2 | 23.7 | 28.1 |
| | 8 | 9.7 | 1.4 | 29.5 | 22.1 | 37.3 |
| | 16 | 8.9 | 2.1 | 27.2 | 24.5 | 37.4 |
| | 200 | 3.0 | 66.4 | 9.1 | 8.6 | 12.8 |
| velocity | | | | | | |
| | 1 | 0.0 | 52.4 | 0.7 | 46.5 | 0.4 |
| | 4 | 0.4 | 41.5 | 4.4 | 48.3 | 5.4 |
| | 8 | 1.8 | 51.7 | 4.4 | 32.3 | 9.8 |
| | 16 | 1.5 | 70.3 | 2.8 | 18.3 | 7.0 |
| | 200 | 0.1 | 98.1 | 0.2 | 1.2 | 0.5 |
| CIV1 | | | | | | |
| | 1 | 7.0 | 14.6 | 27.0 | 47.9 | 3.5 |
| | 4 | 7.7 | 8.1 | 13.0 | 47.9 | 23.3 |
| | 8 | 6.9 | 12.7 | 11.1 | 44.7 | 24.6 |
| | 16 | 6.8 | 13.6 | 11.0 | 44.5 | 24.1 |
| | 200 | 6.9 | 13.8 | 11.0 | 44.3 | 24.1 |
| $R_L - Rtb$ | | | | | | |
| | 1 | 40.4 | 21.0 | 0.1 | 38.5 | 0.1 |
| | 4 | 41.3 | 11.3 | 5.2 | 37.3 | 4.3 |
| | 8 | 40.5 | 11.9 | 6.5 | 36.3 | 4.8 |
| | 16 | 39.6 | 11.9 | 6.7 | 35.7 | 6.1 |
| | 200 | 39.5 | 12.0 | 6.7 | 35.7 | 6.1 |

shock without immediate monetary accommodation. Neither of the other two transitory shocks individually account for more than ten percent of the forecast variance of the interest rate spread at any horizon, and the permanent nominal shock generally accounts for about twelve percent of the forecast variance of the interest rate spread beyond the immediate effect.

The decomposition of the forecast variance of velocity is similar to that observed in previous smaller models. The fraction of the forecast variance attributable to the permanent real output shock is negligible at all horizons. At most horizons, the majority of the forecast variance is attributable to the permanent nominal shock, and this fraction approaches one hundred percent at long horizons. At short horizons, the aggregate demand shock without monetary accommodation is the second most important factor of the forecast variance of velocity, but the importance of this shock declines rapidly over a three year forecasting horizon.

## 8.3 Summary and Conclusions

The expansion of our basic vector error correction model to include five variables and three cointegrating vectors representing an equilibrium demand for real balances, a real interest rate and a stationary term structure relationship generates insight into the dynamics of monetary shocks that is not accessible in the more limited models developed in the previous chapters. First it is possible in the expanded framework to identify aggregate demand shocks with and without immediate monetary accommodation. The impulse response functions and the variance decomposition for these shocks provide some evidence on the short-run influence of transitory monetary shocks. Second, under relatively restrictive assumptions about the structure of a short-run demand function for real balances, it is possible to infer from the different impact responses to the two identified aggregate demand shocks point estimates of the short-run income elasticity and interest rate semielasticity of this function. The available evidence suggests that on quarterly basis the impact income elasticity is probably less than .25, and the impact interest semielasticity may be less than .01 in absolute value.

# Appendix A

# SOME EXTENSIONS OF THE GOODFRIEND ERRORS-IN VARIABLES MODEL

## A.1 Multiple Regressors with Permanent and Transitory Components

Goodfriend (1985) assumes the data generating process (DGP) for real balances is:

$$m_t = a_0 + a_1 y_t^* + a_2 i_t^* + v_t \tag{A.1}$$

with serially correlated transactions variables ($y_t^*$) and interest rate ($i_t^*$) generated by AR(1) processes:

$$y_t^* = \phi_0 + \phi_1 y_{t-1}^* + u_{1t} \tag{A.2}$$

$$i_t^* = \theta_0 + \theta_1 i_{t-1}^* + u_{2t} \tag{A.3}$$

He assumes that $y_t^*$ and $i_t^*$ are not directly observable, and that the available proxy variables, $y_t$ and $i_t$, respectively, are subject to serially uncorrelated errors. $\varepsilon_{1t}$ and $\varepsilon_{2t}$ respectively:

$$y_t = y_t^* + \varepsilon_{1t} \tag{A.4}$$

$$i_t = i_t^* + \varepsilon_{2t} \tag{A.5}$$

He also assumes that $v_t$, $u_{it}$ and $\varepsilon_{it}$ are uncorrelated for $i = 1,2$ and that $v_t$ is not serially correlated.

Let $r_1 = (1-\phi_1^2)^{-1}$ and $r_2 = (1-\theta_1^2)^{-1}$. Goodfriend shows that the normal equations for the regression:

$$m_t = b_0 + b_1 y_t + b_2 i_t + b_3 m_{t-1} + v_t \tag{A.6}$$

given the above assumptions these are:

$$\begin{bmatrix} b_1 \\ b_2 \\ b_3 \end{bmatrix} = \begin{bmatrix} \sigma_{u1}^2 r_1 + \sigma_{\varepsilon 1}^2 & 0 & a_1\phi_1\sigma_{u1}^2 r_1 \\ 0 & \sigma_{u2}^2 r_2 + \sigma_{\varepsilon 2}^2 & a_2\theta_1\sigma_{u2}^2 r_2 \\ a_1\phi_1\sigma_{u1}^2 r_1 & a_2\theta_1\sigma_{u2}^2 r_2 & a_1^2\sigma_{u1}^2 r_1 + a_2^2\sigma_{u2}^2 r_2 + \sigma_v^2 \end{bmatrix}^{-1} * \begin{bmatrix} a_1\sigma_{u1}^2 r_1 \\ a_2\sigma_{u2}^2 r_2 \\ a_1^2\phi_1\sigma_{u1}^2 r_1 + a_2^2\theta_1\sigma_{u2}^2 r_2 \end{bmatrix} \tag{A.7}$$

The determinant of the inverse matrix in (7) is:

$$\begin{aligned} \det &= [\sigma_{u1}^2 r_1 + \sigma_{\varepsilon 1}^2][\sigma_{u2}^2 r_2 + \sigma_{\varepsilon 2}^2][a_1^2\sigma_{u1}^2 r_1 + a_2^2\sigma_{u2}^2 r_2 + \sigma_v^2] \\ &\quad -[a_1\phi_1\sigma_{u1}^2 r_1]^2[\sigma_{u2}^2 r_2 + \sigma_{\varepsilon 2}^2] - [a_2\theta_1\sigma_{u2}^2 r_2]^2[\sigma_{u1}^2 r_1 + \sigma_{\varepsilon 1}^2] \end{aligned} \tag{A.8}$$

When the factors of the three terms in this determinant are multiplied, the resulting expression can be rewritten as:

$$\begin{aligned} \det &= \sigma_{u1}^2\sigma_{u2}^2 r_1 r_2[a_1^2\sigma_{\varepsilon 1}^2 + a_2^2\sigma_{\varepsilon 2}^2] \\ &\quad +\sigma_{\varepsilon 1}^2\sigma_{u2}^2 r_2[a_2^2\sigma_{u2}^2 + \sigma_v^2] + \sigma_{\varepsilon 2}^2\sigma_{u1}^2 r_1[a_1^2\sigma_{u1}^2 + \sigma_v^2] \\ &\quad +\sigma_{u1}^2\sigma_{u2}^2 r_1 r_2[a_1^2\sigma_{u1}^2 + a_2^2\sigma_{u2}^2 + \sigma_v^2] \\ &\quad +\sigma_{\varepsilon 1}^2\sigma_{\varepsilon 2}^2[a_1^2\sigma_{u1}^2 r_1 + a_2^2\sigma_{u2}^2 r_2 + \sigma_v^2] \end{aligned} \tag{A.9}$$

Multiply by $(r_1 r_2)^{-1}$ to get:

$$\begin{aligned} (r_1 r_2)^{-1}\det &= \sigma_{u1}^2\sigma_{u2}^2[a_1^2\sigma_{\varepsilon 1}^2 + a_2^2\sigma_{\varepsilon 2}^2] \\ &\quad +r_1^{-1}\sigma_{\varepsilon 1}^2\sigma_{u2}^2[a_2^2\sigma_{u2}^2 + \sigma_v^2] + r_2^{-1}\sigma_{\varepsilon 2}^2\sigma_{u1}^2[a_1^2\sigma_{u1}^2 + \sigma_v^2] \\ &\quad +\sigma_{u1}^2\sigma_{u2}^2[a_1^2\sigma_{u1}^2 + a_2^2\sigma_{u2}^2 + \sigma_v^2] \\ &\quad +\sigma_{\varepsilon 1}^2\sigma_{\varepsilon 2}^2[a_1^2\sigma_{u1}^2 r_2^{-1} + a_2^2\sigma_{u2}^2 r_1^{-1} + \sigma_v^2(r_1 r_2)^{-1}] \end{aligned} \tag{A.10}$$

The numerators of $b_1, b_2, b_3$ are given by the matrix product of the adjoint matrix in (A.7) and the vector on the right hand side of (A.7):

$$\begin{aligned} (r_1 r_2)^{-1} numb_3 &= \sigma_{u1}^2\sigma_{u2}^2[a_1^2\phi_1\sigma_{\varepsilon 1}^2 + a_2^2\theta_1\sigma_{\varepsilon 2}^2] \\ &\quad +\sigma_{\varepsilon 1}^2\sigma_{\varepsilon 2}^2[a_1^2\phi_1\sigma_{u1}^2 r_2^{-1} \\ &\quad +a_2^2\theta_1\sigma_{u2}^2 r_1^{-1}] \end{aligned} \tag{A.11}$$

$$
\begin{aligned}
(r_1r_2)^{-1}numb_2 \quad = \quad & a_2[a_1^2\sigma_{u1}^4\sigma_{u2}^2 + a_1^2(1-\phi_1\theta_1)\sigma_{u1}^2\sigma_{u2}^2\sigma_{\varepsilon 1}^2] \\
& +a_2[a_2^2\sigma_{u1}^2\sigma_{u2}^4 + a_2^2\sigma_{u2}^4\sigma_{\varepsilon 1}^2 r_1^{-1} \\
& +\sigma_{u1}^2\sigma_{u2}^2\sigma_v^2 + \sigma_{u2}^2\sigma_{\varepsilon 1}^2\sigma_v^2 r_1^{-1}] \qquad \text{(A.12)}
\end{aligned}
$$

$$
\begin{aligned}
(r_1r_2)^{-1}numb_1 \quad = \quad & a_1[a_1^2\sigma_{u1}^4\sigma_{u2}^2 + a_2^2(1-\phi_1\theta_1)\sigma_{u1}^2\sigma_{u2}^2\sigma_{\varepsilon 2}^2] \\
& +a_1[a_2^2\sigma_{u1}^2\sigma_{u2}^4 + a_1^2\sigma_{u1}^4\sigma_{\varepsilon 2}^2 r_2^{-1} \\
& +\sigma_{u1}^2\sigma_{u2}^2\sigma_v^2 + \sigma_{u1}^2\sigma_{\varepsilon 2}^2\sigma_v^2 r_2^{-1}] \qquad \text{(A.13)}
\end{aligned}
$$

$b_1, b_2$ and $b_3$ are computed by taking the ratios of (A.13), (A.12) and (A.11) respectively, to (A.10). We follow Goodfriend (1985) and evaluate the resulting expressions at $\phi_1 = \theta_1 = 1$, i.e. at $r_1^{-1} = r_2^{-1} = 0$ to investigate the case of regressors that are the sums of permanent ($u_{it}$) and transitory ($\varepsilon_{it}$) shocks:

$$b_1 = \frac{a_1[a_1^2\sigma_{u1}^2 + a_2^2\sigma_{u2}^2 + \sigma_v^2]}{[a_1^2\sigma_{\varepsilon 1}^2 + a_2^2\sigma_{\varepsilon 2}^2] + [a_1^2\sigma_{u1}^2 + a_2^2\sigma_{u2}^2 + \sigma_v^2]} \qquad \text{(A.14)}$$

$$b_2 = \frac{a_2[a_1^2\sigma_{u1}^2 + a_2^2\sigma_{u2}^2 + \sigma_v^2]}{[a_1^2\sigma_{\varepsilon 1}^2 + a_2^2\sigma_{\varepsilon 2}^2] + [a_1^2\sigma_{u1}^2 + a_2^2\sigma_{u2}^2 + \sigma_v^2]} \qquad \text{(A.15)}$$

$$
\begin{aligned}
b_3 \quad &= \quad \frac{[a_1^2\sigma_{\varepsilon 1}^2 + a_2^2\sigma_{\varepsilon 2}^2]}{[a_1^2\sigma_{\varepsilon 1}^2 + a_2^2\sigma_{\varepsilon 2}^2] + [a_1^2\sigma_{u1}^2 + a_2^2\sigma_{u2}^2 + \sigma_v^2]} \qquad \text{(A.16)} \\
&= \quad \frac{1}{1+z}, \text{ where } z = \frac{a_1^2\sigma_{u1}^2 + a_2^2\sigma_{u2}^2 + \sigma_v^2}{a_1^2\sigma_{\varepsilon 1}^2 + a_2^2\sigma_{\varepsilon 2}^2}
\end{aligned}
$$

Note that $0 < b < 1$ and $|b_i| = |a_i z/(1+z)| < |a_i|$. As the variances of the transitory components of the regressors get very small relative to the variances of the permanent components, $z$ gets very large and $b_3$ approaches zero, and the $b_i$ approach $a_i$. This is just the standard result that an OLS regression on $I(1)$ variables that are cointegrated is a consistent estimator.

## A.2 Persistence in the Disturbance Shocks

The above results are derived under the assumption that $v_t$ is not serially correlated. The results can be generalized to the case where

$$v_t = \psi_t + \varepsilon_{0t} \text{ where } \varepsilon_{0t} \text{ are not serially correlated and} \qquad \text{(A.17)}$$

$$\psi_t = \rho\psi_{t-1} + u_{0t} \qquad \text{(A.18)}$$

Let $\psi_t$ and $\varepsilon_{0t}$ be independent. Then

$$\sigma_v^2 = \frac{\sigma_{u0}^2}{1-\rho^2} + \sigma_{\varepsilon 0}^2 = \sigma_{u0}^2 r_0 + \sigma_{\varepsilon 0}^2 \text{ where } r_0 = (1-\rho^2)^{-1}. \tag{A.19}$$

(A.19) must be substituted for $\sigma_v^2$ in (A.10) for the generalized analysis. Under (A.17) the covariance of $v_t$ with $v_{t-1}$ is: $\rho\sigma_{u0}^2 r_0$, so the third element of the vector on the right hand side of (A.7) becomes:

$$a_1^2\phi_1\sigma_{u1}^2 r_1 + a_2^2\theta_1\sigma_{u2}^2\sigma_2 + \rho\sigma_{u0}^2 r_0. \tag{A.20}$$

The matrix product of the adjoint matrix in (A.7) and the vector on the right hand side of (A.7) under the generalized specification are:

$$\begin{aligned}(r_1r_2)^{-1}numb_3 &= \sigma_{u1}^2\sigma_{u2}^2[a_1^2\phi_1\sigma_{\varepsilon 1}^2 + a_2^2\theta_1\sigma_{\varepsilon 2}^2] \\ &\quad +\sigma_{u1}^2\sigma_{u2}^2[a_1^2\phi_1\sigma_{u1}^2 r_2^{-1} + a_2^2\theta_1\sigma_{u2}^2 r_1^{-1}] \\ &\quad +[\sigma_{u1}^2\sigma_{u2}^2 + \sigma_{u2}^2\sigma_{\varepsilon 1}^2 r_1^{-1} + \sigma_{u1}^2\sigma_{\varepsilon 2}^2 r_2^{-1} \\ &\quad +\sigma_{\varepsilon 1}^2\sigma_{\varepsilon 2}^2(r_1r_2)^{-1}]\rho\sigma_{u0}^2 r_0 \end{aligned} \tag{A.21}$$

$$\begin{aligned}(r_1r_2)^{-1}numb_2 &= a_2\sigma_{u1}^2\sigma_{u2}^2[a_1^2\sigma_{u1}^2 + a_1^2(1-\phi_1\theta_1)\sigma_{\varepsilon 1}^2 + a_2^2\sigma_{u2}^2] \\ &\quad +a_2[a_2^2\sigma_{u1}^4\sigma_{\varepsilon 1}^2 r_1^{-1} + \sigma_{u1}^2\sigma_{u2}^2\sigma_v^2 + \sigma_{u2}^2\sigma_{\varepsilon 1}^2\sigma_v^2 r_1^{-1}] \\ &\quad -a_2\sigma_{u1}^2\sigma_{u2}^2\theta_1\sigma_{u0}^2\rho r_0 - a_2\theta\sigma_{u2}^2\sigma_{\varepsilon 1}^2\sigma_{u0}^2 r_1^{-1}\rho r_0 \end{aligned} \tag{A.22}$$

$$\begin{aligned}(r_1r_2)^{-1}numb_1 &= a_1\sigma_{u1}^2\sigma_{u2}^2[a_1^2\sigma_{u1}^2 + a_2^2(1-\phi_1\theta_1)\sigma_{\varepsilon 2}^2 + a_2^2\sigma_{u2}^2] \\ &\quad +a_1[a_1^2\sigma_{u1}^4\sigma_{\varepsilon 2}^2 r_2^{-1} + \sigma_{u1}^2\sigma_{u2}^2\sigma_v^2 + \sigma_{u1}^2\sigma_{\varepsilon 2}^2\sigma_v^2 r_2^{-1}] \\ &\quad -a_1\sigma_{u1}^2\sigma_{u2}^2\phi_1\sigma_{u0}^2\rho r_0 - a_2\phi_1\sigma_{u1}^2\sigma_{\varepsilon 2}^2\sigma_{u0}^2 r_2^{-1}\rho r_0 \end{aligned} \tag{A.23}$$

Compute $b_1, b_2$ and $b_3$ by taking the ratios of (A.23), (A.22) and (A.21), respectively, to (A.10) and following Goodfriend evaluate the resulting expressions at $\phi_1 = \theta_1 = 1$, at $r_1^{-1} = r_2^{-1} = 0$ to investigate the case of regressors that are the sums of permanent and transitory shocks:

$$b_1 = \frac{a_1[a_1^2\sigma_{u1}^2 + a_2^2\sigma_{u2}^2 + \sigma_{u0}^2 r_0 + \sigma_{\varepsilon 0}^2 - \sigma_{u0}^2\rho r_0]}{[a_1^2\sigma_{\varepsilon 1}^2 + a_2^2\sigma_{\varepsilon 2}^2] + [a_1^2\sigma_{u1}^2 + a_2^2\sigma_{u2}^2 + \sigma_{u0}^2 r_0 + \sigma_{\varepsilon 0}^2]} \tag{A.24}$$

$$b_2 = \frac{a_2[a_1^2\sigma_{u1}^2 + a_2^2\sigma_{u2}^2 + \sigma_{u0}^2 r_0 + \sigma_{\varepsilon 0}^2 - \sigma_{u0}^2\rho r_0]}{[a_1^2\sigma_{\varepsilon 1}^2 + a_2^2\sigma_{\varepsilon 2}^2] + [a_1^2\sigma_{u1}^2 + a_2^2\sigma_{u2}^2 + \sigma_{u0}^2 r_0 + \sigma_{\varepsilon 0}^2]} \tag{A.25}$$

$$\begin{aligned} b_3 &= \frac{[a_1^2\sigma_{\varepsilon 1}^2 + a_2^2\sigma_{\varepsilon 2}^2 + \rho\sigma_{u0}^2 r_0]}{[a_1^2\sigma_{\varepsilon 1}^2 + a_2^2\sigma_{\varepsilon 2}^2 + \rho\sigma_{u0}^2 r_0] + [a_1^2\sigma_{u1}^2 + a_2^2\sigma_{u2}^2 + (1-\rho)\sigma_{u0}^2 r_0 + \sigma_{\varepsilon 0}^2]} \\ &= \frac{1}{1+z_1}, \\ \text{where } z_1 &= \frac{a_1^2\sigma_{u1}^2 r_0^{-1} + a_2^2\sigma_{u2}^2 r_0^{-1} + (1-\rho)\sigma_{u0}^2 + \sigma_{\varepsilon 0}^2 r_0^{-1}}{a_1^2\sigma_{\varepsilon 1}^2 r_0^{-1} + a_2^2\sigma_{\varepsilon 2}^2 r_0^{-1} + \rho\sigma_{u0}^2} \end{aligned} \tag{A.26}$$

So for $r_0 > 0$ we again have $0 < b_3 < 1$ and

$$b_i = a_i \frac{z_1}{1+z_1}; i = 1, 2 \tag{A.27}$$

so $|b_i| < |a_i|$. If we let the disturbance $v_t$ be the sum of a permanent component ($\rho = 1, r_0^{-1} = 0$) and a transitory component and we hold the variance of the transitory component constant, then $b_3 = 1.0$ and $b_i = 0$, $i = 1, 2$. Alternatively if we let the variance of the transitory component of the disturbance term, $\sigma_{\varepsilon 0}^2$, be proportional to the variance of the permanent component, $\sigma_{\varepsilon 0}^2 = \lambda \sigma_{u0}^2 r_0$ then when $\rho = 1$:

$$b_3 = \frac{1}{1+\lambda} \text{ and again } 0 < b_3 < 1. \tag{A.28}$$

Under this assumption

$$b_i = a_i \left[\frac{\lambda}{1+\lambda}\right] \text{ and } |b_i| < |a_i|. \tag{A.29}$$

## A.3 Differenced Equations

A similar analysis can be constructed for regressions on differenced data. From (A.2) and (A.3).

$$\Delta y_t^* = \phi_0 + (\phi_1 - 1) y_{t-1}^* + u_{1t} \tag{A.30}$$

$$\Delta i_t^* = \theta_0 + (\theta_1 - 1) i_{t-1}^* + u_{2t} \tag{A.31}$$

so

$$\Delta y_t = \phi_0 + (\phi_1 - 1) y_{t-1}^* + u_{1t} + \varepsilon_{1t} - \varepsilon_{1t-1} \tag{A.32}$$

$$\Delta i_t = \theta_0 + (\theta_1 - 1) i_{t-1}^* + u_{2t} + \varepsilon_{2t} - \varepsilon_{2t-1} \tag{A.33}$$

Then it can be shown that the normal equations for the regression

$$\Delta m_t = c_1 \Delta y_t + c_2 \Delta i_t + c_3 \Delta m_{t-1} + \Delta v_t \tag{A.34}$$

imply:

$$c_1 = \frac{a_1}{1+2\lambda_1}; \lambda_1 = \sigma_{\varepsilon 1}^2 / \sigma_{u1}^2 \tag{A.35}$$

$$c_2 = \frac{a_2}{1+2\lambda_2}; \lambda_2 = \sigma_{\varepsilon 2}^2 / \sigma_{u2}^2 \tag{A.36}$$

and:

$$c_3 = \frac{\sigma_{\Delta r \Delta r-1}}{a_1^2 \sigma_{u1}^2 + a_2^2 \sigma_{u2}^2 + \sigma_{\Delta v}^2} \tag{A.37}$$

Therefore, if the $v_t$ shocks are random walks, $c_3 = 0.0$. As the variance of the transitory components of $i$ and $y$ become small relative to the variance of their respective permanent components $(\lambda \to 0)$, $c_i, i = 1, 2$ approach $a_i$.

# Bibliography


[1] Ahn, S.K. and G.C. Reinsel (1990). "Estimation for Partially Nonstationary Autoregressive Models". *Journal of the American Statistical Association.* 85:813-823.

[2] Allen, S. D. and R.F. Hafer (1983). "Money Demand and the Term Structure of Interest Rates: Some Consistent Estimates". *Journal of Monetary Economics.* 11:129-32

[3] Anderson, T. W. (1984). *An Introduction to Multivariate Statistical Analysis.* New York, Wiley

[4] Andersen, L.C. and J.L. Jordan (1968). "Monetary and Fiscal Actions: A Test of their Relative Importance in Economic Stabilization". Federal Reserve Bank of St. Louis *Review* 50:(November) 11-24.

[5] Ando, A. and F. Modigliani (1965). "The Relative Stability of Monetary Velocity and the Investment Multiplier". *American Economic Review.* 55:693-728.

[6] Ando, A, and K. Shell (1975). "Demand for Money in a Portfolio Model in the Presence of an Asset the Dominates Money". in G. Fromm and L. R. Klein (eds.) *The Brookings Model: Perspective and Recent Developments.* Amsterdam: North Holland Publishing Company

[7] Artis, M.J. and M.K. Lewis (1976). "The Demand for Money in the United Kingdom: 1963-1973". *Manchester School.* 44:147-181.

[8] Baillie R.T. (1987). "Inference in Dynamic Models Containing 'Surprise' Variables". *Journal of Econometrics* 35:101-117

[9] Banerjee, A., J. Dolado, J.W. Galbraith and D.F. Hendry (1993). *Co-Integration, Error-Correction, and the Econometric Analysis of Non-Stationary Data.* Oxford University Press: Oxford.

[10] Baumol, W.(1952). "The Transactions Demand for Cash: An Inventory Theoretic Approach". *Quarterly Journal of Economics.* 66:545-556

[11] Bean, C.R. (1983). "Targeting Nominal Income: An Appraisal". *Economic Journal.* 93:806-819.

[12] Belongia, M.T. (1988). "Are Economic Forecasts by Government Agencies Biased? Accurate?". Federal Reserve Bank of St. Louis *Review.* 70:(November/December) 15-23.

[13] Bergman, M., A. Blakemore and D. Hoffman(1995). "Labor Market Dynamics". mimeo. Arizona State University

[14] Beveridge, S. and C.R. Nelson (1981). "A New Approach to Decomposition of Time Series in Permanent and Transitory Components with Particular Attention to Measurement of the Business Cycle". *Journal of Monetary Economics*, 7:151-74

[15] Blanchard, O.J. (1989). "A Traditional Interpretation of Macroeconomic Fluctuations". *American Economic Review.* 79:1146-1164.

[16] Blanchard, O.J. and D. Quah (1989). "The Dynamic Effects of Aggregate Demand and Supply Disturbances". *American Economic Review.* 79:655-73.

[17] Blanchard, O.J. and D. Quah (1993). "The Dynamic Effects of Aggregate Demand and Supply Disturbances: Reply". *American Economic Review.* 83:653-58.

[18] Bomhoff, E.J. (1990). "Predicting the Income Velocity of Money".mimeo. Erasmus University.

[19] Bomhoff, E.J. (1991). "Stability of Velocity in Major Industrial Countries". *I.M.F. Staff Papers.* 38:626-642.

[20] Bomhoff, E.J. and C.J.M Kool (1983). "Forecasting with Multi-State Kalman Filters". in E.J. Bomhoff *Monetary Uncertainty.* Amsterdam: North Holland Publishing Company.

[21] Boorman, J.T. (1976). "The Evidence on the Demand for Money: Theoretical Formulations and Empirical Results". in T.M. Havrilesky and J.T. Boorman (eds.) *Current Issues in Monetary Theory and Policy.* Arlington Heights, IL: AHM Publishing Company. 315-361.

[22] Boswijk, P. H.(1992). *Cointegration, Identification and Exogeneity: Inference in Structural Error Correction Models,* Tinbergen Institute Research Series, No, 37 (University of Amsterdam, Amsterdam)

[23] Box, G.E.P. and G.K. Jenkins (1976). *Time Series Analysis: Forecasting and Control.* (2nd edition) San Francisco: Holden-Day.

[24] Bradley, M.D. and D.W. Jansen (1989). "The Optimality of Nominal Targeting when Wages are Indexed to Prices". *Southern Economic Journal.* 56:13-23.

[25] Bronfenbrenner, M. and T. Mayer (1960). "Liquidity Functions in the American Economy". *Econometrica.* 28:810-834.

[26] Brunner, K. and A.H. Meltzer (1993). *Money and the Economy: Issues in Monetary Analysis.* Cambridge University Press for the Raffaele Mattioli Foundation

[27] Campbell, J.Y. and R.J. Shiller (1987). "Cointegration and Tests of Present Value Models". *Journal of Political Economy.* 95:1062-1088.

[28] Campbell, J.Y. and R.J. Shiller (1988). "Interpreting Cointegrated Models". *Journal of Economic Dynamics and Control* 12:505-22.

[29] Campos, J., Ericsson, N.R. and D.F. Hendry (1993). "Cointegration Tests in the Presence of Structural Breaks". International Finance Discussion Paper . Board of Governors of the Federal Reserve System. (February) No. 440.

[30] Chow, G. (1966). "On the Short-run and Long-run Demand for Money". *Journal of Political Economy.* 74:111-131.

[31] Cooley, T.F. and M. Dwyer (1995). "Business Cycle Analysis Without Much Theory: A Look at Structural VARs". mimeo. University of Rochester.

[32] Cooley, T.F. and S.F. LeRoy (1981). "Identification and Estimation of Money Demand". *American Economic Review.* 71:825-844.

[33] Crowder, W.J. and D. L. Hoffman (1996). "The Long–Run Relationship Between Nominal Interest Rates and Inflation: The Fisher Equation Revisited". forthcoming *Journal of Money Credit and Banking.*

[34] Crowder, W.J. , D.L. Hoffman and R.H. Rasche (1995) "Identification and the Dynamics of a Simple Cointegrated System". mimeo. Arizona State University.

[35] Darby, M. R. (1975). "The Financial and Tax Effects of Monetary Policy on Interest Rates". *Economic Inquiry.* 13:266-269

[36] DePrano, M. and T. Mayer (1965). "Tests of the Relative Importance of Autonomous Expenditures and Money". *American Economic Review.* 55:729-752.

[37] Dewald, W. G., J. G. Thursby and R. G. Anderson (1993). "Replication in Empirical Economics". *American Economic Review.* 76:587-603

[38] Dickey, D.A. and W.A. Fuller (1979). "Distribution of the Estimators for Autoregressive Time Series with a Unit Root". *Journal of the American Statistical Association.* 74:427-31.

[39] Englund, P, A. Vredin, and A. Warne (1991). "Macroeconomic Shocks in Sweden". Manuscript, Trade Union Institute of Economic Research, Stockhom, Sweden

[40] Engle, R.F. and C.W.J. Granger (1987). "Cointegration and Error Correction: Representation, Estimation and Testing". *Econometrica.* 55:251-276. Reprinted in: R.F. Engle and C.W.J. Granger, (eds.) *Long-Run Economic Relations: Readings in Cointegration.* Oxford University Press: New York, 1991.

[41] Engle, R.F. and B.S. Yoo (1987). "Forecasting and Testing in Cointegrated Systems". *Journal of Econometrics.* 35:143-159. Reprinted in: R.F. Engle and C.W.J. Granger, (eds.) *Long-Run Economic Relations: Readings in Cointegration.* Oxford University Press: New York, 1991.

[42] Engle, R.F., D.F. Hendry, and J.F. Richard (1983). "Exogeneity". *Econometrica,* 51:277-304.

[43] Ericsson, N. R., D.F. Hendry and H-A. Tran (1993). "Cointegration, Seasonality, Encompassing, and the Demand for Money in the United Kingdom". International Finance Discussion Papers, Board of Governors of the Federal Reserve System.(October) No. 457

[44] Ericsson, N. R. and J.S. Irons (1994). (eds.) *Testing Exogeneity.* Oxford University Press, New York, New York

[45] Faust, J. and E. M. Leeper (1994) "When Do Long–Run Identifying Restrictions Give Reliable Results?" Working Paper No 94-2, April 1994, Federal Reserve Bank of Atlanta.

[46] Feige, E.L. (1967). "Expectations and Adjustments in the Monetary Sector". *American Economics Review.* 57(May):462-473.

[47] Fisher, F.(1966). *The Identification Problem in Econometrics.* New York, McGraw Hill

[48] Fisher, I. (1930). *The Theory of Interest.* New York, MacMillan

[49] Friedman, B.M. and K.N. Kuttner (1992). "Money, Income, Prices and Interest Rates". *American Economic Review.* 82:472-491.

[50] Friedman, M. (1956). *A Theory of the Consumption Function.* Princeton: Princeton University Press

[51] Friedman, M. (1977). "Time Preference in the Demand for Money". *Scandanivian Journal of Economics.* 79:397-416

[52] Friedman, M. and D. Meiselman (1963). "The Relative Stability of Monetary Velocity and the Investment Multiplier in the United States 1897-1958". Commission on Money and Credit *Stabilization Policies.* Englewood Cliffs, NJ: Prentice-Hall.

[53] Friedman M. and A.J. Schwartz (1982). "The Effect of the Term Structure of Interest Rates on the Demand for Money in the United States". *Journal of Political Economy.* 83:201-12

[54] Friedman, M. and D. Meiselman (1965). "Reply to Ando and Modigliani and to DePrano and Mayer". *American Economic Review.* 55:753-785.

[55] Fuller, W.A. (1976). *Introduction to Statistical Time Series.* New York: Wiley.

[56] Gali, J. (1992). "How Well does the IS-LM Model Fit Postwar U.S. Data". *Quarterly Journal of Economics.* 107:709-738.

[57] Garcia, G. and S. Pak (1979). "Some Clues in the Case of the Missing Money". *American Economic Review.* 69(May):462-473.

[58] Giannini, C. (1992). *Topics in Structural VAR Econometrics.* Berlin: Springer-Verlag.

[59] Goldfeld, S.M. (1973). "The Demand for Money Revisited". *Brookings Papers on Economic Activity.* (3):577-638.

[60] Goldfeld, S.M. (1976). "The Case of the Missing Money". *Brookings Papers on Economic Activity.* (3):683-730.

[61] Goldfeld, S.M. and D.E. Sichel (1987). Money Demand: The Effects of Inflation and Alternative Adjustment Mechanisms". *Review of Economics and Statistics.* 69:511-515.

[62] Gonzalo, J.(1994). "Five Alternative Methods of Estimating Long–Run Equilibrium Relationships". *Journal of Econometrics,* 6:203-233

[63] Gonzalo, J. and C.W.J. Granger (1991). "Estimation of Long-Memory Components in Cointegrated Systems". mimeo. Economics Department. University of California. San Diego.

[64] Goodfriend, M. (1985). "Reinterpreting Money Demand Regressions". *Carnegie-Rochester Conference Series on Public Policy.* 22:207-241.

[65] Granger, C.W.J. (1992). "What Are We Learning About the Long-Run". UCSD Working Paper. (May) No. 22.

[66] Granger, C.W.J. and P. Newbold (1974). "Spurious Regressions in Econometrics". *Journal of Econometrics.* 2:111-120.

[67] Hafer, R.W. and S.E. Hein (1980). "The Dynamics and Estimation of Short-run Money Demand". Federal Reserve Bank of St. Louis *Review.* 62(March):26-35.

[68] Hafer, R.W. and S.E. Hein (1982). "The Shift in Money Demand: What Really Happened". Federal Reserve Bank of St. Louis *Review.* 64(February):11-16.

[69] Hafer, R.W. and D.W. Jansen (1991). "The Demand of Money in the United States: Evidence from Cointegration Tests". *Journal of Money, Credit and Banking.* 23:155-168.

[70] Hall, R. E. and J. B. Taylor (1993). *Macroeconomics.* (4th edition). New York: W.W. Norton and Company

[71] Hamberger M. J. (1977). "Behavior of the Money Stock: Is there a Puzzle?". *Journal of Monetary Economics.* 5:265-88

[72] Hamilton, J.D. (1994). *Time Series Analysis.* Princeton: Princeton University Press.

[73] Hansen, H. and S. Johansen (1993). "Recursive Estimation in Cointgrated VAR–Models". Preprint # 1. Institute of Mathiematical Statistics. University of Copenhagen

[74] Hansen, L.P. and T.J. Sargent (1991). "Two Problems in Interpreting Vector Autoregressions". in L. Hansen and T. Sargent (eds.). *Rational Expectations Econometrics.* Westview: Boulder.

[75] Haraf, W.S. (1985). "Monetary Velocity and Monetary Rules". *The Cato Journal.* 6:641-662.

[76] Haug, A. A.(1994). " Tests for cointegration: A Monte Carlo Comparison". mimeo. Department of Economics, York University.

[77] Hein, S.E. (1980). "Dynamic Forecasting and the Demand for Money". Federal Reserve Bank of St. Louis *Review.* 62(June/July):13-23.

[78] Heller, H. R. and M.S. Khan (1979). "The Demand for Money and the Term Structure of Interest Rates". *Journal of Political Economy.* 87:109-119.

[79] Hendry, D.F. and N. R. Ericsson (1991). "An Econometric Analysis of the UK Money Demand in *Monetary trends in the United States and the United Kingdom* by Milton Friedman and Anna J. Schwartz". *American Economic Review.* 81:8-38

[80] Hester, D.D. (1964). "Keynes and the Quantity Theory: A Comment on the Friedman-Meiselman CMC Paper". *Review of Economics and Statistics.* 46:364-368.

[81] Hoffman, D.L. and R. H. Rasche (1991). "Long-Run Income and Interest Elasticities of the Demand for M1 and the Monetary Base in the Postwar U.S. Economy". *Review of Economics and Statistics.* 73:665-674.

[82] Hoffman, D. L. and C. Tahiri, (1994). "Money Demand in Morroco: Estimating Long–Run Elasticities for a Developing Country". *Oxford Bulletin of Economics and Statistics.* 56:35-24.

[83] Hoffman, D.L., R.H. Rasche and M.A. Tieslau (1995). "The Stability of Long-run Money Demand in Five Industrialized Countries". *Journal of Monetary Economics.* 35:317-339

[84] Horvath, M. and M.W. Watson (1993). "Testing for Cointegration When Some of the Cointegrating Vectors are Known". Working Paper No. 15. Research Department. Federal Reserve Bank of Chicago.

[85] Huizinga, J. and F.S. Mishkin (1986). "Monetary Policy Regime shifts and the Unusual Behavior of Real Interest Rates". *Carnegie-Rochester Conference Series on Public Policy.* 23:231-274.

[86] Hwang , H. (1985). "The Term Structure of Interest Rates in Money Demand: A Revaluation: A Note". *Journal of Money, Credit and Banking,* 17:391-96.

[87] Jansen, D.W. and S.G. Kim (1993). "Targeting Nominal Income: Further Results". *Southern Economic Journal.* 59:385-393.

[88] Johansen, S. (1988). "Statistical Analysis of Cointegrating Vectors". *Journal of Economic Dynamics and Control.* 12:231-254. Reprinted in: R.F. Engle and C.W.J. Granger. (eds.) *Long-Run Economic Relations: Readings in Cointegration.* Oxford University Press: New York.1991.

[89] Johansen, S. (1991). "Estimation and Hypothesis Testing of Cointegration Vectors in Gaussian Vector Autoregressive Models". *Econometrica.* 59:1551-1580.

[90] Johansen, S. (1992a). "A Representation of Vector autoregressive Processes Integrated of Order 2". *Econometric Theory.* 8:188-202

[91] Johansen, S. (1992b). "Identifying Restrictions of Linear Equations". Preprint No. 4: Institute of Mathematical Satistics. University of Copenhagen.

[92] Johansen, S. (1992c). "The Role of the Constant Term in Cointegration Analysis of Nonstationary Variables". Preprint No. 1: Institute of Mathematical Statistics. University of Copenhagen.

[93] Johansen, S. (1992d). "Determination of Cointegration Rank in the Presence of a Linear Trend". *Oxford Bulletin of Economics and Statistics.* 54:383-397.

[94] Johansen, S. (1992e). "Cointegration in Partial Systems and the Efficiency of Single Equation Analysis". *Journal of Econometrics.* 52:389-402.

[95] Johansen, S. and K. Juselius (1990). "Maximum Likelihood Estimation and Inference on Cointegation - With Applications to the Demand for Money". *Oxford Bulletin of Economics and Statistics.* 52:169-210.

[96] Johansen, S. and K. Juselius (1992). "Testing Structural Hypotheses in a Multivariate Cointegration Analysis of the PPP and UIP for the U.K". *Journal of Econometrics.* 53:211-244.

[97] Johansen, S. and B. Nielsen (1993). "Asymptotics for Cointegration Rank Tests in the Presence of Intervention Dummies". mimeo. Institute of Mathematical Statistics. University of Copenhagen.

[98] Judd, J. P. and J.L. Scaddings (1982). "The Search for a Stable Demand for Money Function: A Survey of the Post–1973 Literature". *Journal of Economic Literature.* 20:993-1023

[99] King, R.G., C.I. Plosser, J.H. Stock and M.W. Watson (1991). "Stochastic Trends and Economic Fluctuations". *American Economic Review.* 81:819-840.

[100] Kool, C.J.M. (1989). *Recursive Bayesian Forecasting in Economics: The Multistate Kalman Filter Method.* Nijmegen: Drukkerij SSN

[101] Koopmans, T.C.E. (1950). *Statistical Inference in Dynamic Economic Models.* New York: John Wiley and Sons, Inc.

[102] Koopmans, T. and Hood, W. (1953). *The Estimation of Simultaneous Linear Economic Relationships*, chapter VI. New York: Wiley and Sons, Inc.

[103] Kwiatkowski, D., P.C.B. Phillips, P. Schmidt and Y. Shin (1992). "Testing the Null Hypothesis of Stationarity Against the Alternatives of a Unit Root: How Sure Are We that Economic Time Series Have a Unit Root?". *Journal of Econometrics.* 54:159-178.

[104] Laidler, D.E.W. (1966). "The Rate of Interest and the Demand for Money". *Journal of Political Economy*, 74:545-55

[105] Laidler, D.E.W. (1980). "The Demand for Money in the United States - Yet Again". *Carnegie-Rochester Conference Series on Public Policy.* 12:219-271.

[106] Laidler, D.E.W. (1982). *Monetarist Perspectives.* Deddington: P. Allen.

[107] Laidler, D.E.W. (1985). *The Demand for Money: Theory, Evidence and Problems* (3rd edition). New York: Harper & Row.

[108] Lippi, M. and L. Reichlin (1993). "The Dynamic Effects of Aggregate Demand and Supply Disturbances: Comments". *American Economic Review.* 83:644-652.

[109] Litterman, R.B. and L.M. Weiss (1985). "Money, Real Interest Rates and Output: A Reinterpretation of Postwar U.S. Data". *Econometrica.* 53:129-56.

[110] Lucas, R.E. Jr. (1972). "Expectations and the Neutrality of Money". *Journal of Economic Theory.* 4:103-124.

[111] Lucas, R.E., Jr. (1976). "Econometric Policy Evaluation: A Critique". in K. Brunner and A.H. Meltzer (eds.) *The Phillips Curve and Labor Markets.* Carnegie-Rochester Conference Series, 1. Amsterdam: North Holland Publishing Company. 19-40.

[112] Lucas, R.E., Jr. (1988). "Money Demand in the United States: A Quantitative Review". *Carnegie-Rochester Conference Series on Public Policy,* 29:137-68.

[113] McCallum, B.T. (1988). "Robustness Properties of a Rule for Monetary Policy". *Carnegie-Rochester Conference Series on Public Policy.* 29:173-203.

[114] McNees, S.K. (1988). "How Accurate are Macroeconomic Forecasts?". *New England Economic Review.* (July/August):15-36.

[115] Meltzer, A.H. (1963). "The Demand for Money: The Evidence from the Time Series". *Journal of Political Economy.* 71:405-422.

[116] Meltzer, A.H. (1985). "Variability of Prices, Output, and Money under Fixed and Fluctuating Exchange Rates: An Empirical Study of Monetary Regimes in Japan and the United States". Bank of Japan *Monetary and Economic Studies.*

[117] Meltzer, A.H. (1986). "Size, Persistence, and Interrelation of Nominal and Real Shocks: Some Evidence from Four Countries". *Journal of Monetary Economics.* 17:159-193.

[118] Meltzer, A.H. (1987). "Limits of Short-Run Stabilization Policy". *Economic Inquiry.* 25:1-14.

[119] Mishkin, F.S (1990a). "The Information in the Term Structure about Future Inflation". *Quarterly Journal of Economics.* 105:815- 828.

[120] Mishkin, F.S. (1990b). "What does the Term Structure tell us about Inflation?". *Journal of Monetary Economics.* 25:77-96.

[121] Mishkin, F.S. (1992). "Is the Fisher Effect for Real: A Reexamination of the Relationship Between Inflation and Interest Rates". *Journal of Monetary Economics.* 30:185-215.

[122] Modigliani, F., R.H. Rasche and J.P. Cooper (1970). "Central Bank Policy, the Money Supply and the Short-Term Rate of Interest". *Journal of Money, Credit, and Banking.* 2:166-218.

[123] Muth, J.F. (1960). "Optimal Properties of Exponentially Weighted Forecasts". *Journal of the American Statistical Association.* 55:299-306.

[124] Nelson, C.R. and C.I. Plosser (1982). "Trends and Random Walks in Macro-economic Time Series: Some Evidence and Implications". *Journal of Monetary Economics.* 10:139-162.

[125] Newey, W. and K.D. West (1987). "A Simple Positive Semi Definite, Heteroskedasticity and Autocorrelation Consistent Covariance Matrix". *Econometrica.* 55:703-708.

[126] Osterwald-Lenum, M. (1992). "A Note with Quantiles of the Asymptotic Distribution of the Maximum Likelihood Cointegration Rank Test Statistics". *Oxford Bulletin of Economics and Statistics.* 54:461-471.

[127] Park, J.Y. (1990). "Disequilibrium Impulse Analysis". mimeo. Department of Economics, Cornell University.

[128] Park, J.Y. (1992). "Canonical Cointegrating Regression". *Econometrica.* 60:119-144.

[129] Park, J.Y. and P.C.B. Phillips (1988). "Statistical Inference in Regressions with Integrated Regressors: Part I". *Econometric Theory.* 4:468-497.

[130] Park, J.Y. and P.C.B. Phillips (1989). "Statistical Inference in Regressions with Integrated Regressors: Part II". *Econometric Theory.* 5:95-131.

[131] Perron, P. (1989). "The Great Crash, the Oil Price Shock and the Unit Root Hypothesis". *Econometrica.* 57:1361-1401.

[132] Pesaran, M. H. and Y. Shin (1994). "Long–Run Structural Modelling". mimeo. Department of Applied Economics. University of Cambridge

[133] Pesaran, M. H. and Y. Shin (1995). "An Autoregressive Distributed Lag Modelling Approach To Cointegration Analysis. mimeo. Department of Applied Economics, University of Cambridge

[134] Phillips, P.C.B. (1994). "Some Exact Distribution Theory for Maximum Likelihood Estimators of Cointegrating Coefficients in Error Correction Models". *Econometrica.* 62:73-93

[135] Phillips, P.C.B. (1986). "Understanding Spurious Regression in Econometrics". *Journal of Econometrics.* 33:311-340.

[136] Phillips, P.C.B. (1987). "Time Series Regression with a Unit Root". *Econometrica.* 55:277-301.

[137] Phillips, P.C.B. (1991). "Optimal Inference in Cointegrated Systems". *Econometrica.* 59:283-306.

[138] Phillips, P.C.B. and M. Loretan (1991). "Estimating Long Run Economic Equilibria". *Review of Economic Studies.* 58:407-436.

[139] Phillips, P.C.B. and P. Perron (1988). "Testing for Unit Root in Time Series Regression". *Biometrika.* 75:335-346.

[140] Poole, W. (1970). "Wither Money Demand?". *Brookings Papers on Economic Activity.* 3:485-500.

[141] Poole, W. (1988). "Monetary Policy Lessons of Recent Inflation and Disinflation". *Journal of Economic Perspectives.* 2:73-100

[142] Porter, R.D., T.D. Simpson and E. Mauskopf (1979). "Financial Innovation and the Monetary Aggregates". *Brookings Papers on Economic Activity.* 1:213-229.

[143] Quah, D. (1986a). *Essays in Dynamic Macroeconomics.* PHD dissertation. Harvard University

[144] Quah, D. (1986b). "Estimation and Hypothesis Testing with Restricted Spectral Density Matrices: An Application to Uncovered Interest Parity". Chapter 4 of *Dynamic Macroeconometrics.* Ph.D. Dissertation. Harvard University.

[145] Quah, D (1991). "Identifying Vector Autoregressions: A Discussion of P. Englund, A Vredin, and A. Warne: Macroeconomic Shocks in Sweden 1925-1986. mimeo. Department of Economics. London School of Economics.

[146] Rasche, R.H. (1987). "M1 Velocity and Interest Rates: Do Stable Relationships Exist?". *Carnegie-Rochester Conference Series on Public Policy.* 27:9-88.

[147] Rasche, R.H. (1993) "Monetary Aggregates, Monetary Policy and Economic Activity". Federal Reserve Bank of St. Louis *Review.* 75(March/April):1-35.

[148] Roley, V.V. (1985). "Money Demand Predictability". *Journal of Money, Credit and Banking.* 17:611-641.

[149] Rothenberg, T.J. (1971). "Identification in Parametric Models". *Econometrica.* 39:577-592.

[150] Rothenberg, T.J. (1973). *Efficient Estimation with a priori Information.* Yale University Press, New Haven.

[151] Runkle, D. (1987). "Vector Autoregressions and Reality". *Journal of Business and Economic Statistics.* 5:437-442.

[152] Saving, T.R. (1971). "Transactions Costs and the Demand for Money". *American Economic Review.* 61:407-420

[153] Schwert, G. W. "Effects of Model Specification on Tests for Unit Roots in Macroeconomic Data. *Journal of Monetary Economics.* 20:73-103

[154] Simpson, T.D. (1980). "The Redefined Monetary Aggregates". *Federal Reserve Bulletin.* (February):97-112.

[155] Sims, C.A. (1972). "Money, Income and Causality". *American Economic Review.* 62:540-552.

[156] Sims, C.A. (1980). "Macroeconomics and Reality". *Econometrica.* 48:1-48.

[157] Sims, C.A., J.H. Stock and M.W. Watson (1990). "Inference in Linear Time Series Models with Some Unit Roots". *Econometrica.* 58:113-144.

[158] Stock, J.H. (1987). "Asymptotic Properties of Least Squares Estimates of Cointegrating Vectors". *Econometrica.* 55:1035-1055.

[159] Stock, J. H.(1994). "Unit Roots, Structural Breaks and Trends". in R. F. Engle and D. McFadden (eds.). *Handbook of Econometrics*, Vol 4. ch 46. North-Holland Publishing Company, Amsterdam.

[160] Stock, J.H. and M.W. Watson (1988). "Testing for Common Trends". *Journal of the American Statistical Association.* 83:1097-1107. Reprinted in: R.F. Engle and C.W.J. Granger. (eds.). *Long-Run Economic Relations: Readings in Cointegration.* Oxford University Press: New York. 1991.

[161] Stock, J.H. and M. Watson (1993). "A Simple Estimator of Cointegrating Vectors in Higher Order Integrated Systems". *Econometrica.* 61:783-820.

[162] Teigen, R.L. (1964). "Demand and Supply Functions for Money in the United States: Some Structural Estimates". *Econometrica.* 32:477-509.

[163] Tobin, J. (1956). "The Interest Elasticity of Transactions Demand for Cash". *Review of Economics and Statistics.* 38:241-247.

[164] Warne, A. (1993). "A Common Trends Model: Identification, Estimation and Asymptotics". Institute for International Economic Studies. Seminar Paper No. 555. University of Stockholm.

[165] Watson, M. W. (1994). "Vector Autoregressions and Cointegration". in R. F. Engle and D. McFadden (eds.). *Handbook of Econometrics.* Vol 4. ch 47. North-Holland Publishing Company. Amsterdam.

[166] Wold, H. (1954). "Causality and Econometrics". *Econometrica.* 22:162-177.

[167] Yoshida, T. and R.H. Rasche (1990). "The M2 Demand in Japan: Shifted and Unstable?". Bank of Japan *Monetary and Economic Studies.* 8(September):9-30.

[168] Yule, G.C. (1926). "Why Do We Sometimes Get Nonsense-Correlations Between Time Series". *Journal of the Royal Statistical Society.* 89:1-64.

[169] Zellner, A. and F. Palm (1974). "Time Series Analysis and Simultaneous Equation Econometric Models". *Journal of Econometrics.* 2:17-54.

# Index

## Authors

# Index

## Subject

## G



## H



## I



## J



## L



## M



## N



## P



## R



## S

MIX
Papier aus verantwortungsvollen Quellen
Paper from responsible sources
FSC® C105338

If you have any concerns about our products, you can contact us on
**ProductSafety@springernature.com**

In case Publisher is established outside the EU, the EU authorized representative is:
**Springer Nature Customer Service Center GmbH**
**Europaplatz 3, 69115 Heidelberg, Germany**

Printed by Libri Plureos GmbH
in Hamburg, Germany